BIOLOGY OF THE MAJOR PSYCHOSES:
A Comparative Analysis

Research Publications

Association for Research in Nervous and Mental Disease

Volume 54

Biology of the Major Psychoses:
A Comparative Analysis

*Research Publications:
Association for Research in
Nervous and Mental Disease*

Volume 54

Editor:

Daniel X. Freedman, M.D.
*Louis Block Professor of Biological Sciences
and
Chairman of Psychiatry
University of Chicago
Chicago, Illinois*

Raven Press, Publishers ▪ New York

Distributed in the Eastern Hemisphere by
North-Holland Publishing Co.
Amsterdam

Made in the United States of America

International Standard Book Number 0–89004–034–6
Library of Congress Catalog Card Number 75–14571

ISBN outside North and South America only: 0–7204–7560–0

Publisher's Note

Raven Press has taken over publication of the volumes in this series beginning with volume 53, based on the December 1973 symposium of the A.R.N.M.D. Those interested in purchasing earlier volumes in the series should write directly to the former publisher of the series, the Williams & Wilkins Company, 428 E. Preston Street, Baltimore, Maryland 21202, U.S.A. Titles marked with an asterisk (*) are out of print in the original edition. Some out-of-print volumes are available in reprint editions from Hafner Publishing Company, 866 Third Avenue, New York, N.Y. 10022.

Preface

There are two distinct and exciting lines of progress which promise to redefine emphases in the field of psychiatry. One is a renewed sophistication in diagnosis and classification; the other is the development in the brain sciences of precise measurements of biological processes that can be made in man. Sophistication in clinical characterization of patients and the distinction between trait and state variables are matched by the reliability and sensitivity of biochemical and neurophysiological measures. Much of the work in both areas is rapidly evolving. Thus the intent of the 54th Meeting of the ARNMD [on which this volume is based] was to assess the state of these arts and to ask some specific questions.

An overview was attempted to determine whether there are indeed reliable subpopulations in the major mental illnesses and whether the biological variables being measured are distinctive to those populations. The question was: Is there a general biology of psychosis that would cut across traditional diagnostic lines? Or, on the other hand, are there some measures that may be specific to either the schizophrenic or the manic-depressive psychoses, or to specific aspects of these psychoses? The approach, then, was to ask if there are distinctive differentiations in terms of phenomenology, symptomatology, outcome, heritability, and familial patterns, or in terms of biological response to dysfunction, drugs, or stimuli.

The approach was a comparative one aimed at examining the unity as well as the diversity of clinical phenomena to see what they might reveal about the significance of biological measures and vice versa. And, indeed, in viewing the contents, one finds some measures that seem to relate to the state of being psychotic and others that appear to have promise as biological "markers" (for example, in schizophrenia) for genetic carriers.

One senses that many of the biochemical processes being measured by biologists represent compensatory and adaptive brain responses to the condition of mental illness. Some—such as a possible functional dopamine-receptor overload (perhaps in limbic areas)—may identify a specific component of schizophrenic brain function; others appear to represent imbalances among amines that may represent subgroups of the major mental illnesses.

In perspective, it is interesting to contrast the current era of emphasis on dopamine and biogenic amines with the contents of the last major volume on this topic produced by the ARNMD in 1929, published during an era in which postencephalitic parkinsonian symptoms and the meaning and variety of schizophrenic behaviors were of central interest. Today, it is possible in parkinsonian and mental patients to measure in body fluids central processes that refer to established connections in the CNS and to chemical events at specific synapse systems. The operation of integrative neural systems, hitherto approached only by direct intracerebral recording in animals, appears in some instances to be measured from the body surface, such as "eye tracking" behavior; there are new data clearly indicating reliable peripheral tissue changes in the two major mental illnesses (manic-depressive or schizophrenic psychoses). And the issues of the links between premorbid status, psychotic state and symptoms, and outcome can be put to the test of sophisticated, epidemiologic, clinical, and statistical measures.

Many of these developments appear for the first time to have a potential for direct bearing on clinical and therapeutic practice, so that the symposium on which this volume is based offered a timely review of the rapidly developing sciences and the cogent link of clinical with laboratory investigations.

We express special appreciation for organizing this meeting to Mrs. Hariette Bailie and to Drs. John M. Davis and Herbert Y. Meltzer, and to all the contributors whose candor and explicitness will help the serious student to understand better the nature of pathophysiological events in the psychoses.

Daniel X. Freedman, M.D.
April 1975

Contents

Neurochemical Measures

Contributors

Burton Angrist
Neuropsychopharmacology Research Unit
New York University Medical Center
New York, New York 10016

Malcolm B. Bowers
Department of Psychiatry
Yale University School of Medicine
New Haven, Connecticut 06510

Monte Buchsbaum
Division of Clinical and Behavioral
    Research
National Institute of Mental Health
Bethesda, Maryland 20014

William T. Carpenter, Jr.
Adult Psychiatry Branch
National Institute of Mental Health
Bethesda, Maryland 20014

John W. Crayton
Department of Psychiatry
University of Chicago
Chicago, Illinois 60637

John M. Davis
Department of Psychiatry
University of Chicago
Chicago, Illinois 60637

Barbara Fish
Department of Psychiatry
University of California
Los Angeles, California 90024

F. Gordon Foster
Department of Psychiatry
University of Pittsburgh School of Medi-
    cine
Pittsburgh, Pennsylvania 15261

Daniel X. Freedman
Department of Psychiatry
University of Chicago
Chicago, Illinois 60637

Samuel Gershon
Neuropsychopharmacology Research Unit
New York University Medical Center
New York, New York 10016

J. Glowinski
Groupe de Neuropharmacologie Biochimique
Laboratoire de Neurophysiologie
Collège de France
Paris, France

Frederick K. Goodwin
Section on Psychiatry
LCS/NIMH
Bethesda, Maryland 20014

Angelos E. Halaris
Department of Psychiatry
University of Chicago
Chicago, Illinois 60637

Philip S. Holzman
Department of Psychiatry
University of Chicago
Chicago, Illinois 60637

Harold L. Klawans
Michael Reese Hospital; and
    Department of Medicine
University of Chicago
Pritzker School of Medicine
Chicago, Illinois 60616

David J. Kupfer
Western Psychiatric Institute and Clinic
Pittsburgh, Pennsylvania 15261

Herbert Y. Meltzer
Department of Psychiatry
University of Chicago
Chicago, Illinois 60637

Dennis L. Murphy
Laboratory of Clinical Science
National Institute of Mental Health
Bethesda, Maryland 20014

Robert M. Post
Section on Psychobiology
Adult Psychiatry Branch
National Institute of Mental Health
Bethesda, Maryland 20014

David Rosenthal
Laboratory of Psychology
National Institute of Mental Health
Bethesda, Maryland 20014

Lewis P. Rowland
Department of Neurology
College of Physicians and Surgeons
Columbia University
New York, New York 10032

Edward J. Sachar
Department of Psychiatry
Albert Einstein College of Medicine
Bronx, New York 10461

Charles Shagass
Eastern Pennsylvania Psychiatric Institute
Philadelphia, Pennsylvania 19129

Baron Shopsin
Neuropsychopharmacology Research Unit
New York University Medical Center
New York, New York 10016

John S. Strauss
Department of Psychology
University of Rochester School of Medicine
  and Dentistry
Rochester, Minnesota 14620

Ming T. Tsuang
University of Iowa
College of Medicine
Iowa City, Iowa 52242

Richard J. Wyatt
Laboratory of Clinical Psychopharmacology
National Institute of Mental Health
Bethesda, Maryland 20014

Biology of the Major Psychoses, edited by D. X. Freedman, *Res. Publ. Assoc. Res. Nerv. Ment. Dis.,* Vol. 54. Raven Press, New York 1975.

Clinical Phenomenology in the Functional Psychoses

Malcolm B. Bowers, Jr.

Department of Psychiatry, Yale University School of Medicine, New Haven, Connecticut 06510

The problem of a meaningful nosology in the functional psychoses is an important and persistent one. I emphasize *meaningful,* for it seems to me that we cannot afford cavalier diagnostic exercises in these disorders. Labels, if we use them, should inform treatment, prognosis, and research; they should allow the physician to remain faithful to his foremost duty, not to harm his patient. One need not harbor a bias against diagnostic categories to feel sympathy for the havoc that may be created by the diagnosis of *schizophrenia.* Such a term, once laid on, can deny hope to a family or an individual and seriously limit possibilities for gainful employment. In a society generally uninformed about psychiatric treatment methods in the more severe disorders, the use of this diagnosis carries with it dangers and problems accessory to those inherent in the condition itself. Nor does the negative spin-off of casual diagnostics accrue only to the patient or his family. In academic settings terms can become reified before they have attained practical utility or conceptual validity. Trainees may become comfortable with an easy nosologic shorthand and avoid confronting the multiple inputs to a problem, thereby overlooking ways to offer genuine help in certain problem areas when they cannot effect a complete cure. Researchers, looking at patients from certain distances, may force homogeneities or dichotomies that tend to blur when they take a few steps forward or backward. The configuration of a landscape may have an intriguing and compelling pattern when viewed from the air, quite in contrast to that visible if one is hiking through a field. Thus, whether one examines charts or individuals makes a profound difference. Likewise, whether one sees a patient once or many times throughout the life of the patient may have important consequences for the observer with regard to the way he chooses to set his own observations in order.

My own experience has been as a clinician who supervises the treatment of patients on inpatient services while searching for clinical variables to correlate with certain biologic measurements. I do not claim that this is the best vantage point from which to achieve conceptual clarity, for thinking about either treatment, prognosis, or research. I want to emphasize, however, that my working model has evolved from this kind of setting and in relationship to these tasks. The syndromes encompassed by my discussion are those usually included under the diagnoses of schizophrenia, schizoaffective psychosis, and manic-depressive psychosis.

The so-called functional psychoses can be described as a group of conditions that occur in individuals with a variety of premorbid personality characteristics, characteristics that have as their behavioral phenotypes varying deficits in social role performance, task motivation, and fullness of emotional response. These traits are seen as long-lived personal attributes that have developed over time through an interaction between temperament and experience. Of course, a variety of processes may underlie these traits. A psychosis initially occurs in the lives of these individuals sometime late in the first third or first half of life and is often associated with (although not necessarily caused by) a confrontation with issues of psychobiologic maturation and individuation characteristic of this developmental period. These syndromes present clinically as altered states of consciousness, a general term used to describe a variety of protracted, unusual states of mind which are likely not just an intensification of premorbid states of mind, but may be relatively novel alterations in the individual's experience of himself and the world. From such states of mind a variety of unusual behaviors emerge. These states of mind may subsequently remit to varying degrees and for varying lengths of time. Individuals show varying degrees of awareness of the nonreality of these states, indeed some may even prefer them to "normal" consciousness; therefore, vastly different levels of compliance with therapeutic strategies to diminish their intensity may emerge. The course, status, or outcome of these disorders at any point is actually determined by the degree of persistence of and individual disposition toward these psychotic states of mind taken in conjunction with the status of the prepsychotic trait deficits. These factors constitute the liability with which the individual confronts the continuing tasks of social and economic life (1).

Most nosologic distinctions that have been traditionally proposed for the functional psychoses have emphasized either a set of prepsychotic traits, a group of morbid symptoms or behaviors, or a particular outcome. Thus, schizophrenia has been designated fundamentally as a group of premorbid individual characteristics by some, a set of symptoms or behaviors by others, and as a characteristic outcome by still others. More recently this term has been used to designate a composite of specific criteria in each of these categories; hence, the concept of schizophrenia as a psychosis occurring in a socially incompetent individual, associated with a formal thought disorder and affective blunting, and leading to a poor outcome. Therefore, from the viewpoint of clinical phenomenology, the functional psychoses currently emerge as syndromes composed of three factors, if you will, organized longitudinally into hypothetical diseases (I use the term *factor* here in a descriptive, not a statistical, sense). Thus, it has been frequently assumed that knowledge in any one area (premorbid traits, symptoms, or outcome) can predict the critical data from the other areas. That is, using the longitudinal disease model we think of these syndromes as separate tracks with set articulations between the three factor areas (2).

As a digression, it is important and humbling to recognize that the contrasting heuristic models, which will probably be discussed in this conference, have a rather lengthy heritage. The continental or Kraepelinian "disease" model and the American Meyerian approach have long been creatively opposed in the study of psychotic states. I had occasion to review a book published in 1925 entitled *Schizophrenia (Dementia Praecox),* which actually was the published proceedings of a meeting of the ARNMD, devoted essentially to this same topic (3). It was startling to see the conferees dealing with many of the same conceptual issues. In that conference Karl Menninger pointed to the nonspecificity of schizophreniform states, although the clinical phenomena that he discussed were postinfluenza psychotic reactions and not the psychotomimetic drug syndromes of today.

Therefore, with new and sometimes elegant techniques the old questions continue to be sharpened and investigated, as described in the chapters of this volume. In particular, a number of studies have been reported in the past few years that have again challenged previous notions regarding the pathognomonic character of certain aspects of the psychotic state. For instance, Schneider's so-called first-rank symptoms, which had been considered pathognomonic symptoms of true schizophrenia (4), have been noted to occur in some patients with manic-depressive disorder (or preferably—patients with a psychotic syndrome responsive to lithium) at the height of the psychosis (5,6). Thus, these individuals often do not have marked premorbid social, affect, and drive deficits and may have a relatively favorable outcome despite the fact that they display Schneider criteria when acutely ill. We have reported Schneider symptoms in psychotic reactions precipitated by psychotomimetic drugs (7,8). Indeed, regarding these drug-precipitated psychotic reactions, some observers have argued that such individuals were "already schizophrenic." However, our cases showed relatively good premorbid characteristics compared to a non-drug-induced group of psychotics. Yet some preliminary follow-up observations indicate that a few of these individuals have recurrent and chronic illnesses, not necessarily precipitated by subsequent drug use. This example is an instance in which relatively good premorbid status is associated with an ambiguous symptom picture regarding pathognomonic signs and with an outcome that is at least quite variable.

Other clinical experiences and clinical research during the recent psychotomimetic drug era suggest that there is no rigid lock step relationship between a psychotic state, premorbid traits, or outcome. The fact that amphetamines, the psychotomimetic indoles, and cannabis preparations can produce a schizophreniform state suggests the relative independence of the psychotic state itself from premorbid factors and outcome variables. Moreau in *Hashish and Mental Illness* (9) first seems to have raised the conceptual possibility that endogenous mechanisms for producing "excitement" (in the recent translation) might primarily determine the form of the functional psychoses. Many modern research strategies ranging from abnormalities in methylating processes to possible deficiencies in enzymes that degrade monoamines implicitly employ this model, which is really addressed separately to the psychotic state itself. Traits may, of course, be derived from processes that determine states, just as in Mirsky's model for duodenal ulcer in which increased serum pepsinogen and gastric hyperacidity are seen as possibly determining both the ulcer diathesis *and* the development of psychologic traits of excessive oral dependency in infants (10). We may have seen a related phenomenon in individuals who have used psychotomimetic substances over long periods of time. That is, chronic psychotomimetic drug use in individuals with relatively normal predrug social histories can probably engender long-term changes in motivation, cognition, and affect, traits that resemble the premorbid personality characteristics of the process or poor premorbid functional psychotic disorders (11). Some individuals with this syndrome seem to have very poor outcomes indeed.

The relative independence of the schizophreniform psychotic state of mind from premorbid personality variables is also highlighted in the classic papers of Beard and Slater dealing with the schizophrenic-like psychoses of epilepsy (12). The entire range of symptoms seen in acute schizophreniform disorders was encountered in their cases yet they found "there is no evidence of an unusual abundance of personality traits of a kind which might indicate a predisposition to schizophrenia." Nevertheless, fully 46% of their cases ran a course "towards chronicity, or even to deterioration," whereas in 31% there was "a tendency to improve, even to the point of recovery from the psychosis." Therefore, in the schizophreniform psychoses of epilepsy symptoms, premorbid characteristics, and outcome, as crucial aspects of the structure of the syndrome, seem to be independent factors to a degree. This same general point has been made by Reid (13) in a recent paper in which he proposes the classification of schizophrenia into an idiopathic and a symptomatic group.

The studies of Kety, Rosenthal, Wender, and Schulsinger have shown that the spectrum of psychopathologic disorders in biologic relatives of chronic schizophrenics and borderline schizophrenics included individuals diagnosed as chronic schizophrenics, borderline schizophrenics, and inadequate personalities (14). No instance of a schizophrenic spectrum disorder was found in the biologic relatives of those diagnosed as acute schizophrenic reaction. These findings suggest a discontinuity between acute schizophreniform psychosis and certain long-standing personality characteristics, characteristics that seem to harbor some phenotype in these disorders, as yet undefined, which may be associated with a relatively poor outcome. This evidence points to a role for genetic biology in the *trait* factors of the functional psychoses, rather than in the psychotic state itself. Other genetic processes may be responsible for, or at least may predispose an individual to, psychotic states of mind. The studies of Murphy and Weis (15) and Murphy and Wyatt (16), which deal with monoamine oxidase deficiency in the functional psychoses, would be a relevant example of this model. Genetic conditions that might lead to abnormalities of methylation and the endogenous production of psychotomimetic substances would be another related model whereby genetic variation could underlie psychotic *state* phenomena.

Other recent studies raise questions about the longitudinal model of discrete disease entities in the functional psychoses. In particular, Strauss and Carpenter (17) have recently shown that symptomatic criteria used by several Scandinavian groups to create the category of schizophreniform psychosis do not necessarily predict outcome. These investigators have also shown that outcome itself is not unimodal and that work function, social function, and symptoms do not co-vary as outcome measures (18). Their concept of a "confluence of factors" approach in the functional psychoses is particularly germane to the present discussion. A study by Kendell and Gourlay (19) employing discriminant function analysis of two cohorts of patients diagnosed as suffering from schizophrenia or affective psychosis did not support the view that these were separate entities. Regarding cognitive abnormalities, careful psychologic measurements of thought disorder by Reilly and Harrow (20) have shown considerable variation depending upon the clinical stage of functional psychosis. Other recent studies have found formal thought pathology in a number of depressive syndromes (21).

At the clinical level, at least, we are left with a group of disorders with varying characteristics in three areas—premorbid traits, psychotic state (symptoms and signs), and multidimensional outcome. As an alternative to the longitudinal disease model one can postulate that the panorama of the functional psychoses is determined by combinations of these three factors, which, although inter-related, can also be separately assessed and separately attended to therapeutically. Such an approach leaves the ultimate nosology somewhat in abeyance and allows for the pursuit of clinical care and research differentiations within the component factors. Such a model would argue for a *vertical* as well as a *longitudinal* dimension. Such a model is really different from the Kraepelinian or the Meyerian model. It would include Meyer's attention to life events but would also, with Kraepelin, argue that disease in the sense of a discoverable biologic bias or process might be responsible for aspects of premorbid traits or psychotic states of mind or both. These might be the same or different processes. Their pathogenesis would not have longitudinal or prognostic implications which would be totally predetermining. Biologic processes would therefore be included in this model without the implication of Kraepelin's *Krankheitsvorgang*.

Using this model, one might consider premorbid personality in the following way. Criteria need to be developed for a clearer delineation of the kinds of social incompetence that exist and the processes that underlie them. Some of the "at-risk" studies may be identifying these deficits. Individual differences in exploratory drive or modulation of arousal may antedate problems in the development of social relatedness and contribute to a susceptibility to pathologic rearing patterns. What factors are actually responsible for the problems in building relationships beyond the primary family, which are found in some individuals with psychotic disorders? Have these individuals learned to fear human intimacy through an experience with an abnormally intrusive parent? Or in some ethologic sense do we see their problem as a disorder in the transformation of attachment behavior? Do such individuals suffer from a deficit in responding in behavioral paradigms, which are usually motivated by positive reinforcement? Do they lack a capacity for pleasure? Or, more specifically, for interpersonal pleasure (22)? Can any more highly refined notion of a trait deficit in certain psychotic disorders be related to a basic psychologic response potential? Can such response potential be shown to depend on specific central neurochemical systems as Stein and Wise (23) have postulated for reward behavior? We can, I suggest, greatly improve upon our present level of analysis of such descriptive phrases as *social incompetence*. A similar in-depth examination should be made at such traits as limitation of affect and its possible neurochemical correlates.

With regard to premorbid traits at the level of clinical practice we must know, for instance, how persistent the individual can be during rehabilitation. Will he keep appointments as an initial indication that a working alliance can be established? If he is socially incompetent, can he be taught social skills? Is he willing to try and to experience and tolerate failure as a step necessary to achieving self-confidence? Can he benefit from his mistakes?

Consider the characteristics of the psychotic state itself that leads to researchable questions. What are its pharmacologic response properties? What are the specific agents that ameliorate these states or make them worse? Can drug response, which may cut across current nosologic lines, be profitably used to define a research cohort? Can endogenous mechanisms that lead to an enhanced liability to psychotic states of mind be demonstrated? Some of the contributors to this volume describe currently accumulating information, which may lead to answers to this question. Can state-related processes be demonstrated? Will such processes cut across current nosologic categories? An example in this context would be Meltzer's work, which deals with myopathic phenomena in acute psychotic states (24).

Again, at the clinical level, with regard to the psychotic state we can ask, What is the individual's involvement in his psychotic experience? Is it alien and painful, seen as something he would like to collaborate in getting rid of? Or is it seductive, pleasurable, and convincing as a "higher reality"? Is it easily evoked in response to psychologic challenge? Do its ideational components pose a serious risk of suicide or homicide? In the psychotic state does the individual maintain an "observing ego" or is he swallowed up by the novel experience? Answers to these questions are crucial when one confronts prospects for treatment, and the details of these answers provide the individual configuration or clinical profile for each psychotic individual.

With regard to outcome, its multidimensional character needs to be more fully appreciated. Furthermore, social factors may interact with individual inertia and produce outcomes that are illusory in their apparent simplicity and inevitability. Persistent symptoms may be primarily a problem for adequate drug-maintenance programs and solutions to the myriad problems of treatment compliance in chronic disorders. Work dysfunction may be intimately related to the differential availability and utilization of sheltered work opportunities in different cultures. And social dysfunction may be primarily a matter of loss of familial support and the relative absence of sheltered living communities in our mobile society for a variety of individuals who have been stripped of social ties.

In summary, I have suggested that seen from a clinician's distance the functional psychoses may be assessed through a model of their structure. The model proposed is one which urges a vertical as well as a longitudinal dimension and which focuses upon the *trait* and *state* components of this structure as separate and variable to a degree and not totally predetermining for any aspect of outcome. Whereas certain traits may be frequently associated with certain states, and indeed these pairings with certain outcomes, most individual instances of so-called functional psychotic illness are most practically attended to, and possibly most fruitfully researched, when these aspects of the disorder are independently evaluated.

REFERENCES

1. Bowers, M. B., Jr. (1974): *Retreat From Sanity: The Structure of Emerging Psychosis.* Human Sciences Press, New York.
2. Robins, E., and Guze, S. B. (1970): Establishment of diagnostic validity in psychiatric illness: Its application to schizophrenia. *Am. J. Psychiatry,* 126:983–987.
3. Dana, C. L., Davis, T. K., Jelliffe, S. E., Riley, H. A., Tilney, F., and Timme, W., editors (1925): *Schizophrenia (Dementia Praecox), A.R.N.M.D. Research Publications, Vol. 5.* Hoeber, New York.
4. Taylor, M. A. (1972): Schneiderian first-rank symptoms and clinical prognostic features in schizophrenia. *Arch. Gen. Psychiatry,* 26:64–67.
5. Carpenter, W. T., Jr., Strauss, J. S., and Muleh, S. (1973): Are there pathognomonic symptoms in schizophrenia? *Arch. Gen. Psychiatry,* 28:847–852.
6. Carpenter, W. T., Jr., and Strauss, J. S. (1974): Cross-cultural evaluation of Schneider's first-rank symptoms of schizophrenia: A report from the international pilot study of schizophrenia. *Am. J. Psychiatry,* 131:682–687.
7. Bowers, M. B., Jr. (1973): LSD-related states as models of psychosis. In: *Psychopathology and Psychopharmacology,* edited by J. O. Cole, A. M. Freedman, and A. J. Friedhoff, pp. 1–14. Johns Hopkins Univ. Press, Baltimore and London.
8. Bowers, M. B., Jr. (1972): Acute psychosis induced by psychotomimetic drug abuse. I. Clinical findings. *Arch. Gen. Psychiatry,* 27:437–440.
9. Moreau, J. J. (1973): *Hashish and Mental Illness,* edited by H. Peters and G. G. Nahas. Raven Press, New York.
10. Mirsky, I. A. (1958): Psysiologic, psychologic, and social determinants in the etiology of duodenal ulcer. *Am. J. Dig. Dis.,* 3:285–314.
11. Glass, G. S., and Bowers, M. B., Jr. (1970): Chronic psychosis associated with long-term psychotomimetic drug abuse. *Arch. Gen. Psychiatry,* 23:97–103.
12. Slater, E., Beard, A., and Glitheroe, E. (1963): The schizophrenia-like psychoses of epilepsy. *Br. J. Psychiatry,* 109:95–150.
13. Reid, A. A. (1973): Schizophrenia—disease or syndrome? *Arch. Gen. Psychiatry,* 28:863–869.
14. Kety, S. S., Rosenthal, D., Wender, P. H., and Schulsinger, F. (1968): The types and prevalence of mental illness in the biological and adoptive families of adopted schizophrenics. In: *The Transmission of Schizophrenia,* edited by D. Rosenthal and S. S. Kety, pp. 345–362. Pergamon, Oxford.
15. Murphy, D., and Weis, R. (1972): Reduced monoamine oxidase activity in blood platelets from bipolar depressed patients. *Am. J. Psychiatry,* 128:1351–1357.
16. Murphy, D., and Wyatt, R. (1972): Reduced monoamine oxidase activity in blood platelets from schizophrenic patients. *Nature,* 238:225–226.
17. Strauss, J. S., and Carpenter, W. T. (1974): Characteristic symptoms and outcome in schizophrenia. *Arch. Gen. Psychiatry,* 30:429–434.

18. Strauss, J. S., and Carpenter, W. T. (1974): The prediction of outcome in schizophrenia. II. Relationships between predictor and outcome variables. *Arch. Gen. Psychiatry,* 31:37–42.
19. Kendell, R. E., and Gourlay, J. (1970): The clinical distinction between the affective psychoses and schizophrenia. *Br. J. Psychiatry,* 117:261–266.
20. Reilly, F. E., Harrow, M., and Tucker, G. J. (1973): Language and thought content in acute psychosis. *Am. J. Psychiatry,* 130:411–417.
21. Ianzito, B. M., Cadoret, R. J., and Pugh, D. D. (1974): Thought disorder in depression. *Am. J. Psychiatry,* 131:703–707.
22. Meehl, P. (1962): Schizotaxia, schizotypy, schizophrenia. *Am. Psychol.,* 17:827–838.
23. Stein, L., and Wise, C. (1971): Possible etiology of schizophrenia: progressive damage to the noradrenergic reward system by 6-hydroxydopamine. *Science,* 171:1032–1036.
24. Meltzer, H. Y. (1973): Creatine phosphokinase activity and clinical symptomatology. *Arch. Gen. Psychiatry,* 29:589–593.

Biology of the Major Psychoses, edited by D. X.
Freedman, Res. Publ. Assoc. Res. Nerv. Ment.
Dis., Vol. 54. Raven Press, New York   1975.

The Key Clinical Dimensions of the Functional Psychoses

John S. Strauss and William T. Carpenter, Jr.

*Department of Psychiatry, University of Rochester School of Medicine and Dentistry,
Rochester, New York 14642 and Adult Psychiatry Branch, National Institute of Mental
Health, Bethesda, Maryland 20014*

> It is of little value to be precise in chemistry if we then try to establish correlations
> between exact chemical data and a non-existent clincial abstraction.
>
> Lawrence Kubie (1)

Defining disorders by combining syndromes into concepts that supposedly
reflect underlying pathologic processes has been the common practice throughout
the history of all branches of medicine. Syndromes are first described based on
the clinical impressions of patient characteristics that seem to occur together.
Validation of the syndrome as reflecting a disease process is then attempted by
demonstrating its relationships to underlying etiology, tissue pathology, response
to treatment, and outcome.

In psychiatry, the process of describing syndromes has been common, but
validating them has been particularly difficult. The number of such attempts that
has been made and failed is best reflected in the long list of discarded nosologies
described by Menninger (2) and Stengel (3). The process of arriving at more
definitive diagnostic entities has been made difficult in psychiatry by the absence
of tissue pathology or identified etiologic features that could be used for validation. Because of this problem, the development of meaningful psychopathologic
concepts has rested heavily on less definitive evidence such as symptom co-
occurrence, or on prognosis—criteria for which methodologic error has been
particularly likely to introduce distortion.

Kraepelin (4) entered the history of psychiatry at a period in which a large
number of supposed disorders had been identified on the basis of symptoms alone.
He separated many of these disorders into two discrete groups, using as a validating criterion the deteriorating course found in the one group, schizophrenia, but
not in the other, manic-depressive disorder.

Clinical evidence for the value of these diagnostic concepts has rested on three
kinds of observations: (a) the supposed co-occurrence of the characteristic symptoms of schizophrenia and the absence of these symptoms in manic-depressive
disorder; (b) the supposedly poor prognosis heralded by schizophrenic symptoms
in contrast to the good prognosis presumably indicated by manic-depressive
symptomatology; and (c) the supposed difference in the two disorders in terms
of the individual's ability to relate socially, poor social relationships being considered characteristic of schizophrenia but not of manic-depressive disorder.

This chapter describes recent evidence that suggests that these three characteristics—symptom picture, prognosis, and ability to relate socially—are not so distinctively distributed that they fit the concept of two discrete underlying disease processes—schizophrenia and manic-depressive disorder. The evidence indicates, instead, that although the three component characteristics of these diagnostic concepts are crucial variables, combining them to define two categories of disorder against which to relate biologic and psychologic findings introduces a considerable degree of error into attempts to evaluate patients and discover underlying pathologic processes. This chapter suggests a method for evaluating and describing patients that permits a test of both the roles of the individual components of the diagnostic constructs and the composite categories—schizophrenia and manic-depressive psychosis—as well. Such an approach can maximize the opportunity for finding the relationships between clinical characteristics and the underlying pathologic processes involved in the functional psychoses.

To attain this goal, the distribution patterns and validity of the clinical dimensions of the functional psychoses must first be reevaluated. This is important because improvements in patient evaluation techniques have provided much new information. Kraepelin and other investigators in the past were limited to their own personal observations and descriptive syntheses, often generalizing from data limited to such special groups as patients who had been chronically institutionalized. Recently, however, investigators have collected more accurate data through the use of several methodologic advances. These advances include the use of rating scales and structured interviews that make possible the increasingly reliable collection of clinical data, multivariate techniques to maximize the value of data by providing diverse approaches for analyzing their relationships, and the increasingly sophisticated use of controls and sampling techniques to reduce distortion from unrecognized sampling bias.

Three types of findings have emerged from these improved methodologies to challenge the significance of the clinical stereotypes defined by Kraepelin. These findings are the discovery of so-called "characteristic symptoms" of schizophrenia in diagnostic pictures otherwise considered typical of affective psychoses, the demonstration of only a limited relationship between symptom picture and outcome, and the finding of poor social function as an important prognostic factor, irrespective of the specific symptom picture in which it is found.

OCCURRENCE OF "CHARACTERISTIC SYMPTOMS" IN DIVERSE COMBINATIONS WITH OTHER SYMPTOMS

If symptoms represent a distinctive disease process, they are likely to occur frequently together and not to occur frequently with symptoms that supposedly reflect other disease processes. The following findings suggest that the occurrence of "characteristic symptoms" of schizophrenia separate from symptoms associated with manic-depressive disorder is less common than was originally supposed.

Symptoms considered by some as pathognomonic for schizophrenia such as Kurt Schneider's "first-rank" symptoms, although most helpful in diagnosis, recently have been shown to occur also in patients with predominantly affective symptom pictures and in other patients who have been assigned a variety of nonschizophrenic diagnoses by a diverse group of experienced psychiatrists (5–7).

Many of the most classic and distinctive symptom patterns of schizophrenia and manic-depressive psychosis originally described by Kraepelin and Bleuler have become increasingly rare (8). For example, classic hebephrenic or catatonic schizophrenic pictures are rarely seen.

Many of the alleged key symptoms of schizophrenia, such as flattened affect and certain kinds of thought disorder, appear to be related more to chronic institutionalization than to primary disease process (9).

Affective symptoms such as the "characteristic symptoms" of schizophrenia also appear to occur frequently in mixed pictures, for example, with supposedly schizophrenic types of thought disorder (10).

The co-occurrence of supposedly affective and schizophrenic symptoms does not appear to be limited to rare instances. This is reflected clinically in the common use of the "schizoaffective" diagnostic category. It is suggested also in some controlled studies finding that the distribution patterns of affective and schizophrenic symptoms may in fact reflect not a bimodal but a unimodal pattern (4).

Although the degree of discreteness or mixture of affective and schizophrenic symptomatology remains to be clarified (11,12), most attempts at multivariate analysis of these relationships have suggested considerable overlap between symptoms generally considered characteristic of schizophrenia and those characteristics of manic-depressive disorder as classically defined (13,14).

Taken together, these findings suggest that although examples of discrete syndromes of schizophrenia or manic-depressive psychosis do occur, the different kinds of symptoms putatively representative of these disorders often appear together, and no symptoms appear exclusively in one disorder.

RELATIONSHIP BETWEEN CHARACTERISTIC SYMPTOMS AND COURSE OF DISORDER

If symptoms define a particular disease process, which is validated clinically by a specific outcome, then these symptoms by themselves should predict that outcome. Although Kraepelin noted that there were exceptions to his view that schizophrenic symptoms were related to deterioration, the large number of these exceptions was apparently not recognized. Recent studies of patients first coming to treatment with schizophrenic symptoms show that the symptoms have a limited prognostic importance. The course of illness that they predict, although guarded, is in fact extremely variable. In controlled studies, about 40% of such patients have been shown to recover completely or almost completely (15,16). Even these estimates of recovery may be conservative, however, as sampling techniques and diagnostic practices may exclude from such studies patients with the most transient schizophrenic symptoms.

The frequently reported finding of poor outcome associated with schizophrenic symptoms in many past studies may have been at least partly a result of failure to control for already established chronicity in the patients entering these studies. There is evidence that established chronicity is an indicator of poor prognosis for many symptoms, and so must be controlled if the prognostic importance of the symptoms themselves is to be evaluated (17,18). Recent studies recording prior duration of illness routinely suggest that schizophrenic symptoms in themselves have only limited prognostic importance (16).

Unfortunately, the relationship between affective symptoms and prognosis has been obscured by the tendency to diagnose affective disorder only in the absence of chronicity. This is apparent, for example, in a study by Rennie (19) of outcome in affective disorders in which patients with more chronic, established courses were excluded from the cohort.

Those studies of outcome that have controlled previous duration of symptoms have found a somewhat better outcome in patients who have mostly affective symptoms than for patients who have mostly schizophrenic symptoms. However, the prognosis is less optimistic in affective psychoses than was earlier believed, and there is extensive overlap in outcome with patients who have mainly schizophrenic symptoms. Perhaps the most optimistic study of outcome in affective psychoses is that of Lundquist (20), who reported that 85% of first admissions for affective psychosis did recover. Although sophisticated for its time, this study had important limitations—some outcome data were collected through questionnaire letters sent to patients and through the use of outcome criteria that considered anyone to be recovered who was out of the hospital and back at work, irrespective of symptomatology, level of work, or level of social relationships at follow-up. Recent studies of outcome in affective disorder using more sophisticated methodology have noted that from 11% to about 30% of patients with major affective disorders were moderately to severely impaired at follow-up (21–24).

PREDICTORS OF OUTCOME OTHER THAN SYMPTOMS

If outcome is an important variable for suggesting an underlying pathologic process, as it is in some disorders, then consideration of major predictors of outcome other than symptomatology is crucial to defining that process. The ability to form social relationships has been shown most consistently to be of major importance as such a predictor (16,25). Although most studies of this variable have focused on schizophrenia, there is evidence to suggest that, as with the variable of established chronicity, social relationships are an important predictor in several disorders, irrespective of the specific syndromes involved (26,27). Unfortunately, there are limited data regarding the role of this variable in affective psychoses; however, Rennie (19) did report that those patients in a cohort of manic-depressives who recovered tended to have outgoing personalities.

Taken together, these findings regarding the overlap in the distribution of symptoms, the limited relationship of specific symptoms to outcome, and indications that ability to form social relationships is a prognostic factor transcending particular syndromes, suggest that the conceptualization of the functional psychoses as two distinct disorders may not be the most accurate or valid way of classifying the clinical phenomena; therefore, it might reduce chances to determine the relationship between underlying biologic and psychologic processes and clinical characteristics.

Distortion and constriction is placed on clinical findings by utilizing the two discrete diagnostic categories—schizophrenia and manic-depressive disorder—because the key variables—symptom picture, course of disorder, and social relationships—represent continua and vary relatively independently of one another. The failure to record and analyze each of the variables separately, as well as in combination, may introduce distortion in the process of attempting to define pathologic processes.

This can be illustrated by a brief clinical description. Mrs. D, a middle-aged, married woman, was first hospitalized in her late twenties suffering from depression and the belief that rays were controlling her thoughts. She also felt she was being followed and that people were trying to harm her. The persecutory delusions and the experience of being controlled by an outside force (a first-rank symptom) would be sufficient for many investigators to diagnose her as schizophrenic. She has since been rehospitalized on two occasions with similar symptoms. Between hospitalizations, she has functioned well as a mother and in her professional role, both roles requiring considerable interpersonal skills.

If diagnosed within one of the conventional categories, this woman would be called schizophrenic by some, whereas others would consider her as having a primary depressive disorder. Other investigators might diagnose her as a schizoaffective schizophrenic. For others she might be excluded from studies because she does not fit the classic stereotypes. But these approaches do not provide an optimal solution for discovering relationships between the diverse clinical pictures presented by the three key variables and the underlying pathologic processes. It may be more useful to describe this patient and others in terms of each of the three variables or "axes"—symptoms, course of disorder, and social relationships. This approach permits analysis of biologic and other data in relationship to each clinical dimension, to categories defined by combinations of these axes as well as to classic diagnostic concepts.

VARIABLES (AXES) FOR STUDYING THE FUNCTIONAL PSYCHOSES

Symptoms

Psychotic symptoms can be described on a continuum from a schizophrenic symptom picture at one extreme to a pure affective psychotic picture at the other end. Although the extremes reflect quite different clinical pictures, the middle of the continuum is represented by those patients with both schizophrenic and affective symptomatology. Mrs. D's symptoms of depression and delusions of control and persecution would place her at the middle of this continuum.

Course of Illness

For this variable, a continuum can be represented by a chronic course at one extreme and a single brief episode at the other. This dimension might be defined, e.g., as the percentage of time over a given interval during which an individual has psychotic symptomatology. Mrs. D's remittant course places her toward the middle of this continuum as well.

Social Relationships

In the past, the Phillips Scale of Premorbid Adjustment (28) has been used as a measure of social relationships. This scale has limited reliability, but its success in predicting outcome is a tribute to the power of the concept it defines. A reliable and simpler measure of personal relationships, frequency of meetings with friends in the year prior to evaluation, has been equally or more predictive of outcome than the total Phillips scores in two studies (27,29). Mrs. D's adequacy in social relationships would place her at the "good" end of this continuum.

The three axes described above are represented in Fig. 1.

Although less global than diagnostic categories, these axes are to some degree merely conceptual approximations of reality. As such, they have shortcomings that need further refinement based on more extensive data. Because the axes can be operationalized to fit diverse patients more closely than is possible for diagnostic categories, extreme expectations frequently arise that the dimensions can provide even more concordance between the descriptive concept and the real patient than is possible for any such measure that summarizes a large number of data. In spite of limitations in this regard, using the axes for diagnosis in

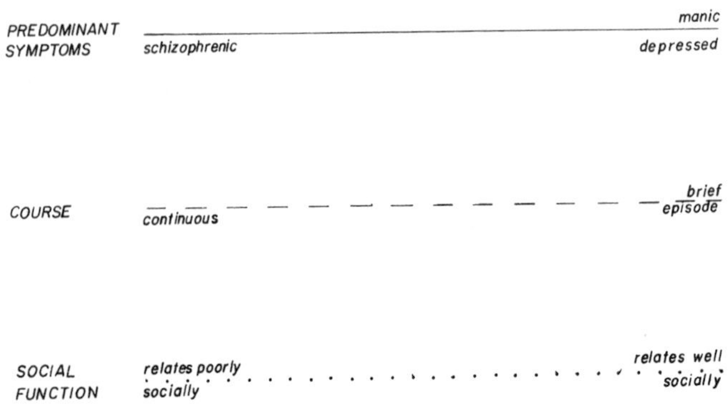

FIG. 1. Three diagnostic axes.

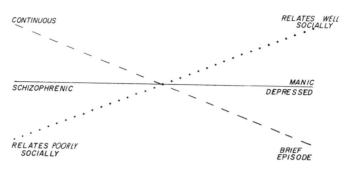

FIG. 2. Classic conception of relationship among diagnostic axes. (—) Predominant symptoms; (- - -) course; (· · ·) social function.

contrast to limiting classification to a small number of diagnostic categories appears to provide a more direct link with clinical findings and prognostic validity, and in this way represents an improved framework for collecting, reducing, and analyzing clinical data (30).

By evaluating and analyzing these axes separately, it is possible, for example, to test Kraepelinian and other assumptions that there is a high correlation among these variables that defines a distinctive type of disorder. The Kraepelinian assumption, as modified slightly by successive schools of psychiatry, can be considered as a conception of the axes as highly correlated. This assumption is reflected diagrammatically in Fig. 2.

If there were no relationship between these axes and Kraepelin were totally incorrect, clinical studies would demonstrate an entirely orthogonal relationship among the axes. A third hypothesis, one that in our opinion is best supported by the available data, is that there is a significant but only partial relationship among the three axes. Such a relationship can best be understood using the systems theory model of open-linked systems. In that view, each of the three axes, although interacting with the others, would be considered as a representation of a separate "system" with its own determinants. This model has the advantage of permitting hypotheses about partial relationships among the variables such as a hypothesis that schizophrenic symptoms are frequently but not exclusively found in individuals with poor social relations; however, when these symptoms and poor social relationships do occur together probability of good outcome is reduced.

Whatever the final conclusions regarding the relationships of the major axes of the functional psychoses, the evaluation system recommended here has the important advantage that it allows the testing of the alternative hypotheses regarding specific disorders, open-linked systems, and independent processes. Routine evaluation of these three axes will help to provide a maximum opportunity for investigators to determine which of the hypotheses relates most closely to biologic and psychologic variables. Abnormal levels of a particular enzyme may be found only in patients who are at an extreme for all three axes, or, in contrast,

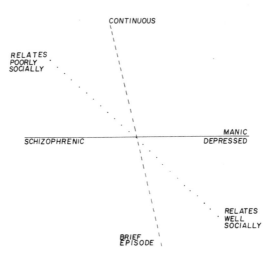

FIG. 3. Revised view of relationship among diagnostic axes. (—) Predominant symptoms; (- - -) course; (· · ·) social function.

who relate only to one of the axes. If these dimensions are routinely evaluated, multivariate techniques such as multiple regression analysis can be utilized to determine the strongest relationships among diverse variables, especially when techniques now available to analyze specific combinations of predictors are used (31). At a time when relatively little is known in this area, such an approach considerably increases the likelihood of discovering the pathologic processes that underlie the clinical characteristics of psychotic patients.

ACKNOWLEDGMENTS

This research was carried out in part in the Department of Psychiatry of the University of Rochester Medical School and was supported by National Institute of Mental Health Grant MH-22836–01.

REFERENCES

1. Kubie, L. S. (1969): Fallacies in the concept of schizophrenia. *Symp. Problems of Psychosis, Montreal.*
2. Menninger, K. (1963): *The Vital Balance.* Viking, New York.
3. Stengel, E. (1960): Classification of mental disorders. *Bull. WHO,* 21:601–663.
4. Kraepelin, E. (1919): *Dementia Praecox,* translated and edited by R. M. Barclay. Livingston, Edinburgh.
5. Carpenter, W. T., Strauss, J. S., and Muleh, S. (1973): Are there pathognomonic symptoms of schizophrenia? *Arch. Gen. Psychiatry,* 28:847–852.
6. Carpenter, W. T., and Strauss, J. S. (1974): Cross-cultural evaluation of Schneider's first-rank symptoms of schizophrenia: A report from the International Pilot Study of Schizophrenia. *Am. J. Psychiatry,* 131:682–687.
7. Taylor, M. A., and Abrams, R. (1973): The phenomenology of mania. *Arch. Gen. Psychiatry,* 29:520–522.

8. Hare, E. H. (1974): The changing content of psychiatric illness. *J. Psychosom. Res.,* 18:283–289.
9. Wing, J. K., and Brown, G. W. (1970): *Institutionalism and Schizophrenia.* Cambridge Univ. Press, London.
10. Breakey, W. R., and Goodell, H. (1972): Thought disorder in mania and schizophrenia evaluated by Bannister's Grid Test for Schizophrenic Thought Disorder. *Br. J. Psychiatry,* 120:391–395.
11. Everitt, B. S., Gourlay, A. J., and Kendell, R. E. (1971): An attempt at validation of traditional psychiatric syndromes by cluster analysis. *Br. J. Psychiatry,* 119:399–412.
12. Kendell, R. E., and Gourlay, J. (1970): The clinical distinction between the affective psychoses and schizophrenia. *Br. J. Psychiatry,* 117:261–266.
13. Lorr, M. (1966): *Explorations in Typing Psychotics,* p. 22. Pergamon, Oxford.
14. Katz, M. M., and Lyerly, S. B. (1963): Methods for measuring adjustment and social behavior in the community. I. Rationale description, discrimination validity, and scale development. *Psychol. Rep.,* 13:503–535.
15. Brown, G. W., Bone, M., Dalison, B., and Wing, J. K. (1966): *Schizophrenia and Social Care.* Oxford Univ. Press, London.
16. Strauss, J. S., and Carpenter, W. T. (1972): The prediction of outcome in schizophrenia I. Characteristics of outcome. *Arch. Gen. Psychiatry,* 27:739–746.
17. Kringlen, E. (1970): Natural history of obsessional neurosis. *Semin. Psychiatry,* 2:403–419.
18. Strauss, J. S., and Carpenter, W. T. (1974): Evaluation of outcome in schizophrenia. In: *Life History Research in Psychopathology,* edited by M. Roff and D. Ricks, Vol. 3. Univ. of Minnesota Press, Minneapolis.
19. Rennie. T. A. C. (1942): Prognosis in manic-depressive psychosis. *Am. J. Psychiatry,* 98:801–814.
20. Lundquist, G. (1945): Prognosis and course in manic-depressive psychosis. *Acta Psychiatr. Neurol.,* Suppl XXXV.
21. Carlson, G. A., Kotin, J., Davenport, Y. B., and Adlord, M. (1974): Follow-up of 53 bipolar manic-depressive patients. *Br. J. Psychiatry,* 124:134–139.
22. Winokur, G. W., Clayton, P. J., and Reich, T. (1969): *Manic-Depressive Illness.* Mosby, St. Louis, Missouri.
23. Bratfos, O., and Haug, J. O. (1968): The course of manic-depressive psychosis. *Acta Psychiatr. Scand.,* 44:89–112.
24. Winokur, and Morrison, J. (1973): The Iowa 500: Follow-up of 225 depressives. *Br. J. Psychiatry,* 123:543–548.
25. Phillips, L. (1966): Social competence, the process-reactive distinction and the nature of mental disorder. In: *Psychopathology of Schizophrenia,* edited by P. H. Hoch and J. Zubin, pp. 471–481. Grune & Stratton, New York.
26. Phillips, L., and Rabinovitch, M. S. (1958): Social roles and patterns of symptomatic behaviors. *J. Abnorm. Psychol.,* 57:181–186.
27. Strauss, J. S., and Carpenter, W. T. (1974): Prediction of outcome in schizophrenia. II. Relationships between predictor and outcome variables. *Arch. Gen. Psychiatry,* 31:37–42.
28. Phillips, L. (1953): Case history data and prognosis in schizophrenia. *J. Nerv. Ment. Dis.,* 135:534–543.
29. Farina A., Garmezy, N., Zalusky, M., and Becker, J. (1962): Premorbid behavior and prognosis in female schizophrenic patients. *J. Consult. Clin. Psychol.,* 26:56–60.
30. Strauss, J. (1974): Towards a multiaxial system for the diagnosis of adult psychopathology. *127th Annual Mtg. of the American Psychiatric Association, Detroit, Michigan.*
31. Koplyay, C., Deene Gott, C., and Elton, J. (1973): *Automatic Interaction Director Version 4 (AID-4) Reference Manual.* Computational Sciences Division of the Air Force Human Resources Laboratory, Lackland, Texas.

Biology of the Major Psychoses, edited by D. X.
Freedman, *Res. Publ. Assoc. Res. Nerv. Ment.
Dis.,* Vol. 54. Raven Press, New York   1975.

The Spectrum Concept in Schizophrenic and Manic-Depressive Disorders

David Rosenthal

Laboratory of Psychology, National Institute of Mental Health, Bethesda, Maryland 20014

It seems somewhat ironic that while representing the U.S. Field Center in the WHO International Pilot Study of Schizophrenia, John Strauss and Will Carpenter were working upstairs at the National Institute of Health Clinical Center, trying to hone a definition of schizophrenia as sharply as they could possibly make it, while Paul Wender and I were working downstairs, in concert with Seymour Kety, in effect broadening the concept of schizophrenic disorder as widely as it may have ever been reasonably conceived before.

If this sounds as though we were working at cross purposes, let me assure you that this was not the case. The two groups of researchers were directing themselves to different goals. Strauss and Carpenter sought to identify a group of symptoms that provided maximal probability of occurrence in schizophrenia and minimal probability of occurrence in nonschizophrenic disorder. Wender, Kety, and I were also concerned with having a maximum likelihood definition of chronic or process schizophrenia, but our major concern was to identify and include all disorders that were genetically associated with process schizophrenia, and eventually to define each of these as succinctly as possible.

While Carpenter and Strauss emphasized the limits or boundaries of the process schizophrenia concept, our group strained to encompass all disorders that shared salient clinical and behavioral manifestations with process schizophrenia and to group these as a spectrum of schizophrenic disorder.

Of course, we did not know which disorders, if any, should be included in such a spectrum to meet the criterion of genetic or familial commonality. Nevertheless, we selected the ones that we thought had the highest probability of meeting this criterion, and introduced them into our research studies as a hypothesis to be tested. It was easy to read through the *APA Diagnostic and Statistical Manual,* second edition, to make such selections. In addition to APA's process schizophrenia with the classic Kraepelinian and schizoaffective subtypes, we included APA's acute schizophrenic episode, which we modified and referred to as acute schizophrenic reaction; schizophrenia, latent type, which we modified and called borderline schizophrenia; and APA's paranoid personality and schizoid personality, and some severe cases of inadequate personality.

Paul Wender rewrote for us the definitions of the respective diagnostic categories, primarily expanding on the APA formulations, adding criteria like "good or poor premorbid adjustment," response to drugs, anhedonia, and other factors not specifically dealt with in DSM II. The category that we elaborated most was borderline schizophrenia, which received relatively sparse treatment and definition in the DSM II characterization of schizophrenia, latent type. Although there were suggestions in the literature that manic-depressive illness and psychopathy might have some genetic association with schizophrenia, we did not consider these disorders to be part of the spectrum, although we have been careful to check out this possibility in our studies.

After having selected the various spectrum disorders, we then had to test their validity. This could be done in two different ways.

1. One can select a group of probands who have spectrum disorders, and a group of controls who do not have such disorders. If the relatives of the spectrum probands have a higher frequency of spectrum disorders than do the relatives of controls, we have presumptive evidence that the spectrum disorders are genetically associated. If, however, the relatives have had life experiences in common with the spectrum probands, one could as well assume that it is the experiential commonality rather than common genes that leads to the increased spectrum frequency in relatives. If the probands are adoptees who were separated from their parents from early age, then the possible effect of similar life experiences is greatly reduced, and the genetic hypothesis takes on high credibility.

2. If we can demonstrate that matings involving one or two spectrum parents lead to increased spectrum disorders in their offspring, as compared to matings of couples without such disorders, then we again have presumptive evidence of a genetic contribution to the spectrum. Moreover, if the offspring have had virtually no experiential associations with the parents, we can infer with a high level of confidence that the increased spectrum frequency in the offspring is genetic in origin.

Finally, to meet the concept of spectrum, we must find an increased frequency among relatives in one or more spectrum disorders when the proband diagnosis involves a specific spectrum disorder. Therefore, we should find more borderlines or schizoid personalities, or both, among the relatives of process schizophrenics than among the relatives of controls.

With respect to all such research, in which the dependent variable is the diagnosis of relatives, it is essential that the diagnostician not know whether the individual examined is related to an index or control proband, especially when the criteria for the spectrum disorders are not as sharply defined as we would like, and because it is easy to be swayed by knowledge regarding index or control status. Studies that do not employ a control group surrender a great deal of their credibility.

Three of our adoption studies were especially relevant to the spectrum concept. In the first of these we begin with spectrum and control probands, and we examine the frequency of the spectrum disorders in the probands' first-degree biologic relatives and half-sibs. The numerical values that I am presenting for today's conference are not final figures but should be close to the final figures. They represent the consensus diagnosis of three judges.

First, the prevalence of all spectrum disorders in the relatives of index probands was about twice as much as that in the relatives of controls, $p < 0.01$. This finding meets our first criterion. When the diagnosis of the index case was process schizophrenia, we found 19 of 104 relatives diagnosed as process, uncertain, or borderline schizophrenia, but none diagnosed as having an acute schizophrenic reaction. When the index case was diagnosed borderline schizophrenia, we found 5 of 38 relatives diagnosed borderline or uncertain schizophrenia, but none diagnosed process or acute schizophrenic reaction. When the proband diagnosis was acute schizophrenic reaction, 4 of 31 relatives were diagnosed as uncertain schizophrenia and one was diagnosed as schizoid personality, but none were diagnosed as acute, process, or borderline schizophrenia. Among the 121 relatives of healthy controls, one was process and one was borderline schizophrenia. Again the index-control differences are statistically significant.

With regard to the spectrum category that includes paranoid, schizoid, and severely inadequate personality, our consensus diagnoses did not produce a statistically significant difference between the relatives of the index and control groups. However, of the three judges who independently diagnosed all relatives, one judge did successfully discriminate the index and control relatives with respect to this category, $p < 0.05$, indicating that it is probable but not certain that this group also belongs in the spectrum. Therefore, the findings suggest that process, uncertain, and borderline schizophrenia behave much the same in their distribution among relatives, that the less salient schizoid category shows a possible but weaker tendency to behave in the same way, and that acute schizophrenic reaction also seems to show a weak genetic association with other spectrum disorders.

In the second study, we compared two groups of adoptees, in which the index group had a biologic parent with a spectrum disorder and the control group did not. Dr. Joseph Welner interviewed and diagnosed both groups without knowing to which group the subject belonged, except perhaps in a few cases. Of the 69 index cases, 22 had a spectrum disorder, approximately one-third. Of the 67 controls, 12 had a spectrum disorder, representing approximately 18%. Hence, the index group had almost twice as many spectrum disorders as the controls, but the χ^2 indicated that the difference was significant only at the 0.05 level, using a one-tailed t-test. Part of the reason for the high rate of such disorders in the controls probably stems from the fact that we had not examined the biologic parents of our controls. We had relied only upon the fact that neither parent had a registered psychiatric disorder; we know now that most people with such disorders do not come to psychiatric attention, and an appreciable number of these parents probably had such a disorder, which they may have transmitted to their offspring. We hope to examine these parents in the future. It should be pointed out in any case that five of the index cases were diagnosed as "schizoid" as compared to two controls, and that of the four index subjects whose biologic parent had a diagnosis of acute schizophrenic reaction, none had a spectrum disorder. The numbers are small, but they are consistent with the findings of the first study. Three index cases were diagnosed process schizophrenia as against zero controls, and fifteen index cases were diagnosed borderline schizophrenia, definite, possible, or probable, as against seven controls. Considering the fact that our controls are probably somewhat contaminated, the differences are appreciable and consistent with those of the first study.

In a third study, we seek to provide a purer test of the hypothesis that the spectrum disorders are genetically related, and we do this by examining *both* biologic parents of our index adoptees. We are especially interested in establishing or ruling out the validity of the category that includes schizoid, paranoid, and severely inadequate personality, the category we call the "soft spectrum." Process, borderline, and doubtful schizophrenia are now well established. The research strategy is a simple one. We divide the parent matings into two types, those in which both parents have a spectrum disorder, which we may designate as assortative or dual matings, and those in which only one parent has a spectrum disorder, which we may designate as nonassortative matings. If dual matings, in which one parent has a soft-spectrum disorder, produce more offspring with spectrum disorders than do nonassortative matings, then the difference must be attributed to the input from the soft-spectrum parent.

In our first analysis, we considered only couples in which one parent was a chronic schizophrenic and in which the co-parent had been given an intensive psychiatric interview which permitted us to make a diagnosis of spectrum, or not spectrum. There were 22 such matings. Of these, 10 were assortative and 12 were nonassortative. In almost all instances, the co-parent had a soft-spectrum diagnosis.

We found that the frequency of spectrum disorder in the offspring of assortative matings was three to five times more frequent than among the offspring of nonassortative matings. A Fisher exact-probability test indicates that the difference is significant at the 0.025 level.

In a second analysis, neither biologic parent had chronic schizophrenia, but at least one parent had a spectrum disorder. Unfortunately, we had only 18 such matings. However, the trend of the findings is similar to that of the previous analysis. There were eight assortative and 10 nonassortative matings. The frequency of spectrum disorder was two to four times greater among the offspring of assortative matings, but the difference does not reach the customary criterion of statistical significance.

However, when we compare all matings in both analyses combined, the numbers are more substantial and we find that among all 40 matings, the frequency of spectrum disorder is three to five times greater among the offspring of assortative than nonassortative matings, and the difference is significant at the 0.006 level.

Therefore although almost every nonassortative co-parent carried a diagnosis of personality, neurotic, or affective disorder, these diagnoses did not contribute to the development of spectrum disorders in the offspring in the same way that assortative spectrum mating did. Because a mating of a chronic schizophrenic and a co-parent with spectrum disorder increases the frequency of spectrum disorders in offspring the genes involved in the spectrum disorders are additive with respect to the gene(s) associated with process schizophrenia itself. Such findings provide evidence that the spectrum concept is probably valid.

Because the spectrum concept regarding schizophrenia seemed to provide a novel and integrated view of the disorders subsumed under it, one could expect that the spectrum idea might be applied to other disorders as well. In fact, Schulsinger (1) proposed a spectrum regarding psychopathic disorders, and Winokur (2,3) and Winokur et al. (4) have proposed a spectrum regarding the affective disorders. Since our concern in this symposium is to evaluate the two major psychoses, schizophrenia and manic-depressive disorder, we will attempt to assess the spectrum concept only as it has been applied to these two disorders.

What Winokur has done is to "divide depressive illness into depression *spectrum* disease and *pure* depressive disease." Depression spectrum disease is the prototype disorder involving "the early onset female who has considerable alcoholism among primary male relatives and more depression in female than male relatives." Its counterpart, *pure* depressive disease, has as its prototype the late-onset male, who has "equal amounts of depression in male and female relatives and no familial increase in alcoholism over ordinary expectation. Depression spectrum disease is characterized also by having a higher degree of total familial illness (alcoholism, sociopathy and depression) than pure depressive disease."

Winokur thinks that there may be a differential response to various treatments between depression spectrum disease and pure depressive disease, and there may also be considerable differences in symptomatology and course of illness.

There are some striking differences between Winokur's spectrum and our own. For example, our spectrum concept is based only on diagnosis, and our view is that the disorders subsumed under it manifest a typologic unity and a gradation of characteristics and symptoms that reflect a single disease category with a common genetic base. Winokur's spectrum splits the depressive disorders into two major groups with the idea that they are genetically distinct. Variables associated with his depression spectrum disease include sex and age at onset. In the schizophrenia spectrum sex and age at onset are not at issue. Whereas we include only diagnoses that have a schizophrenic-like coloring, Winokur includes in the depression spectrum other diagnostic categories such as alcoholism and sociopathy, both of which have been reported to represent separate genetic entities by themselves (Schulsinger, 1; Goodwin et al., 5). Winokur says that "it is entirely likely that alcoholism in a first degree family member could provide a disease marker which would separate one group of patients from another." This sounds like a tall assumption. Moreover, although he sees the spectrum and the pure depressive disorders as two different diseases, he also sees them as "two ends of a continuum," and states that "there must be considerable overlap" regarding them. The distinctions between the spectrum and pure disorders become even more blurred in that "some patients who have depression spectrum disease may actually become ill somewhat later than 40" and "some of the early-onset males may well have depression spectrum disease."

The question we must ask ourselves now is, does the spectrum concept help us in any way to obtain a better understanding of the two major psychiatric disorders? One of the issues we have had to deal with over the years, and which we are attacking head on at this meeting, had to do with the question of whether two different psychoses were involved, or two different manifestations of a single psychosis. Various kinds of evidence have been presented in the past in favor of both possibilities (6). The spectrum concept now suggests some new evidence. Before we can evaluate it, however, we must assume that our schizophrenia spectrum concept and Winokur's depression spectrum disease are both valid, and of course this assumption can be readily challenged. The schizophrenia spectrum concept has been checked out in several ways, but the specific formulation of the concept of depression spectrum disease was proposed only recently, and the opportunity for attempts to validate it has probably been slight. However, if both concepts hold up, we may see more clearly how different the schizophrenic and affective disorders are in their expression.

Perhaps most important, the schizophrenia spectrum disorders diagnostically comprise a relative homogeneity, whereas depression spectrum disease involves a heterogeneous group of diagnostic categories, including depression, alcoholism, and sociopathy. Whereas the spectrum concept suggests that schizophrenic disorders represent a single disease, with the possible exception of some so-called acute schizophrenic reactions, the depression spectrum divides the affective disorders and counterposes to itself a *pure* depression disease. Moreover, if we note that the affective disorders also counterpose genetically the bipolar and unipolar disorders, and suggest as well the possibility of sex linkage, the amount of genetic heterogeneity in these disorders seems to be considerable and messy. Thus, the spectrum concept tends to polarize the schizophrenic and affective disorders even more than before, with schizophrenia looking like a relatively simple entity, from a clinical and genetic standpoint, and the affective disorders appearing to be a highly complex entity from both a clinical and genetic standpoint, even more than was believed by Rüdin in 1916 (7), and by later investigators who also recognized and decried the disordered genetic hodgepodge found in the manic-depressive psychoses. Word of mouth suggestions have been made that the so-called affective disorders do not primarily involve affects at all, but rather that they are primary manifestations of energy anomalies. Perhaps we ought to take a fresh look at this complicated problem and provide it with a new theoretical context.

REFERENCES

1. Schulsinger, F. (1972): Psychopathy: hereditary and environment. *Int. J. Ment. Health,* 1:190–206.
2. Winokur, G. (1972): Depression spectrum disease: Description and family study. *Compr. Psychiatry,* 13:3–8.

3. Winokur, G. (1974): The division of depressive illness into depression spectrum disease and pure depressive disease. *Int. Pharmacopsychiatry,* 9:5–13.

4. Winokur, G., Morrison, J., Clancy, J., and Crowe, R. (1973): The Iowa 500: Familial and clinical findings favor two kinds of depressive illness. *Compr. Psychiatry,* 14:99–106.

5. Goodwin, D. W., Schulsinger, F., Hermansen, L., Guze, S., and Winokur, G. (1973): Alcohol problems in adoptees raised apart from alcoholic biological parents. *Arch. Gen. Psychiatry,* 28: 238–243.

6. Rosenthal, D. (1970): *Genetic Theory and Abnormal Behavior,* pp. 162–168; 215–216. McGraw-Hill, New York.

7. Rüdin, E. (1916): *Zur Vererbung und Neuentstehung der Dementia praecox.* Springer-Verlag, Berlin.

Biology of the Major Psychoses, edited by D. X. Freedman, *Res. Publ. Assoc. Res. Nerv. Ment. Dis.*, Vol. 54. Raven Press, New York   1975.

Schizophrenia and Affective Disorders: One Illness or Many?

Ming T. Tsuang

University of Iowa, College of Medicine, Iowa City, Iowa 52242

It has been nearly 80 years now since Kraepelin (1) delineated dementia praecox and manic-depressive illness. Using available family data, what evidence do we have to support the view that schizophrenia and affective disorder are two genetically distinct illnesses?

EVIDENCE FROM MONOZYGOTIC TWIN STUDIES

Theoretically, monozygotic (Mz) twins share 100% of genes in common. There has been a great deal of evidence to indicate the existence of genetic factors in schizophrenia and affective disorder (2–5). Therefore, if these two conditions are separate illnesses, there should be no pairs of Mz twins in which one twin is schizophrenic and his co-twin is affectively ill. There are many available twin studies that are relevant to our discussion. However, I have selected four studies that present detailed case histories so that the family data may be reanalyzed according to our need.

In a 1953 twin study by Slater (6), case histories were collected of persons born in multiple births from the standing populations of several British mental hospitals. Kringlen's 1967 study (7) selected a twin sample from the Norwegian Birth Register and from the Central Register of Psychosis. The third study by Gottesman and Shields (8) used a study sample from the Twin Register at Maudsley Hospital, London and a blind consensus diagnosis by six psychiatrists who had no knowledge of the twins' relationship. The fourth twin study by Fischer (9) was based on Mz twin probands collected from the Danish Twin Register and the Central Psychiatric Register.

Table 1 shows the pairs of Mz twins in which the proband's diagnosis was either schizophrenia or affective disorder. A review of the case histories of the four studies shows that only those twins with a diagnosis of definite schizophrenia or affective disorder were used in Table 1. The Slater and Kringlen studies have both schizophrenic and affective ill probands, whereas the last two studies included only schizophrenic probands.

According to these studies, there is not a single pair of twins that shows the combination of schizophrenia and affective disorder. Therefore, the evidence from these studies is very convincing that schizophrenia and affective disorder are separate illnesses.

TABLE 1. *Monozygotic twin pairs (proband's diagnosis: Definite schizophrenia or affective disorder)*

SS (%)	SA	SO	S—	Source
22 (55%)	0	12	6	Slater (1953)
14 (31%)	0	18	13	Kringlen (1967)
12 (50%)	0	7	5	Gottesman and Shields (1972)
9 (36%)	0	7	9	Fischer (1973)
AA (%)	AS	AO	A—	Fischer (1973)
4 (50%)	0	1	3	Slater (1953)
2 (33%)	0	2	2	Kringlen (1967)

S, Schizophrenia; A, affective disorder; O, other mental disorder; —, normal.

If the diagnostic criteria of schizophrenia and affective disorder are broadened to include questionable cases, pairs of the combination of schizophrenia and affective disorder can be found. In Slater's study there are two discordant pairs—a schizophrenic-reactive depression pair and an affective disorder-suspected paranoid psychosis pair. In the Kringlen study, there are four discordant pairs—two schizophrenic-neurotic depression pairs, one schizophreniform-neurotic depression pair, and one reactive excitement-borderline schizophrenic pair. In the Gottesman and Shields study, there are two discordant pairs—one schizophrenic–neurotic depression pair and one uncertain schizophrenic–neurotic depression pair. These pairs of twins in which there is a combination of doubtful schizophrenia and affective disorder are quite understandable because of the variation of phenotypic manifestation of schizophrenic or affective genotypes resulting from interaction of genotypes and environment.

The next question we have to ask is whether each of these two illnesses is homogenous or heterogenous. First we will consider the affective disorders.

HETEROGENEITY OF AFFECTIVE DISORDER

Bipolar and Unipolar

Traditionally, manic-depressive illness has been regarded as one illness. However, three separate studies show that manic-depression can be divided into at least two kinds—bipolar and unipolar, as shown in Fig. 1. The three family studies were conducted by Perris (10) in Sweden, Angst (11) in Switzerland, and Winokur and Clayton (12) in the United States. For instance the Perris study, which used clearly defined criteria (evidence of three successive depressive episodes was needed to classify patients as unipolar, whereas those showing at least one manic and one depressive episode were classified as bipolar), found the relatives of bipolar patients had a significantly higher risk for bipolar (16.3%) than for unipolar (0.8%). The relatives of unipolar patients had a significantly

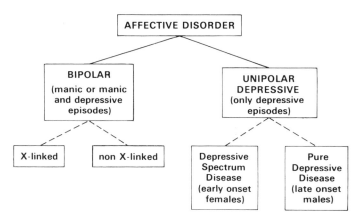

FIG. 1. Heterogeneity of affective disorder. Evidence for subdivision: (———) established; (– – –) presumptive.

higher risk for unipolar (10.6%) than for bipolar (0.5%). The Swiss and American studies found similar differences that strongly suggest that bipolar disorder and unipolar disorder are genetically independent.

Possible Subtypes within Bipolars and Unipolars

Using X-linked markers such as Xg^a blood group and color blindness, Winokur and Tanna (13) showed that bipolars were transmitted by an X-linked dominant gene. This finding was subsequently replicated and confirmed by other workers (14–16). However, there are a number of studies which are incompatible with a strictly X-linked transmission because they indicate the presence of a number of ill-father/ill-son pairs (10,17–22). This raises the question that bipolars are not actually unitary genetically. They may be transmitted by an X-linked dominant, a single autosomal dominant gene or polygenes.

Within unipolars there may be two subtypes, as suggested by Winokur in 1971 (23). Winokur found that in the families of unipolar females with onset before the age of 40, there are more depressives among female relatives than there are among male relatives, whereas among the male relatives there are more alcoholics and sociopaths. In the families of unipolar males with onset after age 40, depressives are fairly equally distributed between males and females, and there is no significant amount of alcoholism or sociopathy in the male relatives. Winokur subtyped these two kinds of unipolars as depressive spectrum disease for the prototype of the early-onset females and pure depressive disease for the prototype of the late-onset males. Subsequent studies seem to support this subclassification of the unipolars (24–27). However, these studies have all been done at the same or at closely related centers. It will be necessary for other centers to confirm this subgrouping. If possible linkage studies for unipolar depressives should be undertaken, as none are available in the literature.

In summary then, it appears affective disorder may be divided into bipolar which may perhaps have X-linked and non-X-linked subgroups, and unipolar which may perhaps be subdivided into depressive spectrum disease and pure depressive disease.

HETEROGENEITY OF SCHIZOPHRENIA

Figure 2 summarizes the ways in which schizophrenia has been delineated by various authors using family studies.

Organic and Idiopathic Schizophrenia

Schizophrenia may be differentiated into two groups on the basis of precipitating factors, namely, organically caused schizophrenia and schizophrenia that has no apparent cause or the cause of which is psychologic. In a 1932 sib study, Schulz (28) found a significantly higher incidence of schizophrenia in the sibs of schizophrenics whose precipitants are either nonorganic or idiopathic (7.5%) than in the families of schizophrenics with somatic precipitating factors (3.7%). Davidson and Bagley (29) summarized the available data in addition to their own study and showed that patients with idiopathic schizophrenia had a higher percentage of family history of schizophrenia (33%) than patients with symptomatic schizophrenia (9.3%). They also found a higher incidence of catatonic symptoms in symptomatic schizophrenia, whereas idiopathic schizophrenia had a higher incidence of flat affect, passivity, thought disorder, auditory and tactile hallucinations, and premorbid schizoid personality. Hence, there is a strong evidence that schizophrenia should be divided into organic or symptomatic schizophrenia and idiopathic or true schizophrenia.

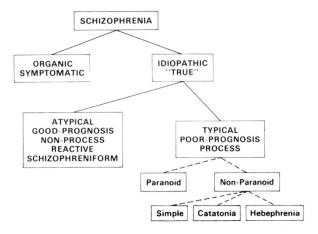

FIG. 2. Heterogeneity of schizophrenia. Evidence for subdivision: (———) established; (– – –) presumptive.

Idiopathic Schizophrenia: Typical and Atypical

Within idiopathic schizophrenia, Mitsuda (30) differentiated typical from atypical cases of schizophrenia. The typical and atypical cases differed clinically in that the typical patients had a gradual onset with symptoms of emotional blunting, high degree of personality deterioration, rigid countenance and posture, disturbed rapport, and a chronic-progressive course, whereas the atypical cases were more episodic with symptoms of delusional perception, disturbed orientation and apprehension, incoherence, confusion or change of consciousness, insight into illness at recovering state, and amnesia as to pathologic experience. Mitsuda found that out of 68 families with a schizophrenic taint, there were 66 families (97%) in which the family members and probands were concordant for typical, and the concordance for atypical was 41 families out of 48 (85%). There were no families in which there was a combination of atypical and typical schizophrenia. Within his family study, Mitsuda also found 140 Mz twin pairs; seven were concordant for typical, 1 was concordant for atypical, and there were no twin pairs with a combination of typical and atypical. He found that 80% of the families with typical probands had a pattern of recessive inheritance in which there was no recognizable taint in the pedigree or only in the sibs. The patterns of inheritance for the families of atypical cases were more evenly distributed among dominant, intermediate, and recessive.

Atypical and typical schizophrenia can also be shown to be different on basis of prognosis, with atypical cases showing good prognosis and typical cases having a poor prognosis. In 1971, McCabe et al. (31) studied the family histories of 28 good-prognosis and 25 poor-prognosis schizophrenics by interviewing family members, without knowledge of whether the proband's prognosis was good or poor. This blind family study showed that the first-degree relatives of good prognosis had a high risk for affective disorder (10.0%) and a lower risk for schizophrenia (3.3%), whereas the relatives of the poor-prognosis group had a low risk for affective disorder (1.5%) and a higher risk for schizophrenia (11.6%). Atypical schizophrenia may also be referred to as nonprocess, reactive, or schizophreniform, whereas typical schizophrenia may be called process schizophrenia.

Possible Subtypes within Typical Schizophrenia

Typical schizophrenia can be divided into simple, catatonic, hebephrenic, or paranoid schizophrenia. Several family studies have found a high concordance rate for these subtypes between probands and family members (32–34). For instance, Kallman (34) found a tendency for the schizophrenic children of hebephrenics to be hebephrenic (60.7%) and for the schizophrenic children of catatonics to be catatonic (52.9%), whereas the subtype distribution for the schizophrenic children of paranoids was more even. Kringlen's Mz twin study (7) showed an even higher subtype concordance (13/14 or 92.9%). These studies were not conducted blindly regarding subtype diagnosis of the proband. However, a blind twin study (35) discovered a similarly high subtype concordance rate (9/11 or 81.8%).

Family studies of hebephrenics and paranoids indicate that the first-degree relatives of hebephrenics have a higher risk for schizophrenia than the families of paranoids. Schulz (28) found a higher risk of schizophrenia for the sibs of hebephrenics than for the sibs of paranoids (18.0% and 5.4%, respectively); Hallgren and Sjogren (36) discovered a similar difference in risk for sibs (7.0% and 4.7%, respectively). Kallman (34) showed that the risk of schizophrenia differed for children of hebephrenics (17.3%) and children of paranoids (8.5%) and for the parents of hebephrenics (6.3%) and the parents of paranoids (2.9%). Winokur et al. (37) discovered risk of 2.8% for the first-degree relatives of hebephrenics and 0.8% for first-degree relatives of paranoids. Whereas these family studies report different risk figures, which are likely the result of variance in samples and methods of diagnosis from one study to another, there is an overall tendency for the relatives of hebephrenics to have a greater risk for schizophrenia that the relatives of paranoids.

Fowler et al. (38) studied paranoid and nonparanoid subtypes using the families of 60 poor-prognosis schizophrenics. The probands were personally interviewed and received concensus subtype diagnosis of paranoid or nonparanoid by four psychiatrists; first-degree relatives were also interviewed and evaluated blindly regarding the proband's subtype diagnosis. The Fowler study found the morbid risk of schizophrenia for first-degree relatives of nonparanoids (13.9%) was almost twice that of the risk for schizophrenia for the relatives of paranoids (7.3%); however, this difference was not significant.

As Fowler's family evidence was not significant to distinguish paranoid and nonparanoid, I conducted a further detailed analysis (39) of the same material to determine the frequency of schizophrenia among each subcategory of first-degree relatives of the paranoid and nonparanoid probands. There was no significant difference in frequency of schizophrenia between family members of paranoids and nonparanoids by subcategories of sibs, children, mothers, or fathers. When the subtype diagnosis of probands was compared to the subtype diagnosis of relatives there was no significant concordance for subtype. Whereas the collection of the material for the Fowler family comparison was blind, the sample size was small and no research criteria were used. Therefore, together with Winokur (40), I developed criteria for the clinical differentiation of hebephrenic and paranoid schizophrenia. Using a group of 260 process schizophrenics who met research criteria for schizophrenia (41) we evaluated the clinical differences between the hebephrenics and paranoids. Based on the results of the analysis of the data and currently available literature, we have proposed clinical research criteria for selecting homogenous subtype groups of hebephrenia and paranoia.

Subsequent to the development of the clinical research criteria, we have developed a numerical computational model for differentiating paranoid from nonparanoid schizophrenia (42). A computer program called best subset discriminant analysis (43) has been used which employs the statistical principles developed by Hocking and colleagues (44,45). The computer program is capable of analyzing a patient's numerically coded responses to 30 discriminating items of information (variables). The program selects whatever number of variables you wish to use to divide the sample into two groups. For example, if you want to use only one of the 30 variables, the program will choose the one that best divides the study sample into two groups; for two variables, the program will select that combination that best divides the sample in two; or for three, the best combination of three variables, and so on. The variables chosen by the program are called the best subset; there are then 30 best subsets, ranging in number of variables from 1 to 30. The principle involved guarantees that all possible subsets will be explored. For example, the best subset of 6 may or may not include the same variables as the best subsets of 1 through 5; the combination of variables determines which ones are included, not the accumulation of variables.

We applied this computer program to 260 process schizophrenics selected according to research criteria (41) who were previously subtyped clinically as paranoid and nonparanoid (38,46). The 30 variables used included such features as age of onset, marriage and employment status, family history of schizophrenia, disorganized thought, affect changes, behavior symptoms, and delusions. We wanted the best subset that produced the highest concordance rate between clinical subtyping and the computer's differentiation in two groups. A comparison of concordance rates found that the best subset of 21 produced the highest concordance rate (87.9%), whereas the rates were slightly lower for the best subsets of 16, 11, and 8. The concordance rate was the same for the best subsets of 3 and 5 (83.3%). As there is only a 4.3% difference in the concordance rate between the best subset of 3 and the best subset of 21, the best subset of 3 yields the highest computer/clinician concordance relative to its size. The three variables in the best subset of three were age of onset, disorganized thought, and affect changes.

Table 2 summarizes the numerical subtyping of two fictional patients. Patient

TABLE 2. Numerical subtyping of two fictional patients using the best subset of three

Variable	Patient I	Patient II
Age of onset ($B_1 = 0.00627$)	20 years: $X_1 = 2$ $B_1X_1 = 0.01254$	30 years: $X_1 = 3$ $B_1X_1 = 0.01881$
Disorganized thoughts ($B_2 = -0.00765$)	Present: $X_2 = 2$ $B_2X_2 = -0.01530$	Absent: $X_2 = 1$ $B_2X_2 = -0.00765$
Affect changes ($B_3 = -0.01253$)	Present: $X_3 = 2$ $B_3X_3 = -0.02506$ $Z_j = -0.02782$ $Z_j < Z_3$	Absent: $X_3 = 1$ $B_3X_3 = -0.01253$ $Z_j = -0.00137$ $Z_j > Z_3$
Diagnosis	Nonparanoid	Paranoid

Discriminant function: $Z_j = B_1X_1 + B_2X_2 + B_3X_3$.
Cutting point: $Z_3 = -0.02017$.
Computer diagnosis: Paranoid $> Z_3 \geq$ nonparanoid.

I is 20 years old ($X_1 = 2$); disorganized thoughts are presented ($X_2 = 2$); and affect changes are present ($X_3 = 2$). Patient II is 30 years old ($X_1 = 3$); disorganized thoughts are absent or not recorded ($X_2 = 1$); and affect changes are absent or not recorded ($X_3 = 1$). Each patient's discriminant function (Z_i) determines the subtype diagnosis relative to a cutoff point for three variables (Z_3). Therefore, patient I is classified as nonparanoid and patient II as paranoid.

The purpose of developing the computational model was to use it to classify family data in a standardized, objective way. The blind data from the previously mentioned Fowler study (38) was analyzed; the family members of 60 poor-prognosis schizophrenics were numerically subtyped as paranoid and non-paranoid. The results showed no significant concordance for subtype between probands and ill first-degree relatives.

There were 26 relatives with definite process schizophrenia and a total of 32 relatives with schizophrenia when probable cases were included. Table 3 shows no significant subtype concordance for the relatives and probands using the numerical model. Therefore, using the numerical model on a blindly gathered sample does not provide any convincing family evidence for the differentiation of paranoid and nonparanoid subtypes. A larger sample size may be needed to produce significant results with the numerical model.

It is quite apparent that a study designed to delineate homogenous subgroups must include certain conditions. The criteria for the selection of a study popula-

TABLE 3. *Pairs of probands and relatives subtyped according to the numerical model*

| | | Probands | | | | Totals | |
| | | Paranoid (%) | | Nonparanoid (%) | | | |
Relatives		I N = 26	II N = 32	I N = 26	II N = 32	I	II
Paranoid	Father	1	2	1	4	2	6
	Mother	4	4	5	6	9	10
	Brother	1	1	1	1	2	2
	Sister	–	–	1	1	1	1
	Son	–	–	–	–	–	–
	Totals:	6(67)	7(64)	8(47)	12(57)	14	19
Nonparanoid	Father	–	1	–	–	–	1
	Mother	–	–	2	2	2	2
	Brother	3	3	3	3	6	6
	Sister	–	–	3	3	3	3
	Son	–	–	1	1	1	1
	Totals:	3(33)	4(36)	9(53)	9(43)	12	13
Totals:		9(100)	11(100)	17(100)	21(100)	26	32

Group I: 26 relatives with definite schizophrenia
Group II: 32 relatives including both definite schizophrenics and probable schizophrenics.

tion should be restricted and well defined; family studies should be conducted blindly with regard to the proband diagnosis; and a nonpsychiatric control group should be included for comparison purposes. If the search for homogenous subgroups is to be truly fruitful, it should include not only a family study, but also a long-term follow-up.

THE IOWA 500 STUDY

Sample Selection

An example of a family study that fulfills the conditions for selecting homogenous subgroups is now being conducted in the Department of Psychiatry at the University of Iowa under my direction. This 3-year project is granted by the National Institute of Mental Health as "Epidemiology: Mania, Depression and Schizophrenia" and is known locally as the Iowa 500.

Figure 3 illustrates the method of sample selection. The psychiatric probands were selected from the inpatient records at the State Psychopathic Hospital for the time period 1934–1944. We selected a study group according to the research criteria for schizophrenia, mania, and depression (41). The final psychiatric proband group includes 200 schizophrenics, 100 manics, and 225 depressives.

The selection of the control group was from general hospital admissions of the same time period. We selected a stratified random sample of 80 appendectomies and 80 herniorrhaphies having a similar sex and socioeconomic status distribution to the study group. Using an estimated average of three family members per proband we hope to contact 2,055 first-degree relatives. Thus, our estimate for the entire study population is 2,740.

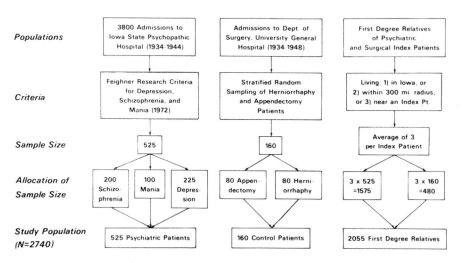

FIG. 3. Selection of Iowa 500 study population.

Data Collection

Contacting our study population based on chart information of 35 years ago requires a considerable amount of detective work on the part of our telephone interviewers. They are usually able to locate one family informant using the 35-year-old addresses in conjunction with current telephone listings. The family informant is then able to provide information on other members of the family concerning location, deaths, and current mental status of the proband. Interviews are arranged with the proband, when living, and with as many family members as possible. The personal interviews are conducted at the residence of the interviewee by another group of trained interviewers using a form specifically designed for the project—Iowa Structure Psychiatric Interview Form (ISPI). The interviews are conducted blindly with regard to the interviewee's status as proband or family member.

Data Analysis

The first step in analyzing the collected data on the ISPI forms involves a blind diagnostic assessment by a pair of psychiatrists and a computer diagnostic assessment. After other validating information is coded there will be a second computer assessment and a final diagnostic assessment, which in turn leads to a final computer assessment. Using all information possible, namely, a combination of clinical characteristics, outcome and family information, further work will be conducted to delineate homogenous subgroups.

Preliminary Findings

In the first year of the study, as of October 25, 1974, nearly 1,000 personal interviews of probands and family members have been completed using the ISPI. We have located 78% of the psychiatric and surgical probands. Of these, 53% are dead. Of the 252 living probands, 201 (80%) are in state.

We have conducted a preliminary analysis of outcome for the located probands. Each proband was rated according to their current status or status at the time of death using three indicators—employment status, physical health, and mental health. In the course of rating each proband, no reference was made to the individual's research diagnosis. According to the ratings for the three indicators, a proband was described as having "severe psychiatric disability," moderate psychiatric disability," or "no psychiatric disability." The typical individual listed with "severe psychiatric disability" was (a) unemployed, (b) physically healthy, and (c) obviously mentally ill. The indications for a rating of obvious mental illness were: residency in a mental institution, death by suicide, mutism at the time of personal interview, unusual or bizarre behavior at interview, or other incapacity for completing the interview. The typical individual listed as having "no psychiatric disability" (a) was employed at full capacity or retired, and (b) had no indication of mental illness.

TABLE 4. *Preliminary evaluation of psychiatric disability among index population*

Diagnostic groups	Severe N (%)	Moderate N (%)	None N (%)
Depression			
145 (100%)	38 (26.2)	40 (27.6)	67 (46.2)
Mania			
55 (100%)	16 (29.1)	19 (34.5)	20 (36.4)
Schizophrenia			
139 (100%)	66 (47.5)	47 (33.8)	26 (18.7)
Control			
83 (100%)	0 (0.0)	9 (10.8)	74 (89.2)
Total:			
422 (100%)	120 (28.4)	115 (27.3)	187 (44.3)

Data for 422 of 685 probands for which there is sufficient information for classification.

Of the located probands, 422 or 61.6% of the total number of probands had sufficient information to allow ratings for all three indicators of outcome. Therefore, the 117 probands with insufficient information and the 146 probands who have not been located are excluded from the preliminary analysis presented in Table 4.

There was no significant difference between the number of depressive and manic probands rated in the severe category, thus both groups may be considered as one, affective disorder, for comparison purposes. None of the control group received ratings in the severe category; this finding is significant when the control group is compared to the affective disorder group or the schizophrenics ($p < 0.0005$). The schizophrenics have a significantly higher proportion of probands in the severe category than the affective disorder group ($p < 0.0005$).

In the category of no psychiatric disability," the depressives and manics again show no significant difference and are combined under affective disorder. The difference between the affective group and the schizophrenics or the controls is significant ($p < 0.0005$) and the difference between the control group and the schizophrenics is also significant ($p < 0.0005$). Further analysis of these data in combination with other variables is needed in order to make a meaningful interpretation of this table.

When we complete our collection of data, with the assistance of computer analysis, using outcome criteria, family data, and other variables, we may be able to delineate homogenous subgroups within schizophrenia and affective disorder for future biologic and psychosocial studies.

ACKNOWLEDGMENT

This work was supported in part by National Institute of Mental Health grant 1-R01-MH-24189-01.

REFERENCES

1. Kraepelin, E. (1896): *Psychiatrie,* 5th ed. Barth, Leipzig.
2. Slater, E., and Cowie V. S. (1971): *The Genetics of Mental Disorders.* Oxford Univ. Press, London.
3. Heston, L. L. (1966): Psychiatric disorders in foster home reared children of schizophrenic mothers. *Br. J. Psychiatry,* 112:819–825.
4. Kety, S. S., Rosenthal, D., Wender, P.H., and Schulsinger, F. (1968): The types and prevalence of mental illness in the biological and adoptive families of adopted schizophrenics. In: *The Transmission of Schizophrenia,* edited by D. Rosenthal and S. S. Kety, pp. 345-362. Pergamon, Oxford.
5. Winokur, G., Clayton, P., and Reich, T. (1969): *Manic Depressive Illness.* Mosby, St. Louis, Missouri.
6. Slater, E. (1953): *Psychotic and Neurotic Illness in Twins.* HM Stationery Office, London.
7. Kringlen, E. (1967): *Heredity and Environment in the Functional Psychoses.* Universitetsforlaget, Norway.
8. Gottesman, I. I., and Shields, J. (1972): *Schizophrenia and Genetics: A Twin Study Vantage Point.* Academic Press, New York.
9. Fischer, M. (1973): *Genetic and Environmental Factors in Schizophrenia.* Munksgaard, Copenhagen.
10. Perris, C. (1973): The genetics of affective disorders. In: *Biological Psychiatry,* edited by J. Mendels, pp. 385–415. Wiley, New York.
11. Angst, J. (1966): Zur ateiologie and nosologie endogener depressiver psychosen. *Monographien aus dem Gesamtgebiete der Neurologie und Psychiatrie,* Vol. 112. Springer-Verlag, Berlin.
12. Winokur, G., and Clayton, P. (1967): Family history studies; II. Two types of affective disorders separated according to genetic and clinical factors. In: *Recent Advances in Biological Psychiatry,* edited by J. Wortis, Vol. 9, pp. 35-50. Plenum, New York.
13. Winokur, G., and Tanna, V. L. (1969): Possible role of X-linked dominant factor in manic depressive disease. *Dis. Nerv. Syst.,* 30:89–93.
14. Mendlewicz, J., Fleiss, J., and Fieve, R. (1972): Evidence for X-linkage in the transmission of manic-depressive illness. *JAMA,* 222:1624–1627.
15. Fieve, R. R., Mendlewicz, J., and Fleiss, J. L. (1973): Manic-depressive illness: Linkage with the X blood group. *Am. J. Psychiatry,* 130:1355–1359.
16. Taylor, M., and Abrams, R. (1973): Manic States. A genetic study of early and late onset affective disorders. *Arch. Gen. Psychiatry,* 28:656–658.
17. Slater, E. (1938): Zur Erbpathologie des manisch-depressiven Irreseins. Die Eltern and Kinder von Manisch-Depressiven. *Z. Gesamte Neurol. Psychiatrie,* 163:1–147.
18. Stenstedt, A. (1952): A study of manic-depressive psychosis. Clinical, social and genetic investigations. *Acta Psychiatr. Scand. (Suppl.),* 79.
19. Von-Greiff, H., McHugh, P. R., and Stokes, P. (1973): The familial history in sixteen males with bipolar manic depressive disorder. *Presented at 63rd Annual Mtg. American Psychopathological Association, New York, New York.*
20. Dunner, D., Gershon, E., and Goodwin F. K. (1970): Heritable factors in the severity of affective illness. *123rd Annual Mtg. APA. San Francisco, California.*
21. Green, R., Goetzl, U., Whybrow, P., and Jackson, R. (1973): X-linked transmission of manic-depressive illness. *JAMA,* 223:1289.
22. Goetzl, U., Green, R., Whybrow, P., and Jackson, R. (1974): X linkage revisited. A further family study of manic-depressive illness. *Arch. Gen. Psychiatry,* 31:665–672.
23. Winokur, G., Cadoret, R., Dorzab, J., and Baker, M. (1971): Depressive disease: A genetic study. *Arch. Gen. Psychiatry,* 24:135–144.
24. Woodruff, R., Guze, S., and Clayton, P. (1971): Unipolar and bipolar primary affective disorder. *Br. J. Psychiatry,* 119:33–38.
25. Marten, S., Cadoret, R. J., Winokur, G., and Ora, E. (1972): Unipolar depression: A family history study. *Biol. Psychiatry,* 4:205–213.
26. Winokur, G. (1973): Diagnostic and genetic aspects of affective illness. *Psychiatr. Ann.,* 3:6–15.
27. Winokur, G., Morrison, J., Clancy, J., and Crowe, R. (1973); The Iowa 500: Familial and clinical findings favor two kinds of depressive illness. *Compr. Psychiatry,* 14:99–107.
28. Schulz, B. (1932): Zur Erbpathologie der Schizophrenie. *Z. Gesamte Neurol. Psychiatr.,* 143: 175–293.

29. Davidson, K., and Bagely, C. R. (1969): Schizophrenia-like psychoses associated with organic disorders of the central nervous system: A review of the literature. In: *Current Problems in Neuropsychiatry: Schizophrenia, Epilepsy, the Temporal Lobe,* edited by R. N. Herrington. Ashford, Kent.
30. Mitsuda, H. (1972): Heterogeneity of Schizophrenia. In: *Genetic Factors in "Schizophrenia,"* edited by A. R. Kaplan, pp. 276–293. Thomas, Springfield, Illinois.
31. McCabe, M. S., Fowler, R. C., Cadoret, R. J., and Winokur, G. (1971): Familial differences in schizophrenics with good and poor prognosis. *Psychol. Med.,* 1:326-332.
32. Garrone, G. (1962): Statistical and genetic study of schizophrenia in Geneva from 1901 to 1950. *J. Génét. Hum.,* II: 89–219, 245.
33. Ødegaard, ø. (1963): The psychiatric disease entities in the light of a genetic investigation. *Acta. Psychiat. Scan.,* Suppl. 169:94–104.
34. Kallman, F. J. (1938): *The Genetics of Schizophrenia.* Augustin, New York.
35 Gottesman, I. (1968): Severity, concordance and diagnostic refinement in the Maudsley–Bethlem schizophrenic twin study. In: *The Transmission of Schizophrenia,* edited by D. Rosenthal and S. S. Kety, pp. 37–48. Pergamon, Oxford.
36. Hallgren, B., and Sjogren, T. (1959): A clinical and genetico-statistical study of schizophrenia and low-grade mental deficiency in a large Swedish rural population. *Acta Psychiat. Scand. Suppl.,* 140.
37. Winokur, G., Morrison, J., Clancy, J., and Crowe, R. (1974): Iowa 500:The clinical and genetic distinction of hebephrenic and paranoid schizophrenia. *J. Nerv. Ment. Dis.,* 159:12–19.
38. Fowler, R. C., Tsuang, M. T., Cadoret, R. J., Monnelly, E., and McCabe, M. S. (1974): A clinical and family comparison of paranoid and non-paranoid schizophrenics. *Br. J. Psychiatry,* 124: 346–351.
39. Tsuang, M. T., Fowler, R. C., Cadoret, R. J., and Monnelly, E. (1974): Schizophrenia among first-degree relatives of paranoid and nonparanoid schizophrenics. *Comp. Psychiatry,* 15:295–301.
40. Tsuang, M. T., and Winokur, G. (1974): Criteria for subtyping schizophrenia: Clinical differentiation of hebaphrenic and paranoid schizophrenia. *Arch. Gen. Psychiatry,* 31:43–47.
41. Feighner, J. P., Robins, E., Guze, S. D., Woodruff, R. A., Winokur, G., and Munoz, R. (1972): Diagnostic criteria for use in psychiatric research. *Arch. Gen. Psychiatry,* 26:57–63.
42. Tsuang, M. T., Leaverton, P. E., and Huang, K. S. (1974): Criteria for subtyping poor prognosis schizophrenia: A numerical model for differentiating paranoid from non-paranoid schizophrenia. *J. Psychiat. Res.,* 10:189–197.
43. Enochson, G. (1971): Best subset discriminant analysis. M. S. Thesis, Industrial and Management Engineering, under the direction of J. S. Ramberg, Univ. of Iowa, Ames, Iowa.
44. Hocking, R. R., and Leslie, R. N. (1967): Selection of best subset in regression analysis. *Technometrics,* 9:531–540.
45. LaMotte, L. R., and Hocking, R. R. (1970): Computational efficiency in the selection of regression coefficients. *Technometrics,* 12:83–94.
46. Morrison, J., Clancy, J., Crowe, R., and Winokur, G. (1972): The Iowa 500. I. Diagnostic validity in mania, depression, and schizophrenia. *Arch. Gen. Psychiatry,* 27:457–461.

Discussion

Question: Where do you place the axes of premorbid manifestation and hereditary background in this scheme?

Strauss: It could be very helpful to have other axes such as genetic background and premorbid characteristics in addition to social relationships. One area we're particularly interested in, for example, has been premorbid work function. But, at the same time, you need some degree of simplicity, too. If you have a multiaxial system that has too many axes, it will be unusable for anyone who does not spend all of his time on the study of diagnosis. So the three-axis system really is a compromise. It's a compromise that we feel is more useful than the single-category model represented by the manic-depressive or schizophrenic diagnostic categories, but it is not so complex that it becomes unwieldy. However, I think that the evaluation of other axes is important and that it would be very useful for an investigator who would be interested in looking at a genetic axis, for example, to do so.

Spitzer: I think one of the difficulties is that it's difficult enough to interpret the data, but often we can't be that clear about whether the actual data are controversial or not. I wonder if I could use Dr. Strauss's presentation as an example. The only reason I pick it is that it lends itself more to this question.

For example, Dr. Strauss says the symptoms are not so clearly separated, that is, the so-called pathognomonic symptoms of Kurt Schneider apparently have been shown to be present in other illnesses. Well, apparently this is Dr. Strauss's view. He may be right. Dr. Wing, in London, though, thinks that he's probably wrong and that the findings in these studies are based on incorrect ratings of those key items; in brief, that there's a question of accuracy of measurement.

Dr. Strauss mentions that 40% of his group of schizophrenics recovered completely, or almost completely. I find that difficult to understand; at issue is the concept of schizophrenia. Very often, in the discussions here, we've heard reference to the criteria in DSMII with which I was involved, so it's easy for me now to take potshots at it. In fact, DSMII really doesn't provide very clear criteria at all. All that is in DSMII is a very general statement that schizophrenia has something to do with thought disorder and that it is somehow different from affective illness. But we really have to know precisely what the criteria are for schizophrenia that, for example, Dr. Strauss uses when he says that 40% recovered completely.

Apparently using different criteria, a Yale group (B. Astrachan, L. Brauer, M. Harrow, and C. Schwartz: *Arch. Gen. Psychiatry* 31:155–160, 1974) recently reported an outcome study of schizophrenia in which almost invariably there were serious residual symptoms and impairment in social functioning at follow-up.

Dr. Strauss mentions that the key symptoms of schizophrenia may not be caused by a primary disease process; that is, flat affect or thought disorder may not be intrinsic to the disease. Well, that again is very controversial. I'm not so sure that it has really been demonstrated that thought disorder of the schizophrenic variety can be attributed to environmental variables so clearly.

It's been mentioned that thought disorder is present in other illnesses. Is that *really* the same kind of thought disorder that one usually speaks of when referring to schizophrenic thought disorder?

One last comment on terminology: It would seem, from Dr. Rosenthal's work, that there is some relationship between many chronic illnesses (inadequate personality being one of them), schizoid personality, and chronic schizophrenia. Why the term "schizophrenia spectrum disease?" Why not a chronic illness spectrum? I'm concerned about calling inadequate personality part of a schizophrenic spectrum.

Rosenthal: The reason we refer to this group of conditions as the spectrum of schizophrenic disorder is simply that we think that: (1) they are genetically related, and (2) they show different degrees of manifestation of what might very well be a common disorder.

To overemphasize the chronic disease aspect implies that we may be giving it too much weight as a diagnostic criterion.

Spitzer: I wasn't referring to chronic physical illness, but it seems the thing that holds these conditions together is a chronic psychiatric disorder that affects general coping and personality functioning. There were really no criteria for inadequate personality noted in DSMII and I don't believe your group has ever specified what your criteria were.

Maybe what you've identified is a general social withdrawal "something," which when it is accompanied by schizophrenia means that the course of the illness is chronic.

Rosenthal: We have not really defined our criteria to the point at which we're ready to publish. That might still be some time off. We seem to have a common conception of what these disorders are, and I say that because we have checked our reliability among the three examiners; we've come out rather well, even without a clear definition of the respective disorders.

Kety: In the spectrum of presentations that we heard this morning, one could find a basis for supporting a variety of beliefs about the validity of the traditional psychiatric concepts, especially schizophrenia or the affective disorders. There has been a great deal of dissatisfaction expressed about some of these and the considerable amount of overlap that exists. I wonder to what extent it might be said of us that we have raised a cloud and are now complaining that we cannot see.

It is my feeling that the problem of psychiatric diagnosis, especially in America, is a highly clouded one and merits some of the criticism and even the pessimism that has been expressed. But it need not be that way, except for the needs of the clinician and some of the needs to use hypotheses instead of phenomenology in order to describe a phenomenologic cluster.

It's easy to understand the difference between the clinician and the research person. The investigator can affort to select only those cases he thinks fit into particular diagnostic categories and to reject the rest. And he can use only those highly selected and well-defined populations for studies of drug effects, biochemical variables, or genetic relationships. He may leave aside a significant number of mentally disordered persons whom he cannot diagnose or fit into these categories.

On the other hand, the clinician can't reject patients because he can't find a diagnosis for them, and because he doesn't like to have no diagnosis or a very meaningless diagnosis, there is an understandable tendency on his part to expand these traditional concepts to include many kinds of patients who would not have been described by the concepts as they were originally developed. We have seen the accretion to the original diagnosis of schizophrenia of such categories as borderline or latent schizophrenia, or acute schizophrenic reaction—although in the latter case I don't really know why it is more meaningful to tell a family that the patient has an acute schizophrenic reaction than it is to say that the patient has an acute psychosis. But these extensions of the original concept should be regarded as hypotheses that remain to be tested.

As a result of this, there has developed some disaffection with diagnostic criteria. And, of course, as Dr. Bowers pointed out, in psychiatry especially, diagnoses carry a certain pejorative connotation. And one should realize that in making a diagnosis in psychiatry one is doing more than identifying a particular syndrome.

Perhaps what the critics of psychiatric nosology should really be urging is two separate nosologic systems—one for the patient and his family with nonpejorative or euphemistic terms acceptable to society, and another nosology representing psychiatric experience and science used by investigators and clinicians for the purpose of advancing knowledge about mental illness. For any case it makes no sense to abandon a heuristic nosology just because it is imperfect.

There is no doubt in my mind that we lose a great deal of information if we do away with nosological categories simply because they carry a pejorative connotation. The concept of general paralysis of the insane was recognized and developed a century or two before the etiology was ever discovered. The discovery of its syphilitic etiology was greatly facilitated by the ability that concept provided to distinguish that group from the rest of the mentally ill. Moreover, if, because syphilis was a disreputable term, that relationship had been suppressed, discovery of the etiology and specific treatment of that disorder would have been long delayed.

Dr. Strauss indicated that symptoms should be pathognomonic of the syndrome rather than common to different kinds of illness. I think that's a requirement that we don't make of any other kind of diagnosis in medicine. The diagnosis of lobar pneumonia was traditionally made on the basis of fever, cough, hemoptysis, and the physical signs of consolidation. Not one of those manifestations is pathognomonic of lobar pneumonia. What is pathognomonic is a combination of all of them. And then, if one is lucky enough eventually to find an etiologic agent, one can even talk specifically about pneumococcal lobar pneumonia. But the characteristics of these psychiatric syndromes is *not* that their individual features are pathognomic but that they contain symptoms in a characteristic kind of cluster which has enabled psychiatrists for several generations to recognize them.

Now, with regard to schizophrenia and the spectrum of schizophrenia, I think we ought to make clear what Dr. Rosenthal said: a distinction between what some of the data seem to demonstrate fairly convincingly and what still remains hypothetical, and what has not been demonstrated.

There are two studies that I know of that provided an opportunity to evaluate traditional diagnoses of schizophrenia against an objective and independent criterion. One of these was the cross-national diagnoses in twins by Gottesman and Shields (I.I. Gottesman and J. Shields: *Schizophrenia and Genetics: A Twin Study Vantage Point,* pp. 207–223, Academic Press, New York, 1972). They had several psychiatrists examine clinical abstracts of monozygotic and dizygotic twins, blind both to zygocity and diagnosis. They found that each did pretty well on the diagnosis of schizophrenia and questionable schizophrenia in finding a high concordance in monozygotic twins and a low concordance in dizygotic twins.

The adoption studies (S. S. Kety, D. Rosenthal, P. H. Wender, F. Schulsinger, and B. Jacobsen: In: *Genetics and Psychopathology,* edited by R. Fisoc, H. Brill, and D. Rosenthal, Johns Hopkins Press, Baltimore, 1975) minimize bias on the part of the investigators but, equally important, the subjects themselves are blind in terms of their relationships to other people who have schizophrenia. This is an important criterion which can only be met by studies in which the genetically related subjects have been reared apart and are unknown to each other. In the adoption studies what has emerged thus far is a very clear concentration of "chronic schizophrenia" (which is very close to Kraeplinian schizophrenia) and what is called "latent schizophrenia" in American psychiatry, among the biologic relatives of chronic and latent schizophrenics. Those diagnosed as having "acute schizophrenic reaction" do not tend to have biologic relatives with schizophrenia.

But what has been clearly demonstrated, I think, in both the Gottesman and Shields studies and in our study is that severe and mild forms of schizophrenia are readily and reliably recognized by psychiatrists. The validity of the diagnosis can now be demonstrated by reference to an independent genetic criterion.

Equally interesting, in the adoption studies, is the fact that no other diagnosis (including organic, neurotic, affective, or personality disorders) is found to be significantly concentrated in the biologic relatives of schizophrenics. So that there appears to be considerable internal consistency in these traditional psychiatric diagnoses, and it will take better arguments than I have heard to date to cause me to discard them.

Harrow: Diagnosis, the value of the diagnostic system, and the value of the label "schizophrenia," are the issues in question. Recently there has been a series of findings, including those of Strauss and Carpenter that raise some doubts about the concept of schizophrenia. It would be most appropriate to look at the label "schizophrenia" and ask about the usefulness of the construct.

At the lowest level of possible value, the classification associated with a diagnostic label (such as the term "schizophrenia") can be used for shorthand, descriptive purposes—a convenient term to describe a group of symptoms, behaviors, or features which (presumably) all patients assigned to this category have in common. The advantage is that it saves time and prevents tedious description. The clinical use of the term "schizophrenia" does give some rough description of a certain specific type of psychotic disorder. There are now three "automatic" systems for rating a diagnosis of "schizophrenia," and hence the old problem of reliability and replicability of a schizophrenic diagnosis is potentially solvable (B. M. Astrachan, M. Harrow, D. Adler, L. Brauer, A. Schwartz, C. Schwartz, and G. Tucker: *Br. J. Psychiatry,* 121:529–539, 1972; W. T. Carpenter, Jr., J. S. Strauss, and J. J. Bartko: *Science,* 182:1275–1278, 1973: R. L. Spitzer and J. Endicott: *Am. J. Psychiatry, 131:*523–530, 1974). Since the symptom picture associated with schizophrenia is more variable and more subject to abuse than many other diagnostic labels in this field, however, the value of the classification "schizophrenia" is clearly limited if it *only* can be justified at this lowest level.

At a second and higher level, there is greater value and justification of such a construct or diagnosis. This level is achieved when the diagnosis or classification carries with it *consequences* or *implications* about the patient that go beyond a description of the directly observable symptom picture. Does the label "schizophrenia" have consequences above and beyond the immediate symptom picture? When patients are assigned the classification of "schizophrenia" does it have any implications about their past, or what kind of treatment to use, or their future?

When we look at the label "schizophrenia" for implications in terms of the past (either through a common "cause" or common childhood occurrences which might have influenced the disorder) we see several possibilities. The ideal for this or any other diagnostic label would be a uniform background factor that might make the whole picture neat and simple, such as a common virus—obviously not the case with schizophrenia. Nevertheless, there is incomplete research that suggests the possibility that there may be some common biochemical factors (e.g., catecholamine disorder or excessive dopamine in certain regions of the brain, etc.). The evidence could suffer the fate of the many previous, seemingly bright, ideas in this area. The work here, however, is more sophisticated and the leads look much more promising than was the case with efforts in this area 15 years ago. Further positive evidence in this area certainly could justify the label "schizophrenia" in a major way.

There is also some strong genetic evidence which is firmly established. Again, however, the genetic factors do not seem to play as great a role in the *overt* picture of schizophrenia as was thought to be the case 15 years ago, with some of the important evidence coming from Dr. Rosenthal's research and his theoretical analysis. But despite alterations in the percent of variance which seems to be accounted for, there is strong evidence that genetic factors play some role.

Another implication of the label "schizophrenia" in terms of the past seeks a common history or set of events that is fairly unique. This would be the case if all such patients were nurtured in a brusque, unfriendly, or inconsistent manner during infancy, or were beaten severely at age five, or came from families with long-term patterns of communicating irrationally or interacting strangely. If the label schizophrenia told us of family events that had *not* occurred in the families of depressives or character disorders, this would be an important implication, adding useful knowledge about schizophrenic patients. There are, in fact, some family studies which are still in dispute (T. Jacob: *Psychol. Bull.* 82: 33–65, 1975; E. Mishler and N. Waxler: *Int. J. Psychiatry,* 2:375–413, 1966). There is evidence that a large percentage of schizophrenics have lived among disturbed families. The problem is to distinguish cause from effect. The question is whether the disturbance among other family members is the result of genetic factors, or whether the patient's years of disordered behavior evoke the family's disturbed interaction, or whether the patient is just a victim of family psychopathology. Most likely all three possibilities have played some role. So again in this area there are a number of controversial issues (and considerable question about the reason for, or how to interpret, the positive data), but at least there is some serious evidence (E. Mishler and N. Waxler: *Int. J. Psychiatry,* 2:375–413, 1966; J. Riskin and E. Faunce: *Family Process,* 11:365–456, 1972).

If we move from patients' past to their current symptom picture, the question arises: Does the term "schizophrenia" imply a common treatment which applies more to patients given this label, or with this particular disorder, than to other disorders? We find it does suggest some uniform features or commonality in treatment. It implies the therapeutic use of phenothiazines or related medications as therapeutic agents. But they are not uniquely effective for schizophrenia, and even though phenothiazines clearly help many, their effect on schizophrenics is not perfectly uniform. Similarly, they often help to reduce symptoms without removing all manifestations of the disorder, or without producing lasting cures. But schizophrenics seem more than others to benefit, and the effect of phenothiazines on schizophrenics is clearly more beneficial than medications such as tricyclics or minor tranquilizers. Thus in regard to treatment, the label does have consequences in terms of implying a type of disorder with some treatment specificity.

Finally, *outcome* is another criterion of the utility of the label schizophrenia as having implications above and beyond the immediate symptom picture. Much of the early thinking about dementia praecox was based on its implications concerning deteriorating or at least very poor outcome. A number of investigators have recently raised doubts about this aspect of the construct [M. Bleuler: In: R. Cancro (Ed.). *The Schizophrenic Syndrome,* Brunner/Mazel, New York; 1971; S. F. Yolles and M. Kramer: In: L. Bellak and L. Loeb (Eds.): *The Schizophrenic Syndrome,* pp. 66–113. Grune & Stratton, New York; 1969 and some of the research by Drs. Strauss and Carpenter (A. B. Hawk, W. T. Carpenter, Jr.,

J. S. Strauss, and W. T. Carpenter, Jr.: *Arch. Gen. Psychiatry*, 27:739–746, 1972), as well as our own work at Yale (M. Harrow, E. Bromet, and D. Quinlan: *J. Nerv. Ment. Disease*, 158:25–36, 1974; M. Harrow, K. Harkavy, E. Bromet, and G. J. Tucker: *Arch. Gen. Psychiatry*, 28:179–182, 1973) has also questioned this assumption.

Thus the extremely negative prognosis originally envisioned by Kraeplin has changed since the early 1930s, partly as a result of the newer organic treatment techniques, and partly as a result of newer social treatments and outlook toward long-term hospitalization [S. F. Yolles and M. Kramer: In: L. Bellak and L. Loeb (eds.); *The Schizophrenic Syndrome*, pp. 66–113. Grune & Stratton, New York, 1969]. Even so, outcome in schizophrenia is still more negative than that of other major disorders such as depression, although there is much more overlap in post-hospital functioning between schizophrenics and other disorders than was originally thought to be the case. Hence there are also some implications concerning outcome attached to the label schizophrenia.

There is one caution that our own research group and Drs. Strauss and Carpenter should take into account in assessing the recent, more mixed findings on schizophrenic outcome. Both of our teams have been working with a large number of acute patients. Most of the previous studies of post-hospital functioning that found strong negative outcomes and large schizophrenic–nonschizophrenic differences in outcome have used a larger percentage of *chronic* schizophrenic patients. Some of these studies have screened out from their samples acute schizophrenics who only had one psychotic break and then showed some degree of recovery, on the basis that these patients are not "true" schizophrenics. Whereas this sometimes involves an after-the-fact procedure, the merits of this technique could be argued *either* way. In this type of procedure, when you have screened out those acute patients who begin to do well after hospital discharge, you have a prediction of negative outcome for *chronic* schizophrenic patients. All one is really predicting in this case, though, is that patients who have a chronic disorder function poorly—not a very remarkable prediction. There is no question that a certain percentage of early schizophrenics will later become chronic patients and do poorly. A key question is, however, do the majority of young, acute, schizophrenics go on to a negative outcome? There are some mixed results in this area, although the weight of evidence still suggests that most acute schizophrenics show decrements in functioning during the post-hospital period and that as a *group*, schizophrenics do have a more negative outcome than do other disordered, but nonschizophrenic patients (C. Astrup and K. Noreik: *Functional Psychoses, Diagnostic and Prognostic Models*. Thomas, Springfield, 1966; J. H. Stephens: *Seminars Psychiatry*, 2: 464–485, 1970). Thus even this implication of the schizophrenic label does have value which goes beyond the immediate clinical picture present at the time of diagnosis (in terms of predicting a negative outcome), although there is more overlap than was once believed.

Overall, when we sum up the value of the diagnostic label schizophrenia, we can see that at present there is some value to this construct. As typically used, at the lowest level of utility it gives a quick description of a patient with a certain type of psychotic disorder, although the symptom picture is often quite variable. More important, though, at a second, higher level it has additional implications, telling us a little about the patient's background or past and possible etiologic factors (there are more likely to be genetic factors in his family background, and he is more likely to come from a home with some disturbed family patterns of interaction). In addition, it suggests more effective use of certain treatments (e.g., phenothiazines are more likely to help than are tricyclics), and it implies the probability of a more pathologic future course.

Thus there is some value associated with the construct, since the label "schizophrenia" provides a series of implications that go beyond the immediate symptom picture. To put the matter into perspective, none of these implications or consequences works perfectly, and some are much less clear than we would like, but all of them seem to have at least a little bit of validity associated with them. Future research and theoretical analysis may suggest a more promising classification system, but until that time, the use of the label "schizophrenia" still carries some utility.

Biology of the Major Psychoses, edited by D. X. Freedman, *Res. Publ. Assoc. Res. Nerv. Ment. Dis.,* Vol. 54. Raven Press, New York   1975

Biologic Antecedents of Psychosis in Children

Barbara Fish

University of California, Los Angeles, California 90024

If we could study the antecedents of schizophrenic and manic-depressive disorders, we would be able to isolate the biology of the genotype from nonspecific correlates of the psychotic state. The different genetic histories of the two disorders suggest that one should find different biologic antecedents. "No case of a child with manic-depressive psychosis has yet been reported in the adoption studies of schizophrenia," and "no instance has ever been reported of clear-cut schizophrenia in one twin and clear-cut manic depressive psychosis in his monozygotic cotwin" (1). To some extent, the studies of children lend support to the concept of two diseases.

There is considerable evidence that a neurobiologic disorder exists in children before the onset of the more chronic forms of *schizophrenic* psychosis. This material is reviewed in the body of this chapter. These severe schizophrenic patients, with more early cognitive and social impairment, lie at the opposite end of the "schizophrenia spectrum" from the schizoaffective disorders (1), and clinically are the most unlike manic-depressives (2). In contrast to schizophrenic patients, manic-depressives typically do not show cognitive impairment before their psychosis, and so far no gross neurobiologic or behavioral disorders have turned up in their childhood histories. A comparison of the army intelligence test scores at induction showed that the pre-illness scores of those who developed manic-depressive psychosis were significantly high, compared to controls who remained well, whereas the scores of the preschizophrenics were significantly low (3). Within the schizophrenic group, those later diagnosed as having simple schizophrenia had even lower pre-illness scores than the hebephrenics, whereas there was no significant lowering of the scores of the paranoid and catatonic schizophrenics.

Robins' study (4) demonstrated that male preschizophrenics had symptoms that required psychiatric attention in childhood, but adult manic-depressive patients did not. Seven percent of boys brought to a child-guidance clinic for a variety of antisocial and non-antisocial symptoms were found to be schizophrenic as adults, whereas none of their matched controls were. However, the former clinic patients did not have a higher rate of manic-depressive disease than did the controls. The biologic antecedents of schizophrenia in children may therefore represent one aspect of the biology of schizophrenia that is distinct from the biology of manic-depressive disorder.

Several bodies of evidence in children that bear on the biology of schizophrenia are reviewed briefly in this chapter. First, is the evidence that childhood schizophrenia is continuous with adult schizophrenia, and that it probably represents the subgroup with the most severe biologic disorder. Then, there is evidence of abnormal neurologic development in infants who were later diagnosed as childhood schizophrenics. Similar but less severe disorders occurred in infants diagnosed as having severe behavior disorders as children, who later became adult schizophrenics.

The occurrence of neurologic deviations from the first day of life certainly implies the presence of a biologic disorder in some infants who manifest schizophrenia later. Characteristics of the disorder in preschizophrenic infants raise questions about the nature of the underlying brain dysfunctions. Finally, the infant disorders suggest a strategy for studying biochemical and neurophysiologic disorders in infants at risk, without waiting 30 to 40 years for the final adult outcome.

CHILDHOOD SCHIZOPHRENIA, THE MOST SEVERE SUBGROUP OF SCHIZOPHRENIA

Neurologic antecedents of childhood schizophrenia are only relevant to the broader problem of schizophrenia if a continuity exists between this condition and schizophrenia in adults. Data from several sources support this continuity.

Similar Clinical Phenomenology: Thought Disorder in Childhood and Adult Schizophrenia

First are the similarities in clinical phenomenology. Schizophrenics of all ages share the critical symptoms of autistic withdrawal and formal thought disorder. Since Bleuler's historic description (5) most authors have viewed "the fragmentation of the thinking as the most significant schizophrenic symptom" (2). The loosening of associations and the interpenetration of personal preoccupations, the difficulties in formulating and using precise abstract categories and in holding a mental set and maintaining the boundaries of a concept, have been demonstrated experimentally in adult schizophrenics by many authors since Vigotsky's work 50 years ago (6–9).

Goldfarb's recent review (10) of the major reports of childhood schizophrenia concluded that all the behavioral symptoms used for diagnosis were encompassed in the nine points of the British working party (11). Gross impairment in human relationships and noncommunicative speech were among the four major symptoms found in all the schizophrenic children. A parsimonious list of diagnostic criteria shows these to be the only two symptoms that can be considered both necessary and sufficient to make the diagnosis of childhood schizophrenia (12).

The differences in the way these cardinal symptoms are expressed by adults and children depend upon the degree of immaturity. The form of the children's psychotic speech is limited by their mental age and can be analyzed quantitatively

(13–16). The words children acquire gradually replace the earlier grunts, babble, and jargon. Unintelligible speech is retained longer by the schizophrenic child, persisting alongside more mature forms (13). The higher the percentage of unintelligible speech, the more retarded is the child compared to age norms and the worse his prognosis (16).

Normally, a child's noncommunicative speech, including expressive speech and echoing, diminishes rapidly during the second year. The schizophrenic child's echoing is retained longer and is pathologically rigid (14). Unlike the imitative echoing of the normal child acquiring speech, the schizophrenic child regurgitates accumulated fragments just as they were heard; he does not reorganize and transform old phrases into new creative sentences, adapted for use in new contexts. Words and sentences are triggered by adventitious and idiosyncratic associations and emitted in inappropriate contexts (15). The greater the percentage of such noncommunicative speech, the worse the outcome (16). In the most severe childhood schizophrenics, even the communicative portion of speech is rigid, stereotyped, and limited to the simplest here-and-now categories (15).

This molecular analysis of their speech reveals a central cognitive disorder in childhood schizophrenia which involves disturbances of association and conceptualization, idiosyncratic and irrelevant referents, a peculiar impairment of the cognitive functions underlying flexible language organization and use. The pattern of speech is primitive in these retarded schizophrenic children under 5 years, but the disturbed organization of thought that is revealed appears analogous in many respects to characteristics found in older schizophrenics.

When the psychotic process begins in the first 2 years, as in early infantile autism, the absence of any normal experience inevitably leads to major mental retardation. The severe cognitive disorder reflected in the beginnings of his speech indicate that the 2- to 3-year old, severely schizophrenic child does not respond to the meaningful patterns and relationships in the world around him in the same way the normal child does. This is also seen in his fragmented play sequences with inanimate objects and in his frequent disregard for their physical properties and normal use (12). His inability to comprehend the meaning of other's speech, to reason logically, and to communicate with others, cuts him off still further from normal learning. The wonder is not that his performance is retarded on many tests of mental functioning, but that he manages to achieve any islands of normality.

This greater cognitive impairment does not necessarily mean that early infantile autism is a separate disease entity from childhood schizophrenia or that childhood schizophrenia is distinct from the adult form. Kanner (17) himself emphasized this in his review 20 years ago: "It has been generally agreed that the earliest from of childhood schizophrenia is probably represented by. . .early infantile autism. . .The clinical manifestations (of childhood schizophrenia) depend upon the time and mode of onset, and the later the onset, the more does the symptom combination resemble that of adult schizophrenia."

In the schizophrenic children who are more advanced in their use of language, the formal thought disorder is indistinguishable from that in severely ill schizophrenic adults. It is readily seen in verbatim samples of their spontaneous speech (18) and in their responses to psychologic tests (19). The content necessarily reflects not only the distorted perceptions and thinking of the schizophrenic, but the special experiences of childhood and the particular child (18). One therefore finds preoccupations with movement and aggression, with the child's own body and its functioning, with his disturbed identification and relationships to others. In the prepuberty schizophrenic child, paranoid ideas are more fragmentary and diffuse than adults' or adolescents' delusions; projection and hallucinations are less significant phenomena than are introjection and the preoccupation with fantasied objects and persons the child experiences as being inside his own body. In childhood schizophrenics, as in adults, the content reflects the individuality of the particular patient; but an analysis of the formal structure of the thoughts reveals a disorganizing process characteristic of schizophrenia.

Genetic Continuity between Childhood and Adult Schizophrenia

Genetic evidence also supports the continuity with adult schizophrenia (see Table 1). Kallman and Roth's (20) study is the only major study of childhood schizophrenic twins. In 52 pairs, the 70.6% uncorrected concordance rate for

TABLE 1. *Percent of relatives of childhood schizophrenics with mental illness*

Relatives of index child	Total no.	Childhood schizophrenics (%)	Total schizophrenics (%)	Severe personality disorders (%)
MZ co-twins (20)	17	70.6	88.2	11.8[b]
DZ co-twins (20)	35	17.1	22.9	25.7[b]
Siblings (20)	199	8.0[a]	9.0[a]	
Parents (20)	204		8.8	
Mothers of (21):				
Onset before 2 years	50		14.0	22.0[c]
Onset after 2 years	50		16.0	28.0[c]
Total:	100		15.0	25.0[c]
Mothers of (22):				
"Organic"	—		21.0	
"Nonorganic"	—		44.0	
Total:	45		29.0	
Fathers of (21):				
Onset before 2 years	50		6.0	30.0[c]
Onset after 2 years	50		8.0	42.0[c]
Total:	100		7.0	36.0[c]
Fathers of (22):				
"Organic"	—		15.0	
"Nonorganic"	—		8.0	
Total:	39		13.0	

[a] Bender reported 24 schizophrenic siblings, 22 of whom were childhood schizophrenics, out of 100 index children. Total number of siblings not reported.

[b] "Schizoid psychopaths" (20).

[c] "Hospitalizable psychopathic, alcoholic, or psychoneurotic" (21).

childhood schizophrenia in monozygotic (Mz) pairs is raised to 88.2%, if one includes co-twins with a later onset. Similarly, the rates for dizygotic (Dz) pairs and siblings are higher when one includes those with adult schizophrenia, as are the gross figures of Bender and Faretra (21) for siblings.

Furthermore, all three major studies of the parents of schizophrenic children (20–22), indicate that the rates for adult schizophrenia in the parents is as high, or higher, than for parents of adult schizophrenics. In other words, adult schizophrenia tends to cluster in the families of childhood schizophrenics, although most of the illness in siblings and co-twins resembles that observed in the index cases and occurs before puberty. Rosenthal (1) concluded that "these findings considered collectively make a strong case for the biologic unity" of preadolescent and adult schizophrenia, and they suggest that "preadolescent schizophrenia is a more virulent form, which has virtually complete penetrance."

Bender's (21) and Goldfarb's (22) data (see Table 1) indicate that there is also a genetic continuity between *early infantile autism* and later onset childhood schizophrenia, with both being continuous with adult schizophrenia. In both series there was a high rate of adult schizophrenia in the parents of schizophrenic children who would be classified as having early infantile autism, as well as in parents of later-onset, less impaired, childhood schizophrenics. The children in Bender's series whose illness began before 2 years of age are those Kanner would diagnose as having early infantile autism. Goldfarb's "organic" subgroup of schizophrenic children constitute 77% of his "very severely impaired" and "severely impaired" groups, whose functioning resembles early infantile autism. However, his "moderately impaired" schizophrenic children have superior intelligence and are clinically more like Bender's later-onset childhood schizophrenics.

Therefore, both Bender and Goldfarb present strong evidence that childhood schizophrenics with an onset before 2 years (21), who have a high incidence of "neurologic" abnormality and severe cognitive and social impairment (22) and who clinically resemble Kanner's early infantile autism, have the same strong genetic family histories for schizophrenia as do the later-onset childhood schizophrenics. Goldfarb (22) attributes this difference from Kanner's report of only 3% incidence of severe psychiatric abnormality to the selective sampling in Kanner's population. Most of Kanner's highly intelligent, professional parents sought his help after he differentiated early infantile autism from simple mental retardation. On the other hand, Bender's and Goldfarb's populations were drawn from city-wide referral agencies; they constituted much more heterogeneous groups, with a majority of the families being in Hollingshead and Redlich's social classes IV and V (22).

Continuity of Childhood and Adult Schizophrenia in Follow-up Studies

Direct evidence that childhood schizophrenia is continuous with adult schizophrenia comes from the follow-up of schizophrenic children into adulthood (Table 2). The most detailed information is available on 100 childhood schizophren-

TABLE 2. *Percent of childhood schizophrenics independently diagnosed schizophrenic as adults*

Number of childhood schizophrenics	Percent schizophrenic as adults (age range, years)
100 (21)	94 (22–45)
19 (24)	85 (15–23)

ics followed by Bender and Faretra (21) to ages 22 to 45 years. Other psychiatrists had confirmed the diagnosis for 94 of the 100 patients in adult life. One was diagnosed as psychosis with psychopathic personality and five were considered to be organically defective. Annell's findings (24) were similar, although she followed a smaller number of schizophrenics only to the age of 23 years and used stricter European criteria for the diagnosis. Almost all of the 19 that she diagnosed as clearly schizophrenic in childhood proved to be schizophrenic as adults. Of the 43 children she diagnosed as "schizophreniform psychosis," only one-third were later diagnosed as schizophrenic; one-third of this milder group adapted as schizoid personality disorders at 15 to 23 years of age.

Bender's (21) detailed report of outcome attests to the severity and chronicity of the disease when schizophrenic symptoms begin early. Twice as many of these childhood schizophrenics (i.e., 63%) remain chronically disabled and institutionalized, compared to schizophrenics first admitted as adolescents or adults (i.e., 33%). Children with an onset of psychosis before 2 years had the highest rate (72%) of chronicity (see Fig. 1). To some extent this increased chronicity was the result of the larger number of early-onset schizophrenics whose verbal intelli-

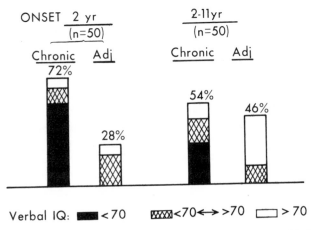

FIG. 1. Verbal I.Q. and outcome of childhood schizophrenics with an onset before or after 2 years (1). Adapted from Bender and Faretra (21). Chronic, Chronically institutionalized; Adj, Some adult adjustment in the community, from "complete psychotic dependency in a tolerant home to various degrees of independence, emotionally, socially, and economically"; Verbal I.Q. <70 ⟷ >70: I.Q. sometimes below and sometimes above 70.

gence quotients (I.Q.s) remained below 70. But children with higher and more variable I.Q.s also required continual institutional care.

When this life course was viewed from the other end, it was found that only 15% of adult schizophrenics who had been brought to a child guidance clinic for a variety of problems, had been diagnosed as schizophrenic in childhood (25). The rest had been diagnosed as having severe behavior disorders. An undetermined number go unrecognized. When elementary and high school records of schizophrenic adults were compared to matched classroom controls, only half of the preschizophrenics could be distinguished by the teachers' comments on their behavior, most of these by 12 to 15 years (26). Either the unrecognized preschizophrenics have symptoms that are ignored by families and schools because they are less troublesome, or they have no clinical features that could have distinguished them from other children. This question can only be answered by very large long-term prospective studies, with direct investigation of the children, rather than postdictive studies of records.

Childhood Schizophrenia: A Biologically More Severe Subgroup

Clinical, genetic, and longitudinal studies, therefore, all indicate that childhood schizophrenia is continuous with the most severe, chronic, adult schizophrenia, which presumably has the largest biologic component. The high concordance rate in twins suggests that the childhood form of schizophrenia has a higher degree of penetrance (1). The long-term course indicates that when schizophrenic thought disorder is present during childhood, and particularly before 2 years, it is much more likely to result in a permanently disabled individual who is likely to show a permanent cognitive deficit. All the differences between the childhood and adult forms of the disease point to the greater severity associated with an earlier onset of psychosis.

Earlier symptoms might produce some greater disability secondarily through the distortion and deficit of early learning. However, the early-onset, poor-outcome childhood schizophrenics all had a later onset of speech or early regression (21), indicating that language and cognition were seriously affected in the first 2 years of life, at the very beginning of the illness, however much they may have been additionally depressed by later experiences. The increased genetic penetrance also supports the view that early-onset schizophrenia reflects a biologically more severe form of the disease that primarily produces a greater disruption of central nervous system (CNS) functioning and more severe developmental deviations, including greater language and cognitive disability.

The greater genetic penetrance and more severe cognitive deficit in childhood schizophrenics parallel the differences between "process" and "reactive" schizophrenics, in an exaggerated form. "Process" schizophrenics have a more insidious onset, with greater cognitive and social impairment by the time they are seen as adults (27). Rosenthal (1) pointed out that "the more benign forms of schizophrenic-like illness belong in the same genetic spectrum as the more malignant forms, since the occurrence of schizophrenia often occurs in relatives at rates that are comparable for both groups," but that there are some data suggesting "a slightly higher heritability for the more typical forms," whether these are categorized as "process" versus "reactive," or as catatonic and hebephrenic versus paranoid.

The evidence indicates that childhood schizophrenia, that is, schizophrenia with an early onset, belongs at the most severe extreme of chronic adult schizophrenia in a spectrum of biologic continuity, and that within childhood schizophrenia the severity also increases, the earlier the onset.

DISORDERS OF EARLY MOTOR DEVELOPMENT IN PRESCHIZOPHRENIC CHILDREN AND CHILDREN GENETICALLY AT RISK FOR SCHIZOPHRENIA

Evidence from several sources points to early disorders of motor development, especially in chronic schizophrenics. Large-scale controlled studies have found motor symptoms in the histories of children with severe personality disorders who later turned out to be schizophrenic. In Robins' follow-up (4,28), difficulty in walking was among the early developmental symptoms that significantly differentiated preschizophrenic children from the others. Less than 25% of these schizophrenics were chronically hospitalized as adults. Only 10% had been suspected of possibly being psychotic when they were seen at a mean age of 14 years (age range 7 to 17). Watt (29) found that severe organic handicaps, including "neurologic disorders," significantly differentiated the preschizophrenics from their classroom controls and constituted one of the 5 factors that postdicted a schizophrenic outcome.

Similarly, Ricks and Nameche (30) found slow motor development and other "symptoms suggesting neurologic impairment" in 20% of the preschizophrenics, compared with 10% of the controls. Because of missing information, they considered these rates to "underestimate the actual frequencies of neurologic deficit in both groups." Furthermore, in the preschizophrenics there was "less evident external or clearly traceable causation" in the form of birth and subsequent neurologic trauma. These neurologic symptoms and estimates of probable brain damage based on neurologic examinations, were more frequent in the chronic preschizophrenic group than in the "released" preschizophrenics (31). In the chronic, withdrawn preschizophrenics, the neurologic symptoms included hypoactivity, rigidity, abnormal gait, poor coordination, and impaired attention. Hyperactivity occurred more frequently in the chronic, delinquent preschizophrenics.

Ricks and Berry (31) concluded that "brain damage, although not essential to the genesis of schizophrenia, is related to its *chronicity.*" They believed that these children were more vulnerable to disorder because of "disorganization and low competence, suggesting poor functioning of the higher integrative brain centers." Regression and chronic hospitalization depended on I.Q. and on social and vocational success. The "best predictors of recovery are measures of competency and integration, including neurological integration."

Children genetically at risk for schizophrenia, as well as preschizophrenics, may show similar early disorders. From the Rosenthal–Nagler project (32), Marcus (33) reported significantly more "soft" neurologic signs in the seven to ten year offspring of schizophrenics, compared to controls who were matched for rearing environments. The population consisted of 50 children, 7½ to 14 years of age, who were born to schizophrenic parents, and matched controls whose parents had no mental disease. Half of the children in each group lived in the city and half lived in kibbutzim and had less contact with their parents. The items that were "significant in differentiating the offspring of schizophrenics from their controls were facial asymmetry, fine motor coordination, left–right orientation, visual perception and auditory–visual integration." Poor overall neurologic functioning characterized half of the schizophrenic offspring under 11 years of age only, suggesting that these functions matured after 11 years, even in the neurologically immature children at risk. Moreover, this younger group consisted mostly of boys reared in cities who presumably had had more contact with their disturbed families.

In a study of obstetric records, Mednick, Mura, Schulzinger, and Mednick (34), found that retarded motor development at 5 days of age and at 1 year differentiated the offspring of schizophrenics from controls. All of this adds up to convincing documentation that disorders and delays of motor development occur more often in preschizophrenics, especially in chronic schizophrenics, and in children at greater genetic risk for schizophrenia, than in controls.

CHARACTERISTICS OF THE PANDEVELOPMENTAL DISORDER IN PRESCHIZOPHRENIC INFANTS AND INFANTS AT RISK FOR SCHIZOPHRENIA

In order to understand the nature of this early neurologic disorder, one must plot the course of development in the first 2 years in more detail. Frequent measurements of several functions yield peculiar curves that reflect a disruption of the normal pattern of neurologic maturation. The disorganization is far more complex than the simple retardation revealed by one or two points on the curve, and it affects not only motor development, but visual– motor, perceptual, and cognitive development, and even physical growth. The major findings from my infant studies that illustrate this point are discussed in the following section. The subjects, methods, predictions, and detailed findings have been reported in earlier papers for the children born in 1952–1953 (35–38) and in 1959–1960 (39–42) and are not repeated here.

Subjects

Briefly, the infants born in 1952–1953 and in 1959–1960 comprise a group of 24 individuals, of whom over half are now 21 to 22 years old (Table 3). The

TABLE 3. *Subjects and families in infant studies*

Description	Infants born in 1952–1953	Infants born in 1959–1960
Subjects		
Random first admissions to NYC "well-baby" clinic	16	0
Consecutive infants born to schizophrenic mothers in two New York State Hospitals	0	13
Followed to present time	14	10
White	9	3
Black	1	4
Puerto Rican	4	3
Boys	5	5
Current age	21–22	14–15
Mothers with chronic schizophrenia	2	9[a]
Mothers with schizophrenia in remission	0	1
Mothers with illegitimate pregnancy	5	10
Pregnancy or birth complications		
Severe (two toxemia; one 3-day labor, 5 days after ruptured membranes, with high forceps, cyanosis)	3[b]	0
Moderate (one bleeding in 1st trimester, one thyroidectomy for hyperthyroidism in first trimester and born with cord around neck of infant)	2	0
Mother under 15 years	0	1
Rearing families of current group		
Psychotic mother + social agency placements	2	1
Stable home, one parent with paranoid or schizoid personality disorder	3	0
Stable, but frequent open derogation of child (after 6 years)	3	1[c]
Stable, generally supportive	6	8[d]

[a] One father hospitalized schizophrenic. Most fathers unknown.

[b] One toxemia in schizophrenic mother ("Conrad").

[c] Maternal grandmother ("Pia").

[d] One maternal grandmother, one paternal grandmother, six permanent adoptive/foster homes.

1952–1953 infants were randomly selected from the Bellevue Hospital well-baby clinic, which served a lower-class neighborhood high in social and psychiatric pathology (37). Recent immigrants who spoke too little English to give the necessary detailed history had to be excluded from the study. This undoubtedly eliminated many psychiatrically normal parents who moved to the neighborhood because of external social circumstances. Because almost all of the 1959–1960 schizophrenic mothers were chronically hospitalized, their offspring were generally reared in carefully selected, permanent adoptive or foster homes, and more of them grew up in stable and supportive homes than in the 1952–1953 group.

There was also a high incidence of pregnancy and birth complications in the

1952–1953 infants (37) compared to the 1959–1960 group (Table 3). However, adequate antepartum records for the first trimester were not available for several mothers in both groups.

Method, Tests, and Measurements in Infancy

The analysis of infant development was based on standard infant tests and measurements and was repeated at key ages 10 times between birth and 2 years of age. Height, weight, head circumference, and overall body growth ("auxodrome") were plotted on the Wetzel grid (43), which enables one to plot changes in the infant's growth curve compared to his own earlier "channel" pattern. Separate developmental quotients (D.Q.s) were obtained for postural–motor, visual–motor, and language development, using the Gesell examination (44). Visual–motor items were analyzed for specific "integrative functions" (42). The analysis of the serial D.Q.s in different functions is comparable to following serial changes in I.Q.s in older individuals.

In the 1959–1960 study, behavioral state was recorded through 16 weeks of age for 1½ hr during the presentation of a standard series of stimuli and the Gesell examination (39,40). Caloric vestibular responses were also tested in this study (41,45), using the maximal stimulus of one minute of cold air at 10°C, which is equivalent to instilling 30 cm³ of icewater for 1 min (46). The duration of nystagmus or tonic deviation after the end of the stimulus was measured in seconds and analyzed according to the initial state of arousal and the infant's age (45).

Independent Psychologic and Psychiatric Evaluations at Follow-up

Independent psychologic and psychiatric assessments were made when the children were 10 and again at 18 years of age. In addition to a standard psychiatric diagnosis, the children were given a global severity rating and were ranked in order of severity. The psychologic tests included the Weschler Intelligence Scale for Children (WISC) or the Weschler Adult Intelligence Scale (WAIS), Rorschach, Thematic Apperception Test, human figure drawings, Bender–Gestalt test, and a perceptual–motor battery.

The distribution of the diagnoses and severity ratings is shown in Table 4. The two schizophrenic children, and one of those with severe personality disorders ("Conrad") (35,37,38), were the only schizophrenic offspring who had any significant contact with their psychotic mothers. Conrad was the only schizophrenic offspring with pregnancy or birth complications (see Table 3).

Brief summaries of the two schizophrenic children have been published. "Peter" was born in 1952 (35–38) and leads a marginal, dependent existence at 22, but has never been hospitalized. His diagnosis of schizophrenia was again independently confirmed at 18 years of age by a second psychologist. "Linda"

TABLE 4. *Independent psychiatric diagnoses at 10 years of schizophrenic offspring and controls*

Children's diagnoses	Schizophrenic mothers	Nonpsychotic mothers
Childhood schizophrenia	2	0
Personality disorder		
Severe	3	1
Moderate	5	2
Mild or no symptoms	2	9
Totals	12	12

was born in 1959 (42), was hospitalized from 7 to 10 years of age and at 15 is slowly improving in a residential treatment center.

The children diagnosed as having severe personality disorders had pathologic disorders of thinking, identification, and personality organization resembling schizophrenia, but without gross psychotic disruption (38,42). In today's terminology, they would fit Meehl's (47) characterization of severe "schizotypic personality disorders," who have so far remained compensated or the severely schizoid, paranoid or inadequate personalities in the "schizophrenia spectrum" described by Kety, Rosenthal, Wender, and Schulzinger (48).

Evidence of a Neurobiologic Disorder: Pandevelopmental Retardation

Analysis of the developmental curves points to an early biologic disorder in the two childhood schizophrenics. Both infants had a major disorganization of neurologic maturation, which involved postural–motor, visual–motor, and physical development as early as the first month of life. There was no fixed neurologic defect, but rather a disorder of the timing and integration of neurologic maturation.

Several features distinguish this from the usual forms of retardation and precocity. First, there was an unusual fluctuation in the rate of development, with marked acceleration and marked retardation succeeding one another (see Fig. 2). Peter's postural–motor development dropped to 45% of normal at 9 months of age and then, without any change in his external circumstances, suddenly accelerated to achieve 5 months' development in the next 2 months, and reached normal levels by 13 months.

Other features differed from the usual patterns in chronic organic brain syndromes. Sometimes there was a temporary loss of a previously acquired ability. At times they showed a reversed cephalocaudal gradient of postural development, with head control lagging months behind the control of trunk and legs. At times a "higher" function, as "Peter's" visual–motor ability (36), remained relatively intact at a time when postural–motor ability was severely retarded. This is the reverse of the pattern in diffuse, chronic brain damage (49). In infants with brain

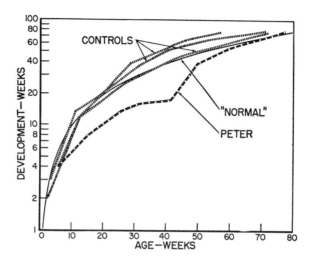

FIG. 2. Comparison between mean postural–motor development of schizophrenic child (Peter) and controls (1). Reprinted with permission from Fish (36). Development (weeks): Age at which postural–motor performance occurs in normal standardization sample (44). "Normal," Development (weeks) equals chronologic age in weeks; Controls, Offspring of nonpsychotic mothers (35, 37). (Copyright 1959, the American Psychiatric Association.)

damage, higher cognitive functions are usually affected first, whereas postural development and physical growth become retarded only when the damage is more severe.

The erratic functioning of these preschizophrenic infants is analogous to the disturbance of older schizophrenic patients who fail easy items on an intelligence test and then succeed on more advanced items during the same session.

In adult schizophrenics, it is difficult to determine which aspects of their peculiar test performance might be disturbances in attention or cognitive function that are specific to schizophrenia, and that result from anxiety or disturbed motivation (8). However, when one sees this disorganized pattern in the first month of life, it is clear that such temporary states of poorly integrated CNS functioning can occur in schizophrenia, long before complex motivational and defensive behaviors have developed.

Pandevelopmental Retardation, Psychiatric Morbidity, and Genetic Risk

The most severe, overall retardation involved physical growth, as well as postural–motor or visual–motor development or both (see Fig. 3). This "pan-developmental retardation" was related to psychiatric morbidity at 10 years. It was most severe in the two preschizophrenic infants, and was most extreme in Peter (Table 5). His onset was earlier and his subsequent cognitive and perceptual disturbances were more severe than Linda's. Children in whom pandevelopmental retardation was milder and shorter were ranked just below the schizophrenic

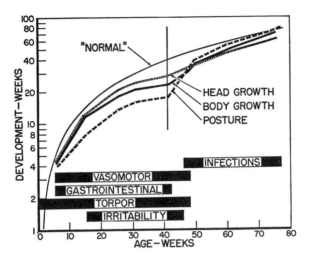

FIG. 3. Relationship between mean postural–motor development, physical growth, and clinical disturbances of schizophrenic child (Peter) (1). Reprinted with permission from Fish (36). Body growth: Auxodrome on Wetzel grid. See text for further explanation. For details of clinical disturbances, see Fish (36). (Copyright 1959, the American Psychiatric Association.)

children in the severity of their psychiatric disturbance at 10 years (Table 6). Children who had no retardation of physical growth had still milder psychiatric disorders at ten years, although one ("Carol") (37) has had moderately severe symptoms since the age of 16.

The offspring of schizophrenic mothers were exposed to fewer pregnancy and birth complications, but they had a higher incidence of pandevelopmental retardation in infancy (χ^2, $p < 0.01$) and of severe to moderate personality disorders at 10 years (χ^2, $p < 0.01$ (see Table 7). Another sequel of early developmental disorder was the occurrence of *specific reading disabilities* with perceptual disor-

TABLE 5. *Comparison of developmental deviations in two schizophrenic children*

Description	"Peter"	"Linda"
Ages with pandevelopmental retardation (in months)	7 to 18	7 to 13
Lowest postural–motor D.Q.	45	75
Lowest visual–motor D.Q.	64	59
Age of onset of schizophrenic symptoms	3	6
I.Q. at 10 years (WISC)		
Full-scale	65	84
Verbal	75	92
Performance	61	78
I.Q. at 18 years (WAIS)		
Full-scale	81	—
Verbal	87	—
Performance	76	—

TABLE 6. *Severity of pandevelopmental retardation and psychiatric outcome at 10 years*

Number of children ($N=23$)*	Lowest motor D.Q. birth to 2 years	Number independently diagnosed at 10 years
I. Pandevelopmental retardation (with growth retardation)		Schizophrenia
1	<70	
1	70–79	} 2
		Personality disorder
6	80–89	{ 3 severe
		3 moderately severe
II. Developmental lags with no growth retardation		
4	60–89	4 moderately mild
		Mild or no symptoms
5	70–89	5
6	>90	6

* Conrad was not examined between 1 and 10 months and is omitted from this table.

ders at 10 years of age (42). These were usually associated with failure on the block-design subtest of the WISC and failures on the perceptual battery, including high Koppitz scores and "organic" types of distortions on the Bender–Gestalt, poor fine coordination, and defective finger schema. These perceptual defects also occurred significantly more often in the offspring of the schizophrenic mothers (χ^2, $p<0.05$), similar to the findings in Marcus' (33) much larger study. Fish's infant data (42) indicate that antecedents can be found before 2 years of age for the perceptual symptoms seen at 7 to 10 years. Failure on the block-design subtest of the WISC at 10 years correlated significantly with failure of form perception at 1½ to 2 years of age, as measured on the form board ($p<0.05$, Fisher test) (42).

TABLE 7. *Disorders in offspring of schizophrenic mothers and controls*

Disorders in children	Mothers	
	Schizophrenic ($N=12$)	No psychosis ($N=12$)
Severe to moderate complications of pregnancy and birth	1	4
Pandevelopmental retardation	7[a]	1
Diagnosed schizophrenic or severe to moderate personality disorder at 10 years	10[a]	3
Reading disability with perceptual dysfunction at 10 years	8[b]	2

[a] χ^2: $p<0.01$.
[b] $p<0.05$.

None of the children with pandevelopmental retardation had had any pregnancy or birth complications. None of the children with pregnancy or birth complications showed regression of development or a peculiar pattern of scatter, and none had pandevelopmental retardation with an overall retardation of physical growth and postural motor development. Pregnancy and birth complications were followed in three of the infants by brief lags in early head control, of a mild degree, which then returned to normal (37). Therefore, in individual infants, as well as in the group data in this study (Table 7), pandevelopmental retardation was significantly related to a genetic history for schizophrenia, but not to pregnancy and birth complications.

SPECTRUM OF NEUROLOGIC "VULNERABILITY" AND PSYCHIATRIC DISABILITY IN INFANT STUDIES AND OLDER PATIENTS

The relationship found in these infants between more severe disruption and retardation of early development, earlier onset of psychiatric symptoms, and more severe cognitive impairment in later childhood recalls the retrospective data in the large studies of schizophrenic children (21,22) and adults (27,30,31) described previously.

The infant data reveal a spectrum of severe to mild irregularity and retardation of physical growth, postural–motor and visual–motor development, which was followed by a corresponding spectrum of severity of psychiatric disorder, ranging from schizophrenia to severe personality disorders. Perceptual and cognitive disorders were associated with the psychiatric disorders in many of the children. The pandevelopmental disorders and their sequelae were significantly related to being at genetic risk for schizophrenia and were not associated with pregnancy and birth complications.

Fish (35–42,50) had hypothesized earlier that this poor integration of neurologic development in infancy was the analogue of the disorders of higher integrative functions seen in older schizophrenic children and adults, and that it constituted a "vulnerability to schizophrenia." Whether a particular vulnerable child became psychotic or developed a less severe personality disorder depended upon the severity of his early deviations interacting with his particular environment.

The relationship in the infant studies between more severe developmental impairment and more severe psychiatric disorder with an earlier onset resembles the spectrum of severity described earlier for the entire range of schizophrenia. The most severely disabled schizophrenics with the most chronic course have the highest frequency of early motor disorders (30,31), the earliest onset, and the most severe cognitive impairment (27). At the furthest extreme of this schizophrenia spectrum are the childhood schizophrenics with an onset before 2 years of age (21,22).

Several large retrospective studies indicate that the spectrum of severity of early neurologic disorders paralleled the later severity of schizophrenia. Ricks and his co-workers (30,31) found more neurologic abnormalities in the childhood records of the more chronic adult schizophrenics. In childhood schizophrenics—the most severe of the chronic schizophrenics—more neurologic abnormalities (22) and more histories of severely retarded and irregular motor development (51,52), were found in the children who have the lowest verbal I.Q.s, and the poorest prognosis with the most chronic course.

There is some genetic evidence that this "schizophrenia spectrum," at its milder end, may also extend to certain severe personality disorders and possibly to other significant psychiatric abnormalities. Kety et al. (48) suggested from their adoption studies that borderline schizophrenia and possibly certain inadequate personality disorders may be milder variants of schizophrenia, occurring in the same genetically determined "schizophrenia spectrum" as chronic schizophrenia. Heston and Denney (53) found that mental retardates, "schizoid psychopaths," and certain emotionally labile neurotics clustered in the adopted offspring of schizophrenic mothers. They raised the possibilities that "a subcritical dose of the pathological genes produces or predisposes to disabilities other than schizophrenia," or that "schizophrenia as a biologic entity is broader than our present clinical entity, . . . the differing manifestations being due to modifying genes or life experiences." The infant data parallel these findings. The infants whose pandevelopmental retardation was less severe than that in the preschizophrenic infants, were diagnosed as having severe personality disorders at 10 years, and showed clinical features similar to those described in the adult studies.

NEUROINTEGRATIVE DEFECT, "SCHIZOTAXIA," AND VULNERABILITY

Meehl (47,54) has formulated most clearly the necessarily indirect "causal chain from gene through biochemical endophenotype to neurophysiological endophenotype (e.g., synaptic slippage) to behavioral dispositions to the ultimate learned behavior" (54). " 'Clinical schizophrenia' as such cannot be inherited because it has behavioral and phenomenal contents which are learned" (47). He postulates that what is inherited is a *"subtle neuro-integrative defect"* (54), which he termed "schizotaxia" (47). All schizotactic individuals develop a "schizotypic" personality organization. If the interpersonal regime is favorable and if the individual also has inherited certain constitutional strengths, he will remain a well compensated schizotype, without symptoms of mental disease, but exhibiting faint signs of "cognitive slippage and other minimal neurological aberrations" (47).

The "endophenotype" will eventually be identified by the biochemical and neurophysiologic aberrations underlying "schizotaxia." Meehl suggested that research on the "exophenotype" should focus on "a refinement and objectification of the 'soft neurology,' as seen in the longitudinal research of Barbara Fish and the ongoing study of Israeli Kibbutz children of schizophrenic mothers."

Pandevelopmental retardation appears to serve as an early "marker" for the inherited neurointegrative defect in schizophrenia. Of the infants genetically at risk, those with the most severe pandevelopmental retardation became schizophrenic, and those with milder forms became "schizotypic" personality disorders, with varying degrees of decompensation in childhood and adolescence.

Changing Manifestations of Neurointegrative Defect with Maturation

The overt manifestations of the neurointegrative defect change with maturation. The age-specific defects are most readily detectable in their most severe form, so that in each age period, mild neurointegrative defects may be found in the entire population at risk, but only a smaller subgroup shows extreme defects.

In the first year, pandevelopmental retardation occurred in about half of the schizophrenic offspring, often accompanied by disorders of state behavior, of the development of reaching and manipulation and of vestibular responsiveness, to be described subsequently. In the retrospective studies of disturbed children and adults, only the most severe motor retardation is recalled, and, therefore these histories cluster in the most severe childhood schizophrenics (22,51,52) and the most chronic adult patients (30,31).

Gross postural–motor retardation cannot be a "marker" once independent locomotion is achieved, but more subtle defects in motor integration can be found. These "soft neurologic" signs appear to identify the population at genetic risk up to 10 years of age, as they occurred in half of the schizophrenic offspring (33). After 10 years, the milder defects in motor integration "mature" and "soft signs" no longer identify the entire population at risk (33). However, certain schizophrenics continue to show "soft neurologic" signs as adolescents (55) and adults, particularly those with thought disorders (56). It is conceivable that finer tests of motor integration might still identify a large adult population genetically at risk (47). The disturbance in oculomotor tracking, which Holzman (57) found in schizophrenic patients with thought disorder and in their relatives, may be such a genetic "marker" in later life.

The spectrum of severe to mild disorders of visual–motor integration also changes its specific manifestations with maturation. The gross retardation of reaching and manipulation in the first year was succeeded by retarded form perception from 2 to 10 years (42). Disorders of visual–motor integration were also among the "soft neurologic" signs that identified half of the seven to 10-year-old schizophrenic offspring in Marcus' study (33). These signs matured and were not detectable after 10 years in the group at genetic risk. However, severe visual–motor disorders on the Bender–Gestalt test and other tasks still persist in many schizophrenics, particularly in the more chronic ones (7).

Similarly, integrative disorders of language and cognitive function change in their manifestations with age. These functions appear to be more sensitive indicators of neurointegrative defect. When they are affected early, massive arrest or permanent retardation may result. The earliest and most severe disorders occur in the early childhood schizophrenics. In the most severely affected, speech begins late (21,52) and continues to be permeated by fragmented, stereotyped, and noncommunicative utterances (13–16). When this early defect is massive, it is reflected in a permanently retarded verbal I.Q. (21). In later-onset schizophrenics, if retardation in I.Q. is present, it is much less severe and occurs predominantly in more severely chronic patients (3,27). However, more sensitive tests can detect subtler evidence of thought disorder in borderline schizophrenic patients who function normally on the WAIS (58) and in many relatives of schizophrenics (59). A "higher percentage" of disordered associations has also been found in the adolescent offspring of schizophrenics (60).

All of these studies point to a neurointegrative defect that can be identified through measures of motor, perceptual, and cognitive integration in individuals genetically at risk for schizophrenia. Poor integration of these functions shows a continuity from birth to adulthood in affected individuals, although the manifestations change somewhat as these capacities mature. Neurointegrative defects can be identified in approximately half the offspring of schizophrenics and may represent an underlying biologic vulnerability to psychiatric disorder. The spectrum of severity of the neurointegrative defect, from infancy on, appears to be related to the spectrum of severity of later psychiatric disorder. The defect is most severe in schizophrenics; with increasing severity of the integrative defect, the psychotic disorder appears earlier and is associated with greater chronicity and cognitive and social disability. Milder defects are followed by severe to moderately severe personality disorders, often associated with perceptual and cognitive deficits.

The development of more refined quantitative measures for the specific motor, perceptual, and cognitive defects would enable us to identify the vulnerable individuals in populations at risk more precisely (54). Such measures would also identify the symptoms that should be targets for early intervention.

DO PREGNANCY AND BIRTH COMPLICATIONS CONTRIBUTE TO PANDEVELOPMENTAL RETARDATION AND A SCHIZOPHRENIC OUTCOME?

Stabenau and Pollin (61), in reviewing their own and other's studies of Mz twins discordant for schizophrenia, found that four times the number of the sick twins were differentiated from their co-twins by birth complications and CNS illness as children, twice as many were differentiated by lighter birth weight, but only 1.8 times as many by slower walking. In this series, externally caused para- and postnatal neurologic disability may have contributed to the development of more severe illness in 17 to 24 of the 100 Mz pairs.

However, Gottesman and Shields (62) doubted that "neurological deficiencies sufficient to account for much of the later psychopathology can be attributed to these differences in birth weight which are not unusual in monozygotic twins" and which sometimes "represent only a trivial portion of the total weight." Furthermore, they pointed out that the "birth weight findings may be accounted for by a bias in sampling," because none of the "twin studies with representative sampling found lower birth weight to distinguish the future schizophrenic or the more severe of a concordant pair. Although there was a tendency for the twin with greater birth complications to be more at risk for schizophrenia in other studies, our evidence, when available, was inconclusive."

Mednick and Schulzinger (60) reported a trend for the birth process to have been accompanied by more difficulties in the offspring of schizophrenic mothers compared to the controls. "Most significant is the fact that abnormal placentas were evidenced by 11.3% of the high-risk subjects and only 1.2% of the controls." However, when they compared the 20 subjects at risk who became psychiatrically ill with matched offspring of schizophrenic mothers who were still well, "there was a slight tendency for the 'sick group' to have had a more difficult birth," but "none of the differences reached statistical significance."

In a later paper, Mednick et al. (34), analyzed more detailed neonatal and developmental data on another group of infants born to schizophrenic parents and controls. In this "OB project," they analyzed perinatal and 1-year follow-up records of 83 offspring of schizophrenics, and compared them to matched controls born to 83 character-disordered parents and 83 parents without recorded psychiatric illness. There were no differences in complications of pregnancy or delivery between the groups, except that more children of schizophrenics had low normal birth weights (2,550 to 3,000 g). Despite this relative absence of increased trauma, the children of schizophrenics tended to have "retarded motor reflexes" at birth that persisted at 5 days of age, although the difficulties in the control infants usually had cleared up by the fifth day. Furthermore, the children of schizophrenics had retarded motor development compared to the controls, including delays in head control (after 4 months), sitting, standing, and walking. But these differences did not quite reach statistical significance.

Genetic or Traumatic Developmental Deviation?

In a discussion of Mednick's paper (34), Fish (63) commented on a number of features in these data which suggested genetically determined motor lags rather than retardation due to trauma. Decreased motor responses on the fifth-day examination differentiated the schizophrenic offspring more than did the immediate neonatal findings. The effects of preanesthetic medication and birth trauma, unless they are very severe, tend to subside after the second or third day, whereas genetically determined immaturity is more likely to persist, as happened in the schizophrenic offspring. In the schizophrenic offspring the decrease in neonatal motor responses occurred in the presence of normal sucking responses, unlike the controls. This dissociation between different measures of "arousal" is like the dissociation seen in the "abnormally quiet" schizophrenic offspring reported by Fish (39,40), but it is different from the more consistent underarousal that can occur with birth injury or severe retardation. A persistence of motor retardation during the first year generally follows only very severe birth injury, but it is frequent with genetically determined developmental lags.

In discussing the paper of Mednick et al. (34), Heston (64) stated that it "adds critical data which supports the hypothesis that immaturity at birth is associated with schizophrenic genotypes in a direct relationship." He noted that "the schizophrenic fathers contributed immature infants in a proportion compatible to their total contribution of offspring," which would not have occurred had the intrauterine environment and the delivery process been the cause of the immaturity.

Although certain pregnancy and birth complications appear to occur more often in the offspring of schizophrenic mothers (60), the evidence cited is not yet conclusive that these trauma increase the risk of the offspring developing schizophrenia as adults. However, in a group of 100 childhood schizophrenics, Bender (21) found that abnormal pregnancies occurred in 44% of the 50 severely impaired children with an onset of psychosis before 2 years, but in only 20% of the later-onset group. Traumatic births occurred in 30% and 20% of the two groups, respectively. Bender concluded that these factors contributed to the severe mental defect in the early-onset schizophrenics.

Genetically Determined Developmental Deviation

An abnormal pregnancy or birth may add organic defect and increase the mental retardation of the young schizophrenic child, as in Bender's series, but it was not responsible for the irregular infant development observed by Fish. None of the infants with pandevelopmental retardation had had any pregnancy or birth complications. Pandevelopmental retardation was, however, significantly related to being a child of a schizophrenic mother. The schizophrenic children in Fish's series had onsets after 2 years and were not as severe as children with early infantile autism. Similarly in Marcus' (33) study, the "soft" neurologic signs in seven to 10-year-old children were significantly related to being born to a schizophrenic parent.

In the 7- to 10-year-old age group, it would be difficult to distinguish on clinical grounds alone, those "soft" neurologic signs that resulted from minimal brain damage from those occurring in a population genetically at risk for schizophrenia. However, in infancy, repeated examinations revealed peculiar regressions in physical growth, postural–motor and visual–motor development which were distinctly different from the patterns seen following pregnancy and birth complications. A much greater number of infants genetically at risk for schizophrenia and infants with benign genetic histories would have to be matched for the presence or absence of pregnancy and birth complications, and then examined frequently from birth to 2 years, in order to determine how reliably regressions, retarded physical growth and erratic patterning of development could differentiate the poor integration in schizophrenic offspring without birth complications, from poor integration in infants at no genetic risk who had suffered brain damage.

DOES THE QUALITY OF MOTHERING CONTRIBUTE TO PANDEVELOPMENTAL RETARDATION AND A SCHIZOPHRENIC OUTCOME?

Certainly in this study the incidence of poorly integrated neurologic development with the characteristics described previously appeared to be increased by a genetic history for schizophrenia. But it would be the height of naiveté to assume from this that the rates of neurologic maturation and the degree of disruption reflected only genetic programming, uninfluenced by environment. The severe sensory deprivation and impoverishment of early institutional care appear to be associated with developmental handicaps in some of the infants subjected to these conditions (65). In that study, gross motor development was affected to a lesser degree than visual–motor, language, and social development.

However, one does not know the genetic histories of many abandoned infants, including those in the Provence and Lipton study (65). It is likely that the incidence of psychiatric pathology in such mothers is higher than in the general population. Provence and Lipton, as well as other authors, have not been able to explain why some infants are much more vulnerable than others to such institutional environments. It is conceivable that some of these infants could have been more vulnerable on a genetic basis, as in Fish's studies. Interestingly, in Heston and Denney's study (53), in which the infants were matched for the duration of institutional care, no gross psychiatric sequelae were dependent on this variable. The authors are careful to state that they could not eliminate the possibility that more subtle emotional impairments existed, which were not reflected in ratings of disability or in the standard psychiatric diagnoses. Their findings add some support to the notion that it may be the genetically vulnerable infants who succumb most to severely impoverished environments. Similarly, in infants studied for "failure to thrive," it is not clear whether genetic factors increase their vulnerability, in addition to the emotional and physical neglect that seem to be implicated.

However, whatever the genetic background of such deprived populations, White and Held (66) demonstrated that the pace and sequence of visual–motor development can be altered significantly by providing specific patterns of early stimulation to the otherwise bleak institutional environment.

Obviously it is much more complicated to assess the effects of environment in a heterogenous population, when the constructive and deleterious factors are not under experimental control. One can therefore draw only the most tentative conclusions from Fish's infant data. These point to both genetic and environmental influences on development. Pandevelopmental retardation not only occurred significantly more often in the offspring of schizophrenic mothers, but it occurred in a severe form in some infants ("Rachel" and "Pia"), reared in optimal environments by mothers who sensitively responded to the particular needs of these vulnerable infants (67). This, as well as the clustering of these severe developmental disorders according to the genetic history, point to a genetic component in these deviations.

However, certain types of rearing experiences may exaggerate or mitigate the severity of particular developmental symptoms in the vulnerable group (67). The most severe pandevelopmental retardation occurred in the two preschizophrenic infants. Both were reared in the most impoverished environments. Peter was reared by a dull, disorganized maternal grandmother and Linda spent her first

4 years in a large foundling institution, as bleak as those described by Provence and Lipton. At 11 months when Peter was unable to sit unsupported, he was able to perform manual tasks optimally "when cradled in the examiner's lap and physically supported. However, his grandmother was emotionally incapable of responding to his needs for special attention and it appeared that he could not practice his nascent skills when left unattended in his crib at home" (35). His spurt in development began in the month prior to his mother's return from the hospital. "The fact that he suddenly began to progress, despite the fact that he was still totally under his grandmother's care, indicates that there must have been an abrupt change in his inner resources" (35). Linda's acceleration in development also occurred spontaneously while she was still on the same large infant ward in the institution. It appears that genetic factors led to the initially poor neurologic integration in these infants and to their spontaneous remissions, but that their impoverished environments could well have added to their early neurologic retardation.

Later outcome appears to depend even more obviously on the child's life experiences interacting with his early developmental assets and impairments. The two preschizophrenic infants had the most severe early impairments and showed the least response to the environmental stimulation and support that they received after 7 years of age. Children with less severe deviations in infancy than this showed a greater capacity to respond to whatever stimulation and support was provided by the environment. Conrad was better integrated than Peter was at 9 years of age, although he had had a traumatic birth history and even much greater disruption of his relationships to parent figures than Peter (37,38). Some children showed remarkably resilient adaptations to severe birth trauma and what are ordinarily considered to be pathogenic environments (37). Rachel, whose early development and cognitive impairment at 10 years were worse than Pia's, is so far coping with her adolescent problems more successfully, apparently because she has been in a warm and continually supportive foster home. Pia has made several adolescent suicide attempts, having been rejected by her grandmother for the academic inadequacies she began to show in grade school. Whereas Conrad's greater competence compared to Peter appears related to his lesser early neurologic vulnerability, the fact that Rachel is coping better than Pia can only point to the positive effect of the environment on a very vulnerable child.

A genetically determined biologic vulnerability is just that—it can be exaggerated by a destructive or impoverished environment and can be compensated for by a constructive environment. Only when the initial neurobiologic disorder is of devastating proportions, as in the most severe of the early-onset childhood schizophrenics, is it the overriding determinant of outcome that is virtually uninfluenced by variations in family environments, or by the most potent pharmacologic and educational measures currently available (52).

The necessary influence of a genetic predisposition has been clearly demonstrated by the adoption studies (48,53) and the twin studies (62). To go beyond this and attempt to evaluate the precise influences in the environment that cause one vulnerable "schizotypic" individual to decompensate and that help another to compensate, presents enormous complications. The issues are still unclear, even in the studies of discordant monozygotic twins, when the genetic component can be held constant (54,62). To study the effects of different rearing experiences in prospective studies of infants, when the genetic risk cannot be equated so precisely, one would need to match the infants according to their different profiles and the degrees of severity of early developmental impairments, and also for their compensating developmental assets.

If we are to match environments for their constructive and destructive effects on different types of infants, we need much more information regarding what effects specific differences in the environment can have on specific developmental symptoms. At the present time we can only rate the most extreme differences in early mothering. The impact of different patterns of nurturing will be different on vulnerable infants with different degrees of vulnerability, and with different profiles of other developmental assets and liabilities. A depressed or withdrawn mother may have a more devastating effect on an apathetic infant than on an oversensitive, irritable one. An agitated, tense, or chaotic mother may be more disorganizing for the latter type of infant (67).

The variables to be measured increase exponentially if we then want to compare the effects of subsequent life experiences on children with different early developmental assets and handicaps. One would need some understanding of the destructive or constructive meaning of these events for individual children, in the light of their own particular past experiences (54).

Rather than embark on such enormously complicated studies of long-term outcome of infants at risk, I believe it is more appropriate and economical at the present stage of our knowledge to study first the nature of the biologic antecedents of schizophrenia in more detail in infants at risk. If we knew more about the mechanisms whereby the early motor, perceptual, and cognitive handicaps were produced, one could study the effects of specific early interventions on specific developmental impairments, as White and Held (66) have done in institutionalized infants. If early interventions could be developed that could prevent, arrest, or compensate for the perceptual and cognitive impairments these infants often show before 2 years, one might interrupt the sequence of cumulative academic and vocational failure which makes for a more chronically disabled adult who retreats into "despair and apathy" (30).

OTHER FEATURES OF THE NEUROINTEGRATIVE DISORDER IN INFANTS AT RISK

Abnormally "Quiet State"

In addition to pandevelopmental retardation, three other abnormal patterns in the first months raise neurophysiologic questions. The first was an "abnormally quiet" state found in four offspring of schizophrenic mothers (see Table 8). From

TABLE 8. *Other features of the neurointegrative defect in infancy*

Abnormally "quiet" state: birth to 4 weeks

1. Continuous visual alertness: 15 to 80 min (versus 2 to 5 min) (without a pacifier)
2. Marked decrease in spontaneous crying
3. No crying with postural manipulation of body or extremities (decreased response to proprioceptive stimulation)
4. Normal or increased responses to visual, auditory and tactile stimuli
5. Muscles "doughy" to palpation (like Down's syndrome)
6. Flaccid, overextensible at joints
7. Deep tendon reflexes 2+ to 3+, loose, pendular
8. Decreased caloric nystagmus when awake: 0.5 sec (versus 37.2 sec)
9. Severe psychopathology at 10 years in three out of four "quiet" infants

Failure of midline bimanual skills ("hand-to-hand" items)

1. Related to severe to moderate psychopathology at 10 years (in all eight infants; $p = 0.022$)
2. Related to decreased caloric vestibular response: at 4 months: $p = 0.008$, 7 months: $p = 0.071$, 10 months-random)

Decreased caloric nystagmus (0 to 6 sec) occurred with:

1. "Quiet" state (0 to 1 month)
2. Failure of midline bimanual skills (4 to 7 months)
3. Pandevelopmental retardation (0 to 24 months)

---

birth to 4 weeks of age, these infants differed from the others in their ability to maintain an unbroken state of quiet, visual alertness for up to 1 hr and 20 min, as early as 18 hr of age (39,40). In contrast, the normally active infants spontaneously cried when awake and could only remain alert for 2 to 5 min without a pacifier, at under 2 months of age. The abnormally quiet infants did not cry in the first month, even with vigorous postural manipulation, unlike the others, although their responses to visual, auditory, and tactile stimuli were normal or increased.

These features were observed clinically in the first schizophrenic infant, Peter, in 1952 (35,36). In the 1959–1960 study, the difference in spontaneous activity and in responses to stimuli were measured under standard conditions (39,40). These "quiet" infants also had extreme underactivity, flaccidity, and overextensibility of the joints. Their muscle tone was as doughy as that of infants with Down's syndrome. This hypotonia was apparently of central origin, as their deep tendon reflexes were two- to three-plus, loose, and pendular.

The "quiet" infants also differed following caloric stimulation in the first month (45). Their mean nystagmus when awake was only 0.5 sec, compared to 37.2 sec for the active infants. Decreased nystagmus is a very sensitive indicator of slight decreases in arousal (68,69). But in these "abnormally quiet" infants, the decrease in nystagmus, spontaneous motor activity, and the response to manipulation, all occurred in the presence of normal or increased visual fixation and following. The "abnormally quiet" state was characteristic of these infants between examinations, as well. It therefore appeared to be a sustained, but relatively "focal" depression of CNS functioning in the first month, limited to gross motor, proprioceptive and vestibular systems.

In three of the four quiet infants, this abnormally quiet behavior was a precursor of severe psychopathology at 10 years. But Linda, who became grossly psychotic by six years, had appeared normally active in her first month. One should note here that all the abnormally "quiet" infants were white, whereas all of the black infants were active, including Linda.

Visual–Motor Disorders and Failures of Integrated Bimanual Skills

Visual–motor performance revealed several severe disturbances that will not be reviewed in detail here (35,38,42). These included delays in visual fixation on objects held in the infant's own hand, in contrast to normal attention to objects seen in space; severe delays in reaching and manipulation in the first year, apraxia and retarded form perception in the second year, as well as a variety of failures on perceptual tests at 10 years.

Gross irregularity, or "scatter," in integrative visual–motor tasks during infancy occurred only in children with severe to moderate psychiatric disorders at 10 years (42). Only one item, failure of "hand-to-hand" integration was similarly correlated with the presence of later severe to moderate psychiatric impairment ($p = 0.022$, Fisher test) (70). This integrated functioning of one hand with the other at the midline normally begins with mutual fingering of one hand by the other at 16 weeks, followed by the transferring of objects from one hand to the other at 28 weeks, and finally at 40 weeks to the simultaneous grasp of one object in each hand and approximating them. Failure in these specific bimanual skills occurred in all eight of the children rated as having severe to moderate psychiatric impairment at 10 years, but they were not failed by either of the two children rated as having mild to no impairment.

There was also a significant relationship between the times when midline bimanual skills were failed and when vestibular response was reduced on one or both sides (45). This relationship was significant at 16 weeks ($p = 0.008$, Fisher test). It declined at 28 weeks ($p = 0.071$) and appeared at random at 40 weeks. The schizophrenic infant, Linda, had the most severe retardation in these "hand-to-hand" items (42) and in the associated vestibular hyporeactivity (45). Although finger dexterity developed normally, her hands did not engage at the midline like a normal 16-week infant, even when she was 28 weeks old, and she did not transfer objects like a 28-week-old, even when she was 58 weeks of age.

Decreased Vestibular Responses

Decreased to absent vestibular responses were associated with the periods of pandevelopmental retardation between birth and 2 years, with the "abnormally quiet" state in the first month, and with the failures of bimanual skills in the fourth and seventh months (45). The transitory nature of the absent responses rules out the possibility of an organic lesion of the vestibular system. Rather, it appeared to be a sensitive indicator of periods when several different CNS functions manifested integrative disorder. This suggests that transitory states of decreased CNS activity, which depressed gross motor, proprioceptive, and vestibular functions, but not vision, accompanied periods when CNS integration was disrupted.

On most of these occasions there were no overt behavioral changes to suggest the presence of a decreased arousal, which might have explained the failures in performance and the decreased nystagmus. The infants usually appeared visually intent and focused in their attention to the performance materials. The hypoactivity of the "abnormally quiet" babies in the first 4 weeks, which was accompanied by decreased nystagmus, has been discussed above. There were also four occasions when waking infants who had decreased nystagmus showed some degree of behavioral apathy. Although they were visually alert on these four occasions, three infants did not cry during the 60 sec of caloric stimulation, which was the usual response. They showed complete absence of nystagmus on these occasions. This exceptional underresponsiveness occurred in the three infants who were seriously disturbed at ten years. Furthermore, these four instances occurred at the age when pandevelopmental retardation was most severe in these infants. The absence of the usual irritability with caloric stimulation suggests some covert state of decreased arousal. However, the association of this state with the periods of the worst pandevelopmental retardation, when physical growth was maximally retarded, testifies to a cumulative phenomenon that had begun one or more months before. This means that the poor central nervous system integration at these times was not a momentary phenomenon, but part of a continuing, profound process.

NEUROINTEGRATIVE DEFECT IN INFANTS AT RISK: A DYSREGULATION OF MATURATION AT ALL LEVELS

In summary, these infants had periods when several different CNS functions manifested integrative disorder. The biologic disorder during these periods disrupted the normal timing, sequences, and spatial organization of development. It was a disorder of the overall regulation and patterning of the orderly progress of maturation, not a disorder of isolated traits or responses. The normal temporal pattern was changed in a disorderly fashion, so that the rate alternated between being excessively slow and excessively fast, or even went into reverse. The spatial patterning was disrupted, as seen in the temporary reversal of the cephalocaudal gradient and the failures of midline integration of the hands. The peculiar "scatter" in functioning resulted in a profile of successes and failures on any single exam unlike that seen in chronic brain syndromes (see Table 9).

Finally, this integrative disorder affected many systems under control of the CNS, including physical growth, gross motor, visual–motor, vestibular functioning, and possibly arousal. The biologic disorder in preschizophrenic and vulnerable infants is a disorder of the total organism.

One could construct a theory of schizophrenia based on any one of the disturb-

TABLE 9. *Neurointegrative defect in infancy: signs of dysregulation of maturation in many systems*

Periods of decreased CNS integration
1. Alternately retarded and accelerated development
2. Regression of development; loss of function
3. Reversed cephalocaudal gradient
4. Failure of integration of midline bimanual skills
5. Profile of failures unlike chronic brain syndromes

Involvement of many systems
1. Retarded physical growth with most severe, overall retardation *(pandevelopmental retardation)*
2. Decreased muscle tone, activity, crying ("quiet" state)
3. Decreased response to proprioceptive stimuli ("quiet" state)
4. Retarded postural–motor development
5. Decreased vestibular response to caloric stimulation (decreased "arousal"?)
6. Retarded visual–motor development
7. Retarded cognitive development

Severity of neurointegrative defect related to outcome
1. Pandevelopmental retardation (0 to 24 months) related to schizophrenia and severe personality disorders (10 years)
2. Visual–motor retardation (Form-board, 18 to 24 months) related to visual–spatial deficit (Block design, 10 years)

---

ances that occur. Disorders of autonomic function, affect and "drive," proprioception and vestibular function, attention, perception, and cognition, all occurred in the preschizophrenic infants, as they do in older schizophrenic children and adults. Each of these dysfunctions has been put forward at some time as "the" fundamental defect in schizophrenia. These early disturbances very likely predispose to particular schizophrenic symptoms (35,42,50,71). The various developmental disorders also point to different aspects of brain function that should be studied, using neurophysiologic and biochemical methods. However, I do not believe that we will unlock the riddle of schizophrenia until we understand how the biologic disorder disrupts the total integrative functioning at all levels of central nervous system functioning, from physical growth and motor development up to perception and abstract reasoning.

STRATEGY FOR STUDYING NEUROPHYSIOLOGIC AND BIOCHEMICAL ABNORMALITIES IN INFANTS AT RISK

The infant data provide a strategy for studying the underlying neurophysiologic and biochemical abnormalities in infants at risk, using pandevelopmental retardation as a "marker" for the inherited neurointegrative defect in schizophrenia. If neurophysiologic or biochemical changes were studied longitudinally in infants genetically at risk, pandevelopmental retardation would identify the infants most vulnerable to later schizophrenia or severe personality disorders. Furthermore, the periods of severe retardation appear to reflect increased "activity" of the schizophrenic process. These measurable fluctuations in development would underscore the significance of any associated neurophysiologic or biochemical changes that occurred at these times. Without an external marker, the latter would be more difficult to distinguish from random variations. A series of 2-year studies could screen the most promising measures to be used in later controlled, long-term studies of infants at risk.

Severe neurointegrative disorders in infancy delineate a biologic continuum of genetic vulnerability, extending from chronic schizophrenia to severe personality disorders in the "schizophrenia spectrum" (48). So far no gross neurologic, psychologic, or behavioral disorders have turned up in the infancy or childhood of acute schizophrenics or manic depressives. Because developmental lags without growth retardation occur in many different conditions, ranging from no psychiatric disorder to moderately severe adult disorders (i.e., "Carol"), I suspect that development alone is too gross and nonspecific a measure to delineate the more covert biologic antecedents of acute schizophrenia and manic-depressive disease. More specific biochemical or neurophysiologic measures will probably be required in order to identify the biologic antecedents of these disorders.

ACKNOWLEDGMENTS

This study was supported in part by a grant from the Harriett Ames Charitable Trust, New York. The New York State Department of Mental Hygiene cooperated with this study.

REFERENCES

1. Rosenthal, D. (1970): *Genetic Theory and Abnormal Behavior.* McGraw-Hill, New York.
2. Redlich, F. C., and Freedman, D. X. (1966): *The Theory and Practice of Psychiatry.* Basic Books, New York.
3. Mason, C. F. (1956): Pre-illness intelligence of mental hospital patients. *J. Consult. Clin. Psychol.,* 20:297–300.
4. Robins, L. N. (1966): *Deviant Children Grown Up.* Williams & Wilkins, Baltimore, Maryland.
5. Bleuler, E. (1950): *Dementia Praecox or the Group of Schizophrenias,* translated by J. Zinken. International Universities Press, New York.
6. Kasanin, J. S., editor (1944): *Language and Thought in Schizophrenia.* Univ. of California Press, Berkeley and Los Angeles.
7. Payne, R. W. (1961): Cognitive abnormalities. In: *Handbook of Abnormal Psychology,* edited by H. J. Eysenck, pp. 193–261. Basic Books, New York.
8. Shakow, D. (1963): Psychological deficit in schizophrenia. *Behavioral Science,* 8:275–305.
9. Salzinger, K., Portnoy, S., and Feldman, R. S. (1966): Verbal behavior in schizophrenics and some comments toward a theory of schizophrenia. In: *Psychopathology of Schizophrenia,* edited by P. Hoch and J. Zubin, pp. 99–128. Grune & Stratton, New York.
10. Goldfarb, W. (1970): Childhood psychosis. In: *Carmichael's Manual of Child Psychology, Third Edition, Vol. 2,* pp. 765–830. Wiley, New York.
11. Creak, M. (1961): Schizophrenic syndrome in childhood: Report of a working party. *Br. Med. J.,* 2:889–890.
12. Fish, B. (1971): The "one child, one drug" myth of stimulants in hyperkinesis. Importance of diagnostic categories in evaluating treatment. *Arch. Gen. Psychiatry,* 25:193–203.
13. Shapiro, T., and Fish, B. (1969): A method to study language deviation as an aspect of ego organization in young schizophrenic children. *J. Am. Acad. Child Psychiatry,* 8:36–56.

14. Shapiro, T., Roberts, A., and Fish, B. (1970): Imitation and echoing in young schizophrenic children. *J. Am. Acad. Child Psychiatry,* 9:548–567.
15. Shapiro, T., Fish, B., and Ginsberg, G. (1972): The speech of a schizophrenic child from two to six. *Am. J. Psychiatry,* 128:1408–1413.
16. Shapiro, T., Chiarandini, I., and Fish, B. (1974): Thirty severely disturbed children. Evaluation of their language development for classification and prognosis. *Arch. Gen. Psychiatry,* 30:819–825.
17. Kanner, L. (1954): General concept of schizophrenia at different ages. (In: *Neurology and Psychiatry in Childhood.*) *Res. Publ. Assoc. Nerv. Ment. Dis.,* 34:451–453.
18. Bender, L. (1947): Childhood schizophrenia. *Am. J. Orthopsychiatry,* 17:40–56.
19. Des Lauriers, A., and Halpern, F. (1947): Psychological tests in childhood schizophrenia. *Am. J. Orthopsychiatry,* 17:57–69.
20. Kallman, F., and Roth, B. (1956): Genetic aspects of preadolescent schizophrenia. *Am. J. Psychiatry,* 112:599–606.
21. Bender, L., and Faretra, G. (1972): The relationship between childhood schizophrenia and adult schizophrenia. In: *Genetic Factors in Schizophrenia,* edited by A. R. Kaplan, pp. 28–64. Thomas, Springfield, Illinois.
22. Goldfarb, W. (1968): The subclassification of psychotic children: Application to a study of longitudinal change. In: *The Transmission of Schizophrenia,* edited by D. Rosenthal and S. S. Kety, pp. 333–342. Pergamon, London.
23. Kanner, L. (1953): To what extent is early infantile autism determined by constitutional inadequacies? (In: *Genetics and the Inheritance of Integrated Neurological Psychiatric Patterns.*) *Res. Publ. Assoc. Nerv. Ment. Dis.,* 33:378–385.
24. Annell, A. (1963): The prognosis of psychotic syndromes in children. A followup of 115 cases. *Acta Psychiatr. Scand.,* 39:235–297.
25. Garmezy, N. (1974): The study of children at risk—A research strategy whose time has come. *Schizophrenia Bull., No. 8,* pp. 14–90. DHEW Pub 1. No. HSM 73–9006, Superintendent of Documents, U.S. Government Printing Office, Washington, D.C.
26. Watt, N. F. (1972): Longitudinal changes in the social behavior of children hospitalized for schizophrenia as adults. *J. Nerv. Ment. Dis.,* 155:42–54.
27. Garmezy, N. (1968): Process and reactive schizophrenia: Some conceptions and issues. In: *The Role and Methodology of Classification in Psychiatry and Psychopathology,* edited by M. M. Katz, J. O. Cole, and W. E. Barton, pp. 419–466. Superintendent of Documents, U. S. Government Printing Office, Washington, D. C.
28. O'Neal, P., and Robins, L. N. (1958): Childhood patterns predictive of adult schizophrenia: A 30-year follow-up study. *Am. J. Psychiatry,* 115:385–391.
29. Watt, N. F. (1974): Childhood and adolescent routes to schizophrenia. In: *Life History Research in Psychopathology, Vol. 3,* edited by D. F. Ricks, A. Thomas, and M. Roff, pp. 194–211. Univ. of Minnesota Press, Minneapolis.
30. Ricks, D. F., and Nameche, G. (1966): Symbiosis, sacrifice and schizophrenia. *Ment. Hyg.,* 50:541–551.
31. Ricks, D. F., and Berry, J. C. (1970): Family and symptom patterns that precede schizophrenia. In: *Life History Research in Psychopathology, Vol. 1,* edited by M. Roff and D. F. Ricks, pp. 31–50. Univ. of Minnesota Press, Minneapolis.
32. Kety, S. S., and Matthysse, S. (1972): Prospects for research on schizophrenia. *Neurosci. Res. Program Bull.,* 10:370–507.
33. Marcus, J. (1970): Neurological and physiological characteristics of the children of schizophrenic parents. *7th Congress of the International Association of Child Psychiatry and Allied Professions, Jerusalem, August 4.*
34. Mednick, S. A., Mura, M., Schulzinger, F., and Mednick, B. (1971): Perinatal conditions and infant development in children with schizophrenic parents. *Soc. Biol.,* 18:S103–S113.
35. Fish, B. (1957): The detection of schizophrenia in infancy. *J. Nerv. Ment. Dis.,* 125:1–24.
36. Fish, B. (1959): Longitudinal observations of biological deviations in a schizophrenic infant. *Am. J. Psychiatry,* 116:25–31.
37. Fish, B., Shapiro, T., Halpern, F., and Wile, R. (1965): The prediction of schizophrenia in infancy. III. A ten-year follow-up report of neurological and psychological development. *Am. J. Psychiatry,* 121:768–775.
38. Fish, B., Shapiro, T., Halpern, F., and Wile, R. (1966): The prediction of schizophrenia in infancy. II. A ten-year follow-up of predictions made at one month of age. In: *Psychopathology of Schizophrenia,* edited by P. Hoch and J. Zubin, pp. 335–353. Grune & Stratton, New York.

39. Fish, B., and Alpert, M. (1962): Abnormal states of consciousness and muscle tone in infants born to schizophrenic mothers. *Am. J. Psychiatry,* 119:439–445.

40. Fish, B. (1963): The maturation of arousal and attention in the first months of life: A study of variations in ego development. *J. Am. Acad. Child Psychiatry,* 2:253–270.

41. Fish, B., and Alpert, M. (1963): Patterns of neurological development in infants born to schizophrenic mothers. In: *Recent Advances in Biological Psychiatry, Vol. 5,* edited by J. Wortis, pp. 37–42. Plenum, New York.

42. Fish, B., and Hagin, R. (1973): Visual–motor disorders in infants at risk for schizophrenia. *Arch. Gen. Psychiatry,* 28:900–904.

43. Wetzel, N. C. (1946): The baby grid. *J. Pediatr.,* 29:439–454.

44. Gesell, A. (1947): *Developmental Diagnosis, 2nd edition.* Harper (Hoeber), New York.

45. Fish, B. (1975): Vestibular hyporeactivity and associated developmental disorders in infants born to schizophrenic mothers. *(In preparation.)*

46. McNally, W. J., and Stuart, E. A. (1953): *Examination of the Labyrinth in Relation to its Physiology and Nonsuppurative Diseases.* Am. Acad. Ophthalmol. Otolaryngol., Douglas Printing Company, Omaha, Nebraska.

47. Meehl, P. E. (1962): Schizotaxia, schizotypy, schizophrenia. *Am. Psychol.,* 17:827–838.

48. Kety, S. S., Rosenthal, D., Wender, P. H., and Schulzinger, F. (1968): The types and prevalence of mental illness in the biological and adoptive families of adopted schizophrenics. In: *The Transmission of Schizophrenia,* edited by D. Rosenthal and S. S. Kety, pp. 345–362. Pergamon, London.

49. Paine, R. S., and Oppé, T. E. (1966): *Neurological Examination of Children.* Spastics Society Medical and Information Unit–Heinemann Medical Books, London.

50. Fish, B. (1960): Involvement of the central nervous system in infants with schizophrenia. *Arch. Neurol.,* 2:115–121.

51. Fish, B. (1961): The study of motor development in infancy and its relationship to psychological functioning. *Am. J. Psychiatry,* 117:1113–1118.

52. Fish, B., Shapiro, T., Campbell, M., and Wile, R. (1968): A classification of schizophrenic children under five years. *Am. J. Psychiatry,* 124:1415–1423.

53. Heston, L. L., and Denney, D. (1968): Interaction between early life experience and biological factors in schizophrenia. In: *The Transmission of Schizophrenia,* edited by D. Rosenthal and S. S. Kety, pp. 363–376. Pergamon, London.

54. Meehl, P. E. (1972): A critical afterword. In: *Schizophrenia and Genetics. A Twin Study Vantage Point,* by I. I. Gottesman and J. Shields, pp. 367–415. Academic Press, New York.

55. Hertzig, M. A., and Birch, M. G. (1968): Neurologic organization in psychiatrically disturbed adolescents. *Arch. Gen. Psychiatry,* 19:528–537.

56. Tucker, G. J., Campion, E. W., and Silberfarb, P. M. (1975): Sensorimotor functions and cognitive disturbance in psychiatric patients. *Am. J. Psychiatry,* 132:17–21.

57. Holzman, P. S., Proctor, L. R., Levy, D. L., Yasillo, N. J., Meltzer, H. Y., and Hurt, S. W. (1974): Eye-tracking dysfunctions in schizophrenic patients and their relatives. *Arch. Gen. Psychiatry,* 31:143–151.

58. Gunderson, J. G., and Singer, M. T. (1975): Defining borderline patients: An overview. *Am. J. Psychiatry,* 132:1–10.

59. Singer, M. T., and Wynne, L. C. (1963): Differentiating characteristics of parents of childhood schizophrenics, childhood neurotics and young adult schizophrenics. *Am. J. Psychiatry,* 120: 234–243.

60. Mednick, S. A., and Schulzinger, F. (1968): Some premorbid characteristics related to breakdown in children with schizophrenic mothers. *Psychiatr. Res.,* 6 (Suppl. 1): 267–291.

61. Stabenau, J. R., and Pollin, W. (1967): Early characteristics of monozygotic twins discordant for schizophrenia. *Arch. Gen. Psychiatry,* 17:723–734.

62. Gottesman, I. I., and Shields, J. (1972): *Schizophrenia and Genetics. A Twin Study Vantage Point.* Academic Press, New York.

63. Fish, B. (1971): Discussion: Genetic or traumatic developmental deviation? *Soc. Biol.,* 18: S117–S119.

64. Heston, L. L. (1971): Discussion: Schizophrenia in infancy? *Social Biol.* 18:S114.S116.

65. Provence, S., and Lipton, R. C. (1962): *Infants in Institutions.* International Universities Press, New York.

66. White, B. L., and Held, R. (1967): Plasticity of sensori-motor development in the human infant. In: *Exceptional Infant, Vol. 1: The Normal Infant,* edited by J. Hellmuth, pp. 291–313. Brunner/Mazel, New York.

67. Fish, B. (1975): Infants at risk for schizophrenia: Developmental deviations from birth to ten years. In: *Infant Psychiatry,* edited by L. Sander and T. Shapiro. Yale Univ. Press, New Haven, Connecticut. *(In press.)*
68. Pendleton, M. E., and Paine, R. S. (1961): Vestibular nystagmus in human infants. *Neurology (Minneap.),* 11:450–458.
69. Collins, W. E. (1963): Manipulation of arousal and its effects on human vestibular nystagmus induced by caloric irrigation and angular acceleration. *Aerosp. Med.,* 54:124–129.
70. Dixon, W. J., and Massey, Jr., F. J. (1969): *Introduction to Statistical Analyses, Third Edition.* McGraw-Hill, New York.
71. Fish, B. (1971): Contributions of developmental research to a theory of schizophrenia. In: *Exceptional Infant, Vol. 2: Studies in Abnormalities,* edited by J. Hellmuth, pp. 473–482. Brunner/Mazel, New York.

Discussion

Meltzer: My studies of muscle abnormalities in psychotic patients show a commonality across the major psychoses, whereas Dr. Fish's observations indicate that only children of schizophrenic mothers show problems such as decreased motor tone or problems in the development of muscles.

Could it be that the children of the manic-depressives and the acute schizophrenics were from the benign end of the spectrum that Drs. Strauss, Carpenter, Bowers, and Tsuang pointed out, rather than from those with a more severe form of the illness with poor outcome? I think in Dr. Tsuang's study there were 35 or 40% of manic-depressives with a poor outcome. Have you looked at your data in the manic-depressive and acute schizophrenic groups from that perspective?

Fish: No, I never did a study of the offspring of manic-depressives. I have tried to review the slim evidence—and it's really minimal—in the sense that it's negative evidence. Studies now being launched, both in Iowa and at NIH, will look carefully at the primary relatives of manic-depressive patients and begin to work back to the younger age groups. We don't even have any decent studies that tell us what manic-depressive patients, or their primary relatives, look like in early childhood, much less in infancy. So it is an open question. I have only hypothesized that—since nothing gross has yet turned up in the retrospective studies of hospitalized patients' earlier clinic or school records—that apparently the manic-depressive patients did not look behaviorally disordered early in life, and did not have any gross neurologic deficits. But there's a clear need for such studies.

Holzman: There is an aspect of Dr. Fish's presentation—vestibular responsiveness—which deserves underscoring.

There have been a whole series of studies of vestibular responsiveness in adult schizophrenia, going back to the early 1950s. And all of these, with exception of the report by Arnold Friedhoff (W. I. Rosenblum and A. J. Friedhoff: *J. Nerv. Ment. Dis.* 133:104–107, 1961) have shown hyporesponsivity.

In our laboratory, we have tried to replicate these several studies, and our results are negative. Dr. Fish reports in her presentation that the high-risk children did not manifest any vestibular disease or lesion of the vestibular system. And I think this accurately reflects the true state of affairs. Her subjects did show *phasic* hyporesponsivity. And I think the reason for this is that there are two major variables that have not been controlled in this whole series of vestibular studies in adults. The first is the state of the subject's attention, and the second is the subject's opportunity for visual fixation. If you don't control these two variables, you're going to get hyporesponsivity.

Test vestibular responsiveness of the catatonic schizophrenic in stupor, and who stares and has poor attention, and one finds hyporesponsivity. The patient is hyporesponsive not because of a vestibular lesion but because of procedural artifacts.

Now, Dr. Fish reports that her infants showed phasic diminution of the vestibular response. This could mean that they are phasically inattentive, and this could reflect a phasic appearance of the psychosis in these infants. Does she have some clinical evidence or support for the fact that when the hyporesponsivity occurred there was something clinically going on that may have been associated either with increased staring or with diminished attention, both of which could be reflections of a general organismic disturbance like a psychosis?

Fish: Without detailing the whole methodology, the answer is a qualified "yes." The responses were timed nystagmus, as visually observed. This is generally not a very reliable measure of vestibular response. As far as fixation is concerned, usually the procedure produces crying, with eye closure and manifest behavioral activation, so that the infants did not fixate.

The instrumentation was limited to whatever could be carried on my back out to the state hospitals, so electronystagmography was not possible. Nor was it possible to get EEGs done to measure finer fluctuations in arousal, through alpha- or slow-wave rhythms.

The only other study of infant nystagmus that properly controlled for state behavior was by Pendleton and Paine (M. E. Pendleton and R. S. Paine: *Neurology,* 11:450–458, 1961). They found that decreased nystagmus preceded drowsiness and behavioral depression of arousal, and it also preceded even the first EEG signs of beginning drowsiness (so possibly, even if we had been able to add the EEG, it wouldn't have added much to our behavioral measures of state).

Clinically and behaviorally there was no change in state during most of the periods when the nystagmus dropped to either zero or a few seconds.

There were only four occasions in which there was clinically some decreased activation in the sense of decreased crying. These occurred in three infants who were diagnosed independently as being the only ones with severe psychiatric disorder on the 10-year follow-up.

On these four occasions in the first year-and-a-half, when they showed real depression, when they didn't even arouse or cry with the test procedure, their pandevelopmental retardation was at its lowest point, including postural–motor and visual–motor D.Q.s and physical growth. I assume this means that whatever was happening in the nervous system was a more sustained, total disorganization of maturation. If we had only seen the vestibular response you could say, maybe this was a very brief episode of decreased arousal. But it was part of a process involving months of decline in physical growth. Reactivity did not change *clinically* during these months, except for this lowest point.

So one should not dismiss the decreased vestibular responses that have been found as simply being secondary to a form of superficial attentional disorders, or motivation, in schizophrenia. I think this state of consciousness and total state of CNS functioning is probably a very fundamental aspect of the psychotic state in schizophrenia, which is most exaggerated in catatonic stupor, and that we should look at the disturbance in consciousness as one of the phenomena of CNS dysfunction in schizophrenia, rather than just simply dismissing it as if it were only a lack of motivation. But I think we have to study it with much more specific electrophysiologic techniques.

Kety: I was very much impressed with Dr. Fish's findings of neurologic and psychologic deficits in the infants and children of schizophrenic mothers. It seemed to me that this was more common in her sample than the diagnoses of schizophrenia to be expected in such offspring later in their development.

Such deficits could be the result of a genetic factor that the mother has also transmitted to the child. Alternatively, they could be the result of environmental factors, especially *in utero,* birth trauma or postnatal environment. Or, of course, some combination of both.

Fish: Of course one cannot make an epidemiologic and genetic statement from 24 infants. To separate genetic and environmental factors one needs the sort of large studies with separate rearings, as in the adoption and twin studies.

But keeping that in mind, I'm inclined to feel that there is a genetic component to the neurointegrative disorder that I found. It's true that the two schizophrenic offspring of schizophrenic mothers did have significant contact with their psychotic mothers. In these two children one certainly could not split the genetic influence from the very traumatic, disorganizing home environments.

With one exception, all of the other offspring of schizophrenics were reared apart. These include all of those who were independently rated as having severe and moderately severe personality disorders. Most of them had not even the most casual contact with their biologic mothers. They knew they had a mother who was too sick to care for them, but they were generally in optimal adoptive and foster homes. Yet they turned up as early as three and four years of age with severe symptoms which made their parents seek psychiatric help, and they were independently treated by a series of psychiatrists, sent to residential schools, and so on. This makes me think that something had happened before birth.

Now, one still doesn't know how much was some intrauterine toxicity or other damage. When one analyzes Mednick's obstetric data, I think there are several things there that point to this as being part of a developmental *neurointegrative* deficit, rather than what we think of as birth trauma. For one, his immediate neonatal data did not differentiate the index offspring from the controls. It was at five days, when generally the most immediate effects of birth have disappeared, that the offspring of schizophrenics were differentiated, and also at one year. Usually it's only the most severe organic damage that leads to persistent motor lags at one year. Otherwise one thinks of genetically determined lags at that age.

We had some infants with very severe prenatal and perinatal damage in the 1952 study. One of these was also the offspring of a schizophrenic mother; he developed a severe personality disorder later. But neither of the schizophrenic children had had birth complications, nor did any of the other schizophrenic offspring.

The infants who did have pregnancy and birth abnormalities generally showed very brief, simple motor lags, if anything, but no growth lag. And they compensated rather rapidly and came up to normal levels. One of them had a minimal perceptual problem at age ten that made the independent psychologist suspect that there may have been some damage earlier. But there was no trace of a schizophrenic spectrum disorder in the children with poor birth histories, except for the one with a schizophrenic mother.

Biology of the Major Psychoses, edited by D. X.
Freedman, Res. Publ. Assoc. Res. Nerv. Ment.
Dis., Vol. 54. Raven Press, New York   1975.

Drugs, Diagnosis, and Disease

Samuel Gershon, Burton Angrist, and Baron Shopsin

Neuropsychopharmacology Research Unit, New York University Medical Center, New York,
New York 10016

We thought we might approach this problem by exploring the effects of
pharmacologically active agents as tools in modifying behavior in the different
disease states, in the hope that this might resolve questions of psychoses as either
a continuum or as separate and distinct disorders.

This chapter clearly stipulates the pharmacologic aspects and the use of specific
drugs as provocateurs in these studies. However, we are faced with semantic and
diagnostic ambiguities and quite fundamental difficulties in dealing with the other
aspect of our task—the issues of diagnosis and disease state.

We must at the outset clearly state that diagnostic vagary, semantic confusion,
and looseness of criteria for diagnosis have made a definition of the populations
studied exceedingly difficult. For example, between the affective disorders and
the schizophrenias it is becoming increasingly difficult to reach agreement on
specific criteria of dysfunction. Recent publications have taken the view that if
a patient with overactivity responds to treatment with lithium he must be a manic;
this view overlooks the possibilities of placebo response or natural remission. The
use of drugs in this retrospective uncontrolled fashion cannot aid us in our present
task, but on the contrary, will further aggravate clarification of such issues. The
problem is further compounded by transcultural differences, and important differences in diagnostic practice exist between the United States and other countries,
particularly Great Britain and Western Europe. Recent research has documented
the considerable differences that exist in the criteria by which affective disease
and schizophrenias are diagnosed (1).

Because of these diversities, an investigator can obtain almost any clinical
response to the administration of a drug by altering the composition of the patient
population. Having stated these problems, we will try to explore the extent to
which we can utilize drugs to perform pharmacologic dissections of diagnoses
and disease states in psychiatry.

DRUG-INDUCED SWITCHES AND PSYCHOPATHOLOGY

Although many psychoactive drugs, such as the minor tranquilizers, have
similar sedative effects in most individuals, the effects of other psychophar-
macologic agents appear to depend upon the preexisting state of the individual.
For example, whereas imipramine leads to marked improvement in mood and

motor activity in depressed patients, but is not a euphoriant or stimulant in normals, when given to schizophrenics, a significant incidence of activation of schizophrenic psychopathology occurs, and in bipolar manic-depressives a precipitation of a manic episode may result. These pharmacologic effects upon behavior are of particular interest when the biologic changes produced by the drug can provide evidence concerning the biochemical mechanisms involved in the behavioral change and can highlight any specific relationships to diagnosis and disease state.

L-DOPA

L-DOPA (L-3, 4-dihydroxyphenylalanine) is the direct amino acid precursor of the neurotransmitter catecholamines, dopamine and norepinephrine. However, its indirect effects on other transmitters such as serotonin cannot be excluded.

Investigators who treated parkinsonian patients with L-DOPA soon pointed out that psychiatric side effects occurred frequently. Reviewing these reports, both Brogden et al. (2) and Goodwin (3) have estimated that such side effects occur in approximately 20% of parkinsonian patients treated with L-DOPA. The behavioral effects most often encountered have been confusion, depression, agitation, paranoid delusions, and hypersexuality. Impulsivity, increased anxiety, insomnia, vivid dreams, and lethargy were also noted.

In studies in our unit, L-DOPA was administered to six nonpsychotic psychiatric inpatients in large doses (mean daily dose, 8.8 g/day). The behavioral effects noted were quite similar in quality and range to those seen in nonpsychotic parkinsonian patients (hypersexuality in one patient, dysphoric stimulation in two, toxic confusion in one patient, no psychologic effects in one, and a paranoid schizophreniform psychosis in one nonschizophrenic patient (4).

However, when L-DOPA was administered to 10 schizophrenic patients, a clear deterioration of psychiatric status occurred in all (5). In three patients it was judged that nonspecific stimulant effects (such as those seen after low doses of amphetamine) led to more intense and inappropriate verbalization of original psychotic preoccupations. However, the remaining seven showed either a clear and dose-related intensification of original base-line psychopathology (along with superimposed stimulant effects as in the first three) or a development of *de novo* symptoms, such as bizarre symbolic motor mannerisms and auditory hallucinations. This change occurred at a much lower dose (mean, 5 g/day L-DOPA) than that for which behavioral effects were noted in the nonschizophrenic patients in the prior study. The data from those two studies, as well as some biochemical data regarding cerebrospinal fluid homovanillic acid levels (CSF HVA levels), are summarized by Angrist et al. (6).

Therefore, L-DOPA can both induce a paranoid psychosis in nonpsychotics and dramatically aggravate the predrug psychopathology of schizophrenic patients. Its effect on schizophrenics was seen at lower doses than those required for effects in the nonschizophrenic group. After discontinuation of this drug, its behavioral effects gradually cleared completely after approximately 72 hr.

A second diagnostic group that shows a rather specific and predictable behavioral response to L-DOPA is manic-depressive disorder.

A much higher incidence of one specific side effect, mania, occurs in patients with manic-depressive disorder. Bipolar manic-depressive patients (those with histories of previous manic episodes) seem especially prone to develop typical, brief, hypomanic behavioral changes that are very similar to the individual patient's spontaneous hypomanic episodes (7).

The episodes reported were characterized by a sudden, clearly defined onset of increased speech, hyperactivity, increased social interaction, intrusiveness, sleeplessness, and some euphoria and grandiosity.

L-DOPA-induced hypomania is not only behaviorally very similar but is also associated with many of the biologic changes noted in spontaneous episodes—(a) urinary catecholamine excretion is increased by L-DOPA administration, and is further increased during the hypomanic episode (8); (b) urinary cyclic-AMP excretion is increased by L-DOPA (9); (c) REM sleep is decreased (10,11); and (d) Visual-evoked EEG responses show a pattern of augmentation during L-DOPA just as they do during mania (12).

Amphetamines and Methylphenidate

Amphetamine and methylphenidate are similar to L-DOPA in that they both cause a schizophreniform psychosis in nonschizophrenics and can cause dramatic exacerbation of predrug symptomatology in schizophrenics (13–17).

Moreover, their capacity for inducing these effects is much more dramatic than that of L-DOPA in terms of both milligram-for-milligram potency and rapidity of onset. Hence, *de novo* psychoses have been seen at doses of under 200 mg amphetamine and after less than 24 hr. (For L-DOPA, a daily dose of 9 g attained after a 28-day administration was required for a *de novo* psychosis.) Exacerbation of psychotic symptomatology in schizophrenics was noted after single intravenous doses of *d*-amphetamine and methylphenidate of 20 and 29 mg, respectively (17), whereas the schizophrenics who showed these effects after L-DOPA administration on our unit (5) received the drug for a mean of 21 days at a mean daily dose of just over 5 g.

It should also be noted that the comparative potency of the stereoisomers of amphetamine, both for inducing psychosis in nonpsychotics (18) and for exacerbating the predrug symptoms of some schizophrenics (17), are of a comparable order.

Therefore, the dramatic clinical effects of amphetamine and methylphenidate made them important drugs in the investigation of psychotogenic mechanisms. An extensive body of evidence reviewed by Snyder (19) suggests that these mechanisms are mediated by dopamine. However, in some pharmacologic respects it appears that there are differences among amphetamine, methylpheni-date, L-DOPA, and the clinically similar central nervous system (CNS) stimulant phenmetrazine (20–22).

In addition, dopamine receptor stimulants such as apomorphine have quite different clinical effects.[1] These dopamine receptor stimulants cause emesis at very low doses—an effect that appears to make aggressive investigation of their psychotogenic potency all but impossible. Why amphetamine does not cause emesis is a question seldom raised.

Intermediate in clinical effects between L-DOPA and apomorphine is the dopa-mine receptor stimulant ET 495. It can both activate schizophrenic symptoms and cause psychotic states *de novo,* yet frequently it also is too potent an emetic for these effects to be well documented (23).

Hence, L-DOPA can cause a schizophreniform psychosis in some, but not all, nonschizophrenics. This parallels our experience with amphetamine (15) in which some subjects received large (over 900 mg) cumulative doses of the drug without psychosis. It appears, then, that among nonschizophrenics a continuum exists as to the level of pharmacologic dopaminergic stimulation that can be tolerated without psychotic effects.

In contrast, patients with manifest schizophrenia show a markedly increased sensitivity to both L-DOPA and amphetamine, but within this group as well, sensitivity to these agents varies among individuals, with some showing marked activation of psychosis at relatively low doses whereas others do not.

This suggests a continuum of sensitivity to psychosis caused by these agents in both groups, but indicates some discontinuity in this spectrum, in that schizo-phrenics appear clearly more vulnerable.

MAOI

These agents may act as behavioral activating agents through effects on the neurotransmitter amines. They can precipitate manic episodes and produce ex-acerbations of psychotic symptomatology in some schizophrenic patients (24–26). They appear to potentiate the psychotomimetic effects of some amino acids, including L-methionine and possibly L-DOPA (27–29).

Imipramine

The administration of tricyclic compounds may also precipitate a manic epi-sode in bipolar manic depressive patients (30).

A review of the literature makes it appear fairly clear that the production of a manic episode is highly associated with a history of manic-depressive disorder.

---

[1] For example, in a recent study on our unit, apomorphine emesis was blocked by administering 20 mg metaclopromide IV. This permitted i.v. administration of 24 mg apomorphine, after which clear sedative effects were documented—not CNS stimulation, as one might anticipate.

The mechanism by which imipramine might act as a trigger for mania in some cases is not clear. It is possible that there is some commonality in the underlying biochemical effects produced by both the tricyclic antidepressants and L-DOPA in their interactions with manic-depressive and schizophrenic substrates, albeit, the incidence of such activation effects in both diagnostic categories seems higher, more predictable, and consistent with L-DOPA than with the tricyclics.

It has been reported that imipramine hydrochloride activates the psychotic process in schizophrenic patients (31–34).

Therefore it seemed plausible that imipramine might be used as a pharmacologic tool to reveal differences among diagnostic subgroups in order to contribute to some further understanding of psychotic processes (35). Three different diagnostic groups were studied—(a) 15 schizophrenic patients (six chronic with deterioration—apathetic, withdrawn, anergic, inactive; seven responsive and still showing some evidence of active schizophrenic processes; and two whose diagnosis was not unanimous); (b) seven nonschizophrenic patients (two chronic brain syndromes with syphilis, two chronic brain syndromes with alcoholism, one epileptic, and two uncertain) with psychotic reaction; and (c) eight nonschizophrenic nonpsychotic (five sociopaths and three alcoholics).

Psychiatric Observation

Imipramine was given in a dose of 3 mg/kg body weight. The six chronic deteriorated patients did not show any specific change in their clinical condition, whereas the other nine schizophrenics showed some degree of activation of their psychotic state with either appearance or increase in delusions, hallucinations, and disturbed behavior. Psychotic material was produced freely and there was an increase in general activity; in some subjects there was evidence of hostility. The response was particularly interesting in those cases (two) in whom the diagnosis was uncertain. An overt psychotic picture, with freely produced delusions and ideas of reference, aggressiveness, hostility, and uncooperativeness emerged.

The seven psychotic nonschizophrenic subjects showed increased psychotic activity, with the exception of an epileptic on Dilantin and phenobarbital, who became more drowsy. The remainder of the group in varying degrees became more aggressive, hostile, abusive, overactive, and generally more difficult to manage. Hallucinatory phenomena became clearly apparent in two subjects in whom it could previously be deduced only from their behavior. One subject began to write voluminous notes and incessantly replied to his hallucinations almost to the point of breathlessness.

The eight nonpsychotic subjects showed no striking changes nor did they exhibit any psychotic features (35).

There have been no reports of imipramine-induced psychotic manifestations in character disorders (36) or neurotics (37,38). Klein and Fink noted that 19% of their schizophrenic group developed a pattern of "agitated disorganization" and a "manic" pattern in 6% of the schizophrenics, whereas in 20% of manic-depressive patients a manic episode occurred. Pilkington reported on the effect of imipramine in mental defectives; in his group with schizophrenic traits 72% developed florid schizophrenic symptoms (39).

The Lithium Ion

Therapeutic specificity intimately depends on diagnostic accuracy. In order to appreciate the specific therapeutic effects of lithium, it should be prescribed for patients showing a clear diagnostic indication for this drug. The manic phase of manic-depressive illness is the prime indication for lithium treatment. The ambiguities surrounding the diagnosis of manic illness, and especially that shadowy interface between manic phase, manic-depressive disorder and schizophrenia, schizoaffective type, excited phase, present a diagnostic dilemma in that both illnesses share large components of both affective as well as behavioral disturbance. The resolution of this problem of differential diagnosis is critical, however, because several studies have indicated that patients do not do as well on lithium when the manic picture is clouded with "atypical" features (40–42). This "atypical" group includes subjects with schizophrenic symptoms, and the significance of such differential drug responsiveness has been underlined in several recent studies (43–45). In discussing their trial of lithium, Aronoff and Epstein (44) noted that some of their schizoaffective cases, which they acknowledged might well have been designated "atypical manic-depressive illness" by others, showed only moderate response or symptom aggravation under lithium treatment. It is on this sort of explicitness about diagnostic ambiguities that progress in delineating the therapeutic usefulness of lithium depends. The studies by Johnson et al. (43) and Shopsin et al. (45) underscore the specificity of action of lithium; both investigations indicate strongly that lithium has no apparent sedative or neuroleptic properties and that it can, in fact, precipitate or contribute to further decompensation of schizophrenic symptomatology.

Central to the issue of lithium specificity, our group (46) reported toxic-confusional states as well as activating effects in a considerable number of schizophrenic patients (11 of 17) receiving lithium carbonate. Significant features in these cases are a general worsening of previously manifest psychoses with the appearance of bizarre affect and behavior patterns, inconsistent changes in psychomotor activity, aggravation of delusional thought, and florid hallucinatory phenomena. The frequently concomitant appearance of reduced comprehension, clouding of sensorium with confusion, memory impairment, and disorientation indicate organic brain dysfunction in these patients.

Blood lithium levels were quite modest in all instances (mean 0.750 mEq/liter) and, paradoxically, the common lithium effects or toxic manifestations were not consistently present. The most consistent laboratory abnormalities consisted of EEG changes including alterations in the alpha activity, diffuse slowing, accentuation of previous focal abnormalities, or the appearance of previously absent focal changes or both. The occurrence of neurotoxicity corresponds, therefore, to the presence and severity of EEG changes.

Previous reports of psychotogenic effects and confusion during lithium treatment have appeared in the literature (47–54).

Several studies have offered convincing evidence of changes in electrical activity of the brain during lithium treatment, relating these changes to electrolyte effects or shifts (55–57). Johnson et al. (58) noted that the most significant changes in EEG during chronic lithium administration were seen in individuals showing base-line abnormalities (Fig. 2). Underlining the possible relevance of premorbid conditions to such changes, Rochford et al. (59) indicated that neurologic abnormalities were found in nearly 40% of young adult psychiatric patients, significantly more than in controls (5%). The incidence of neurologic impairment did not differ significantly from one diagnostic group to another, except for those patients with affective disorders. It is interesting that no neurologic abnormality was found among subjects in this latter diagnostic category. One would anticipate from such findings that neurotoxicity following lithium administration would be highest in patients with other than primary affective disorders, that is, in subjects not diagnosed as having manic-depressive illness. This is supported by the findings in two double-blind studies using lithium or chlorpromazine in schizophrenic patients (45,60). Indications are that such patients, whether by differential handling (excretion), differences in electrolyte or endocrine substrate, or "abnormal" base-line neuropathy, exhibit a decreased threshold tolerance or sensitivity for the lithium ion, which exposes them to CNS toxicity at moderate to low levels of serum lithium.

Acetylcholine

Diisopropyl fluorophosphonate (DFP) is an anticholinesterase with 30 times the potency of physostigmine. It is an irreversible inhibitor of acetylcholinesterase. It produces in animals and man effects similar to the muscarinic and nicotinic actions of acetylcholine. Grob et al. (61), after acute administration of DFP, have described EEG changes in man and mental symptoms such as tremulousness, insomnia, nightmares, and confusion. Rountree et al. (62) examined the effects of this agent given chronically (13 mg i.m. over 7 days) to schizophrenic and manic-depressive patients and to a group of controls.

Changes in blood pressure were significantly different in the two psychotic groups. In all the manic-depressive patients (nine, except for the two in a euthymic phase), there was a gradual fall of blood pressure from the beginning of the injection period until approximately 7 days after the withdrawal of the drug.

In the schizophrenic patients (13), however, there was a tendency for the blood pressure to rise. No schizophrenic patient showed a progressive fall in blood pressure, and no manic-depressive patient showed a progressive rise.

Although the schizophrenic and manic-depressive patients received the same total dosage of DFP and showed comparable cholinesterase inhibition, both the incidence and severity of the muscarinic effects were considerably less in the schizophrenic group. The remarkable tolerance to the drug exhibited by certain schizophrenic patients is exemplified by one patient who received a total dosage of 63 mg of DFP over 35 days without showing any characteristic effects of the drug. The few schizophrenics who showed a response to DFP comparable with that of the manic-depressive group were of the paranoid type.

In general, the EEG changes were much more marked in the manic-depressive than in the schizophrenic patients, particularly in the appearance of slow activity.

Mental Changes

In six of the 17 schizophrenic patients, a most pronounced mental effect was observed. This consisted of an "activation" of the psychosis or of the reappearance in chronic cases of the florid symptoms that had characterized the onset of the illness—bizarre behavior, thought disorder, ideas of reference, and auditory hallucinations—without impairment of consciousness. These changes persisted for a number of months after withdrawal of DFP.

Of the manic-depressive group, the two euthymic cases showed only slight mental changes. Sleeplessness and increased dreaming occurred, and slight depression in one. Two of the six hypomanic cases were unaffected by the drug. In the remainder (four hypomanic and one depressed), significant mental changes occurred, with the appearance of a marked depressant effect.

In the normal subjects, a very characteristic picture of clinical depression, irritability, lassitude, and apathy appeared. They looked dejected and felt unhappy. They were retarded and talked little and despondently.

After this report, in 1961, Gershon and Shaw (63) reported the results of an accidental series of chronic exposures to organophosphorus insecticides. Sixteen cases were reported—three were scientists studying the efficacy of sprays, eight worked in these test greenhouses, and five were farm workers. Of the 16 cases, seven were depressive and five schizophrenic; in one, a fugue state was the presenting symptom.

The fact that only two forms of psychiatric illness were induced—depressive and schizophrenic reactions—suggests that perhaps some interaction with a specific substrate produces a particular psychiatric response pattern. Follow-up of our cases showed that the effects persisted for about 6 months after the exposure ceased.

DISCUSSION

In attempting to synthesize the effects of this array of drugs on the various diagnostic entities and disease substrates, we find that certain limited conclusions may be offered—that some drugs have an apparent specific interaction with different diagnostic and disease substrates. When the organophosphorus insecticides interact with manic-depressive disorder, a change is produced in the direction of depression, and when given to schizophrenic states an activation of psychopathology is induced. Then, when administered to normal individuals, two distinct diagnostic patterns emerge—schizophrenia and depression. This example would tend to support the view that a continuum does not exist across diagnoses, but that there is a continuum in those predisposed individuals from normal through to manifest illness.

We have one class of agents—L-DOPA, the amphetamines and related agents, and imipramine—which may be considered together.

L-DOPA, in its interaction with three diagnostic types—schizophrenics, manic-depressives, and nonpsychotic subjects—seems to induce a threshold response pattern. That is, in schizophrenics, an activation of psychosis is seen in most subjects at about one-half the dose given to nonpsychotics and in whom only a very low incidence of psychosis appears, which exhibits the form of a schizophrenic reaction when it appears. In a manic-depressive population, the reaction pattern is of a manic type.

Imipramine essentially follows this reaction pattern, i.e., in manic-depressives, the pathologic reaction is that of mania; in schizophrenics, about 20 to 30% show an activation of their psychosis. The nonpsychotics, given the same dose and duration of administration, showed no pathologic reaction patterns.

The amphetamines and related agents in schizophrenic and nonschizophrenic groups demonstrate responses similar to those seen with L-DOPA. That is, these agents demonstrate a lower threshold of psychotogenicity in the schizophrenic substrate than in the nonschizophrenics, but there exists a continuity of the reaction across both groups that is somewhat dose- and time-dependent.

These data might support a concept of disease and diagnosis specificity; the drugs employed here produce reaction patterns based on the specificity of the substrate.

The therapeutic responses with lithium in manic, schizophrenic, and schizoaffective patients suggest a degree of specificity also.

The cholinergic activation data again seemed to suggest a specific drug interaction with diagnosis, but no simple biochemical explanations can be made.

ACKNOWLEDGMENTS

This research was supported by USPHS Grant No. MH-04669 and the Supreme Council 33, A.A. Scottish Rite Northern Masonic Jurisdiction.

REFERENCES

1. Cooper, J. E., Kendall, R. E., Gurland, B. J., Sartorius, N., and Farkas, T. (1969): Cross national study of diagnoses of mental disorders. *Am. J. Psychiatry,* 125:21–29.
2. Brogden, R. N., Spieght, T. M., and Avery, G. S. (1971): Levodopa: A review of its pharmacological properties and therapeutic uses with particular reference to Parkinson's disease. *Drugs,* 2:257–408.
3. Goodwin, F. K. (1972): Behavioral effects of L-DOPA in man. In: *Psychiatric Complications of Medical Drugs,* edited by R. I. Shader, pp. 149–174. Raven Press, New York.

4. Sathananthan, G., Angrist, B. M., and Gershon, S. (1973): Response threshold to L-DOPA in psychiatric patients. *Biol. Psychiatry,* 7:139–149.
5. Angrist, B., Sathananthan, G., and Gershon, S. (1973): Behavioral effects of L-DOPA in schizophrenic patients. *Psychopharmacologia,* 31:1–12.
6. Angrist, B. M., Sathananthan, G., Wilk, S., and Gershon, S. (1973): Behavioral and biochemical effects of L-DOPA in psychiatric patients. In: *Frontiers in Catecholamine Research,* edited by E. Usdin and S. Snyder, pp. 991–994. Pergamon, Oxford.
7. Murphy, D. L., Brodie, H. K. H., Goodwin, F. K., and Bunney, W. E., Jr. (1971): L-DOPA: Regular induction of hypomania in bipolar manic-depressive patients. *Nature,* 229:135–136.
8. Goodwin, F. K., Murphy, D. L., Brodie, H. K. H., and Bunney, W. E., Jr. (1970): L-DOPA, catecholamines and behavior: A clinical and biochemical study in depressed patients. *Biol. Psychiatry,* 2:341–366.
9. Paul, M. I., Cramer, H., and Bunney, W. E., Jr. (1971): Urinary cyclic AMP in the switch process from depression to mania. *Science,* 171:300–303.
10. Fram, D. H., Murphy, D. L., Goodwin, F. K., Keith, H., Brodie, H., Bunney, W. E., Jr., and Snyder, F. (1970): L-DOPA and sleep in depressed patients. *Psychophysiology,* 7:316–317.
11. Wyatt, R. J., Chase, T. N., and Engleman, K. (1970): Effect of L-DOPA on the sleep of man. *Nature,* 228:999–1001.
12. Buchsbaum, M., Goodwin, F., Murphy, D. L., and Borge, G. (1971): Average evoked response in affective disorders. *Am. J. Psychiatr.,* 128(1):19–25.
13. Connell, P. H. (1958): *Amphetamine Psychosis.* Maudsley Monographs No. 5, Oxford Univ. Press, London.
14. Griffith, J. J., Cavanaugh, J. H., and Oates, J. A. (1970): Psychosis induced by the administration of *d*-amphetamine to human volunteers. In: *Psychotomimetic Drugs,* edited by D. H. Efron, p. 28. Raven Press, New York.
15. Angrist, B. M., and Gershon, S. (1970): The phenomenology of experimentally-induced amphetamine psychosis. Preliminary observations. *Biol. Psychiatry,* 2:95–107.
16. Spensley, J., and Rockwell, D. A. (1972): Psychosis during methylphenidate abuse. *New Engl. J. Med.,* 286:880–881.
17. Davis, J. M., and Janowsky, D. S. (1973): Amphetamine and methylphenidate psychosis. In: *Frontiers in Catecholamine Research,* pp. 977–981. Pergamon, Oxford.
18. Angrist, B. M., Shopsin, B., and Gershon, S. (1971): The comparative psychotomimetic effects of stereoisomers of amphetamine. *Nature,* 234:152–153.
19. Snyder, S. H. (1973): Amphetamine psychosis: a "model" schizophrenia mediated by catecholamines. *Am. J. Psychiatry,* 130:61–67.
20. Angrist, B., Gershon, S. (1974): Dopamine and psychotic states: Preliminary remarks. In: *Advances in Biochemical Psychopharmacology,* Vol. 12, edited by E. Usdin, pp. 211–219. Raven Press, New York.
21. Lewander, T. (1974): Effect of chronic treatment with central stimulants on brain monoamines and some behavioral and physiological functions in rats, guinea pigs and rabbits. In: *Advances in Biochemical Psychoparmacology,* Vol. 12, edited by E. Usdin, pp, 221–239. Raven Press, New York.
22. Wallach, M. B. (1974): Drug induced stereotyped behavior: similarities and differences. In: *Advances in Biochemical Psychopharmacology,* Vol. 12, edited by E. Usdin, pp. 241–260. Raven Press, New York.
23. Angrist, B. M., Thompson, H., Shopsin, B., and Gershon, S. (1975): Clinical studies with dopamine receptor stimulants. *(In preparation.)*
24. Rees, L., and Benaim, S. (1960): An evaluation of iproniazid in the treatment of depression. *Br. J. Psychiatry,* 106:193–202.
25. Greenblatt, M., Grosser, G. H., and Wechsler, H. (1962): A comparative study of selected antidepressant medications and EST. *Am. J. Psychiatry,* 119:144–153.
26. Brune, G. G., Pscheidt, G. R., and Himwich, H. E. (1963): Different responses of urinary tryptamine and of total catecholamines during treatment with reserpine and isocarboxazid in schizophrenic patients. *Int. J. Neuropharmacol.,* 2:17–23.
27. Pollin, W., Cordon, P. V., and Kety, S. S. (1961): Effects of amino acid feedings in schizophrenic patients treated with iproniazid. *Science,* 133:104–105.
28. Turner, W., and Merlis, S. (1964): A clinical trial of pargyline and DOPA in psychotic subjects. *Dis. Nerv. Syst.,* 24:538–541.

29. Berlet, H. H., Matsumoto, K., Pscheidt, G. R., Spaide, J., Bull, C., and Himwich, H. E. (1970): Biochemical correlates of behavior in schizophrenic patients. *Arch. Gen. Psychiatry,* 13: 521–531.

30. Bunney, W. E., Jr., Murphy, D. L., Goodwin, F. K., and Borge, G. F. (1970): The switch process from depression to mania: Relationship to drugs which alter brain amines. *Lancet,* 1:1022–1027.

31. Feldman, P. E. (1959): The treatment of anergic schizophrenia with imipramine. *J. Clin. Exp. Psychopath.,* 20:235.

32. Kuhn, R. (1958): The treatment of depressive states with G-22355. *Am. J. Psychiatry,* 115:459.

33. Kuhn, R. (1957): Uber die Behandlung depressiver Zustande mit einem Iminobenzyldervat. *Schweiz. Med. Wochenschr.,* 87:1135.

34. Pollack, B. (1959): Clinical findings in the use of Tofranil in depressive and other psychiatric states. *Am. J. Psychiatry,* 116:312.

35. Gershon, S., Holmberg, G., Mattsson, E., and Mattsson, N. (1962): Imipramine hydrochloride. *Arch. Gen. Psychiatry,* 6:96–101.

36. Goldner, R. D. (1961): Control of minor sexual compulsions with imipramine and amine oxidase regulators. *Third World Congr. Psychiatry,* 2:1155.

37. Klein, D. F. (1964): Delineation of two drug-responsive anxiety syndromes. *Psychopharmacologia,* 5:397.

38. Leyberg, J. T., and Denmark, J. C. (1959): The treatment of depressive states with imipramine hydrochloride. *Br. J. Psychiatry,* 105:1123.

39. Pilkington, T. L. (1962): A report on "Tofranil" in mental deficiency. *Am. J. Ment. Defic.,* 66:729.

40. Schou, M., Juel-Nielson, N., Stromgren, E., and Boldby, H. (1954): The treatment of manic psychoses by the administration of lithium salts. *J. Neurol. Neurosurg. Psychiatry,* 17:250.

41. Hartigan, G. P. (1963): The use of lithium salts in affective disorders. *Br. J. Psychiatry,* 109:810.

42. Fries, H. (1969): Experience with lithium carbonate treatment at a psychiatric department in the period 1964–1967. *Acta Psychiatr. Scand.* (Suppl), 207:41.

43. Johnson, G., Gershon, S., and Hekimian, L. J. (1968): Controlled evaluation of lithium and chlorpromazine in the treatment of manic states: An interim report. *Compr. Psychiatry,* 9:563.

44. Aronoff, M. S., and Epstein, R. S. (1969): Lithium failure in mania: A clinical study. *Annual Mtg. of American Psychiatric Association, Bal Harbor, Florida.*

45. Shopsin, B., Kim, S. S., and Gershon, S. (1971): A controlled study of lithium vs. chlorpromazine in acute schizophrenics. *Br. J. Psychiatry,* 119:435–440.

46. Shopsin, B., Johnson, G., and Gershon, S. (1970): Neurotoxicity with lithium; differential drug responsiveness. *Int. Pharmacopsychiatry.*

47. Greenfield, I., Zuger, M., Bleak, R. M., and Bakal, S. F. (1950): Lithium chloride intoxication. *New York State J. Med.,* 50:459.

48. Glessinger, B. (1954): Evaluation of lithium in treatment of psychotic excitement. *Med. J. Aust.,* 41:277.

49. Sivadon, P., and Chanoit, P. (1955): Clinical experience with lithium treatment of psychomotor excitation. *Ann. Medicopsychol.,* 113:790.

50. Schou, M. (1959): Lithium in psychiatric therapy. *Psychopharmacologia,* 1:65.

51. Mayfield, D., and Brown, R. G. (1966): The clinical laboratory and electroencephalographic effects of lithium. *J. Psychiatr. Res.,* 4:207.

52. Lehmann, H. E., and Ban, T. A. (1970): Clinical use of other antipsychotic agents. In: *Principles of Psychopharmacology,* edited by W. G. Clark and J. del Giudice, p. 621. Academic Press, New York.

53. Baldessarini, R. J., and Stephens, J. H. (1970): Lithium carbonate for affective disorders. *Arch. Gen. Psychiatry,* 22:72.

54. Spring, G. K., Schweid, D., Gray, C., Steinberg, J., and Harwitz, M. (1970): A double blind comparison of lithium and chlorpromazine in the treatment of manic states. *Am. J. Psychiatry,* 126:1306.

55. Moracci, E. (1931): Azione di alcuni sali applicati direttamente sui centri corticali sensitivo— Motori del cane. *Arch. Fisiol.,* 29:487.

56. Araki, I., Ito, M., Kostyuk, P., Oscarsson, O., and Oshima, I. (1965): The effects of alkaline cations on the responses of cat spinal neurons and their removal from the cell. *Proc. R. Soc. Lond. (Biol.),* 162:319.

57. Pfeiffer, C. Z., Singh, M., and Goldstein, L. (1969): Single dose–effect relationship of lithium on the electrical activity of cerebral cortex and of the heart. *J. Clin. Pharmacol.,* 9:298.

58. Johnson, G., Hekimian, L., and Gershon, S. (1970): Differential drug responsiveness in psychiatric subjects. *8th Annual ACNP Mtg., San Diego, California.*
59. Rochford, J. M., Detre, T., Tucker, G. J., and Harrow, M. (1970): Neuropsychological impairments in functional psychiatric disease. *Arch. Gen. Psychiatry,* 22:114.
60. Johnson, G., Gershon, S., and Hekimian, L. J. (1968): Controlled evaluation of lithium and chlorpromazine in the treatment of manic states: an interim report. *Compr. Psychiatry,* 9:563.
61. Grob, D., Harvey, A. M., Langworthy, O. R., and Lilienthal, J. R., Jr. (1947): The administration of di-isopropyl fluorophosphate (DFP) to man. III. Effect on the central nervous system with special reference to the electrical activity of the brain. *Johns Hopkins Med. J.,* 81:217.
62. Rountree, D. W., Nevin, S., and Wilson, A. (1950): The effects of diisoprophylfluorophosphonate in schizophrenia and manic depressive psychosis. *J. Neurol. Neurosurg. Psychiatry,* 13:47–62.
63. Gershon, S., and Shaw, F. H. (1961): Psychiatric sequelae of chronic exposure to organophosphorus insecticides. *Lancet,* 1:1371–1374.

Discussion

Calloway: I seem to remember that at the Army Chemical Center when occasional massive doses of organophosphates were given and before the subsequent iatrogenic atropine psychosis intervened, these people were not depressed but were rather giggly and silly. Is there a difference between acute and chronic DFP administration?

Gershon: Yes, that's crucial. Usually with the acute toxicity they're really so sick from cholineomimetic activity that they are sort of intoxicated. After the acute intoxication and sickness they have some nightmares. But that's it. The ones we studied were chronic, insofar as on any day *none* manifested acute cholineomimetic overactivity such that it was reported as a side effect. Therefore in these cases which we observed the effect endured for many months, and for some weeks in the ones that Rountree reported. I think it's very different.

The problem of central cholinesterase inhibition was rasied by Dr. Lipton who recalls that animals showed little behavioral effects in Russel's pioneer work (R. W. Russel: In: *Drugs and Behavior,* edited by L. Uhr and J. S. Miller. Wiley, New York, 1960). Man and animal may differ or detection of behavioral effects may not be as easy in animals.

Cholinesterase blood levels were measured by Rountree in a prospective study. There was inhibition, but it was not dramatic; they weren't vomiting or acutely sick. The chronic central effects of this irreversible inhibitor obviously are of some significance because there were both gross EEG as well as clinical changes. The degree of inhibition was essentially the same in the schizophrenic group and manic-depressive groups. In our study—which was a retrospective study—there were no peripheral cholinesterase level changes at all at the time we saw patients.

Snyder: Though you cautioned against using drug-response to diagnose, it seems to me that this is the logical extension of your research as well as that of Dr. Davis. It should be possible to establish in a definitive experiment whether or not the exacerbation of symptoms by methylphenidate (Ritalin®) is a *sine qua non* for the diagnosis of schizophrenia.

Gershon: The point I was making was only the retrospective point with lithium in single cases. There is an abundance of literature now trying to give lithium to everybody and justify it by labeling them manic-depressive.

We presume, in the grandiose delusionary system in which we work, that our diagnostic criteria are good—but are still limited. Therefore, we couldn't do it retrospectively per case, but we would be prepared to do it for group response, if there are group response differences.

Snyder: Do you feel that any drugs may be diagnostic tools in psychiatry? Could you comment on whether the transitory improvement of depressed patients to amphetamine predicts therapeutic response to imipramine?

Gershon: I would not be prepared to use an amphetamine test for a single case, because as has been pointed out in Dr. Angrist's work the dose required to produce response is highly variable. That is, you might get an exacerbation with 10 or 20 milligrams of the agent. And another patient at 1,000 milligrams will produce no change.

But for group responses and research activity, in the way I tried to present it relating to diagnostic groups and disease substrate, I think it is indeed highly appropriate. But I don't think you can go per patient yet. It might indeed be a worthwhile *additional* test, certainly, if I may take the risk of offending some people, as worthwhile as doing projective tests!

Freedman: That's a blot on this discussion! Dr. Davis has had experience with this.

Davis: I took Dr. Gershon's cautionary remarks as warning, in part, against circularity. Those of us who use drugs as a tool should watch out that we don't define all lithium responders as manics or all nonresponders as nonmanics. This applies to research on schizophrenia, also. A broad or narrow diagnosis of schizophrenia might lead to a similar circularity; so the same methodologic caution applies to diagnostic and natural history studies as well as to drug studies. For example, if in the definition of schizophrenia there is the implicit criterion that it be chronic, then for the investigator to argue that his criteria are correct because his criteria predict chronicity is circular.

Much new research needs to be done for the diagnostic use of methylphenidate (Ritalin®) as a test to predict schizophrenia. Patients can change with drugs in a variety of ways, and a slight difference in emphasis in the psychologic variables measured could make the difference between good prediction and no prediction. Let me illustrate this by an example. Some years ago I treated schizophrenics with large doses of L-DOPA and found that they became worse in terms of their psychotic symptomatology. However, I particularly remember one case in which the ward nurses requested that the patients stay on DOPA. To us, the physicians, the DOPA appears to have caused the patients to become more delusional. One particular patient felt the dogs of war were gnawing a hole in her side. To the nurses—who saw the DOPA activating a very retarded, uncommunicative, chronic schizophrenic to a patient who is more lively and interested in life, and possibly able to live outside the hospital—the patient was seen as better. This patient had been in the state hospitals for some 15 years continuously but was discharged from our research ward, partly because of benefits she received from a drug which made her symptomatically worse.

For a pharmacologic provocative test to be clinically useful, it would be really important to be precise in pinning down the qualitative dimension that might predict diagnosis and to develop a reliable method for measuring this dimension quantitatively. Hence thus, there is a lot of work involved in use of drugs as tools to predict diagnosis when used clinically. It may, indeed, prove to be possible to predict accurately enough so that one considers such predictions as clinically useful for the individual cases, but in the present state of the art it is doubtful that we are really close to doing it for single case.

Friedhoff: The use to which drugs can be put in making a diagnosis is dependent on the basis used for establishing nosologic categories. In psychiatry, at the present time, most diagnostic categories are based primarily on symptom constellation and history. Many symptoms, hallucinations or agitation for example, are common to a number of diagnostic entities. The psychotropic drugs now known to us are generally active against a given symptom, more or less independent of the illness with which it is associated. We should not conclude from this that psychotropic drugs, in particular, the antipsychotic drugs, are simply useful for "papering-over" symptoms. There is ample reason to feel that antipsychotic drugs are interacting with an important component of the pathophysiologic mechanism involved in the formation of specific symptoms. Therefore, categories based on drug response are likely to reflect homogeneity of symptom pathogenesis, but would be even less likely to reflect illnesses with a common etiology than do the present descriptive categories.

Spitzer: I guess I would have to disagree. I don't think the evidence suggests that psychotropic drugs are really effective at the symptom level. The phenothiazines are not useful just for delusions or hallucinations. They are useful for the syndrome which we generally call schizophrenic—delusions and hallucinations—with withdrawal or agitation.

For example, anxiety in a schizophrenic is helped by psychotropic medication. The same kind of medication is not very effective in the anxiety that is seen in the anxious neurotic. So phenothiazine may not be effective at the disease level, but certainly operates at the syndromic level.

Freedman: What is meant, Dr. Davis, when somebody is given methylphenidate and is "more schizophrenic" or the symptoms are "intensified?" There is a thought disorder that we haven't yet mentioned, in schizophrenia. What component, process, or dimension of behaviors affected by these drugs is Dr. Gershon's battery getting at? Can it be pinned down?

Davis: I think it can, but in trying to do this with physostigmine to raise brain acetylcholine with reference to the cholinergic story or with methylphenidate (Ritalin®) to release dopamine, I found that we did not have the psychologic measuring instruments to really pin down what was happening to the patient qualitatively and quantitatively. Our present instruments are crude behavioral ratings and are not precise instruments to make a qualitative distinction. So, it indicates that more work is to be done on the phenomenologic level in order to get the full impact of these pharmacologic studies, which brings us back to the first few of these presentations on phenomenology and diagnosis.

Gershon: What we saw giving impramine or Ritalin® to schizophrenics—I don't know what the explanation is—was nothing other than schizophrenic pathology. These people were more deluded; they spoke about delusions when before they weren't speaking, and the staff would have to infer whether they were deluded and were hallucinating. This material became overtly manifest.

The same profile occurred in the people with cholinergic activation. In that study the initial diagnoses were never made by us. They had seen dozens of doctors and were referred. So the diagnosis was clearly made and essentially they were made without relating to the apparent causative agent. And all cases cleared up, the organophosphorus ones, after about six months. It didn't matter what treatment they got; about six months later, presumably when the enzyme centrally was resynthesized, they cleared up.

Snyder: I'd like to comment on the theoretical underpinnings of Dr. Gershon's study. He has employed several drugs to determine whether the drug-mediated exacerbation of schizophrenic symptoms involves one or the other of the two brain catecholamines, norepinephrine and dopamine. Methylphenidate (Ritalin®) and amphetamine affect both catecholamines, while L-DOPA primarily increases dopamine formation. ET-495 (Biperidol®) selectively stimulates dopamine receptors. Since both L-DOPA and ET-495 are active, the exacerbation of symptoms probably involves dopamine and not norepinephrine. Interestingly the therapeutic effects of phenothiazines and butyrophenones correlate with blockade of receptors for dopamine and not norepinephrine. This evaluation of neurotransmitter specificity might be extended to other drugs. For instance, clonidine selectively stimulates norepinephrine receptors. One would predict that it ought not worsen schizophrenic symptoms.

Kety: In thinking about drugs and diagnosis, I might suggest that we not attempt to draw any diagnostic conclusions from the drug effects alone. Yet these are tremendously important in that we keep them constantly in our thinking and in the development of hypothetical breakdowns of diagnostic categories. Thus I don't think it would be proper to say that an activation by methylphenidate should be a *sine qua non* for diagnosis of schizophrenia. On the other hand, I think it would be extremely valuable to have a subcategory of schizophrenia which is activated by methylphenyidate and keep that as a separate entity until more is known about what methylphenydate is doing.

I think we can learn a great deal from the rest of medicine and what has happened to medical models of illness. Suppose, before the pneumococcus was identified, that one had discovered one of the chemotherapeutic agents, let's say sulfapyridine. And let us suppose that this drug had a dramatic therapeutic effect in a substantial number of patients with lobar pneumonia. That wouldn't mean that all lobar pneumonias would respond to the drug, and yet it would have been extremely valuable in terms of later developments and later thinking to have recognized that there was a kind of lobar pneumonia that responded to an agent that was known to have an effect upon a particular group of bacteria. That, in itself, could have facilitated the discovery of the pneumococcus.

Biology of the Major Psychoses, edited by D. X. Freedman, Res. Publ. Assoc. Res. Nerv. Ment. Dis., Vol. 54. Raven Press, New York   1975.

EEG and Evoked Potentials in the Psychoses

Charles Shagass

Temple University Department of Psychiatry and Eastern Pennsylvania Psychiatric Institute, Philadelphia, Pennsylvania 19129

In 1875, Richard Caton (1) first recorded both the "spontaneous" rhythms of the EEG and sensory evoked potentials from the exposed brain of an animal. A half-century elapsed before Hans Berger (2) demonstrated that the EEG can be recorded from the human scalp surface, and two more decades before George Dawson (3) showed how evoked potentials can be measured in man. The pioneering work of Berger (2) and Dawson (3) made it possible to record electrical brain activities in the conscious human subject, capable of reporting his experiences, and offered psychiatry exciting new avenues for elucidating the nature of disordered brain functions in mental illness. At the onset of the EEG era one could even hope that EEG records might contain waveforms specific for schizophrenia, as indeed they did for some convulsive disorders. The evidence soon dispelled such optimistic, and perhaps naive, expectations. No EEG waves were found that could be taken as the electrical "signature" of a psychosis. The same is true for evoked potentials, although it is unlikely that similarly optimistic hopes prevailed when it became possible to record them.

In the absence of qualitatively distinct electrical signs of psychosis, psychiatric EEG investigators began to search for quantitative differences. In addition to seeking such differences in the "resting" EEG, they looked for differential reactivity of the EEG to agents such as sensory stimuli and drugs. Liberson (4) gave the name "functional electroencephalography," to such efforts, and the term easily encompasses the subsequently developed evoked potential techniques. However, even though many quantitative EEG studies were performed, it remained for the development of computer technology, which also facilitated evoked potential recording, to provide the means for adequate, and previously impossible, quantitative analysis of large masses of EEG data. Computer methods thereby inaugurated a new era of psychiatric electrophysiology, an era which is still in its early stages. Although psychiatric EEG research has a 40-year history, it is actually a very young field, and the material covered in this chapter should be evaluated from that perspective.

A selective survey of findings of interest obtained to date in EEG and evoked potential studies of adult schizophrenic and affective psychoses will be presented here. An attempt will also be made to consider the evidence in relation to the issue of electrophysiologic differences between the psychoses.

METHODOLOGY

Several books describe the technical aspects of EEG and evoked response (ER) recording procedures in detail (5–7). Because methodologic issues play a crucial role in relation to the data of this field, it seems worthwhile to draw attention to some of the important problems.

Artifact Control

It should be emphasized that studies of disturbed psychiatric patients require special strategies for coping with biologic artifacts, such as muscle potentials and eye movements. Ideally, subjects should be managed during testing in such a way as to reduce artifact to a minimum, but some artifact is unavoidable. In modern investigations, which depend heavily upon automatic quantification methods by means of digital computers, there may be an even greater need for adequate ways of dealing with artifacts than there was when measurements were based entirely on visual inspection. There are two reasons for this: (a) sensitive computer measurements can detect small, consistent artifactual effects, which the eye would disregard, and give them undue weight; (b) the trained eye is better at some kinds of artifact detection than available computer algorithms. Visual inspection of data before computer analysis is probably still highly desirable.

Subject Factors

Most of the studies to be reviewed involve comparisons of clinical populations, usually a patient group and a nonpatient control group. Although the concept of a control group, matched to the patient group in all respects except illness, is well understood and accepted, few, if any, studies really meet this standard. The practical difficulties of matching groups for all possibly relevant variables are obvious. However, those subject factors that have been found to be correlated with electrophysiologic measurements cannot be ignored. These include age, sex, handedness, and probably intellectual level.

A methodologic problem, which is of special importance in the present context, results from the fact that hospitalized patients with schizophrenia and affective psychoses often differ with respect to age and sex distributions. Patients with affective psychoses tend to be older and more often female than patients with schizophrenias. This is an important determinant of the fact that there are so few comparative studies of properly matched groups with these disorders. Most of the available data are of indirect type, each patient group being matched with a nonpatient control group, thus permitting some indication of the ways in which each differs from the controls. It is also noteworthy that electrophysiologic measurements can differ with respect to age and sex in one group and not in another. For example, we found such differences in chronic schizophrenics, even though they were absent in normals (8). To demonstrate such interactions between age, sex, and clinical state, one must use statistical designs involving properly proportioned groups.

Transitory Factors

Some of the more transitory factors that can affect electrophysiologic results are time of day, caffeine intake, smoking habits, and time since the last cigarette (9,10). The blood sugar level (time since last meal) may be important. Drowsiness changes both EEG and ER characteristics. Although continuous monitoring of the EEG can serve to indicate gross changes with drowsiness and sleep, investigators may have considerable difficulty in detecting and controlling minor variations in attention; these can also be associated with significant electrophysiologic changes, particularly in ER.

The issue of psychoactive drug effects is of critical importance. Most investigators find it difficult to obtain for study sufficient numbers of psychotic patients who are assuredly free of drug influence. Also, the exact length of time that a patient should be drug-free is not certain. The findings of Ulett et al. (11) suggest that this may be up to 3 months for EEG. A comparable time has not been established for ER. Some indication of drug effects per se can be obtained if clinically unchanged patients are studied with and without drugs in a longitudinal fashion.

EEG STUDIES

Resting EEG

The "resting" EEG is taken with the subject reclining or seated, eyes closed, awake, and "relaxed." This is the usual clinical EEG recording. Comprehensive reviews of clinical EEG findings in psychiatric disorders are to be found in the volume edited by Wilson (12). Although no distinctive EEG patterns characterize any "functional" psychiatric illness, a relatively high incidence of abnormal EEGs in psychiatric populations has often been reported. The interpretation of these reports is frequently difficult because the criteria of "abnormality" are poorly specified, and the populations compared are not matched for important subject characteristics.

Affective Psychoses

Workers from Berger on have concluded that there are no specific EEG abnormalities associated with affective psychoses. On the contrary, the discovery of specific abnormalities in patients presenting with depressive symptoms, has generally been taken as grounds for revision of the original diagnosis. This is documented by case reports of EEG diagnosis of intracranial neoplasm (13) and convulsive disorders (14,15) in patients with depression. The incidence of such cases appears to be quite low.

In contrast to the low incidence of specific EEG abnormalities among patients with affective psychoses, a number of workers have reported a relatively high incidence of nonspecific "abnormality," consisting of excessive fast or slow activity outside of the alpha range. For example, Davis and Davis (16) found that psychotic patients, of whom about one-quarter were manic-depressive, had low percentage time alpha compared to nonpatients, and a higher incidence of irregular records. Davis (17, 18) reported data comparing the EEG in manic-depressive psychosis and schizophrenia. She found very little change in the EEG when patients shifted from one phase of the illness (depressed or manic) to the other, except when level of consciousness was altered. Patients with erratic slow wave disturbances were those whose behavior was unpredictable, regardless of diagnosis. Most of the depressives had alpha frequencies of 10 Hz or slower, whereas alpha frequencies tended to be faster in the manics. In comparison with schizophrenics, manic-depressives more often had records in which alpha rhythm was predominant, while low-voltage fast records were more common in the schizophrenics. The predominant alpha frequency tended to be slower in the manic-depressives than in the schizophrenics, whereas alpha voltage was about equally distributed in both groups. Davis (19) designated disorganized low-voltage fast activity (26 to 50 Hz) as "choppy"; this was much more common in schizophrenics, a difference apparently not attributable to age. The contribution of muscle activity to the "choppy" pattern remains in question, although Davis (19) believed that the activity was of brain origin.

Lemere (20) found a greater incidence of high voltage, "strong" alpha rhythm in manic-depressives than in normals, who, in turn, showed more than schizophrenics. He found no difference between manic and depressed patients. He interpreted his data to indicate that there was an overproduction of energy in the manic-depressives, a conclusion exactly opposite to the one reached by P. Davis (18) from similar findings.

The EEG findings in 1,593 psychiatric patients were reviewed by Greenblatt et al. (21); their sample included 145 manic-depressive, depressed, 82 manic, and 70 involutional psychotic patients. They considered as "abnormal" records in which the predominant rhythm was outside the limits of 8 to 12 Hz or there was a marked hyperventilation response or both. According to these criteria, the percentages of "abnormality" were as follows: manic-depressive, depressed, 31; manic-depressive, manic, 42; involutional psychosis, 51; control group (young), 10; schizophrenia, 23; senile and arteriosclerotic psychoses, 54. They found a significant amount of fast activity in the manic-depressive, depressed, and in the involutional psychotic patients. Recognizing the importance of the age factor, these authors related the incidence of "abnormality" to age, and found that the lowest incidence was in the middle years from 25 to 45. Slow activity was more common in young patients, and fast activity in older ones. They concluded that the EEG findings in the various neuropsychiatric conditions were largely explained by changes associated with age.

Finley (22) paid particular attention to fast activity in psychiatric patients. In a large series of cases, which included 89 manic-depressives and 53 involutional psychotics, he found the rapid patterns with high frequency in all diagnostic groups; they were much more common than in a control group of 300 nonpatients. The greatest incidence of excessive fast activity was in the involutional psychoses (50 to 75%); manic and depressive types had an equal incidence at 25 to 40%.

It seems probable that the statistical differences between patients with affective psychoses and other groups are largely attributable to changes with age. Maggs and Turton (23) compared 82 normal control patients over 60 years of age with 96 cases of depression. They were unable to demonstrate any difference between the patients and the controls, but they did find more abnormalities in the patients whose illness began at the age of 60 or above. Their data revealed a considerable number of abnormal and borderline records in both controls and patients, which they considered to be an expression of a general aging process, not limited to any one specific symptom complex or disorder.

Schizophrenia

Although there has been general agreement that specific EEG abnormalities are rare in affective psychoses, there have been numerous reports of a high incidence of such abnormalities in schizophrenic patients. A comprehensive review of EEG studies in schizophrenia (24) indicated wide variation in the reported incidence of abnormal patterns, which include the "choppy" pattern described by P. Davis (19)—sharp waves, slow wave bursts, and temporal lobe spikes. Should it be true that paroxysmal EEG abnormalities occur with high frequency in schizophrenic patients, this would provide support for the view held by some that there is an intimate relationship between schizophrenia and epilepsy. The extreme form of this view is that schizophrenia may be a form of epilepsy. An opposing interpretation would be that some fraction of patients with convulsive disorders present with schizophrenic-like symptoms. The idea that schizophrenia is related to epilepsy is supported by observations in schizophrenic patients chronically implanted with electrodes (25). Apparently, schizophrenics frequently have paroxysmal discharges in deeply placed structures, such as the septal area, although such discharges may not appear in surface recordings. The incidence of such discharges in normals is, however, not known. The most striking aspect of the clinical EEG evidence is that different series have reported the incidence of abnormalities to range from 5 to 80%. This suggests that the incidence of abnormalities is likely determined by the origin of the study sample. Higher incidence would be expected in populations composed of individuals who had EEGs performed only upon referral because of suspected convulsive or other cerebral disorders. This view is supported by the results obtained with relatively unselected large samples, such as the 1,000 cases of Colony and Willis (26); they found the incidence of epileptiform EEGs in the general schizophrenic population to be no different that that of controls. The author feels that the balance of the evidence favors the view that some portion of patients with convulsive disorders present with schizophrenic symptoms, rather than that schizophrenia is a form of epilepsy. Gibbs and Gibbs (27) have reinterpreted their own early positive findings in schizophrenia in accordance with this view.

There is one interesting and rather consistent EEG finding in schizophrenia, which has been reported by workers from many different countries. If one relates the course of schizophrenic illness to EEG pattern, patients with chronic illness of "process" type tend to show a considerably higher incidence of excessively stable and well regulated EEGs than patients considered to be "reactive" (28). There is some evidence that the EEGs of such patients are also resistant to change by therapy with psychoactive drugs; furthermore, the EEG resistance appears to be paralleled by therapy-resistance, the patients showing little clinical response to pharmacotherapy (29).

"Activated" EEG

Activation procedures in the clinical EEG setting are designed to test the EEG for normal reactivity, e.g., alpha blocking when the eyes are opened, or to bring out latent convulsive activity. The commonly used activation procedures include eye opening, hyperventilation, intermittent photic stimulation, natural or drug-induced sleep, and injection of metrazol or other convulsants.

Visual Stimulation

Liberson (4) found that, among psychiatric patients, prolonged reduction of alpha activity in response to visual stimulation was most prominent in involutional melancholics and psychopaths. Wilson and Wilson (30) observed that alpha blocking to light flashes lasted longer in depressives than in normals, while d'Elia et al. (31) found prolonged blocking duration in depressives to be reduced after treatment. Schizophrenics do not differ from normal in alpha blocking (32).

Intermittent flash stimulation at rates of 5 to 30 Hz may produce EEG waves at the frequency of flash stimuli; this is called photic driving. Hurst et al. (33) found that manic-depressives showed more photic driving than normals over the 4 to 20 Hz range, but not in the 21 to 26 Hz range. The manic patients tended more often to show harmonics and flicker following in the beta range than the depressive group. In our laboratory we compared the relative amount of driving at flash rates of 10 and 15 Hz in controls and patients with anxiety and depression (34). Patients with depressive psychoses showed relatively more driving with 10 Hz flicker than with 15 Hz flicker, so that the 15:10 ratio was lower in them than in the other two groups; patients with anxiety states had the highest 15:10 ratio, and controls were intermediate. However, these differences were significant only for female subjects.

Drug Activation

Gastaut (35) devised an activation method that combined intermittent photic stimulation with stepwise injections of metrazol. The amount of drug required to produce epileptiform discharges in the EEG was taken as the photometrazol threshold. Lieberman et al. (36) found that the photometrazol threshold was lower in patients with catatonic schizophrenia, epilepsy, and narcolepsy than in psychoneuroses and noncatatonic schizophrenias. They concluded that the test had little diagnostic value.

Goldman (37) described a method of activating the EEG by means of intravenous pentothal. His technique was based upon assessment of EEG changes, primarily in the beta frequency, that occur within a 5-min period after the intravenous injection of 300 mg of pentothal. He reported that paroxysmal rhythms were elicited more often in schizophrenics than in patients with other psychiatric diagnoses. He also found that chlorpromazine blocked the paroxysmal effects. Sila et al. (38) attempted to verify Goldman's findings; they used a frequency analyzer for objective measurement of the EEG. Their original sample consisted of 39 schizophrenic and 19 psychotic depressive patients; prior to pentothal administration the average spectra of the groups did not differ. During the first minute after the injection, activity over almost the entire frequency range increased to a greater extent in schizophrenics than in depressives, in agreement with Goldman's (37) results. However, when patients with overlapping symptomatology were eliminated, so that comparisons were made only between 12 clear schizophrenics and 12 clear depressives, the groups no longer differed significantly.

Sleep

"Sleep activation" studies have produced some tantalizing findings. Gibbs and Gibbs (27) described an EEG pattern in sleep that appears to correlate with psychosis. They called this the "mitten" pattern, because the slow wave and spike resemble the hand and thumb of a mitten. Mittens occur only during sleep, and are found mainly in the frontal areas, but usually spread to the parietal areas, do not repeat rythmically, and have not been seen in subjects under 15 years of age. Gibbs and Gibbs (27) subdivide these patterns into the A-mitten, in which the fast component lasts longer than 100 msec, and the B-mitten, in which it lasts between 80 and 100 msec. Both patterns were rare in healthy subjects; the B-mitten was frequent in psychotic patients without epilepsy, whereas A-mittens were most common in patients with Parkinson's disease. The B-mitten pattern was found in 37% of schizophrenic subjects; the incidence was nearly as high in patients with paranoid psychoses, and higher in epileptic patients with psychoses. The incidence did not differ with respect to subtype of schizophrenia. B-mittens occurred in about 20% of involutional depressions and manic-depressive, manic, patients in the Gibbs and Gibbs series (27).

Struve and his colleagues have attempted to relate the B-mitten pattern to clinical aspects of schizophrenia. Struve and Becka (39) found the B-mitten pattern in 8 of 11 male "reactive" schizophrenics, whereas only 1 of 10 male "process" patients had it. Subsequently, they reported on 67 patients, including both sexes (40). The data showed the B-mitten pattern in 41% of 46 reactive schizophrenics, and in only 5% of 21 process schizophrenics. No other EEG findings discriminated between the process and reactive schizophrenic groups. It is noteworthy that, among nonschizophrenic patients, the distinction in B-mitten incidence does not relate to process-reactive premorbid history, although about 30% of the nonschizophrenic group also displayed the pattern.

Another psychiatrically interesting EEG sign during sleep, also first recognized by Gibbs and Gibbs (41), is the 14- and 6-/sec positive spike pattern, which they interpreted as evidence of thalamic and hypothalmic epilepsy. There have been many clinical reports relating the 14 and 6 pattern to psychiatric symptoms, such as aggressiveness, affective impulsivity, and driven behavior. The 14 and 6 pattern appears to be highly variable in different reported populations, depending upon degree of attention to the essential recording conditions, namely sleep and monopolar montages. Niedermeyer and Knott (42) found that 14 and 6 positive patterns were most frequent in psychiatric patients, and Schmidt and Andrews (43) reported a relatively high incidence in schizophrenic patients. However, other workers failed to find associations between the 14 and 6 phenomenon and behavioral manifestations in psychiatric patients (44). The 14 and 6 pattern is seldom seen after age 25. Of some relevance to considerations of the EEG in psychosis is the evidence that the presence of 14 and 6 positive spiking may relate to suicidal ideation and attempts. Struve et al. (45) compared EEG findings in patient groups selected for suicidal ideation, suicide attempts, and assaultive–destructive acts. This study gave careful attention to independence of ratings, and the groups compared were of the same age and sex. The results showed a significantly higher incidence of 14 and 6 positive spikes in the symptom groups. The findings in this study are in accord with earlier results reported in a smaller sample by Greenberg and Pollack (46), which indicated that schizophrenic patients with 14 and 6 positive spiking presented a greater suicidal risk, and displayed more aggressive behavior.

Sedation Threshold

My sedation threshold method, although not really an activation procedure, may be mentioned in the present context (47). The threshold is the amount of intravenous amobarbital required to produce a near-maximal increment in frontal 15 to 30 Hz activity, usually associated with onset of dysarthria. The mean sedation threshold in normals is about 3 mg/kg. In patients with depressive neuroses, thresholds tend to be considerably higher than normal, whereas in patients with depressive psychoses, they tend to be about the normal level. In acute schizophrenic patients, they also tend to be at about the normal level, whereas they are significantly elevated in chronic schizophrenia, i.e., with duration of 1 year or longer (48). Using a galvanic skin response indicator of threshold, Perez-Reyes (49) compared neurotic and psychotic depressions, and confirmed my results; thresholds were low in the psychotics and high in the neurotics. The method used by Perez-Reyes (49) seems to be more sensitive than my EEG indicator of sedation threshold, since he was also able to distinguish normals from psychotic depressives, the patients having lower thresholds.

Quantified EEG

One of the earliest devices for automatic EEG quantification was a Fourier analyzer developed by Grass, which Gibbs (50) employed in studies of schizophrenia. The Walter frequency analyzer, introduced in the 1940s, was used for automatic EEG quantification by many investigators; it displays integrated voltage in a selected series of frequency bands, essentially a power spectrum. The Drohocki integrator is a simpler device, which sums voltage across all frequencies. Period analyzers concentrate upon the frequency domain, and measure wave duration. Recently general purpose computers have been used for all forms of EEG quantification.

Although Gibbs (50,51), using the Grass analyzer, found that schizophrenics had less alpha activity and more fast activity than normal subjects, he subsequently concluded that these findings resulted from a greater amount of muscle artifact in the patients (27). Gibbs' skepticism about the validity of his own quantitative EEG data in schizophrenia needs to be borne in mind in relation to evaluating the data of other investigators who may not have been so critical.

Affective Psychoses

Hurst et al. (33) used the Walter-type analyzer to study manic-depressive patients. They found that mean alpha frequency was lower in patients with predominantly depressed phases than in those with predominantly manic phases of the disorder, and that this difference was present regardless of the clinical phase at the time of the test. They were unable to demonstrate a correlation between alpha frequency and clinically assessed degree of depression or mania. They also found that low-voltage fast records were more frequent in the psychotic group than in normals. In addition, they observed that the amplitude of theta activity (4 to 7.5 Hz) was greater, and the incidence less than in normal. In recent data from our laboratory, we were unable to find significant differences between manic-depressive, depressed patients and normals of the same age and sex, with respect to EEG frequency or amplitude characteristics (52).

Schizophrenia

Kennard and Schwartzman (53) compared the frequency analyzed EEGs of schizophrenic patients and controls, and studied changes after treatment. Their recordings involved an array of electrodes covering the head. They found that in patients alpha activity was less sharply defined; there was a greater frequency spread within the alpha range, and there was more nonalpha activity. Furthermore, anteroposterior gradients were less marked in patients than in controls, and there was less synchrony between the right and left hemispheres; "poor organization" was therefore more common among the patients. Shifts toward the normal pattern occurred with clinical improvement. An abnormal, poorly organized frequency graph was associated with acute and severe onset of disturbance, and with greater degree of dissociation with immediate environment. Fink et al. (54) compared single-channel frequency analyses of schizophrenic and depressed patients, and found greater amounts of slow and fast activity in the schizophrenics. However, there were significant effects of age and sex, which were not controlled and may have led to spurious diagnostic differences.

Bruck (55) measured amplitude and synchrony between records from different head areas by a hand method. He found significantly lower amplitudes in schizophrenics, particularly in the occipital area, than in nonschizophrenic patients. Bruck did not find that his synchrony measures differentiated between schizophrenics and nonpatients, but they did differ, to some extent, between schizophrenic and nonschizophrenic patients.

Itil et al. (56) obtained both power-spectrum (Walter-type frequency analyzer) and period analysis for the right occipital EEG of 100 nondrugged schizophrenics and 100 age- and sex-matched controls. With both forms of analysis, schizophrenics showed significantly more activity above and below the alpha range. These workers also did a systematic visual analysis of the entire eight channels recorded, and obtained a number of significant differences between the patient and control groups. A discriminant function analysis indicated that the visual examination of the EEG provided greater discrimination between groups than the quantitative findings, but the visual observations were based on eight channels, and the measurements on only one. Itil et al. (57) subsequently carried out repeat studies, using both power-spectrum and period analysis, in chronic schizophrenics and age- and sex-matched normal volunteers. Again, the schizophrenics showed more slow and fast, and less alpha activity than normals. The first derivative in the period analysis, indicative of superimposed waves, showed less slow and more fast activity in the schizophrenics. The schizophrenics also had less amplitude variability than normals. The differences between the groups remained very stable over a period of three months. The data also indicated that the EEG patterns of normals were more consistent over time than those of chronic schizophrenics.

Giannitrapani and Kayton (58) compared 10 schizophrenics with 10 age- and sex-matched controls, with respect to multiple channel spectral analyses. The schizophrenics showed lower dominant alpha frequency, greater alpha spread, more 19 and 20 Hz activity, and less interhemispheric asymmetry than the normals. The frequency results agree with our own recent data, which show significantly lower mean frequency in chronic schizophrenics than in matched normals (52).

Goldstein and his co-workers (59) used the Drohocki integrator to sum the voltage of 30 consecutive 20-sec left occipital EEG samples; although mean amplitudes of male chronic schizophrenics did not differ from those of normal men, the coefficient of variation of the 30 measurements was less in the patients, indicating reduced variability over the 10-min period of recording. These results were essentially confirmed by Marjerrison et al. (60) and Lifshitz and Gradijan (61). The latter workers examined different frequency bands separately; their data suggested that the greater variability of controls resulted mainly from more activity in the slow bands. This would indicate that controls more often became drowsy, a finding in agreement with the visual observations of Itil et al. (56). These results seem to support the view that schizophrenics are more "aroused" than normals, but it appears uncertain as to whether such "hyperarousal" can be taken to reflect more than a normal correlate of emotional disturbance. Our own amplitude data are based on consecutive 1-sec integration epochs for a 10-min left parietal recording (52). Our male chronic schizophrenics did not differ significantly from male controls, but both mean amplitude and coefficient of variation were much greater in our schizophrenic than in our control females.

Interhemispheric Comparisons

There has been considerable recent interest in comparing the activity of right and left hemispheres. Goldstein et al. (62) compared integrated amplitudes from left and right occipital recordings in 67 normal volunteers and 173 unselected psychiatric patients. Amplitudes tended to be greater in the right hemisphere in normals, whereas the reverse tendency was found in the patients. However, the results may have been influenced by drugs, as Serafetinides (63) showed that chlorpromazine tends to produce greater voltage increases in the left hemisphere in schizophrenic patients. D'Elia and Perris (64) found that EEG amplitudes were about the same on both sides before and after treatment in depressive patients, but that the variance was less on the left side before treatment than it was after.

EVOKED POTENTIAL STUDIES

Evoked Responses to Single Stimuli

In early studies, we employed several intensities of median nerve shock to evoke somatosensory evoked responses (SER) (65). We found that, at all intensities, the amplitude of early components was greater than normal in all types of psychiatric patients, except nonpsychotics with anxiety, depression, and somatic complaints (dysthymics). Using a single intensity, SER amplitude differences between clinical groups were not significant in a subsequent study (66). However, more recently (67) in a study using several stimulus intensities, the earlier results were essentially confirmed for schizophrenia. SER amplitudes for the first 100 msec following the stimulus were lower in controls than in chronic paranoid, chronic undifferentiated, and schizoaffective schizophrenics. However, amplitudes were as in controls in patients with acute and latent subtypes of schizophrenia. In these studies we also attempted to relate the symptom patterns of schizophrenic patients to SER measurements (68). The data revealed that, within a heterogeneous schizophrenic population, SER amplitudes were significantly greater in patients rating high on florid manifestations of psychosis, such as hallucinations, unusual thoughts, bizarreness, etc., and low on depressive mood. In contrast, amplitudes were normal in patients who were rated high on depression, but low on overt psychotic symptoms.

Auditory evoked responses (auditory ER) have been compared in schizophrenic patients and in nonpatients by several workers. There appears to be a relatively uniform finding indicating lower amplitudes of the components occurring after 50 msec in the patients (69–71). Saletu et al. (71) also found that times of occurrence of auditory ER peaks (latencies) were earlier in the schizophrenics; schizophrenics with thought-process disorder were most deviant from normal.

Studies of responses to visual stimuli have yielded variable results. We found greater amplitudes in a heterogeneous group of psychiatric patients than in controls, with the highest amplitudes in nonpsychotics; the patients, particularly schizophrenics, also had faster latencies for the initial visual evoked response (visual ER) positive peak, occurring at about 45 msec (72). With eyes closed, the typical flash visual ER contains rhythmic afteractivity, which commences at about 300 msec, and may continue for more than 1 sec. In schizophrenics, we found less visual evoked response rhythmic afteractivity than in any other group (72). Since similar results were obtained in elderly patients with chronic brain syndromes (73), the finding of reduced visual ER afteractivity is not specific for schizophrenia. Visual ER amplitude and latency differences have either not been found by other workers (74), or were in opposite direction (75,76). Some of the discrepancies in findings may be accounted for by lead differences, failure to immobilize the pupils (77), and by sample differences, particularly in relation to subtype and chronicity.

Augmenting–Reducing

Buchsbaum and Silverman (78) employed visual ER to several intensities of light flash to develop an ER test of Petrie's (79) perceptual dimension, called "augmenting-reducing." The particular aspect of visual ER that they found most relevant to their purpose, was measured in the monopolar vertex recording between a positive deflection at about 100 msec and a negative one at about 140 msec. The amplitude of this visual ER wave increased with greater stimulus intensity in subjects who were "augmenters" by Petrie's (79) behavioral test of kinesthetic figural aftereffect; in contrast, visual ER amplitude tended to become lower with more intense stimuli in subjects who tested behaviorally as "reducers." Buchsbaum and Silverman (78) took the slope of the curve relating amplitude to stimulus intensity (intensity–response function) as their ER index of augmenting–reducing. Although visual ER recordings are prone to contamination by ocular factors, such as pupillary diameter and blink potentials, we recently demonstrated that such factors do not significantly influence the ER measures of augmenting–reducing (80).

Interesting clinical correlates of the visual ER augmenting–reducing measurement have been found in depression. Buchsbaum et al. (81) reported that bipolar manic-depressive patients (history of mania) were augmenters, whereas unipolar depressive patients (depressions only) were reducers. Lithium therapy tended to decrease the amount of augmentation in both groups. Buchsbaum et al. (82) paid special attention to factors of age and sex in further studies of evoked potential augmenting–reducing in affective disorders. They found that the reducing tendency in unipolar depressives occurred primarily in male, but not female, patients. Furthermore, although visual ER amplitude is normally greater in females than in males, the sex difference was reversed in unipolar depressive patients. Although smaller visual ER amplitudes were associated with high ratings of depression, bipolar and unipolar patients with equivalent depression ratings still differed with respect to augmenting, which was greater in the bipolar group. These workers also found that unipolar depressives had shorter visual ER latencies than bipolar depressives, who, in turn, had shorter latencies than normals. In addition, they measured monoamine oxidase (MAO) activity in platelets, and found higher platelet MAO activity in unipolar than bipolar patients. Within the unipolar group, the slope of the visual ER intensity–response function was lower when MAO activity was greater.

Buchsbaum and Silverman (78) found marked reducing, i.e., negative slope tendency with increasing light intensity, in a small group of male nonparanoid schizophrenic subjects. However, the idea that nonparanoids are reducers was not strongly supported by the results of Inderbitzin et al. (83), who compared 12 long-term-process schizophrenics with 11 paranoid early-term-reactive male schizophrenics. Although there was a tendency for more augmenting in the paranoids than the nonparanoids, the difference was not statistically significant. Greater differences between the two schizophrenic subgroups were found when the degree of replication of ER measurements with different intensities of stimulation was used as an index, the paranoids showing greater stability, particularly at higher stimulus intensities. It is possible that because the patients were on drugs there was less manifestation of evoked potential reducing than in the original study. A recent study of undrugged acute schizophrenic patients from the same laboratory showed significantly more reducing tendency in schizophrenics than in normals or bipolar depressives of the same age and sex (76). Schizophrenics with marked visual ER reducing also showed greater improvement and relatively good premorbid histories.

Spatial Distribution

There have been few studies of the spatial distribution of ER in psychiatric patients. That attention to topography may be rewarding is suggested by recent data of Perris (84) and Perris and d'Elia (85). These workers recorded visual ER to flash from the two occipital areas, and found that the amplitude of the right visual ER exceeded that of the left more often in psychotic depressive patients than in either neurotic depressives or chronic schizophrenics. Treatment with tricyclic antidepressants shifted the asymmetry in the psychotic depressives toward left predominance. They concluded that the dominant hemisphere is functionally involved in depression.

Evoked Response Variability

The measurement of variation in the wave shape of ER from one averaging sequence to another was introduced to psychiatric investigation by Callaway and his colleagues (70,86). Their measure of variability was the product-moment correlation coefficient between corresponding data points in different auditory ERs. They found that schizophrenics had greater variability of auditory ER than normals; furthermore, in individual patients, reduction of psychopathology accompanied reduction in variability. Similar evidence of greater variability in auditory ER, in schizophrenics, was obtained by Cohen (69); it is noteworthy that Cohen's schizophrenic population was drug-free. Lifshitz (87) demonstrated greater than normal visual ER variability in schizophrenics. As mentioned previously, Inderbitzin et al. (83) obtained evidence of greater visual ER variability in nonparanoid than in paranoid schizophrenics. The studies cited reflect the variation in time of auditory and visual ERs recorded from a single lead. Greater variation between visual ERs recorded from different leads at the same time, i.e., spatial variability, has been shown in schizophrenics than in normals by Rodin et al. (77). Increased variability of auditory ER wave shape is not specific to schizophrenia; it occurs also in brain syndromes (88).

In our own studies with SER, we found *less* variability during the first 100 msec in chronic schizophrenics than in normals, neurotics, and acute or latent schizophrenics (89). In addition, within the schizophrenic population, we found the lowest variability in nondepressed, overtly psychotic patients; depressed schizophrenics with low ratings on other psychotic symptoms had variability measures within the normal range (69). Although at first glance our results appear to be at odds with the results of other workers, which showed greater than normal variability in schizophrenics, it may be pointed out that our data also showed a definite trend for increased SER variability after 100 msec in the sicker schizophrenics. This finding reconciles our results with those obtained by others with auditory and visual ERs since the main portion of overall response variability in these other studies occurred after 100 msec, and variability was not measured separately before 100 msec. Consequently, it appears that, in seriously ill schizophrenics, the early portion of the evoked response, presumably concerned with initial input processes, may be more stable, or perhaps "rigid," whereas the later portion, presumably more concerned with analysis of information, may be more variable than normal.

We found no significant differences between manic-depressive, depressed patients and nonpatients of the same age and sex, with respect to SER variability. In contrast, SER variability during the first 100 msec was significantly less in a group of manic-depressed, manic, patients than in controls of the same age and sex.

It should be noted that ER variability would be increased by artifact such as muscle potentials. Consequently, when less variability is found in a disturbed group than in normals, it would be difficult to attribute this to greater artifact generation by the patients. It is also noteworthy that we have failed to demonstrate significant drug effects on our SER variability measures.

Recovery Functions

Recovery functions are usually measured by administering paired "conditioning" and "test" stimuli, the intervals separating these stimuli being varied in different averaging sequences. The basic idea of recovery determinations is that the initial stimulus alters central nervous system responsiveness, and that the time course of return to base line will be reflected in the changes in the response to the test stimulus (R2); the base-line response (R1) is measured when there is no conditioning stimulus. With full recovery, measurements of R2 and R1 are equal, giving an R2:R1 ratio of 1.0. In our earliest work on SER recovery functions, we found that the recovery curve for the initial negative–positive component (15 to 30 msec) was biphasic in normal subjects with interstimulus intervals to 200 msec (90). The first recovery phase occurred before 20 msec, with R2:R1 ratios reaching 1.0 in most normal subjects; the second phase of recovery occurred at about 100 msec, R2 being relatively decreased between the two phases. Our main finding was that, in the initial (20-msec) phase, recovery was less than normal in patients with schizophrenias, psychotic depressions, and personality disorders, but not in dysthymic neuroses. In patients with psychotic depressions, serial measurements showed that recovery normalized with clinical improvement caused by electroconvulsive therapy or drugs (91). This indicated that reduced recovery is not a fixed biologic characteristic, but rather a correlate of clinical state. Two later studies confirmed the finding of reduced SER amplitude recovery in psychiatric patients (92, 66); the second of these studies incorporated a number of methodologic improvements, including measurements of several SER peaks in addition to the initial ones. Reduced amplitude recovery in patients was found for all peaks, but latency recovery was more rapid in patients than in controls. This suggests that different processes may underlie amplitude and latency recovery. In a recent study, we also found more rapid latency recovery in both schizophrenic and manic-depressive, depressed patients (67).

Several workers have studied visual ER recovery with flash stimuli. Although our own results (72) were relatively negative, Speck et al. (74) and Floris et al. (93) found reduced visual ER amplitude recovery in schizophrenic patients. Ishikawa (94) found reduced visual ER amplitude recovery in schizophrenics only when hallucinations were present. Visual ER amplitude recovery in psychotic depressives appears normal (95).

Satterfield (96) measured auditory ER recovery in depressed patients and matched normals. Auditory ER recovery measurements were more widely distributed in the patients. Patients with extreme low recovery had a positive family history of depression more frequently than patients with high recovery.

In recent years, we have used a modification of the conventional SER recovery procedure. The interval between stimuli is kept constant at 10 msec, but the intensity of the conditioning stimulus is varied, whereas test stimulus intensity remains the same from one averaging sequence to the next. In addition to a single conditioning stimulus, a train of nine conditioning stimuli is applied (7). Also, the test design permits measurement of intensity–response functions and wave shape stability. Most of the positive results obtained in our studies with this modified recovery procedure were derived from single ER and variability measures, and have been presented under those headings. A significant finding, specifically contributed by the recovery procedure, was that test response amplitudes changed less with different conditioning stimulus intensities in nondepressed, more floridly psychotic schizophrenic patients than in the more depressed, less floridly psychotic ones (69). This evidence of "restricted dynamic range of responsiveness" was obtained particularly in male schizophrenic patients.

Long Latency and Slow Potentials

This group of potentials appears to be determined more by the psychologic meaning, or context, of stimuli than by their physical properties.

P3 (P300) is a positive wave seen at latencies of 300 to 500 msec in auditory and visual ERs, particularly when the subject is not certain about the nature of the forthcoming stimulus (97). Roth and Cannon (98) reported that P3 can be demonstrated under passive attention conditions in normals, but apparently not in schizophrenics. A recent report by Levit et al. (99) indicates that the P3 wave, as recorded under active information processing conditions, is of lower amplitude in schizophrenics than in depressives or normals. The data indicated that conditions of uncertainty affect the P3 in normals more than in schizophrenics, and that shifts between visual and auditory stimuli increased P3 in normals and depressives, but reduced it in schizophrenics. Although drugs did not seem to affect P3 results, clinical remission of one patient was associated with normalized P3 waves.

The contingent negative variation (CNV) is a slow negative shift, generally measured in a reaction time situation; it occurs after the alerting signal, and before the signal to which response is required. It is reduced by distraction. When the response to the "imperative" signal takes place, CNV generally terminates, with a return to base line or an overswing toward positivity. Although there is little doubt that the CNV phenomenon is real, it is easily contaminated by a number of events, recordable from the same electrodes and with the same general appearance. The most important of these contaminants are probably the electrooculo-gram (EOG), which reflects eye movements and eye blinks, and the electrodermal response (GSR). The problems of artifact control render psychiatric studies of CNV difficult, but much data of interest have accumulated (100).

CNV appears to be of lower amplitude and to show greater effects of distraction in anxiety neuroses, process schizophrenia, and psychopathy (101–103). Small and Small (104) compared normals with manic-depressives and schizophrenics. These workers found that both the manic and depressed patients showed very little discrimination between recordings in which they were required to make a response and those in which this requirement was not imposed. In essence, patients with affective psychosis, on the average, appeared to give no indication of a potential associated with response contingency. Small and Small (104) found that schizophrenic patients gave more variable results; they tended to have smaller CNVs, and with some persistence of negativity after the motor response was made. McCallum (102) subdivided schizophrenics according to the presence or absence of Schneider's first-rank symptoms; CNVs in the Schneider-positive patients were smaller and showed greater effects of distraction than in normals and the other schizophrenic subgroup.

Timsit et al. (105), in their CNV studies with psychiatric patients, focused on the duration of negativity following response to the imperative stimulus. Or-dinarily, the negativity decreases precipitously at this time, but they found that it was prolonged in patients. The most prolonged durations of negativity were found in acute schizophrenic patients, but prolonged negativity occurred more frequently in "process" than in "residual" schizophrenics (106). Although Tim-sit-Berthier (106) found some distinctions between different kinds of psychoses, Dongier et al. (107) were unable to distinguish between mania, depression, schizo-phrenia, and paranoid states with relation to prolongation of negativity. In studies which carefully attempted to control for common artifacts, they confirmed the higher incidence of prolonged negativity in psychosis than in neurosis or normals. Abnormalities appeared to be greatest in acute cases, and to decrease with dura-tion of illness.

Kornhuber and Deecke (108) described a "readiness" potential consisting of negativity associated with the intention to perform and preceding a motor act. Timsit-Berthier (106) found that, with button pressing, this readiness potential occurred in only 23% of 80 psychotics, compared to 85% of controls, and 71% of neurotics. However, there was persistent negativity following the motor act in the majority of psychotics, and in very few controls or neurotics.

DISCUSSION

EEG Comparisons between Schizophrenic and Affective Psychoses

The main EEG findings reviewed here are listed in Tables 1 and 2 for schizo-phrenic and affective psychoses, respectively. The principal EEG differences

TABLE 1. *Summary of EEG findings in schizophrenia*

---

1. Abnormalities: Incidence ranges from 5 to 80%. Sample selection phenomenon?
2. "Process" cases: Hyperstable, hypernormal records
3. Lower photometrazol threshold in catatonics
4. Greater pentothal response (Goldman)
5. Sleep "activation"
   a. More B-mittens
   b. B-mittens mainly in "reactive" cases
   c. Fourteen and 6 positive spikes in suicidal, assaultive cases
6. Low sedation threshold in acute, high in chronic
7. Power spectrum and period analysis
   a. Greater alpha frequency spread
   b. Lower alpha frequency
   c. Less alpha activity
   d. More non-alpha activity
   e. "Poor" organization across leads
8. Amplitude analysis (time series)
   a. Low temporal variability (CV)
   b. Less drowsiness than normals
   c. Greater amplitude in females
   d. Deviant interhemispheric asymmetry

---

between the two groups of disorders are listed in Table 3. Unresolved methodologic issues prompt due caution, but it seems possible to state the following conclusions. (a) The waking EEGs of schizophrenics differ from normal in several quantitative characteristics. (b) Both waking and sleep EEG records of schizophrenics tend to differ with respect to degree of chronicity of the psychosis and whether the case is "process" or "reactive." (c) Within the affective psychoses, there is some tendency for the EEGs of manics to differ from those of depressives, with faster background frequencies, and higher frequency response to intermittent flash in the manics. (d) Generally, the EEG characteristics of manic-depressive, depressed patients tend to be more similar to those of normals of the same age than those of schizophrenics. (e) Reactions to single light flashes or trains of flashes tend to be greater than normal in depressive patients, and not in schizophrenics.

The evidence suggests that the two major groups of psychoses differ statistically in their EEG characteristics; the differences are obviously not of great magnitude. Furthermore, their meaning in terms of underlying mechanism is not

TABLE 2. *Summary of EEG findings in affective psychoses*

---

1. Abnormalities: Nonspecific and probably related to age
2. Alpha frequency faster in mania than in depression
3. Prolonged alpha blocking to flash in depression
4. More photic driving
5. Higher frequency photic driving in manics than depressives
6. B-mittens higher than normal, less than schizophrenics
7. Lower sedation threshold in psychotic than neurotic depressives
8. Power spectrum: More fast activity

TABLE 3. *Probable EEG differences between schizophrenic and affective psychoses*

1. More low-voltage, "choppy" records in schizophrenics
2. Longer alpha blocking to flash in depressives
3. More B-mittens in schizophrenics
4. Quantitative differences (frequency, amplitude, variability) from matched normals more prevalent in schizophrenics

obvious. Although they could reflect some essential differences from normal in the organization of brain function, particularly in the schizophrenias, it is also possible that the EEG differences are secondary to variations in general psychologic accompaniments of the psychoses. The waking EEG findings in the schizophrenias are suggestive of a heightened state of "arousal" or "hyperalertness," which may not be present at all, or to lesser degree, in the depressive psychoses. Another, and not entirely different, interpretation of similar nature would relate the EEG findings to general personality predispositions. The results of Saul et al. (109) suggest that high alpha EEGs are characteristic of individuals with a passive, dependent, receptive attitude toward other persons. One could speculate that such a personality pattern may occur with greater frequency in patients with affective psychoses than it does in schizophrenic disorders. Without regard to explanation, however, the EEG evidence does provide some support for the view that there are electrophysiologic differences between the major psychoses.

ER Comparisons between Schizophrenic and Affective Psychoses

The main positive evoked potential findings obtained in studies of schizophrenic and affective psychoses are shown in Tables 4 and 5, respectively. The relatively short list of findings in manic states probably reflects the fact that only small numbers of such patients have been studied. Comparing Tables 4 and 5, it will be seen that lower CNV amplitude and prolonged slow potential negativity have been found in all three groups of psychoses. Evoked potential deviations from normal that have been reported for both the schizophrenic and depressive psychoses include faster visual ER latency; reduced SER amplitude recovery; and faster SER latency recovery. Manics appear to differ from schizophrenics with respect to SER wave-shape variability in the first 100 msec, the manics having greater and the schizophrenics less than normal variability. The visual ER reducer tendency in schizophrenics contrasts with the "augmenter" tendency in bipolar depressives, discriminating these groups from normal in opposite directions. The following variables have been found to differentiate schizophrenics, but not depressives, from normal—lower auditory ER amplitude, shorter auditory ER latency, less visual ER afterrhythm, greater wave-shape variability after 100 msec, and reduced P3. Table 6 lists probable evoked potential differences between schizophrenic and affective psychoses.

It appears that some ER measurements may be generally deviant from normal

TABLE 4. *Evoked potential findings in schizophrenia*

---

1. SER amplitude
   a. Higher in chronic than in acute or latent
   b. Higher in nondepressed, floridly psychotic
2. Auditory ER
   a. Amplitude lower than normal
   b. Latency faster than normal
3. Visual ER
   a. Amplitude varies
   b. Latency faster
   c. Less after-rhythm
   d. Tend to be "reducers"
4. Waveshape variability
   a. Less in chronics before 100 msec (SER)
   b. Greater in chronics after 100 msec (all)
5. Reduced SER and visual ER amplitude recovery (visual ER recovery, less, particularly in hallucinated patients)
6. Faster SER latency recovery
7. Reduced P3, less effect of uncertainty
8. CNV
   a. Lower amplitude
   b. Prolonged negativity
9. Prolonged negativity and less "readiness" potential with motor responses

---

in all psychoses, and that others are more specifically deviant for one group. Clearly, conclusions about diagnostic specificity are at best tentative at this time, considering the paucity of studies on directly comparable clinical groups, and the fact that many of the findings require replication. One can say only that there are indications of at least some degree of diagnostic specificity in ER measurements.

Some guidance for future research is given by the findings showing significant ER differences between subgroups of patients within the same general diagnostic category, e.g., unipolar versus bipolar depressions, and depressed versus nondepressed schizophrenics. It seems probable that gross diagnostic grouping may be

TABLE 5. *Evoked potential findings in affective psychoses*

A. Depressives
   1. Bipolar are visual ER "augmenters," male unipolar are "reducers"
   2. Shorter visual ER latencies, more in unipolar
   3. Right visual ER > left visual ER before treatment
   4. Reduced SER amplitude recovery
   5. Faster SER latency recovery
   6. Less auditory ER recovery with positive family history
   7. Low CNV
   8. Prolonged slow potential negativity

B. Mania
   1. Greater than normal SER variability before 100 msec
   2. Low CNV
   3. Prolonged slow potential negativity

TABLE 6. *Probable evoked potential differences between schizophrenic and affective psychoses*

---

1. Auditory ER in schizophrenics
   a. Lower amplitude
   b. Shorter latency
2. Visual ER
   a. Less after-rhythm in schizophrenics
   b. Schizophrenics are "reducers," bipolar depressives are "augmenters"
3. Wave shape variability
   a. Before 100 msec—less than normal in schizophrenic, greater in mania
   b. After 100 msec—greater in schizophrenic
4. Reduced P3 in schizophrenic

---

a less appropriate clinical criterion for correlation with ER phenomena than the clinical factors upon which subgrouping is based. This, of course, imposes a demand for larger samples of patients who can be appropriately subdivided according to various clinical criteria.

OVERVIEW

Most of the material reviewed in this chapter deals with the validity of electrophysiologic indicators for distinguishing between clinical groups. It should be made explicit that the validity results to be expected from cross-sectional group comparisons are limited by the reliability, or stability, of the measures. Available data indicate that, given relatively uniform recording conditions, both EEG and ER measures are quite stable over time (7,57,110). Although variability is not inconsequential, particularly in EEG, the reliability is sufficiently great to have prompted genetic studies involving comparisons of similarity between monozygotic and dizygotic twins. These twin studies have provided evidence favoring significant genetic determination of both EEG and ER characteristics (111–113). For example, Dustman and Beck (112) found a median correlation of 0.88 between wave shapes of monozygotic twins, whereas the median was only 0.37 for dizygotic twins.

Genetic determination may impose a further limitation on psychiatric electrophysiologic research, if such determination is not related to psychopathology. Perhaps more than one-half of individual differences in EEG and ER characteristics appears to be genetically determined, and a substantial portion of the remaining variability may be due to uncontrolled factors, i.e., "noise." This suggests at least three possibilities. (a) If illness affects only that portion of the variance left after the genetic factors and "noise" are accounted for, differences between clinical groups are likely to be small and distributions of measurements will overlap considerably. (b) If genetic determinants of electrophysiology are linked to factors leading to expression of illness, differences could be large. (c) If illness produces effects of such magnitude that they override the electrophysiologic expression of genetic determinants, differences would also be large. The nature of the majority of the results reviewed here suggests that they may reflect the first possibility, i.e., that illness can affect only a relatively small portion of the total variance. Thus, in general, expectations from cross-sectional clinical group comparisons should probably be modest. Implications of the second and third possibilities are that significant effects obtained in group comparisons, whether weak or strong, should be further explored in longitudinal studies of the same patients in health and in illness. Longitudinal studies would permit distinction between temporary and permanent differences. Permanent differences, which could be genetically determined, may provide evidence of electrophysiologic expression of genetic factors involved in illness. These could be further elucidated by studying identical twins, concordant and discordant for illness.

It has been stated earlier that psychiatric electrophysiology is still in an early stage of development. Although computer methods have made possible the handling of large quantities of data, the potentialities of these methods have so far been realized to a minimal extent. This is most clear in relation to the dimension of spatial distribution. Sophisticated quantitative analyses of EEG and ER data have been conducted on recordings from leads placed over the entire head in very few studies. One of these is the EEG study of Giannitrapani and Kayton (58), but they examined only 10 patients, five of whom were on drugs. Adequate investigation of clinical psychiatric correlates of differences in topographic distribution in EEG and ER events lies in the future. The issue of interhemispheric relationships and differences is a special aspect of such topographic investigation. A further set of problems arises from the largely unexplored area of relating EEG and ER events. There is some indication that such relationships may have functional behavioral significance (114). A major technical problem to be solved in studies of spatial distribution and of interrelationships between different electrical events, is to devise adequate methods for quantifying topographic and relationship data.

One may look forward with some confidence to future development and application of increasingly sophisticated and adequate methods of electrophysiologic analysis. The really crucial determinants of success or failure in psychiatric electrophysiologic research will probably lie in the clinical area. What dimensions of clinical phenomena are appropriate criteria for correlation with EEG and ER events? The evidence that subtyping yields more significant relationships with EEG and ER measurements than gross diagnostic category alone is encouraging. However, our current modes of clinical conceptualization may need considerable change before they parallel neurophysiologic dimensions. It is possible that studies in this field may be of some value in fostering development of new clinical concepts.

The fact that many statistically significant electrophysiologic differences between patients and normals have been found, and that some even suggest diagnostic specificity, seems encouraging from the perspective of the embryonic state of the field. Continued efforts appear justified, although expectations of very rapid progress would seem to be unrealistic.

SUMMARY

EEG and evoked potential (ER) findings in schizophrenic and affective psychoses were selectively reviewed. Both groups of psychoses appear to differ from normal in a number of EEG and ER characteristics; however, diagnostic specificity was suggested by relatively few findings. More encouraging results with respect to specificity have been obtained by subtyping the psychotic groups, e.g., process versus reactive schizophrenic, unipolar versus bipolar depression. Methodologic issues and directions for future research were discussed.

ACKNOWLEDGMENTS

Professional collaborators include Drs. M. Amadeo, D. A. Overton, and J. J. Straumanis, Jr. Research of the author supported (in part) by grant MH12507 from the U.S. Public Health Service.

REFERENCES

1. Caton, R. (1875): The electric currents of the brain. *Br. Med. J.,* 2:278.
2. Berger, H. (1929): Uber das elektrenkephalogramm des Menschen. *Arch. Psychiatr.,* 87:527–570.
3. Dawson, G. D. (1947): Cerebral responses to electrical stimulation of peripheral nerve in man. *J. Neurol. Neurosurg. Psychiatry,* 10:134–140.
4. Liberson, W. T. (1944): Functional electroencephalography in mental disorders. *Dis. Nerv. Syst.,* 5:357–364.
5. Hill, D., and Parr, G. (1963): *Electroencephalography: A Symposium on Its Various Aspects.* Macmillan, New York.
6. Regan, D. (1972): *Evoked Potentials in Psychology, Sensory Physiology and Clinical Medicine.* Chapman and Hall, London.
7. Shagass, C. (1972): *Evoked Brain Potentials in Psychiatry.* Plenum, New York.
8. Shagass, C., Overton, D. A., and Straumanis, J. J. (1972): Sex differences in somatosensory evoked responses related to psychiatric illness. *Biol. Psychiatry,* 5:295–309.
9. Hall, R. A., Rappaport, M., Hopkins, H. K., and Griffin, R. (1973): Tobacco and evoked potential. *Science,* 180:212–214.
10. Murphree, H. B. (1974): Electroencephalographic effects of caffeine, nicotine, tobacco smoking, and alcohol. In: *Psychotropic Drugs and the Human EEG. Modern Problems of Pharmacopsychiatry, Vol. 8,* edited by T. M. Itil, pp. 22–36. Karger, Basel.
11. Ulett, G. A., Heusler, A. F., and Word, T. J. (1965): The effect of psychotropic drugs on the EEG of the chronic psychotic patient. In: *Applications of Electroencephalography to Psychiatry,* edited by W. P. Wilson, pp. 241–257. Duke Univ. Press, Durham, North Carolina.
12. Wilson, W. P., editor (1965): *Applications of Electroencephalography to Psychiatry.* Duke Univ. Press, Durham, North Carolina.
13. Strauss, H. (1955): Intracranial neoplasms masked as depressions and diagnosed with the aid of electroencephalography. *J. Nerv. Ment. Dis.,* 122:185–189.
14. Weil, A. A. (1955): Depressive reactions associated with temporal lobe-uncinate seizures. *J. Nerv. Ment. Dis.,* 121:505–510.
15. Williams, D. (1954): The electroencephalogram in affective disorders. *Proc. Soc. Med.,* 47: 779–782.
16. Davis, P. A., and Davis, H. (1939): Electroencephalograms of psychotic patients. *Am. J. Psychiatry,* 95:1007–1025.
17. Davis, P. A. (1941): Electroencephalograms of manic-depressive patients. *Am. J. Psychiatry,* 98:430–433.
18. Davis, P. A. (1942): A comparative study of the EEGs of schizophrenic and manic-depressive patients. *Am. J. Psychiatry,* 99:210–217.

19. Davis, P. A. (1940): Evaluation of the electroencephalogram of schizophrenic patients. *Am. J. Psychiatry,* 96:851–860.
20. Lemere, F. (1941): Cortical energy production in psychoses. *Psychosom. Med.,* 3:152–156.
21. Greenblatt, M., Healey, M., and Jones, G. A. (1944): Age and electroencephalographic abnormality in psychiatric patients. A study of 1593 cases. *Am. J. Psychiatry,* 101:82–90.
22. Finley, K. H. (1944): On the occurrence of rapid frequency potential changes in the human electroencephalogram. *Am. J. Psychiatry,* 101:194–200.
23. Maggs, R., and Turton, E. C. (1956): Some EEG findings in old age and their relationship to affective disorder. *Br. J. Psychiatry,* 102:812–818.
24. Shagass, C. (1969): Neurophysiological studies. In: *The Schizophrenic Syndrome,* edited by L. Bellak and L. Loeb, pp. 172–204. Grune & Stratton, New York.
25. Heath, R. G. (1966): Schizophrenia: Biochemical and physiologic aberrations. *Int. J. Neuropsychiatry,* 2:597–610.
26. Colony, H. S., and Willis, S. E. (1956): Electroencephalographic studies of 1,000 schizophrenic patients. *Am. J. Psychiatry,* 113:163–169.
27. Gibbs, F. A., and Gibbs, E. L. (1963): The mitten pattern: An electroencephalographic abnormality correlating with psychosis. *J. Neuropsychiatry,* 5:6–13.
28. Igert, C., and Lairy, G. C. (1962): Prognostic value of the EEG in the course of the development of schizophrenics. *Electroencephalogr. Clin. Neurophysiol.,* 14:183–190.
29. Itil, T. M. (1968): Electroencephalography and pharmacopsychiatry. In: *Clinical Psychopharmacology. Modern Problems in Pharmacopsychiatry, Vol. 1,* edited by F. A. Freyhan, N. Petrilowitsch, and P. Pichot. pp. 163–194. Karger, Basel.
30. Wilson, W. P., and Wilson, N. J. (1961): Observations on the duration of the photically elicited arousal responses in depressive psychoses. *J. Nerv. Ment. Dis.,* 133:438–440.
31. d'Elia, G., Laurell, B., and Perris, C. (1974): EEG photically elicited alpha blocking responses in depressive patients before and after convulsive therapy. *Acta Psychiatr. Scand.*
32. Hein, P. L., Green, R. L., and Wilson, W. P. (1962): Latency and duration of photically elicited arousal responses in the electroencephalograms of patients with chronic regressive schizophrenia. *J. Nerv. Ment. Dis.,* 135:361–364.
33. Hurst, L. A., Mundy-Castle, A. C., and Beerstecher, D. M. (1954): The electroencephalogram in manic-depressive psychosis. *Br. J. Psychiatry,* 100:220–240.
34. Shagass, C. (1955): Differentiation between anxiety and depression by the photically activated electroencephalogram. *Am. J. Psychiatry,* 112:41–46.
35. Gastaut, H. (1950): Combined photic and metrazol activation of the brain. *Electroencephalogr. Clin. Neurophysiol.,* 2:249–261.
36. Lieberman, D. M., Hoenig, J., and Hacker, M. (1954): The metrazol-flicker threshold in neuropsychiatric patients. *Electroencephalogr. Clin. Neurophysiol.,* 6:9–18.
37. Goldman, D. (1959): Specific electroencephalographic changes with pentothal activation in psychotic states. *Electroencephalogr. Clin. Neurophysiol.,* 11:657–667.
38. Sila, B., Mowrer, M., Ulett, G., and Johnson, M. (1962): The differentiation of psychiatric patients by EEG changes after sodium pentothal. In: *Recent Advances in Biological Psychiatry, Vol. IV,* edited by J. Wortis, pp. 191-203. Plenum, New York.
39. Struve, F. A., and Becka, D. R. (1968): The relative incidence of the B-mitten EEG pattern in process and reactive schizophrenia. *Electroencephalogr. Clin. Neurophysiol.,* 24:80–82.
40. Struve, F. A., Becka, D. R., and Klein, D. F. (1972): B-mitten EEG pattern and process and reactive schizophrenia. *Arch. Gen. Psychiatry,* 26:189–192.
41. Gibbs, E. L., and Gibbs, F. A. (1951): Electroencephalographic evidence of thalamic and hypothalamic epilepsy. *Neurology,* 1:136–144.
42. Niedermeyer, E., and Knott, J. R. (1961): Uber die Bedeutung der 14 and 6/sec positiven Spitzen im EEG. *Arch. Psychiatr. Nervenkr.,* 202:266–280.
43. Schmidt, H. O., and Andrews, R. C. (1961): Notes on the 6- and 14- positive spikes in the EEG. *Psychol. Rep.,* 9:399–400.
44. Small, J. G., and Small, I. F. (1964): Fourteen- and six-per-second positive spikes. *Arch. Gen. Psychiatr.,* 11:645–650.
45. Struve, F. A., Klein, D. F., and Saraf, K. R. (1972): Electroencephalographic correlates of suicide ideation and attempts. *Arch. Gen. Psychiatry,* 27:363–365.
46. Greenberg, I. M., and Pollack, M. (1966): Clinical correlates of 14- and 6-per-second positive spiking in schizophrenic patients. *Electroencephalogr. Clin. Neurophysiol.,* 20:197–200.

47. Shagass, C. (1954): The sedation threshold: A method for estimating tension in psychiatric patients. *Electroencephalogr. Clin. Neurophysiol.,* 6:221–233.
48. Shagass, C. (1959): A neurophysiological study of schizophrenia. *Report of 2nd International Congress for Psychiatry, Vol. 2,* pp. 248–254.
49. Perez-Reyes, M. (1972): Differences in sedative susceptibility between types of depression: Clinical and neurophysiological significance. In: *Recent Advances in the Psychobiology of the Depressive Illnesses,* edited by T. A. Williams, M. M. Katz, and J. A. Shields, pp. 119–130. U.S. Government Printing Office, Washington, D.C.
50. Gibbs, F. A. (1939): Cortical frequency spectra of schizophrenic, epileptic, and normal individuals. *Trans. Am. Neurol. Assoc.,* 65:141–144.
51. Gibbs, F. A. (1940): Spectra from eight cortical areas of normal adults, epileptics, parents of epileptic and schizophrenic patients. *Trans. Am. Neurol. Assoc.,* 66:211–212.
52. Shagass, C., Straumanis, J. J., and Overton, D. A. (1974): Psychiatric correlates of some quantitative EEG variables. *Proc. 1st World Congress of Biological Psychiatry,* Buenos Aires, Argentina.
53. Kennard, M. A., and Schwartzman, A. E. (1957): A longitudinal study of electroencephalographic frequency patterns in mental hospital patients and normal controls. *Electroencephalogr. Clin. Neurophysiol.,* 9:263–274.
54. Fink, M., Itil, T., and Clyde, D. (1966): The classification of psychoses by quantitative EEG measures. In: *Recent Advances in Biological Psychiatry, Vol. VIII,* edited by J. Wortis, pp. 305–312. Plenum, New York.
55. Bruck, M. A. (1964): Synchrony and voltage in the EEG of schizophrenics. *Arch. Gen. Psychiatry,* 10:454–468.
56. Itil, T. M., Saletu, B., and Davis, S. (1972): EEG findings in chronic schizophrenics based on digital computer period analysis and analog power spectra. *Biol. Psychiatry,* 5:1–13.
57. Itil, T. M., Saletu, B., Davis, S., and Allen, M. (1974): Stability studies in schizophrenics and normals using computer-analyzed EEG. *Biol. Psychiatry,* 8:321–335.
58. Giannitrapani, D., and Kayton, L. (1974): Schizophrenia and EEG spectral analysis. *Electroencephalogr. Clin. Neurophysiol.,* 36:377–386.
59. Goldstein, L., Murphree, H. B., Sugerman, A. A., Pfeiffer, C. C., and Jenney, E. H. (1963): Quantitative electroencephalographic analysis of naturally occurring (schizophrenic) and drug-induced psychotic states in human males. *Clin. Pharmacol. Ther.,* 4:10–21.
60. Marjerrison, G., Krause, A. E., and Keogh, R. P. (1968): Variability of the EEG in schizophrenia: Quantitative analysis with a modulus voltage integrator. *Electroencephalogr. Clin. Neurophysiol.,* 24:35–41.
61. Lifshitz, K., and Gradijan, J. (1972): Relationships between measures of the coefficient of variation of the mean absolute EEG voltage and spectral intensities in schizophrenic and control subjects. *Biol. Psychiatry,* 5:149–163.
62. Goldstein, L., Sugerman, A. A., Marjerrison, G., and Stoltzfus, N. (1973): Interhemispheric EEG relationships in mental patients and in normal subjects under modified behavioral states. *Annual Mtg. of Society of Biological Psychiatry,* Montreal, Canada.
63. Serafetinides, E. A. (1972): Laterality and voltage in the EEG of psychiatric patients. *Dis. Nerv. Syst.,* 33:622–623.
64. d'Elia, G., and Perris, C. (1973): Cerebral functional dominance and depression. *Acta Psychiat. Scand.,* 49:191–197.
65. Shagass, C., and Schwartz, M. (1963): Psychiatric disorder and deviant cerebral responsiveness. In: *Recent Advances in Biological Psychiatry, Vol. V.,* edited by J. Wortis, pp. 321–330. Plenum, New York.
66. Shagass, C. (1968): Averaged somatosensory evoked responses in various psychiatric disorders. In: *Recent Advances in Biological Psychiatry, Vol. X,* edited by J. Wortis, pp. 205–219. Plenum, New York.
67. Shagass, C., Overton, D. A., and Straumanis, J. J. (1974): Evoked potential studies in schizophrenia. In: *Biological Mechanisms of Schizophrenia and Schizophrenia-like Psychoses,* edited by H. Mitsuda and T. Fukuda, pp. 214–234. Igaku-Shoin, Tokyo.
68. Shagass, C., Soskis, D. A., Straumanis, J. J., and Overton, D. A. (1974): Symptom patterns related to somatosensory evoked response differences within a schizophrenic population. *Biol. Psychiatry,* 9:25–43.
69. Cohen, R. (1973): The influence of task-irrelevant stimulus variations on the reliability of

auditory evoked responses in schizophrenia. In: *Human Neurophysiology, Psychology, Psychiatry: Average Evoked Responses and Their Conditioning in Normal Subjects and Psychiatric Patients,* edited by A. Fessard and G. Lelord, pp. 373–388. Inserm, Paris.

70. Jones, R. T., and Callaway, E. (1970): Auditory evoked responses in schizophrenia. A reassessment. *Biol. Psychiatry,* 2:291.

71. Saletu, B., Itil, T. M., and Saletu, M. (1971): Auditory evoked response, EEG, and thought process in schizophrenics. *Am. J. Psychiatry,* 128:336–344.

72. Shagass, C., and Schwartz, M. (1965): Visual cerebral evoked response characteristics in a psychiatric population. *Am. J. Psychiatry,* 121:979–987.

73. Straumanis, J. J., Shagass, C., and Schwartz, M. (1965): Visually evoked cerebral response changes associated with chronic brain syndrome and aging. *J. Gerontol.,* 20:498–506.

74. Speck, L. G., Dim, B., and Mercer, M. (1966): Visual evoked responses of psychiatric patients. *Arch. Gen. Psychiatry,* 15:59–63.

75. Rappaport, M., Hopkins, H. K., Hall, K., and Belleza, T. (1973): Averaged visual evoked potential differences between normal and schizophrenic subjects: Maximum amplitude, frequency of peaks, and phenothiazine effects. *Proc. Am. Psychol. Assoc.,* 8:1041–1042.

76. Landau, S. G., Buchsbaum, M. S., Carpenter, W., Strauss, J., and Sacks, M. (1975): Schizophrenia and stimulus intensity control. *Arch. Gen. Psychiatry (in press).*

77. Rodin, E., Grisell, J., and Gottlieb, J. (1968): Some electrographic differences between chronic schizophrenic patients and normal subjects. In: *Recent Advances in Biological Psychiatry,* edited by J. Wortis, pp. 194–204. Plenum, New York.

78. Buchsbaum, M., and Silverman, J. (1968): Stimulus intensity control and the cortical evoked response. *Psychosom. Med.,* 30:12–22.

79. Petrie, A. (1967): *Individuality in Pain and Suffering.* Univ. of Chicago Press, Chicago, Illinois.

80. Soskis, D. A., and Shagass, C. (1974): Evoked potential tests of augmenting-reducing. *Psychophysiology,* 11:175–190.

81. Buchsbaum, M., Goodwin, F., Murphy, D., and Borge, G. (1971): AER in affective disorders. *Am. J. Psychiatry,* 128:51–57.

82. Buchsbaum, M., Landau, S., Murphy, D., and Goodwin, F. (1973): Average evoked response in bipolar and unipolar affective disorders: Relationship to sex, age of onset, and monoamine oxidase. *Biol. Psychiatry,* 7:199–212.

83. Inderbitzin, L. B., Buchsbaum, M., and Silverman, J. (1970): EEG-averaged evoked response and perceptual variability in schizophrenics. *Arch. Gen. Psychiatry,* 23:438–444.

84. Perris, C. (1974, in press): Averaged evoked responses (AER) in patients with affective disorders. A pilot study of possible hemispheric differences in depressed patients. *Acta Psychiatr. Scand.*

85. Perris, C., and d'Elia, G. (1974): Electroencephalographic hemispheric differences and affective disorders. *Proc. 1st World Congress of Biological Psychiatry, Buenos Aires, Argentina.*

86. Callaway, E., Jones, R. T., and Layne, R. S. (1965): Evoked responses and segmental set of schizophrenia. *Arch. Gen. Psychiatry,* 12:83–89.

87. Lifshitz, K. (1969): An examination of evoked potentials as indicators of information processing in normal and schizophrenic subjects. In: *Average Evoked Potentials: Methods, Results and Evaluations,* edited by E. Donchin and D. B. Lindsley, pp. 318–319 and 357–362. National Aeronautics and Space Administration, Washington, D.C.

88. Malerstein, A. J., and Callaway, E. (1969): Two-tone average evoked response in Korsakoff patients. *J. Psychiatr. Res.,* 6:253–260.

89. Shagass, C. (1973): Evoked response studies of central excitability in psychiatric disorders. In: *Human Neurophysiology, Psychology, Psychiatry: Average Evoked Responses and Their Conditioning in Normal Subjects and Psychiatric Patients,* edited by A. Fessard and G. Lelord, pp. 223–252. Inserm, Paris.

90. Shagass, C., and Schwartz, M. (1961): Reactivity cycle of somatosensory cortex in humans with and without psychiatric disorder. *Science,* 134:1757–1759.

91. Shagass, C., and Schwartz, M. (1962): Cerebral cortical reactivity in psychotic depressions. *Arch. Gen. Psychiatr.,* 6:235–242.

92. Shagass, C., and Schwartz, M. (1963): Psychiatric correlates of evoked cerebral cortical potentials. *Am. J. Psychiatry,* 119:1055–1061.

93. Floris, V., Morocutti, C., Amabile, G., Bernardi, G., and Rizzo, P. A. (1968): Recovery cycle of visual evoked potentials in normal, schizophrenic and neurotic patients. In: *Computers and Electronic Devices in Psychiatry,* edited by N. S. Kline and E. Laska, pp. 194–205. Grune & Stratton, New York.

94. Ishikawa, K. (1968): Studies on the visual evoked responses to paired light flashes in schizophrenics. *Kurume Med. J.,* 15:153–167.
95. Floris, V., Morocutti, C., Amabile, G., Bernardi, G., and Rizzo, P. A. (1969): Cerebral reactivity in psychiatric and epileptic patients. *Electroencephalogr. Clin. Neurophysiol.,* 27:680.
96. Satterfield, J. H. (1972): Auditory evoked cortical response studies in depressed patients and normal control subjects. In: *Recent Advances in the Psychobiology of the Depressive Illnesses,* edited by T. A. Williams, M. M. Katz, and J. A. Shield, pp. 87–98. U.S. Government Printing Office, Washington, D.C.
97. Sutton, S., Braren, M., and Zubin, J. (1965): Evoked-potential correlates of stimulus uncertainty. *Science,* 150:1187–1188.
98. Roth, W. T., and Cannon, E. H. (1972): Some features of the auditory evoked response in schizophrenics. *Arch. Gen. Psychiatry,* 27:466–471.
99. Levit, A. L., Sutton, S., and Zubin, J. (1973): Evoked potential correlates of information processing in psychiatric patients. *Psychol. Med.,* 3:487–494.
100. McCallum, W. C., and Knott, J. R. editors (1973): Event-related slow potentials of the brain. *Electroencephalogr. Clin. Neurophysiol.,* Suppl. 33.
101. McCallum, W. C., and Walter, W. G. (1968): The effects of attention and distraction on the contingent negative variation in normal and neurotic subjects. *Electroencephalogr. Clin. Neurophysiol.,* 25:319–329.
102. McCallum, W. C. (1973): Some psychological, psychiatric and neurologic aspects of the CNV. In: *Human Neurophysiology, Psychology, Psychiatry: Average Evoked Responses and Their Conditioning in Normal Subjects and Psychiatric Patients,* edited by A. Fessard and G. Lelord, pp. 295–324. Inserm, Paris.
103. McCallum, W. C. (1973): The CNV and conditionability in psychopaths. *Electroencephalogr. Clin. Neurophysiol.,* Suppl. 33:337–343.
104. Small, J. G., and Small, I. F. (1971): Contingent negative variation (CNV) correlations with psychiatric diagnosis. *Arch. Gen. Psychiatry,* 25:550–554.
105. Timsit, M., Koninckx, N., Dargent, J., Fontaine, O., and Dongier, M. (1970): Variations contingentes negatives en psychiatrie. *Electroencephalogr. Clin. Neurophysiol.,* 28:41–47.
106. Timsit-Berthier, M. (1973): CNV, slow potentials and motor potential studies in normal subjects and psychiatric patients. In: *Human Neurophysiology, Psychology, Psychiatry: Average Evoked Responses and Their Conditioning in Normal Subjects and Psychiatric Patients,* edited by A. Fessard and G. Lelord, pp. 327–366. Inserm, Paris.
107. Dongier, M., Dubrovsky, B., and Garcia-Rill, E. (1974): Slow cerebral potentials in psychiatry. *Can. Psychiatr. Assoc. J.,* 19:177–183.
108. Kornhuber, H. H., and Deecke, L. (1965): Cerebral potential changes in voluntary and passive movements in man: Readiness potential and reafferent potential. *Eur. J. Physiol.,* 284:1–17.
109. Saul, L. J., Davis, H., and Davis, P. A. (1949): Psychologic correlations with the electroencephalogram. *Psychosom. Med.,* 11:361–376.
110. Shagass, C. (1972): Electrical activity of the brain. In: *Handbook of Psychophysiology,* edited by N. S. Greenfield and R. Sternbach, pp. 262–328. Holt, New York.
111. Lennox, W. G., Gibbs, F. A., and Gibbs, E. L. (1942): Twins, brain waves and epilepsy. *Arch. Neurol. Psychiatry,* 47:702–706.
112. Dustman, R. E., and Beck, E. C. (1965): The visually evoked potential in twins. *Electroencephalogr. Clin. Neurophysiol.,* 19:570–575.
113. Buchsbaum, M. S. (1974): Average evoked response and stimulus intensity in identical and fraternal twins. *Physiol. Psychol.,* 2:365–370.
114. Häseth, K., Shagass, C., and Straumanis, J. J. (1969): Perceptual and personality correlates of EEG and evoked response measures. *Biol. Psychiatry,* 1:49–60.

Biology of the Major Psychoses, edited by D. X. Freedman, Res. Publ. Assoc. Res. Nerv. Ment. Dis., Vol. 54. Raven Press, New York   1975.

Average Evoked Response Augmenting/Reducing in Schizophrenia and Affective Disorders

Monte Buchsbaum

Division of Clinical and Behavioral Research, National Institute of Mental Health, Bethesda, Maryland 20014

Average evoked response (AER) techniques provide a kind of mathematical depth electrode which in humans has the potential of getting closer to measuring the specific function of a specific brain area noninvasively than any other current biochemical or physiologic method. Shagass has pointed out in his comprehensive review that there are several replicated AER differences between normal individuals and psychotic patients, and that the major challenge that now confronts us is to elucidate the neurobiology underlying these differences. One approach may be to take advantage of the saltatory strides that have been made in the fields of neuropharmacology and neurochemistry by my colleagues at the National Institute of Mental Health and elsewhere. Neurochemical and evoked response (ER) techniques have two complementary defects in their approaches to the problem of human psychiatric dysfunction. Although many basic biochemical mechanisms are understood, measurement in intact human subjects is often indirect, depending on metabolic products and reflecting slow responses of the whole brain (and often of the body as well). The ER is a more empirical measure for which the underlying neurophysiology is not fully understood. Nevertheless, it has the advantage of affording examination of the response of specific brain areas to brief psychologic events.

Two areas of contact between human electrophysiology, discussed by Shagass, and neurochemical studies seem especially promising. First, AER stability studies are gaining importance because of experimental interest in stable (stereotypical) behavior in animals treated with amphetamine or dopamine receptor blockers. Does this stereotyped behavior extend to the perceptual system, causing a more similar, less variable neuroelectric response from stimulus to stimulus? Callaway (1) was the first to recognize the importance of studying AER stability in schizophrenics, but a truly satisfactory mathematical resolution of the problem of separating response variability from background noise has been elusive. Recent developments in signal-processing mathematics (2) are promising, but their empirical application is fraught with problems (3).

The second strategy for connecting human AER and neurochemical techniques involves exploitation of the wide individual differences seen among both normal and psychiatric patients with both types of measures.

INDIVIDUAL DIFFERENCES AND THE AER

One of the first features observed in connection with human evoked responses was their extreme variability from person to person—not just in waveform and amplitude, but also in their systematic changes with the physical parameters of the stimulus. For this reason, conventional neurophysiology initially tended to minimize the value of the technique and credit the variations to artifacts or to poor stimulus control. But those of us studying human behavior in health and disease were mindful of the remarkable differences between people in their responses to similar environmental stimuli, and we were intrigued.

An example of such an individual difference is shown in Fig. 1. On the left is an individual whose visual AER increases in amplitude with increasing stimulus intensity. On the right are AERs from an individual whose AER *decreases* in amplitude with increasing stimulus intensity—for the P100–N140 component. We have labeled the people with increasing amplitude "augmenters" and the people with decreasing amplitude "reducers," terms borrowed from Petrie (4). Based on research using kinesthetic figural aftereffects, Petrie hypothesized two different ways of accepting sensory input—augmenting, the tendency to increase the perceived intensity of stimuli, and reducing, the tendency to decrease it. Petrie

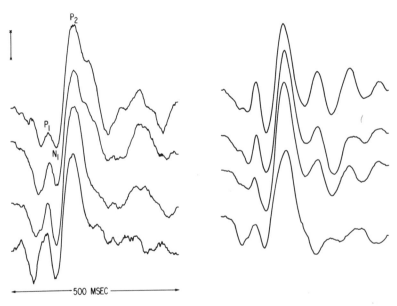

FIG. 1. Typical adult average evoked responses (AERs) to four intensities of light flashes, presented in random order. The response to the dimmest light is at the top and the brightest at the bottom. Responses are recorded vertex (C_z) to right ear (drawn positive up with 2-μV calibration in upper left). An augmenter is shown on the left with amplitude of component **P1–N1** increasing with increasing intensity. In contrast, the reducer on the right shows the reverse—a systematic *decrease* in amplitude with increasing stimulus intensity. Component **N1–P2** does not show such striking individual differences.

found reducers to be pain-tolerant (5); reports from other investigators have supported this hypothesis (6,7). Methodologic problems with Petrie's kinesthetic figural aftereffect procedure (8) for measuring augmenting/reducing have led us and even recently Petrie herself (9) to use a neurophysiologic measure of sensory response to stimuli at different intensities. AER techniques have been used by a number of authors to measure augmenting/reducing in man (10–15) and in animals (16).

In awake adults, visual AERs to light flashes generally increase in amplitude with increasing stimulus intensity up to an intermediate level, then level off or even decrease; individual differences are quite prominent (17–22). Similarly, sinusoidal modulation demonstrates that individual differences in amplitude/intensity relationships are prominent (23,24) and that cortical response may decrease as the intensity of stimulation increases (25–27).

Decreases in amplitude with increasing intensity cannot be attributed to poor stimulus control because electroretinographic changes recorded simultaneously do not show such a pattern (18). Peripheral factors such as pupillary diameter do not appear to explain these decreases because the vertex AER is uninfluenced by pupillary diameter in humans (28,29), visual AER augmenting/reducing is unchanged by pilocarpine (13), and in animals such as the pigeon (30) no AER changes with pupillary diameter were observed. The finding of AER reducing from vertex but not occipital leads (12) and the high correlation between amplitude/intensity slopes obtained with randomized and blocked presentation of stimulus intensities (31) also tends to mitigate against peripheral factors as being solely responsible. Single-unit recordings from the lateral geniculate body in cats showed the decrease in amplitude with increasing stimulus intensity even under the rigid stimulus control of Flaxedil administered to cats wearing corneal contact lenses with artificial pupils (32).

GENETIC FACTORS

Both augmenting and reducing have been found to be relatively stable individual traits (12,13,33). This tendency to augment or reduce is partly set genetically (34) as has also been found to be true of waveform shape in animals (35) and in man (36–39). Figure 2 shows visual AERs for two sets of normal Mz twins; both members of the twin pair on the left are augmenters; the pair on the right are reducers. Heritability estimates for the AER amplitude/intensity slope on a group of 30 monozygotic (Mz) and 30 dizygotic (Dz) normal adult twins ranged from 0.52 for the P100–N140 component measured visually to 0.68 for certain quantitative measures of the same component. Initially, it was the heritability of the AER waveform and the amplitude/intensity gradient that encouraged our clinical studies of schizophrenia. Figure 3 shows AERs from two adult Mz twins concordant for schizophrenia who were studied at the National Institute of Mental Health (40, pair 24). Both twins are strong reducers for the P100–N140 component.

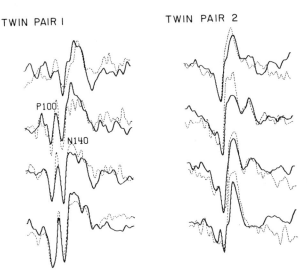

FIG. 2. Visual AERs in two pairs of Mz twins collected as in Fig. 1. For each pair, the AER is shown as a solid line for one twin and as a dotted line for the co-twin. Both members of twin pair 1 are augmenters for the **P100** (P1)–**N140** (N1) component, showing a marked increase with increasing stimulus intensity. In pair 2, the same component shows a marked decline in amplitude with increasing intensity especially between the third and fourth intensities.

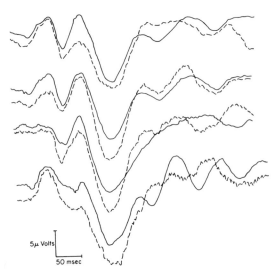

FIG. 3. Visual AERs for four intensities of light in a pair of Mz twins concordant for schizophrenia. The solid line indicates AER for one twin and the dotted line the curve for the other twin. AERs collected at higher intensity levels than Fig. 1 and 2 and presented negative up in this illustration. Note that the P100–N140 component shows marked reducing.

TOLERANCE FOR PAIN

Is the tendency to reduce AER amplitude associated with adaptive protective mechanisms for withstanding sensory overload and pain? Two current studies suggest that AER reducers are indeed pain- and noise-tolerant. Individual differences in pain response were studied by means of brief electrical stimuli (constant current 1-msec square waves) administered to the left forearm using the Tursky (41) electrode.

Stimuli of four different intensities (2,9,16, and 23 mA) were delivered 1 sec apart with 64 randomized presentations of each intensity; AERs to these stimuli were collected. Subjective pain ratings were also obtained in a separate run in which stimuli (1 to 31 mA in 1-mA steps) were presented three times each in random sequence. Subjects rated each stimulus on a four-point scale (1 = just noticeable; 2 = distinct; 3 = unpleasant; and 4 = painful) using a special keyboard. The EEG was recorded from vertex (C_z-right ear), and AER amplitude was measured using Shagass' technique for mean deviation (42) over two time bands centered on P100 (76 to 112 msec) and P200 (168 to 248 msec).

This technique generally has yielded results similar to those obtained with peak-to-trough measurments. Shock-response rating data were analyzed according to simple nonparametric analogues of signal-detection parameters C_x and d'. As subjects differed widely in the shape, symmetry, and size of the dispersion of their judgments of the four categories, the usual mathematical assumptions underlying signal-detection analysis did not appear to be well met. A measure of response criterion (C_x) was obtained for the distinct/unpleasant categories by locating the stimulus strength for which the least overlap between the categories occurred. A measure of sensitivity (d') was the percent of total responses in error according to the above criterion. Mean ratings for the 6- to 12, 13- to 19, and

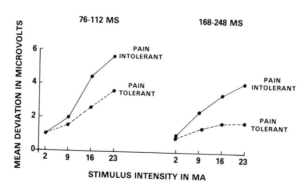

FIG. 4. Mean somatosensory AER amplitude for four intensities of electric shock for the 76- to 112-msec and 168- to 248-msec time bands (generally equivalent to P100 and P200). Subjects were divided into pain-tolerant and -intolerant groups on the basis of their subjective ratings of shock unpleasantness. Note that the pain-tolerant subjects are relative reducers, i.e., they have lower rates of increase in AER amplitude with increasing stimulus intensity. Group differences are greatest at the highest intensities.

20- to 26-mA range were also computed, each value being based on 21 judgments.

Figure 4 shows the somatosensory ER amplitudes of normal college students divided into pain-tolerant ($N = 18$) and pain-intolerant ($N = 18$) groups on the basis of their falling above or below the median on their mean rating for the 20- to 26-mA-range stimuli. As anticipated, individuals with reducing or relatively low amplitude/intensity slopes were pain tolerant, and augmenters were pain intolerant. These slope differences were confirmed statistically using two-way analysis of variance ($p < 0.05$, group by intensity interaction). Individual criterion measures (C_x) for the distinct/unpleasant division were correlated −0.48 with the amplitude/intensity slope for P100. The d' measure was not significantly correlated. The criterion measure has been previously linked to placebo and suggestion effects (43), and our neurophysiologic correlates may be related to these phenomena.

TOLERANCE FOR NOISE

As with the pain-tolerance experiment, we expected reducers to be noise tolerant; to test this hypothesis, noise studies were carried out in collaboration with Dr. John Molino at the National Bureau of Standards. Noise tolerance was assessed by measuring the rate at which subjects pressed a key to decrease noise while using a teaching machine (44).

In a separate session, AERs were collected in a manner similar to that used in the pain-tolerance study, i.e., random presentation of four intensities of noise bursts.

Individuals showed wide variation in tolerated noise—56 to 112 dB. Individuals who were relatively tolerant of noise on the key-pressing task were reducers on the AER (Fig. 5), whereas noise-intolerant individuals were augmenters. Again, this was statistically confirmed by two-way analysis of variance on the two groups and by correlations between the noise-tolerance score (in decibels) and the slope of the AER amplitude/intensity function for P100.

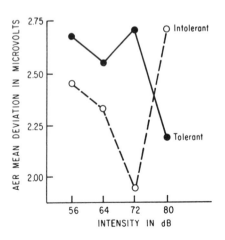

FIG. 5. Mean auditory AER amplitudes for noise stimuli at four intensities for the 76- to 112-msec interval (equivalent to P100). Subjects were divided into pain-tolerant and pain-intolerant groups on the basis of an avoidance-conditioning measure of noise tolerance. Note that the noise-tolerant subjects are reducers, as were pain-tolerant subjects.

Based on this finding of reducer tolerance to sensory overload and on the finding of reducer sensitivity to weak stimuli (45) we have hypothesized a model of a central nervous system mechanism that modulates the intensity of incoming sensory signals. In this model the reducer is thought to be protecting himself from sensory overload, perhaps as a compensatory adjustment for hypersensitivity at low levels. Whereas the tendency to reduce sensation might be useful as a means of coping with painful stimulation, its excessive or inappropriate application might be either a mechanism or symptom in psychopathology. Similarly, augmentation might be valuable for surviving sensory isolation but it is maladaptive for dealing with sensory inundation.

Evidence that psychiatric patients may be different in controlling intense sensory input comes from a number of experimental studies. Malmo, Shagass, and Smith (46) and Hall and Stride (47) found that schizophrenics had higher pain thresholds than normals. Hemphill, Hall, and Crookes (48) and Hall and Stride (47) found that depressive patients also had high pain-tolerance levels. Schizophrenics were found to be reducers in many studies that used kinesthetic figural aftereffects (51–55).

Sensory overload experiments in normals using high levels of light and sound stimulation have yielded reports of schizophrenic-like effects with perceptual distortion, diminished reality testing, and personal disorganization (49,50). It therefore seemed appropriate to look for differences in stimulus-intensity control in both schizophrenic and affective disorder patients.

CLINICAL STUDIES OF SCHIZOPHRENIC AND AFFECTIVE DISORDER PATIENTS

The patients studied all come from the metabolic research wards at the National Institute of Mental Health, and the results are the fruits of my collaborations with the other "NIMHers" at this meeting—Drs. Carpenter, Goodwin, Murphy, Strauss, and Wyatt. Patients were tested after having been off all psychoactive medications for at least 2 weeks. The AER procedure consisted of presenting four intensities of light (2, 30, 80, and 240 foot lamberts) in a pseudorandom sequence. Each intensity was presented 64 times for a total of 256 stimuli. Stimuli were generated and responses averaged by an on-line computer system (56,57). The light flashes were 500 msec long, followed by a 500-msec interstimulus interval. The subjects viewed the flashes on a large translucent screen rear-illuminated by the computer-controlled fluorescent tubes. EEG was recorded between vertex (C_z) and right ear. AERs were measured peak-to-trough (as indicated in Figs. 1 and 3) from P1 (P100) to N1 (N140) and from N1 (N140) to P2 (P200).

The primary affective disorder group (31) consisted of 63 patients (24 males and 39 females) divided into bipolar and unipolar groups. The schizophrenic group (58) consisted of 19 acutely psychotic patients (8 males and 11 females). Normal controls were selected from various volunteer groups to age and sex

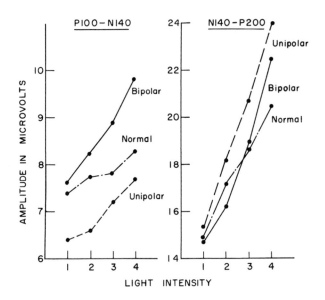

FIG. 6. Mean visual AER amplitude as a function of stimulus intensity for components P100–N140 and N140–P200 for 63 bipolar and unipolar patients with affective disorders and age- and sex-matched normal groups. Note that component P100–N140 shows bipolars to have greater amplitudes and amplitude/intensity slopes than unipolar patients, whereas component N140–P200 shows little difference.

match with the patients. Figure 6 illustrates the finding that unipolar patients were AER reducers for peak P100–N140 in comparison with normal controls, whereas bipolar patients were clear augmenters. Figure 7 shows the strong reducing of the schizophrenic group for peak P100–N140 in comparison with another appropriately age- and sex-matched control group. In each case these differences were confirmed as statistically significant. Note that the N140–P200 peak does not exhibit these diagnostic group differences (left half of Figs. 6 and 7), which demonstrates the relative specificity of the finding. This specificity of the P100–N140 component for stable group differences is extended to studies of patients with Turner's syndrome or chromatin-negative gonadal dysgenesis (59). Figure 8 illustrates how group differences based on sex chromosome status are reflected in AER amplitude/intensity slope differences on the P100–N140 peak, but not on the N140–P200 peak. Our clinical studies are summarized in Table 1. Considerable overlap between normals and the patient groups occurs, but we were intrigued by an aspect of the data that seemed to suggest some complementarity between the AER findings and ongoing studies of platelet monoamine oxidase (MAO) by Murphy and Wyatt.

AER AND PLATELET MAO

In the AER studies, biopolar patients show greater augmenting than do normals, whereas unipolar patients, like schizophrenics, show reducing. In MAO

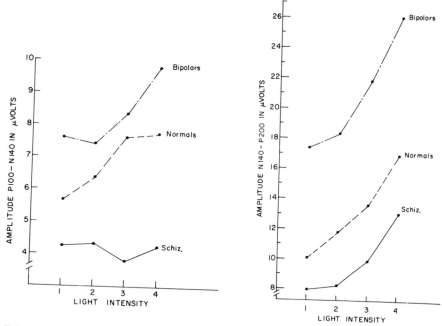

FIG. 7. Mean visual AER amplitude as a function of stimulus intensity for components P100–N140 and N140–P200 for 21 bipolar, and 21 schizophrenic patients and their matched normal controls. Note that, as with the affective disorder patients, marked amplitude/intensity slope differences appeared for P100–N140 and not for N140–P200.

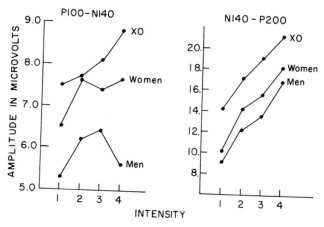

FIG. 8. Mean visual AER amplitude for normal male, female, and chromatin-negative gonadal dysgenesis (XO) groups. Male and female groups are age-matched to the 45XO group. Again, as with the schizophrenic/bipolar groups, amplitude/intensity group differences appear for P100–N140 but only amplitude differences are shown for N140–P200.

studies, chronic schizophrenics have shown low MAO levels (60) as have bipolar patients, (61), whereas unipolar patients have shown normal or high levels. Therefore, the AER could best distinguish schizophrenics from bipolars, and the MAO could best distinguish unipolars from schizophrenics; used together, the AER and MAO measurements could be a powerful, diagnostic tool. We decided to investigate this possibility.

TABLE 1. *Clinical findings with visual AER measure of augmenting/reducing*

Patient group	Reference
Augmenters	
Bipolar affective disorder	(31)
Acting-out adolescents	(73)
45XO patients	(59)
Women	(59,12)
Reducers	
Unipolar affective disorder	(31)
Schizophrenia	(10,58)
Pseudohypoparathyroidism	(72)
Men	(12)

Multivariate discriminant analysis was used to separate a group of 51 bipolar, unipolar, and schizophrenic patients from a group of 49 age- and sex-matched normal controls; platelet MAO levels and the four-intensity visual AERS had been obtained in both patient and normal control groups. AERs were recorded as described earlier. Venipuncture was performed at another session, and MAO activity levels were assayed using [^{14}C]tryptamine as described by Murphy (*this volume*). Both amplitude and amplitude/intensity slopes for P100 (76 to 112 msec), N140 (116 to 152 msec), and P200 (168 to 248 msec) together with platelet MAO levels were entered into multivariate discrimination program BMD05M (62). Amplitude was measured as described in the section on pain tolerance (page 133) using the area integration technique of Shagass. This was done in order to achieve as much consistency as possible across experiments and subject groups. This quantitative technique also eliminated any observer bias in peak identification. The six AER variables were the mean amplitude across intensities for each of the three peaks and the amplitude/intensity slopes for each of the three peaks. The seventh variable was platelet MAO level. The addition of unipolar patients made full age and sex matching with the other patient groups difficult, but each patient was matched with a normal. Multivariate analysis identified 42% correctly in this four-group problem when the sexes were not separated, but 61% were identified correctly when the analysis was run separately for each sex (both statistically significant, $p < 0.01$) (Table 2). Most classification errors were biopolars and normals classified as schizophrenics, which is interesting from the standpoint of Rosenthal's schizophrenia spectrum concept (this volume).

TABLE 2. *Multivariate discriminant analysis using AER and MAO measurements (7 variables)*

Patient category	7-variable Multivariate diagnosis			
	BP	UP	*N*	S
Bipolar	14*	3	4	6
Unipolar	2	10*	2	1
Normal	8	5	28*	8
Acute schizophrenic	0	1	0	9*

61% correct diagnosis for 101 subjects.
* Indicates correct diagnosis.

These results indicate that the joint use of biochemical and psychophysiologic measures may greatly improve their ability for identifying patient groups. The interaction between individual differences in neurochemistry and individual differences in electrophysiology may be valuable in identifying biologically homogeneous patient groups and in explaining the lack of pathology in normal individuals whose neurochemical findings overlap with those for patient populations. Furthermore, measures such as augmenting/reducing may provide links between both neurochemical abnormalities and behaviorally oriented theories and observations. A number of authors have stressed the importance for mental health of controlling sensory input (63–67). Many clinical theories impute a causative role to sensory overload in the psychoses. Venables (68) describes the acute schizophrenic as "characterized by an inability to restrict the range of his attention so that he is flooded by sensory impressions. . . ." Reducing might be the kind of backup system postulated by Mirsky (69) for sensory overload protection, which some psychotic patients are able to fall back upon when faults in the ascending reticular activating system appear. AER reducing is also reminiscent of McReynolds' (70) hypothesized "reduction in the tendency to obtain novel or variable percepts" as the basis for schizophrenic withdrawal. Epstein and Coleman (71) actually characterize many of the major theories of schizophrenia (e.g., those of Pavlov, Freud, Mednick, Broen and Storms, Venables) as assuming "that the basic defect in schizophrenia consists of a low threshold for disorganization under increasing stimulus input."

REFERENCES

1. Callaway, E., Jones, R., and Layne, R. (1965): Evoked responses and segmental set of schizophrenia. *Arch. Gen. Psychiatry*, 12:83–89.

2. Bershad, N. J., and Rockmore, A. J. (1974): On estimating signal to noise ratio using the sample correlation coefficient. *IEEE Trans. Inform. Theory,* 20:112.

3. Schimmel, H., Rapin, I., and Cohen, M. M. (1974): Improving evoked response audiometry with special reference to the use of machine scoring. *Audiology,* 13:33–65.

4. Petrie, A. (1967): *Individuality in Pain and Suffering.* Univ. of Chicago Press, Chicago, Illinois.

5. Petrie, A., Collins, W., and Solomon, P. (1958): Pain sensitivity, sensory deprivation and suscepti- bility to satiation. *Science,* 128:1431–1433.

6. Blitz, B., Dinnerstein, A. J., and Lowenthall, M. (1966): Relationship between pain tolerance and kinesthetic size judgment. *Percept. Mot. Skills,* 22:463–469.

7. Sweeney, D. R. (1966): Pain reactivity and kinesthetic aftereffect. *Percept. Mot. Skills,* 22: 763–769.

8. Platt, D., Holzman, P. S., and Larson, D. (1971): Individual consistencies in kinesthetic figural aftereffects. *Percept. Mot. Skills,* 32:787–795.

9. Petrie, A. (1974): Reduction or augmentation? Why we need two "planks" before deciding. *Percept. Mot. Skills,* 39:460–462.

10. Buchsbaum, M., and Silverman, J. (1968): Stimulus intensity control and the cortical evoked response. *Psychosom. Med.,* 30:12–22.

11. Spilker, B., and Callaway, E. (1969): "Augmenting" and "reducing" in averaged visual responses to sine wave light. *Psychophysiology,* 6:49–57.

12. Buchsbaum, M., and Pfefferbaum, A. (1971): Individual differences in stimulus intensity re- sponse. *Psychophysiology,* 8:600–611.

13. Soskis, D. A., and Shagass, C. (1974): Evoked potential test of augmenting-reducing. *Psychophysi- ology,* 11:175–190.

14. Zuckerman, M., Murtaugh, T., and Siegel, J. (1974): Sensation seeking and cortical augmenting- reducing. *Psychophysiology,* 11:535–542.

15. Hall, R. A., Rappaport, M., Hopkins, H. K., and Griffin, R. (1973): Tobacco and evoked potential. *Science,* 180:212–214.

16. Hall, R. A., Rappaport, M., Hopkins, H. K., Griffin, R., and Silverman, J. (1970): Evoked response and behavior in cats. *Science,* 170:998–1000.

17. Rietveld, W. J. (1963): The occipitocortical response to light flashes in man. *Acta Physiol. Pharmacol. Neerl.* 12:373–407.

18. Armington, J. C. (1964): Adaptational changes in the human electroretinogram and occipital response. *Vision Res.,* 4:179–192.

19. Shagass, C., Schwartz, M., and Krishnamoorti, S. (1965): Some psychologic correlates of cerebral responses evoked by light flash. *J. Psychosom. Res.,* 9:223–231.

20. Vaughan, H. G., and Hull, R. C. (1965): Functional relation between stimulus intensity and photically evoked cerebral response in man. *Nature,* 206:720–722.

21. Shipley, T., Jones, R. W., and Fry, A. (1966): Intensity and the evoked occipitogram in man. *Vision Res.,* 6:657–667.

22. Jacobson, J. H., Kawasaki, K., and Hirose, T. (1969): The human electroretinogram and occipital potential in response to focal illumination of the retina. *Invest. Ophthalmol.,* 8:545–556.

23. Kitajima, H. (1967): On the cerebral evoked response in man as a function of the intensity of flicker stimulation. *Electroencephalogr. Clin. Neurophysiol.,* 22:325.

24. Pfefferbaum, A., and Buchsbaum, M. (1971): Handedness and cortical hemisphere effects in sine wave stimulated evoked responses. *Neuropsychologia,* 9:237–240.

25. Il'yanok, V. A. (1961): Effect of intensity and depth of pulsation of flickering light on the electrical activity of the human brain. *Biofizica,* 6:72–82.

26. Van der Tweel, L. H., and Verduyn Lunel, H. F. E. (1965): Human visual responses to sinusoi- dally modulated light. *Electroencephalogr. Clin. Neurophysiol.,* 18:587–598.

27. Montagu, J. D. (1967): The relationship between the intensity of repetitive photic stimulation and the cerebral response. *Electroencephalogr. Clin. Neurophysiol.,* 23:152–161.

28. Kooi, K. A., and Bagchi, B. K. (1964): Observation on early components of the visual evoked response and occipital rhythms. *Electroencephalogr. Clin. Neurophysiol.,* 17:638–643.

29. Richey, E. T., Kooi, K. A., and Waggoner, R. W. (1966): Visually evoked responses in migraine. *Electroencephalogr. Clin. Neurophysiol.,* 21:23–27.

30. Samson, H. H., and Young, M. L. (1973): The relation of flash intensity and background illumination to the photic evoked potential in the pigeon's optic tectum. *Vision Res.,* 13:253–261.

31. Buchsbaum, M., Landau, S., Murphy, D. L., and Goodwin, F. (1973): Average evoked response in bipolar and unipolar affective disorders: Relationship to sex, age of onset and monoamine oxidase. *Biol. Psychiatry,* 7:199–212.

32. Hamasaki, D. I., and Winters, R. W. (1973): Intensity-response functions of visually deprived LGN neurons of cats. *Vision Res.,* 13:925–936.
33. Stark, L. H., and Norton, J. C. (1974): The relative reliability of average evoked response parameters. *Psychophysiology,* 11:600–602.
34. Buchsbaum, M. (1974): Average evoked response and stimulus intensity in identical and fraternal twins. *Physiol. Psychol.,* 2:365–370.
35. Creel, D. J., Dustman, R. E., and Beck, E. C. (1973): Visually evoked responses in the rat, guinea pig, cat, monkey and man. *Exp. Neurol.,* 40:351–356.
36. Dustman, R. E., and Beck, E. (1965): The visually evoked potential in twins. *Electroencephalogr. Clin. Neurophysiol.,* 19:580.
37. Osborne, R. T. (1970): Heritability estimates for the visual evoked response. *Life Sci, II,* 9: 481–490.
38. Lewis, E. G., Dustman, R. E., and Beck, E. C. (1972): Evoked response similarity in monozygotic, dizygotic and unrelated individuals: A comparative study. *Electroencephalogr. Clin. Neurophysiol.,* 23:309–316.
39. Young, J. P. R., Lader, M. W., and Fenton, G. W. (1972): A twin study of the genetic influences on the electroencephalogram. *J. Med. Genet.,* 9:13–16.
40. Mosher, L. R., Pollin, W., and Stabenau, J. R. (1971): Identical twins discordant for schizophrenia. *Arch. Gen. Psychiatry,* 24:422–430.
41. Tursky, B., and Watson, P. D. (1964): Controlled physical and subjective intensities of electric shock. *Psychophysiology,* 1:151–162.
42. Shagass, C. (1972): *Evoked Potentials in Psychiatry,* Plenum, New York.
43. Clark, W. C., and Goodman, J. (1974): Effects of suggestion on d' and C_x for pain detection and pain tolerance. *J. Abnorm. Psychol.,* 83:364–372.
44. Molino, J. (1974): Equal aversion levels for pure tones and $1/3$ octave bands of noise. *J. Acoust. Soc. Am.,* 55:1285–1289.
45. Silverman, J., Buchsbaum, M., and Henkin, R. (1969): Stimulus sensitivity and stimulus intensity control. *Percept. Mot. Skills,* 28:71–78.
46. Malmo, R. B., Shagass, C., and Smith, A. A. (1951): Responsiveness in chronic schizophrenia. *J. Pers.,* 19:359–375.
47. Hall, K. R. L., and Stride, E. (1954): The varying response to pain in psychiatric disorders: A study in abnormal psychology. *Br. J. Med. Psychol.,* 27:48–60.
48. Hemphill, R. E., Hall, K. R. L., and Crookes, T. G. (1952): A preliminary report on fatigue and pain tolerance in depressive and psychoneurotic patients. *Br. J. Psychiatry,* 98:433–440.
49. Ludwig, A. M. (1972): "Psychedelic" effects produced by sensory overload. *Am. J. Psychiatry,* 128:114–117.
50. Gottschalk, L. A., Haer, J. L., and Bates, D. E. (1972): Effect of sensory overload on psychological state changes in social alienation–personal disorganization and cognitive-intellectual impairment. *Arch. Gen. Psychiatry,* 27:451–457.
51. Wertheimer, M., and Jackson, C. W. (1957): Figural aftereffects, "brain modifiability," and schizophrenia: A further study. *J. Gen. Psychol.,* 57:45–54.
52. Kelm, H. (1962): The figural after-effect in schizophrenic patients. *J. Nerv. Ment. Dis.,* 135: 338–345.
53. Petrie, A., Holland, T., and Wolk, I. (1963): Sensory stimulation causing subdued experience: audio-analgesia and perceptual augmentation and reduction. *J. Nerv. Ment. Dis.,* 137:312–321.
54. Silverman, J. (1964): Perceptual control of stimulus intensity in paranoid and nonparanoid schizophrenia. *J. Nerv. Ment. Disease,* 139:545–549.
55. Houpt, J. L., Tucker, G. J., and Harrow, M. (1972): Disordered cognition and stimulus processing. *Am. J. Psychiatry,* 128:1505–1510.
56. Gips, J., Pfefferbaum, A., and Buchsbaum, M. (1971): Use of a small process control computer in a psychophysiological laboratory. *Psychophysiology,* 8:538–542.
57. Maugh, T. H. II, (1973): Medium sized computers: Bringing computers into the lab. *Science,* 182:270–272.
58. Landau, S. G., Buchsbaum, M., Carpenter, W., Strauss, J. and Sacks, M. (1975): Schizophrenia and stimulus intensity control. *Arch. Gen. Psychiatry. (In press.)*
59. Buchsbaum, M., Henkin, R. I., and Christiansen, R. L. (1974): Age and sex differences in averaged evoked responses in a normal population with observations on patients with gonadal dysgenesis. *Electroencephalogr. Clin. Neurophysiol.* 37:137–144.
60. Murphy, D. L., and Wyatt, R. J. (1972): Reduced MAO activity in blood platelets from schizophrenic patients. *Nature,* 238:225–226.

61. Murphy, D. L., and Weiss, R. (1972): Reduced monoamine oxidase activity in blood platelets from bipolar depressed patients. *Am. J. Psychiatry,* 128:1351–1357.
62. Dixon, W. J., editor (1971): *BMD Biomedical Computer Programs,* Univ. of California Press, Berkeley, California.
63. Miller, J. G. (1960): Information input overload and psychopathology. *Am. J. Psychiatry,* 116: 695–704.
64. Silverman, J. (1967): Variations in cognitive control and psychophysiological defense in the schizophrenias. *Psychosom. Med.,* 29:225–251.
65. Ludwig, A. M. (1971): Self-regulation of the sensory environment. *Arch. Gen. Psychiatry,* 25: 413–418.
66. Lipowski, Z. J. (1973): Affluence, information inputs and health. *Soc. Sci. Med.,* 7:517–529.
67. Grimes, C., and McGhie, A. (1973): Stimulus overload in schizophrenia. *Can. J. Behav. Sci.,* 5:101–110.
68. Venables, P. H. (1964): Input dysfunction in schizophrenics. *Prog. Exp. Pers. Res.,* 1:1–47.
69. Mirsky, A. F. (1969): Neuropsychological bases of schizophrenia. *Annu. Rev. Psychol.,* 20: 321–348.
70. McReynolds, P. (1960): Anxiety, perception and schizophrenia. In: *The Etiology of Schizophrenia,* edited by D. D. Jackson. Basic Books, New York.
71. Epstein, S., and Coleman, M. (1970): Drive theories of schizophrenia. *Psychosom. Med.,* 32: 113–140.
72. Buchsbaum, M., King, C., and Henkin, R. I. (1972): Average evoked responses and psychophysical performance in patients with pseudohypoparathyroidism. *J. Neurol. Neurosurg. Psychiatry,* 35:270–276.
73. Silverman, J., Buchsbaum, M., and Stierlin, H. (1973): Sex differences in perceptual differentiation and stimulus intensity control. *J. Pers. Soc. Psychol.,* 25:309–318.

Biology of the Major Psychoses, edited by D. X.
Freedman, Res. Publ. Assoc. Res. Nerv. Ment.
Dis., Vol. 54. Raven Press, New York   1975.

The Sleep of Psychotic Patients: Does It All Look Alike?

David J. Kupfer and F. Gordon Foster

*Department of Psychiatry, University of Pittsburgh School of Medicine and Western
Psychiatric Institute and Clinic, Pittsburgh, Pennsylvania 15261*

Within the last decade, the study of sleep has emerged as a valuable research and diagnostic tool. Much of this work had focused on just "functional" psychiatric disorders, but it has now been extended to narcolepsy and to other sleep disorders attendant to the "organic" diseases of the central nervous system (CNS).

As we discuss the relationship of sleep EEG patterning to the major psychoses, and in particular to the changes observed in schizophrenic states and psychotic depression, we must, at the same time, stress that EEG measurement cannot be considered a primary diagnostic tool in identifying a specific disease. Although we feel that the techniques of sleep EEG, and even more recently, telemetric motor activity measurements, eventually may provide useful leads for diagnostic classification of mental disorder and subsequent prediction of clinical response to treatment, at present we can only regard such measurements as aids to differential diagnosis. In this sense, EEG sleep data are comparable to laboratory data as applied in other medical specialties.

DEFINITION OF PSYCHOSIS

For the purpose of our investigations, we define psychosis by three rather simple criteria: (a) the presence of bizarre or idiosyncratic thinking, (b) the presence of egosyntonic delusions or hallucinations, and (c) a marked impairment in social or work functioning. Only when at least two of the three criteria are present can we state with some conviction that we are discussing a patient who is "psychotic." A seizure, for example, can be associated with delusions or hallucinations, but these are rarely egosyntonic.

Using the above definition it becomes clear that we can distinguish at least eight categories of psychoses in which the relationship of mental state to sleep patterns can be examined: (a) schizophrenia, (b) the depressive disorders, (c) mania, (d) acute and chronic intoxications (amphetamines, mescaline, hallucinogens), (e) acute withdrawal states of CNS depressants (also scopolamine), (f) toxic–metabolic encephalopathies (unrelated to the use of drugs), (g) end-stage dementiform states, and (h) psychosis associated with mental retardation. This chapter is limited to the first three categories, but it should be remembered that all of the disorders named are legitimately labeled "psychotic" illnesses, and that clinicians have long reported sleep disorders associated with these states.

The strategy used by many investigators has been to search for certain unique features in the EEG sleep pattern that are present in all psychotic states. Such an approach seems justified, for it is known that a generalized disturbance in sleep–wakefulness regulation occurs in all psychotic states (1). However, the literature on this subject and our own findings on schizophrenic, manic, and depressive patients lead one to conclude that there does not seem to be a specific EEG marker common to all psychoses (2). Although at first glance this finding appears disappointing if not outright discouraging, in fact, the opposite may be true. What clinicians need most is not a method to aid in the identification of psychosis per se, but a method for identifying the various types of psychosis. Therefore, the delineation of specific EEG sleep markers within types of psychosis may have considerable heuristic value. With this in mind, we approached the problem by looking at EEG sleep patterns in various kinds of psychiatric conditions along with clinical ratings.

DATA COLLECTION

The subjects described in these investigations were studied on the clinical psychiatric research services of the National Institute of Mental Health, Yale University, and the University of Pittsburgh. All patients were selected on the basis of independent evaluations by at least two attending psychiatrists and had been drug-free for a minimum of 2 weeks prior to the study. Systematic assessment of behavioral dimensions, with emphasis on depressive and psychotic symptoms, was obtained throughout the periods of study through the use of self-rating and clinical rating scales, both of which have been described previously (3–5). All patients were studied by continuous nightly recordings of their electroencephalogram (EEG), horizontal electro-oculogram (EOG), and submental electromyogram (EMG) in their own rooms on the research service. Unless specified, the results reported do not refer to the first two nights of the study period. These results were discarded to allow acclimation to the recording methods.

All sleep records were evaluated according to the standard criteria by a scorer who was unaware of the patient's drug or clinical status (6). In addition to the EEG categorization of sleep stages, each minute of REM sleep was scored on a nine-point scale (0 to 8) for intensity of REM patterns which reflect both the amplitude and the number of conjugate eye movements (7). We were particularly interested in monitoring the length of the REM latency in depressed patients. REM latency is the amount of time asleep prior to the onset of the first REM period. A REM latency is usually considered normal if it is above 60 min. To obtain a measure of sleep fragmentation, a ratio of minutes of time spent asleep (TSA) over of total recording period (TRP) in minutes, also known as "sleep efficiency," was utilized.

SCHIZOPHRENIA

Because of the similarities between dreams and psychotic thought, sleep EEG research in schizophrenic patients has received considerable attention and has led to speculations that the physiologic processes associated with dreaming especially in these patients might be related to daytime hallucinations. The results obtained prior to 1970 suggested that the acute schizophrenic episode might not be associated with consistent sleep alterations (8). Studies subsequent to 1970 have shown, however, that if one is able to record the sleep of the disturbed patient early in the course of an acute episode, there does seem to be a significant reduction in total sleep time, especially a reduction in REM sleep time and REM activity (intensity). In 1970, we reported several longitudinal cases from the National Institute of Mental Health confirming that the period of acute psychosis was associated with particular reductions in REM sleep and REM intensity (9) (Fig. 1). Subsequent investigations have shown that such a reduction in REM time and REM activity can be observed not only early in the acute schizophrenic psychosis but in chronic schizophrenia during acute exacerbations. This 1970

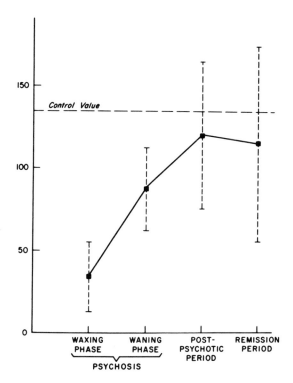

FIG. 1. REM activity in acute schizophrenia. Each black square represents the mean sleep value for the six patients plotted against their clinical course. Standard deviations of the sleep values are shown by the dotted vertical lines. Normal control values are indicated by the dotted lines.

study showed that REM recovery or compensation did not occur following prolonged periods of REM deprivation, suggesting that an abnormality in REM sleep may, in turn, reflect an alteration in biogenic amine mechanisms of the brain. A number of REM-deprivation experiments in acute schizophrenic patients subsequently confirmed the absence of REM rebounds, giving further support to this hypothesis (10,11). Moreover, in a preliminary communication published recently, we reported that the amplitude and intensity of eye movements in a small group of schizophrenic patients prior to treatment were significantly different from those in post-treatment states, as well as from patients suffering from depression either prior to or during treatment (12). This particular investigation was performed with an automated REM analyzer, a method that may prove of considerable value for characterizing the types of eye movements in schizophrenia (13).

Recent reviews of sleep research in mental illness have pointed to the lack of adequate clinical data regarding the subtypes, length, and intensity of the illness in studies on schizophrenic patients (2,10). We have just completed an investigation in which we attempted to remedy these inadequacies by examining sleep disturbance in well-defined subtypes of schizophrenia (14). Using the three criteria of psychosis mentioned earlier, we labeled "borderline" those patients who had a history of a brief 48- to 72-hr psychotic episode and who presented with evidence of subtle but continuous bizarre idiosyncratic thinking and multiple neurotic symptoms (15,16). In order to distinguish it from primary bipolar disease, we defined the schizoaffective psychosis as one in which the episode has (a) a marked affective component and (b) idiosyncratic thinking persisting during so-called symptom-free intervals.

We found that the major differences between the acute and borderline schizophrenic patients were that the borderline group slept longer by 70 min and more efficiently (14% more in TSA/TRP) with increased non-REM sleep as well as REM sleep, but with no differences in REM% or in the REM intensity (Tables 1 and 2). The sleep architecture of the acute schizophrenic and borderline schizophrenic was otherwise fairly similar except that there was a general tendency for the stages of delta sleep and REM% to be somewhat greater in the latter group. When both the borderline and acute schizophrenic groups were compared to nonpatients, the REM sleep time and, in the acute schizophrenic group, the REM% as well, were significantly lower than in age-matched controls during the first two nights of study (Table 3; Fig. 2).

The differences between the schizoaffective group and the acute or borderline group of schizophrenic patients were more distinct (Tables 4 and 5). First, the REM latency was significantly shorter (31.7 min) and the REM intensity higher in the schizoaffective group. As shown in Fig. 3, the REM latency in the schizoaffective group was less than 50% of the REM latency in either the borderline or the acute schizophrenic group. This phenomenon was present not only in the first two nights of study but later on in the hospital course. All three groups of

TABLE 1. Non-REM sleep parameters in schizophrenia

Sleep parameters	Acute (N = 14)	Borderline (N = 9)	Acute vs. borderline (p)
Total recording period*	431.3 ± 15.7	430.0 ± 9.2	NS[a]
Sleep latency	79.6 ± 18.4	43.4 ± 5.7	NS
Early morning awakening	13.1 ± 4.3	6.0 ± 2.4	NS
Intermittent awakening	30.1 ± 10.0	6.2 ± 3.4	NS
Time spent asleep	305.1 ± 16.4	374.7 ± 11.4	0.05
TSA/TRP ratio	0.72 ± 0.04	0.87 ± 0.02	0.05
Non-REM sleep	250.9 ± 14.9	295.2 ± 9.5	0.05
Stage 1	26.4 ± 4.3	29.8 ± 5.3	NS
Stage 2	194.7 ± 11.8	220.8 ± 10.8	NS
Delta (stages 3 and 4)	28.9 ± 5.7	43.3 ± 7.7	NS

* Minutes except where indicated.
[a] NS = Not significant.

TABLE 2. REM sleep parameters in schizophrenia

Sleep parameters	Acute (N = 14)	Borderline (N = 9)	Acute vs. borderline (p)
REM latency	97.9 ± 11.0	81.0 ± 12.0	NS
Stage 1-REM (RT)	54.0 ± 5.6	74.8 ± 5.6	0.05
Stage 1-REM (%)	17.4 ± 1.6	20.0 ± 1.4	NS
REM activity units (RA)	85.9 ± 11.0	110.8 ± 12.2	NS
RA/RT ratio	1.6 ± 0.1	1.5 ± 0.1	NS
RA/TSA ratio	0.27 ± 0.03	0.30 ± 0.03	NS

TABLE 3. Selected REM sleep parameters for the first 2 nights

Sleep parameters	Normal controls	Acute schizophrenic	Borderline schizophrenic
REM latency	109.0 ± 11.6	100.5 ± 19.2	125.9 ± 10.9
REM time	75.3 ± 8.2	37.6 ± 7.2*	47.8 ± 8.5*
REM activity	110.3 ± 11.4	56.5 ± 12.4†	80.0 ± 20.2

* $p < 0.05$.
† $p < 0.01$.

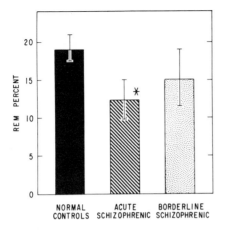

FIG. 2. REM % levels in acute and borderline schizophrenic states indicating that the REM % in the acute group is significantly lower than in the normal controls (based on first two nights) (* $- p < 0.05$).

TABLE 4. *REM sleep parameters*

Sleep parameters	Acute ($N = 14$)	Borderline ($N = 9$)	Schizo-affective ($N = 6$)	Acute vs. schizoaf. (p)	Borderline vs. schizoaf. (p)
Stage 1-REM (RT)	54.0 ± 5.6	74.8 ± 5.6	81.0 ± 10.5	0.05	NS
Stage 1-REM (%)	17.4 ± 1.6	20.0 ± 1.4	23.2 ± 1.9	NS	NS
REM activity units (RA)	85.9 ± 11.0	110.8 ± 12.2	174.2 ± 33.2	0.01	NS
RA/RT ratio	1.6 ± 0.1	1.5 ± 0.1	2.2 ± 0.2	0.05	0.05
RA/TSA ratio	0.27 ± 0.03	0.30 ± 0.03	0.54 ± 0.08	0.01	0.05

TABLE 5. *Non-REM sleep parameters*

Sleep parameters	Acute ($N = 14$)	Borderline ($N = 9$)	Schizo-affective ($N = 6$)	Acute vs. schizoaf. (p)	Borderline vs. schizoaf. (p)
TRP	431.3 ± 15.7	430.0 ± 9.2	475.5 ± 26.5	NS	NS
Sleep latency	79.6 ± 18.4	43.4 ± 5.7	102.2 ± 17.7	NS	0.01
Early morning awakening	13.1 ± 4.3	6.0 ± 2.4	9.3 ± 3.2	NS	NS
Intermittent awakening	30.1 ± 10.0	6.2 ± 3.4	14.7 ± 5.7	NS	NS
TSA	305.1 ± 16.4	374.7 ± 11.4	345.8 ± 28.4	NS	NS
TSA/TRP ratio	0.72 ± 0.04	0.87 ± 0.02	0.73 ± 0.04	NS	0.01
Non-REM sleep	250.9 ± 14.9	295.2 ± 9.5	267.8 ± 24.4	NS	NS
Stage 1	26.4 ± 4.3	29.8 ± 5.3	34.2 ± 8.9	NS	NS
Stage 2	194.7 ± 11.8	220.8 ± 10.8	217.8 ± 18.3	NS	NS
Delta (Stages 3 and 4)	28.9 ± 5.7	43.3 ± 7.7	18.2 ± 4.5	NS	0.05

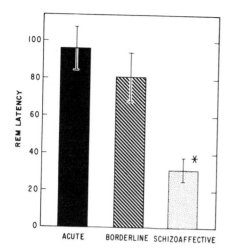

FIG. 3. REM latency (time asleep to the onset of the first REM period) is significantly reduced in the schizoaffective group as compared to the other two groups (*$p < 0.01$ with the borderline group and $p < 0.001$ with the acute group).

schizophrenic patients showed decreased delta sleep, unrelated to the age of the subjects (Table 5).

Although using REM percentages, it would appear that REM sleep time is lower in the acute than in other subgroups of schizophrenia, this is not entirely true. It is more likely that REM activity and particularly REM intensity measures reflect more faithfully phasic REM changes and in fact, seem to differentiate clearly the schizoaffective group from the acute and borderline groups. In conclusion then, the REM cycles may be intact (tonic component) in schizophrenia, but the phasic component as measured by REM activity is especially "weak." On the basis of the available literature on REM deprivation it would be expected that during remission there would be a significant REM rebound or compensation, but in fact, such compensatory activity fails to occur (10).

In order to assess the value of base-line sleep measurements for predicting treatment response we studied the type and dosage of drugs administered to the schizophrenic patients during hospitalization and at the time of discharge. The results of the base-line REM latency findings in the patient subgroups may be of further interest even though they were obtained by retrospective analysis of the records. Of a group of 29 patients, the seven patients (three schizoaffective and four acute schizophrenic) who were discharged on antidepressant medication had a base-line REM latency of 45.4 min as against the 22 patients who were not discharged on antidepressants who had a REM latency of 89.6 min (significant at the 0.05 level). If one examines only the 14 acute schizophrenic patients in the sample, the four patients discharged on tricyclic antidepressants had a REM latency of 59.2 min as opposed to the 10 patients who were not discharged on antidepressant medication who showed a mean REM latency of 113.4 min (significant at the 0.05 level). Because we do not have follow-up data showing whether long-term tricyclic antidepressant medication was clinically efficacious, this finding should be viewed with caution. Nevertheless, it is quite possible that a continuing investigation of sleep parameters in schizophrenic patients may help identify a subgroup of patients who either will suffer from a prolonged post-psychotic depressive syndrome or who are actually presenting with a concurrent affective syndrome that mandates combined treatment.

Previous investigations have shown very tenuous relationships between clinical symptoms and sleep EEG patterns in schizophrenia. In an attempt to shed further light on these issues, we examined the clinical ratings in relation to the sleep parameters. When the 29 schizophrenic patients in this investigation were rated for hallucinations and delusions, the relationship between clinical symptoms and the individual sleep parameters was weak. It was found that delusions correlated inversely with TSA ($r = -0.43$; $p < 0.05$) and the measure of sleep efficiency (TSA/TRP) ($r = -0.42$; $p < 0.05$) as well as REM time ($r = -0.45$ $p < 0.05$).

We examined the clinician ratings of overall cognitive disorganization in relation to the sleep parameters in another group of schizophrenic patients ($N = 16$), and found essentially that the degree of cognitive disorganization relates inversely ($p < 0.05$) to the amount of REM time ($r = -0.50$) and the REM% ($r = -0.54$), a finding that has emerged consistently since our first study of acute schizophrenic patients was reported in 1970 (17). In this new study we defined cognitive disorganization as including disorganized speech, unusual or bizarre expressive behavior, explicitly delusional thinking, hyperalertness, easy distractability, and hallucinatory experience described by the patient, or behavior strongly suggestive of hallucinations. When we examined symptoms indicative of cognitive disorganization, we found that bizarre expressive behavior and hallucinatory experience correlate inversely with the number of REM periods ($r = -0.52$). In contrast, the severity of anxiety (rated by the clinician), which is said to be very high in disorganized schizophrenics, did not relate significantly either to REM sleep time or to REM%. This apparently contradictory finding may be interpreted to mean that the quality of anxiety may be different in schizophrenics than in neurotics who usually show these relationships (18). In schizophrenia the anxiety is perhaps secondary to cognitive disorganization, thereby accounting for the relationship between the cognitive disorganization and certain REM parameters.

DEPRESSION

For almost half a decade we have been engaged in the study of the sleep patterns of depressed patients who require hospitalization as well as a smaller number of patients who have needed outpatient treatment. The current findings in this area can be summarized briefly as shown in Table 6.

It is generally accepted that there are two types of nonpsychotic depressions —unipolar and bipolar—both of which have been well described in the clinical literature. Nonpsychotic unipolar patients spend relatively less time asleep during the severe stages of their illness than they do during the state of remission. The unipolars have a marked sleep-continuity disturbance consisting of intermittent wakefulness and early morning awakening, findings repeatedly verified by EEG

TABLE 6. *Primary depressive states*[a]

State	TSA	Waking (%)	Delta (%)
Nonpsychotic depression			
Unipolar (hyposomnic)	Low	High	Low
Bipolar (hypersomnic)	High	Low	Low
Psychotic depression	Very low	High	Very low

[a] REM latency: short in all primary depressive states.

recordings (19, 20). In addition, such patients usually have low delta sleep, a clear proponderance of the lighter stages of sleep (stages 1 and 2), and most distinctively shortened REM latency, the extent of which appears to be inversely correlated with the severity of their illness (21) (Fig. 4). Short REM latency is not only found in hospitalized patients but also in depressed outpatients (Fig. 5). As indicated in Fig. 6, still another group of depressed patients studied at the University of Pittsburgh (including bipolar and unipolar depressives) exhibited reduction in the REM latency that was not reduced in other psychiatric states.

In studies at Yale and Pittsburgh, data obtained from our clinical patients all-night sleep and telemetric motor activity have shown, however, that in the vast majority of cases the depressive phase of bipolar illness has biologic characteristics markedly different from those seen in typical unipolar depressions. Sleep time in bipolar depressives, rather than being discontinuous or decreased, tend to be unchanged or even increased (22, 23). In the past few years we have performed several investigations to characterize further the sleep profiles in so-called "hypersomnic" depressives.

In one pilot study of nine depressed patients who reported little if any wakefulness during the night, all subjects had a history of either bipolar illness or a history of recurrent depression accompanied by severe anergia, rather than anxiety and agitation typically observed in unipolar depressions (24). Sleep EEG studies revealed that these patients fell asleep immediately, had almost no awakenings, and averaged more than 8 hr sleep per night. However, it is interesting that both delta sleep (stages 3 and 4) and the REM latency were reduced, as they are in patients with hyposomnic depressions.

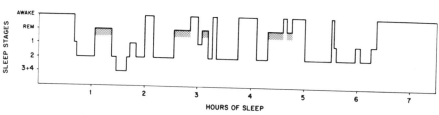

FIG. 4. The features of psychotic depression are represented in this graph based on actual patient sleep data illustrating short REM latency, scarcity of delta sleep (stages 3 and 4), multiple awakenings, and a final early morning awakening.

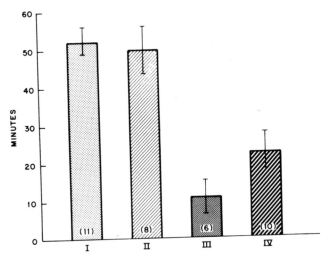

FIG. 5. The REM latency is shortened in all four groups of depressed patients as compared to normals or to other psychiatric patients. I, mild depression; II, moderate depression; III, severe depression; IV, severe depression with psychosis. Number of patients is enclosed in parentheses.

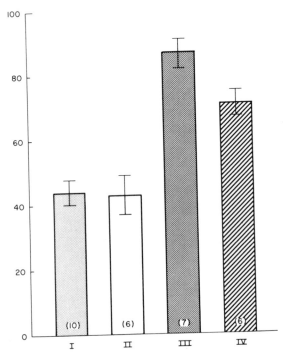

FIG. 6. REM latency is shortened in both unipolar and bipolar depression. I, Unipolar depression; II, bipolar depression; III, nonpsychotic–nondepressive states; IV, psychotic–nondepressive states. Number of patients is enclosed in parentheses.

TABLE 7. *Nonpsychotic depression*

Sleep parameter	Hyposomnic	Hypersomnic
Age	40.8 ± 3.6	41.6 ± 5.1
Delta sleep	22.2 ± 5.6	17.2 ± 6.0
REM latency	39.9 ± 5.9	42.7 ± 6.3

In order to minimize the problems of a biased selection, we conducted a second study comparing depressed patients whose sleep pattern was marked by a lack of fragmentation with those who showed the intermittent wakefulness and early morning awakening typically seen in patients with recurrent depression (25). Of the 35 patients, the 10 patients with psychotic depression all had the typical fragmentation of sleep, whereas only 16 of the 25 patients with nonpsychotic depression (unipolar and bipolar) had this pattern. When these 16 nonpsychotic patients with the "typical" hyposomnic pattern were compared to the other nine nonpsychotic patients who had no sleep-continuity disturbance, the results once again showed that whereas the nonfragmented group also slept longer (100 min) and had an increased stage 1 percentage, both types of patients had a short REM latency and reduced delta (stages 3 and 4) sleep. This suggested that, at least in nonpsychotic depression, decreased sleep time with frequent awakenings is not an obligatory feature (Table 7; Fig. 7).

In the process of separating hyposomnic and hypersomnic types of depressions, we have shown that the sleep pattern in psychotic depressive states is an exaggeration of what the sleep pattern in severe nonpsychotic unipolar depressions appears to be. However, in patients with marked hypersomnia, psychotic features (as defined earlier in this chapter) are apparently not present. As shown in Table

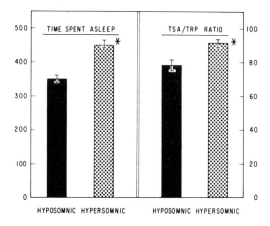

FIG. 7. EEG sleep time in nonpsychotic depression. Both time spent asleep and the TSA/TRP ratio ("sleep efficiency") are significantly greater (*$p < 0.001$) in the hypersomnic group than in the hyposomnic group despite similarities in the sleep architecture.

TABLE 8. *Psychotic depression* ($N = 9$)

Sleep parameter	N
TSA*	262.9 ± 23.7
Early morning awakening	41.1 ± 12.7
Wakefulness	54.5 ± 13.4
TSA/TRP ratio†	0.61 ± 0.05
REM latency	36.0 ± 7.2
REM time	51.3 ± 7.0
REM %	19.6 ± 2.4
REM activity/TSA ratio	0.46 ± 0.08
REM cycle length (T1–2)	130.8 ± 20.3
REM cycle length (T-A 1–2)	100.3 ± 14.2
Delta	4.4 ± 2.2
Delta %	1.6 ± 0.85

* Minutes except where indicated.
† Time spent asleep/Total recording period.

8, there is a profound fragmentation of sleep characterized by severe intermittent wakefulness with early morning awakenings in psychotic depression. This considerable amount of wakefulness means that less than two-thirds of the more than 7 hr available for sleep was actually spent in sleep. In psychotic depression, other findings include shortened REM latencies (36 min), a disruption in the REM cycle frequently associated with decreases in REM sleep (51.3 min, but a normal REM% of 19.6%) and a decreased percentage of delta sleep (1.6%). It should be noted, however, that although reduced delta sleep was thought to occur most frequently in the depressive disorders, it is not specific to the depressive syndromes. In fact, recent studies indicate that delta sleep changes are pervasive throughout most psychotic states and have been noted in many nonpsychiatric conditions as well. The interval between the first and second REM period seems prolonged in psychotic depression, but this is secondary to increased wakefulness. In other words, when a correction is made for the amount of wakefulness (30.5 min), the REM cycle length is within the normal range. Although sleep-continuity disturbance may be related in part to the age of the patient, even when age-related effects are accounted for, these findings are still characteristic of psychotic depression and nonpsychotic unipolar depressive syndromes. As Fig. 7 shows, when hyposomnic and hypersomnic depressives are compared, even though the mean patient age in both groups was similar, a very different type of sleep-continuity change is observed. It should also be pointed out that the typical changes in psychotic depressive states can be noted even in the first few nights of EEG sleep study. As shown in Table 9, the characteristic changes observed in psychotic depression are manifest in nights 1 and 2 as well as nights 3 and 4 (26). In fact, there is a suggestion in our patient samples that even though the patient may become more "comfortable" after several nights in hospital, the sleep parameters do not reflect this increasing state of comfort. The fact that the clinical symptomatology of psychotic depressives did not improve during this

TABLE 9. *Psychotic depression (N = 9) (first 4 nights)*

Sleep parameter	Nights 1 and 2	Nights 3 and 4
TSA	309.6 ± 24.0	290.1 ± 12.0
Early morning awakening	34.6 ± 10.6	46.6 ± 13.8
Wakefulness	65.0 ± 11.5	81.5 ± 26.7
TSA/TRP	68.8 ± 4.0	68.8 ± 4.0
REM latency	17.8 ± 5.0	32.7 ± 6.2
REM time	57.9 ± 9.8	66.6 ± 9.1
No. of REM periods	3.8 ± 0.5	3.9 ± 0.5
Delta sleep time	13.9 ± 6.0	7.6 ± 2.6

initial base-line study period supports the notion that the changes in sleep are related to changes in clinical state, although one cannot be certain that this lack of change in some cases is not caused by prolonged states of withdrawal from alcohol and other CNS depressants that persist even after the 2-week drug-free period.

The profound REM sleep changes observed in affective states have received considerable attention. In several longitudinal cases of psychotic depression we have followed, it appears that despite alterations in the degree of sleep fragmentation, the changes in REM sleep time and, in fact, the intensity of REM sleep are correlated with particular stages of the clinical course (27–29). For example, it appears that in the early stages of depression, there is a decrease in total REM time with a greater decrease usually found in the second half of the night. With the lifting of the depression, the total REM sleep time begins to increase during the first half of the night. In a longitudinal study of a 54-year-old female, the patient's REM intensity as measured by REM activity increased considerably (113%), particularly in the final third of the night during a state of partial remission (30). This increase in REM time, accompanied by an increase in REM intensity, was then followed by a more pronounced increase during the second half of the night. It is interesting to note that such intense REM periods (so-called REM storms), observed at the end stage of psychotic depression, are similar to those seen in the delirious states, most particularly in states of acute alcoholic withdrawal. But it would be premature to conclude that they are invariably related to psychotic states, nor are there careful measurements available to determine at what point a REM rebound should be considered a REM storm (31).

There have been many speculations about the significance of REM sleep alterations and possible rearrangement during clinical states of depression. The meaning of the relationship between short REM latency found in depressive states and REM deprivation is yet unclear. Recent work suggests that REM deprivation may, in fact, improve the clinical state of depression (32). On the other hand, it may be that the short REM latency is a function of natural REM deprivation, which, in turn, reflects a state of "suspended animation" for the CNS until such time that the depressive state begins to remit. Another possibility is that the shortened REM latency may simply mirror a significant alteration in the cir-

TABLE 10. *Sleep in psychotic depression and schizoaffective states*

Sleep parameter	Psychotic depression	Schizo-affective	p
TSA*	262.9 ± 23.7	345.8 ± 28.4	NS
Early morning awakening	41.1 ± 12.7	9.3 ± 3.2	NS
Wakefulness	54.5 ± 13.4	14.7 ± 5.7	0.05
TSA/TRP ratio†	0.61 ± 0.05	0.73 ± 0.04	NS
REM latency	36.0 ± 7.2	31.7 ± 5.7	NS
REM time	51.3 ± 7.0	81.0 ± 10.5	0.05
REM %	19.6 ± 2.4	23.2 ± 1.9	NS
REM activity/TSA ratio	0.46 ± 0.08	0.54 ± 0.08	NS
REM cycle length (T1–2)	130.8 ± 20.3	88.5 ± 9.7	NS
REM cycle length (T-A 1–2)	100.3 ± 14.2	85.5 ± 10.3	NS
Delta	4.4 ± 2.2	18.2 ± 4.5	0.05
Delta %	1.6 ± 0.85	4.8 ± 1.2	NS
Mean age (years)	58.2 ± 1.1	38.8 ± 5.5	NS

* Minutes except where indicated.
† Time Spent Asleep/Total Recording Period.

cadian rhythm. There has been much speculation and some evidence from endocrine studies that such an alteration exists (33). Whatever the relationship, it may be said that depression is characterized by rearrangement of REM sleep with marked changes in the REM cycle, whereas in schizophrenia there is a disturbance in the quality of REM sleep.

Before we turn briefly to sleep and mania, it is worthwhile to comment on the relationships between the sleep of schizoaffective patients and that of psychotically depressed patients. A comparison of these two groups as shown in Table 10 indicates that the sleep of these two groups is quite similar, especially with regard to REM latency and REM intensity. Because the schizoaffective patient's sleep-continuity disturbance is characterized by difficulty in falling asleep, rather than by intermittent wakefulness, and the architecture of sleep in both these states is comparable, the sleep of the schizoaffective patient may be more akin to the sleep of a depressed individual than to the sleep of an acute schizophrenic patient. These findings may be viewed as corroborating recent clinical reports that schizoaffective disease is closer to primary affective disease than to other forms of schizophrenia (34).

MANIA

Only very few studies have been reported on mania, perhaps because of the difficulties of studying such patients longitudinally in a drug-free state. However, the available studies suggest that the sleep of the manic patients is somewhat different both from that of the schizophrenic patient and from that of the depressed patient (30, 35). Whether there are short REM latencies or other alterations in REM cycle lengths in such patients is still subject for debate. In our own longitudinal investigations, as typified by a 22-year-old woman with definite mood swings, the sleep of the manic patients is somewhat similar to that of the acute schizophrenic patient in that during the so-called stage 3 mania (mania and psychosis) there is a marked difficulty falling asleep (98 min) (36). During a 6-night period this patient did not sleep at all for two nights; on the nights on which she slept, she averaged 307 min with an average of 19% REM sleep. Once asleep, the extent of severe REM sleep time reduction and REM intensity reduction seen in acute schizophrenic patients was not apparent in the manic patient. However, apparently we do not know enough even to attempt a characterization of sleep patterns in this disorder.

CONCLUSION

There are several additional points that should be made before concluding this chapter. First, we should comment on the so-called lack of adaptation evidenced in sleep studies of psychotic patients. In general, nonpsychotic patients and those patients with manifestations of acute anxiety or other neurotic symptoms, show a great deal of variability in their sleep over the first several nights of EEG study, with a tendency toward normalization of sleep. Similarly, we have noted that there is a certain degree of adaptation or change in sleep between the first and second night in borderline schizophrenic patients. But we have not seen these changes in patients clearly diagnosed with psychotic depression or schizophrenic psychosis (27). One can speculate that given a novel situation that initially produces some degree of anxiety, there will be adaptation. But in psychotic inpatients who suffer from severe impairment of functioning and who report many symptoms there is no such adaptational syndrome. This may be caused by the severity of the disorder or a type of biologic fatigue.

The final point to be made is that although we have emphasized sleep and its relationship to psychosis throughout this discussion, we are convinced that motor activity measured telemetrically also holds considerable promise as still another easily measurable psychophysiologic index (37–39). Because there are a number of relationships already established between sleep EEG parameters and motor activity, this second objective measurement offers another tool with which the functional psychotic states can be classified.

In closing, we should again mention the caveat that we alluded to earlier in the chapter. Measurements such as sleep and motor activity eventually may provide objective data that can be used in understanding the functional psychoses. In fact, we expect that some day these types of measurements will diminish the clinician's almost exclusive dependence upon amnestic data and psychologic observations made on the patient's behavior. At the present time, however, efforts to correlate specific measurements with specific behaviors are greatly hindered by the relative lack of attention to the precise collection of clinical data. We hope that in the next few years as much emphasis will be given to clinical and psychologic measurements as to sleep and motor activity studies.

Only then will be be in a position to develop a more comprehensive approach to problems of diagnosis in psychiatric disorders.

ACKNOWLEDGMENTS

This research was supported in part by research grant MH24652–01A1 from the National Institute of Mental Health. Although many colleagues have contributed in these research activities, the authors would like especially to acknowledge the assistance of Ms. Patricia Coble, Dr. Thomas Detre, Ms. Ellen Frank, and Mr. Richard McPartland in the preparation of this chapter.

REFERENCES

1. Hawkins, D., and Mendels, J. (1973): The psychopathology and psychophysiology of sleep. In: *Biological Psychiatry,* edited by J. Mendels, pp. 297–330. Wiley, New York.
2. Snyder, F. (1972): Electroencephalographic studies of sleep in psychiatric disorders. In: *The Sleeping Brain,* edited by M. H. Chase, pp. 376–393. Brain Information Service/Brain Research Institutes, Los Angeles.
3. Kupfer, D. J., and Detre, T. P. (1971): Development and application of the KDS-1 in inpatient and outpatient settings. *Psychol. Rep.,* 29:607–617.
4. Kupfer, D. J., and Detre, T. P. (1971): *The KDS System.* New Haven, Connecticut.
5. Kupfer, D. J., and Detre, T. P. (1972): KDS-1 scale for symptom discrimination. *Psychol. Rep.,* 30:915–919.
6. Rechtschaffen, A., and Kales, A. A. (1968): *A Manual of Standardized Terminology, Techniques and Scoring Systems for Sleep Stages of Human Subjects.* National Institute for Nervous Diseases and Blindness, Bethesda, Maryland.
7. Kupfer, D. J., Reynolds, C. F. III, Weiss, B. L., and Foster, F. G. (1974): Lithium carbonate and sleep in affective disorders: Further considerations. *Arch. Gen. Psychiatry,* 30:79–84.
8. Feinberg, I. (1969): Recent sleep research: Findings in schizophrenia and some possible implications for the mechanism of action of chlorpromazine and for the neurophysiology of delirium. In: *Schizophrenia: Current Concepts in Research,* edited by D. V. S. Sankar, pp. 739–750. PJD Publications, Hicksville, New York.
9. Kupfer, D. J., Wyatt, R. J., Scott, J., and Snyder, F. (1970): Sleep disturbance in acute schizophrenic patients. *Am. J. Psychiatry,* 126:1213–1220.
10. Wyatt, R., Termini, B. A., and Davis, J. (1971): Biochemical and sleep studies of schizophrenia: A review of the literature. 1960–1970. Part II. Sleep studies. *Schizophr. Bull.,* 4:45–66.
11. Gillin, J. C., Buchsbaum, M. S., Jacobs, L. S., Fram, D. H., Williams, R. B., Vaugn, T. B., Jr., Mellon, E., Snyder, F., and Wyatt, R. J. (1974): Partial REM sleep deprivation, schizophrenia, and field articulation. *Arch. Gen. Psychiatry,* 30:653–662.
12. McPartland, R. J., Weiss, B. L., and Kupfer, D. J. (1974): An objective measure of REM activity. *Physiol. Psychol.,* 2:441–443.
13. McPartland, R., Kupfer, D. J., and Foster, F. G. (1973): Rapid eye movement analyzer. *Electroencephalogr. Clin. Neurophysiol.,* 34:315–318.
14. Reich, L., Weiss, B. L., Coble, P., McPartland, R., and Kupfer, D. J. (1975): Sleep disturbance in schizophrenia: A revisit. *Arch. Gen. Psychiatry, (In press).*
15. Detre, T. P., and Jarecki, H. G. (1971): *Modern Psychiatric Treatment.* Lippincott, Philadelphia, Pennsylvania.
16. Pfeiffer, E. (1974) Borderline states. *Dis. Nerv. Syst.,* 35:212–219.
17. Foster, F. G., and Kupfer, D. J.: Psychomotor activity as a correlate of depression and sleep in acutely disturbed psychiatric inpatients. *Am. J. Psychiatry (Submitted for publication.)*
18. Monroe, L. J. (1967): Psychological and physiological differences between good and poor sleepers. *J. Abnorm. Psychol.,* 72:255–264.
19. Mendels, J., and Hawkins, D. R. (1967): Sleep and depression: A controlled EEG study. *Arch. Gen. Psychiatry,* 15:344–354.

20. Hawkins, D. (1972): Sleep research and depression. In: *Recent Advances in Psychobiology of the Depressive Illnesses,* edited by T. Williams, Katz, M., and Shields, J., pp. 141–146. DHEW, Washington, D.C.

21. Kupfer, D. J., and Foster, F. G. (1972): Interval between onset of sleep and rapid eye movements sleep as an indicator of depression. *Lancet,* 2:684–686.

22. Detre, T. P., Himmelhoch, J., Swartzburg, M., Anderson, C. M., Byck, R. and Kupfer, D. J. (1972): Hypersomnia and manic-depressive disease. *Am. J. Psychiatry,* 128:1303–1305.

23. Kupfer, D. J., Detre, T. P., and Himmelhoch, J. (1973): Classification of depressions—A guide for the clinician. *Symposium Advances in the Treatment of Affective Disturbances, Rutgers Univ. Nov. 14–15, 1973.*

24. Kupfer, D. J., Himmelhoch, J., Swartzburg, M., Anderson, C., Byck, R., and Detre, T. P. (1972): *Dis. Nerv. Syst.,* 33:720–724.

25. Kupfer, D. J., Foster, F. G., and Detre, T. P. (1973): Sleep continuity disturbances in depression. *Dis. Nerv. Syst.,* 34:192–195.

26. Kupfer, D. J., Weiss, B. L., Detre, T. P., and Foster, F. G. (1974): First night effect revisited: A clinical note. *J. Nerv. Ment. Dis.,* 159:205–209.

27. Snyder, F. (1968): Electroencephalographic studies of sleep in depression. In: *Computers and Electronic Devices in Psychiatry,* edited by N. S. Kline and E. Laska, pp. 272–301. Grune & Stratton, New York.

28. Snyder, F. (1969): Dynamic aspects of sleep disturbance in relation to mental illness. *Biol. Psychiatry,* 1:119–130.

29. Snyder, F. (1972): NIH studies of EEG sleep in affective illness. In: *Recent Advances in The Psychobiology of the Depressive Illnesses,* edited by T. Williams, M. Katz, and J. Shields, pp. 171–192. DHEW, Washington, D.C.

30. Kupfer, D. J., and Foster, F. G. (1973): Sleep and activity in a psychotic depression. *J. Nerv. Ment. Dis.,* 156:341–348.

31. Gross, M. M., Goodenough, D., Tobin, M., Halpert, E., Lepore, D., Perlstein, A., Sirota, M., DiBianco, J., Fuller, R., and Kishner, I. (1966): Sleep disturbances and hallucinations in the acute alcoholic psychoses. *J. Nerv. Ment. Dis.,* 142:493–514.

32. Vogel, G. W., Thurmond, A., Gibbons, P., Moore, S., Edwards, K., Sloan, K., Sexton, K., Boyd, M., Walker, M., Miller, S., and Deen, L. (1975): The effects of REM sleep reduction on depression syndromes. *Arch. Gen. Psychiatry (In press.)*

33. Sachar, E. J., Hellman, L., Roffwarg, H. P., Halpern, F. S., Fukushima, D. K., and Gallagher, T. F. (1973): Disrupted 24-hour patterns of cortisol secretion in psychotic depression. *Arch. Gen. Psychiatry,* 28:19–24.

34. Welner, A., Croughan, J. L., and Robins, E. (1974): The group of schizoaffective and related psychoses—Critique, record, follow-up and family studies. I. A persistent enigma. *Arch. Gen. Psychiatry,* 31:628–631.

35. Mendels, J., and Hawkins, D. R. (1971): Longitudinal sleep study in hypomania. *Arch. Gen. Psychiatry,* 25:274–277.

36. Carlson, G. A., and Goodwin, F. K. (1973): The stages of mania. *Arch. Gen. Psychiatry,* 28:221–228.

37. Kupfer, D. J., Detre, T. P., Foster, F. G., Tucker, G. J., and Delgado, J. (1972): The application of Delgado's telemetric mobility recorder for human studies. *Behav. Biol.,* 7:585–590.

38. Kupfer, D. J., Weiss, B. L., Foster, F. G., Detre, T. P., Delgado, J., and McPartland, R. J. (1974): Psychomotor activity in affective states. *Arch. Gen. Psychiatry,* 30:765–768.

39. Weiss, B. L., Foster, F. G., Reynolds, C. F., III, and Kupfer, D. J. (1974): Psychomotor activity in mania. *Arch. Gen. Psychiatry,* 31:379–383.

Discussion

Roffwarg: In this discussion, we hear attempts to learn more about various kinds of psychopathologic states by means of electrophysiologic exploration. What is requested by the investigator is that the brain confess that certain neurophysiologic (or neuroendocrinologic) phenomena are specific to a disease entity or syndrome.

In addition to better refining our indices of differentiation, one hopes also to improve the definition of the condition in question. The fundamental intent of all these lines of research, lest they get bogged down in parametric and correlative materials, is as Drs. Shagass and Kupfer point out, in the first instance, to find biologic parameters to delineate types of syndromes. However, what more can be learned about basic mechanisms underlying the different conditions constitutes the real gold mine of these researches. For example, picking up where Dr. Kupfer left off, we can mention how sleep researchers have thrown some light on essential nervous system mechanisms involved in endogenous depression. Perhaps there are more direct ways to the ultimate understanding of these mechanisms than through sleep polygraphic variables, but many roads lead to Rome. Our knowledge in the end will undoubtedly be most veridical if and when a number of roads have led to the same conclusions.

A cardinal finding in Kupfer's work is that the sleep of depressives, whether unipolar or bipolar, is marked by a significantly reduced latency to REMS. It is probably reflective of what sleep researchers, for want of a better term, like to call evidence of increased "REMS pressure." Some sleep researchers have believed that the term could be readily translated to other models such as the neurochemical, but I have always thought it was necessary to be cautious because increased "REMS pressure" has not always covaried smoothly with levels and turnover rates of dopamine and norepinephrine. [There had been a prevailing opinion that REMS triggering depends, at least in part, on catecholamine nuclei in the brainstem, and the implication grew that catecholamines are utilized in REMS (M. Jouvet: Biogenic amines and the states of sleep. *Science,* 163:32,1969). But Hartman (E. Hartmann: Antidepressants and sleep, clinical and theoretical implications, in: *Sleep—Physiology Pathology,* edited by A. Kales, p. 308. Lippincott, Philadelphia, 1969.) has marshaled evidence to support the hypothesis that REMS provides a neurophysiologic matrix for the synthesis of norepinephrine.] A diminished REMS latency seems to be unique to endogenous depression. It is not seen in anxious patients, who generally show a prolongation of the time to the first REMP, or in schizophrenics, except for the depressed schizoaffectives whose sleep patterns resemble depressives more than schizophrenics.

What does a diminished REMS latency mean? It signifies that the depressed patient is partially REMS deprived, and has a progressively increasing quantity of damned up REMS; in other words, he has a heightened "REMS pressure." The severity of the depression appears to co-vary with the extent of the REMS deprivation. This descriptive truth now takes on additional meaning, however, when we look elsewhere.

Dr. Gerald Vogel, in a landmark series of well controlled studies of the effects of REMS deprivation, by manual awakenings, on endogenous depression has found that this procedure alleviates depression in those patients who can reduce their REMS latency, thereby showing an elevated "REMS pressure" (G. Vogel, F. Thompson, A. Thurmond, and B. Rivers: The effect of REM deprivation on depression. *Psychosomatics,* 14:104, 1973). The practical efficacy of these findings are less relevant than their heuristic value. For they begin to make our speculations more firm about the mechanisms in REMS deprivation. We know that the antidepressant drugs, and electroconvulsive treatment—perhaps (M. H. Ebert, R. J. Baldessarini, J. F. Lipinski, K. Berv: *Arch. Gen. Psychiatry,* 29:397–401, 1973)—elevate available stores of intracerebral norepinephrine. What is more, these clinically therapeutic modalities also tend to reduce REMS. Dr. Vogel's studies raise the likelihood that blocking the expression of REMS tends also to increase norepinephrine, the Hartmann hypothesis (1963), notwithstanding.

Accordingly, a captivating possibility emerges with respect to the disordered sleep patterns of depressed individuals. Could it be that the increased REMS "pressure" in their sleep reveals evidence of a process of "auto-REMS deprivation"? Perhaps the slow buildup of a REMS debt constitutes a restitutive attempt of the brain (at first homeopathic, perpetually imperfect and costly) designed to increase catecholamine levels by the only means at its command. It is known that depression is a self-limited disease. It will be an exciting instance of the art of self-healing if it turns out to be true that the slow REMS deprivation process ultimately brings norepinephrine levels to the point at which spontaneous recovery from depression is possible. Certainly, the evidence is that REMS deprivation by drugs, ECT, or experimental awakenings seems to speed up the process.

Whether the subtle EEG sleep finding of a reduced REMS latency is linked to noradrenergic mechanisms is still uncertain. However, recent evidence from another source strangely suggests an effect of REMS deprivation on the augmentation of brain catecholamines. There are a great deal of data to the effect that intracranial self-stimulation (ICSS) is mediated critically by catecholamine mechanism (S. J. Ellman, R. F. Ackermann, J. Farber, L. Mattiace, and S. S. Steiner: *Physiol. Psychol.* 2:31, 1974). Ellman and coworkers have shown a crossover between the systems regulating ICSS and the system regulating REM sleep (Ellman et al., 1974). The Nucleus Locus Coeruleus turns out to be a site for ICSS. Destruction of this nucleus not only blocks ICSS but, in most though not all studies, sharply reduces REMS sleep as well. An animal who is REMS deprived will bar press more frequently to lower stimulus intensities, and REMS-deprived animals with access to ICSS will show a reduced REMS rebound. Furthermore, if animals are allowed to self-stimulate, they are not likely to go into REMS for 2 to 3 hours, exceedingly long for the rat.

We are just beginning to join our neurophysiologic and neurochemical frontiers. We should be aware that even seemingly trifling, electrophysiologic parameters, in this case the shortened REMS latency, may turn out to be important clues. They may lead ultimately to fresh sources of confirmatory evidence about aberrantly functioning neurophysiologic or neurochemical mechanisms. In this fashion, intersecting modes of investigation afford the greatest hope of establishing the fundamental mechanisms at work in depression as well as in the other psychobiologic pathologies.

Callaway: Some of my friends in neurochemistry say that electrophysiologists talk like fifth-graders having show and tell. They demand mechanisms and so the discussions of both Drs. Kupfer and Roffwarg are certainly most welcome.

For those of us who like to record brain waves, hope also comes from work by Adey and colleagues at UCLA. They show that imposed voltage fields on the order of those that give rise to the EEG can change GABA and calcium efflux from the mammalian brain (L. K. Kaczmarek and W. R. Adey: Weak electric gradients change ionic and transmitter fluxes in cortex. *Brain Res.,* 66:537–540, 1974). Similar fields induced in the brain either by electromagnetic radiation (S. M. Bawin, R. J. Gavalas-Medici, and W. R. Adey: Effects of modulated very high frequency fields on specific brain rhythms in cats. *Brain Res.,* 58:365–384, 1973) or by electrostatic fields, can modify behavior. These fields are on the order of microvolts per centimeter, and the synapse operates in the kilovolts per centimeter range. It's very strange that the brain is operating this way, but then, it's a very strange organ.

All this is to say that maybe we have been seeing actual signals used in data processing when we look at brain waves. Now that, I think, is encouraging.

Whether or not we get to the mechanisms as all of us hope, I think that the work of Drs. Shagass and Buchsbaum will provide what J. Stoyva and J. Kamiya have called convergent data. (Electrophysiological studies of dreaming as the prototype of a new strategy in the study of consciousness. *Psychol. Rev.,* 75: 192–205,1968). Any piece of behavior can be produced by a variety of underlying brain states so long as they act through some final common pathway. And any particular patterns of electrical potentials at the top of the head can also be produced by a variety of underlying brain states, again so long as they happen to sum out the same way.

But if we take a piece of behavior and a concomitant electrical state at the top of the head, then we're likely to be talking about a much more homogeneous situation than we were when we were just talking about either electrical pattern or the behavior. For example, looking at "schizophrenics with slow activity" perhaps as opposed to "schizophrenics with fast activity" may give us a better way of more exactly defining clinical populations for further studies.

Shagass: I have been asked to reiterate a point concerning my attempts to delineate the realistic expectations that one can have in electrophysiologic studies. Dr. Buchsbaum presented fascinating data that showed the great similarity between evoked potentials in identical twins. It's not as well known that in the early days of EEG research, people did twin studies and obtained similar results for EEG. The literature on both evoked potentials and EEG, comparing identical and nonidentical twins, shows generally that the identical twins come out as similar to their co-twins as the same person comes out like himself on another occasion. And this is quite different from nonidentical twins or unrelated people.

The upshot of this is that we are dealing with phenomena in which there appears to be pretty good evidence that genetic determinants can probably take care of at least half the variance. Beyond the genetically determined variance, there is a long list of factors which require control and are never completely controlled; in other words, there is an awful lot of "noise."

Now, when a clinical group, such as schizophrenic patients, is compared with another group, one possibility is that there is *no* relationship between the illness and the genetically determined variance of the electrophysiologic measurements. If this be so, the only margin for demonstrating a difference is in what's left after you take out both the very big genetic factor, and the perhaps not quite as big, but usually substantial, "noise" factor. And that may be *a very small margin.*

If that's the case, you're going to get a lot of overlapping between groups and small differences.

Now, the second possibility is that the illness factor is related to the electrophysiologic expression of the genetic factor or some portion of these genetic factors. In that case you are likely to get big differences between clinical groups.

The third possibility is that the illness factor will override the electrophysiologic *expression* of the genetic factor. In that case you can also get big differences.

Considering these possibilities, one can draw some implications for what one should do in research. After that first step of comparing groups to see if there is anything there at all, and if one does find differences, whether big or small, longitudinal study of the same people in health and disease is warranted. Such longitudinal studies will separate out temporary from permanent differences. The last step, which is both the most difficult and the most desirable, is to study twins concordant and discordant for illness to find out what part of any permanent difference is genetic and what part isn't.

Biology of the Major Psychoses, edited by D. X. Freedman, Res. Publ. Assoc. Res. Nerv. Ment. Dis., Vol. 54. Raven Press, New York 1975.

Neuromuscular Abnormalities in the Major Mental Illnesses. I. Serum Enzyme Studies

Herbert Y. Meltzer

Department of Psychiatry, University of Chicago, and The Illinois State Psychiatric Institute, Chicago, Illinois 60637

A series of reports from this laboratory has presented evidence for skeletal muscle and subterminal motor neuron abnormalties in the majority of patients with both schizophrenic and affective psychoses. This evidence includes (a) increased activity in serum of skeletal muscle-type creatine phosphokinase (CPK) and aldolase activity (1-8) and more recently, pyruvate kinase activity (Meltzer and Pscheidt, *unpublished data);* (b) abnormal extrafusal muscle fibers in skeletal muscle biopsies (7,9-13); and (c) abnormalities of subterminal motor nerves (14, 15).

In light of the theme of this book, this chapter and the succeeding one compare the current results of our studies of serum enzymes, the morphology of skeletal muscle fibers and the morphology of subterminal motor nerves in patients with acute and chronic schizophrenia, unipolar and bipolar affective psychoses, non-psychotic psychiatric patients, and normal controls. This chapter also considers potential causes of the increased serum CPK activity in acutely psychotic patients and the relationship of these increases to comparable findings in patients with unequivocal acute brain diseases.

METHODS

We have studied consecutive voluntary admissions to a research ward at the Illinois State Psychiatric Institute from 9/1/68 to 12/31/73. Informed consent was obtained from all patients and their families. Only data from the first admission of each patient to this study are reported, excluding data from readmitted patients.

Patient Population

Patients were generally accepted into this project because of the recent onset of grossly psychotic symptoms. e.g., delusions, hallucinations, and bizarre behavior. Clinical diagnoses were made by two psychiatrists and a social worker, at the time of discharge, without any knowledge of the research biologic data. The criteria used for the diagnosis of manic-depressive illness and psychotic depression have been described elsewhere (7). The criteria used for the diagnosis of

TABLE 1

Factor	Non-psychotic	Acute schizo-phrenic	Chronic schizo-phrenic	Bipolar manic phase	Psychotic depression
Age					
Range	17–55	15–49	18–47	19–47	29–63
Median	26	24	25	29	36
Sex–Race					
Black males	3	34	6	1	1
White males	2	24	12	2	3
Black females	9	43	14	4	5
White females	5	22	8	5	3
Total N	19	123	40	12	12

schizophrenia are those of the New Haven Schizophrenia Index (16). Chronic schizophrenics were those schizophrenics with poor premorbid personalities, minimal remission of symptoms after previous psychotic episodes, and no greater improvement after treatment on our unit than the limited adjustment achieved prior to the onset of the current episode. Generally, these patients had been ill for at least 2 years prior to admission. At the time of study, however, they were usually experiencing an acute exacerbation of their psychosis with a marked intensification of delusions, hallucinations, and bizarre behavior. Acute schizophrenic patients are those psychotic patients having generally good premorbid personality, without a history of mood disorder, and with a relatively abrupt onset of delusions, hallucinations, formal disorders of thinking, and bizarre behavior, none of which is typical of the symptomatology characteristic of manic or depressed patients, and who usually go on to near-complete remission of symptoms during the course of hospitalization. Family history data are not explicitly used in making diagnoses. Schizophrenic patients were further divided into paranoid and nonparanoid types on the basis of the presence or absence of delusions of persecution or grandeur, and pervasive ideas of reference.

Nonpsychotic patients generally had very severe anxiety or depressive symptoms in the absence of delusions, hallucinations, bizarre behavior, or formal disorder of thinking. These patients had no first degree relatives with a history of psychotic illness.

Table 1 gives the number of subjects in each diagnostic group, their median age, race, and sex. The oldest subject in the study was 63 years old, but the majority were under 25. We did not include data from patients who had histories of alcoholism or who had received any type of intramuscular injection within 2 weeks prior to admission.

Clinical Assessment

At the time of admission, the prognosis of each psychotic patient was evaluated by the Stephans–Astrup scale (17). Only the data from the patients who received a discharge diagnosis of schizophrenia were utilized in relating overall prognosis scores to serum CPK activity.

Each patient was rated by two of six raters, Monday through Friday, using a 14-item version of the rating scale devised by Hargreaves (18). Of these 14 items, four were significantly intercorrelated with each other and three pairs of other items were significantly intercorrelated. Thus, the eight items that were essentially independent are reported on: Depression, Anger, Anxiety, Psychotic Behavior, Paranoia, Hyperactivity, Underactivity, and Effective Contact with People. Each item was related on a scale of 0 to 9, with descriptive guideposts for rating of 0, 1 to 3, 4 to 6, and 7 to 9. The highest ratings indicated the most aberrant behavior or lack of effective contact. The rating team consisted of six raters who based their ratings on observations of the patient during the day shift. The mean pooled interrater reliability for all six raters over 14 items was 0.906 ± 0.051.

We investigated the possibility that the peak dose of phenothiazine which was prescribed might differentiate those schizophrenic patients with and without increased serum CPK activity at any time during hospitalization. All patients were placed on placebo for the first week of hospitalization, unless very bizarre behavior made immediate treatment necessary. Thereafter, schizophrenic patients were treated with chlorpromazine (Thorazine®), trifluoperazine (Stelazine®), or thioridazine (Mellaril®), which were generously supplied by Smith, Kline, and French, Inc. and Sandoz, Ltd. in the form of pink capsules identical to the placebo. Each patient received three capsules b.i.d. throughout hospitalization. If patients required parenteral medication, fluphenazine enanthate (Prolixin Enanthate®) was given subcutaneously. (We have found that this is one form of parenteral antipsychotic medication that does not raise serum CPK activity.) Rarely was intramuscular Thorazine® given. To assess the minimal dose of medication required to bring about remission, each patient was begun on 200 mg chlorpromazine orally, or its equivalent: 10 mg trifluoperazine, or 200 mg thioridazine.

Fluphenazine enanthate was considered to be 24 times more potent than chlorpromazine. The medication was then raised by the equivalent of 200 mg of chlorpromazine every fifth or sixth day, until it appeared that no further remission of psychotic symptomatology was brought about by increasing the dosage. The prescribing physician had no knowledge of serum CPK levels. The staff making daily ratings had no knowledge of which medication was ordered or dosage. The peak dose prescribed for each patient, in chlorpromazine equivalents, was used for an assessment of the amount of medication required to treat schizophrenic patients with and without increased serum CPK activity. It was not possible to use drug dosage as a parameter for differentiating patients with affective psychoses.

Length of hospitalization was also considered as a parameter that might distinguish patients with and without increased CPK activity. Each patient's discharge was given as soon as maximal clinical improvement and arrangement for outpatient treatment had occurred. These discharge decisions were independent of any knowledge of serum CPK levels or muscle biopsy results.

Laboratory Methods

Small amounts of plasma were obtained Monday through Friday on each patient from the day of admission to discharge, when possible. Serum CPK activity was determined by the method of Rosalki (19) using reagents obtained from Calbiochem as preweighed kits. Control sera of known activity are determined periodically in order to validate the assay. The coefficient of variation for duplicate determinations was 5%. The 95% upper limits of normal for serum CPK activity in our laboratory are 50 IU/liter for white females; 70 IU/liter for black females and white males; and 110 IU/liter for black males. These norms are based on the study of 145 healthy subjects undergoing pre-employment examinations and 436 newly admitted nonpsychotic psychiatric patients or non-acutely psychotic, chronic schizophrenic patients (3,20). These limits are slightly higher than those usually used by other laboratories (19,21).

The isoenzymes of CPK were determined by the method of Van der Veen and Willebrands (22).

RESULTS

Incidence of Serum CPK Elevations

The incidences of increased serum CPK activity at admission and later in hospitalization are given in Table 2. None of the 19 non-psychotic patients had increased serum CPK activity at admission. One of the 19 nonpsychotic patients had increased serum CPK activity later in hospitalization—an increase of small magnitude that was present in only one sample. At admission 47.1% of all psychotic patients had increased serum CPK activity; the percentage varied from 20 to 56% for particular diagnostic groups. Some of the psychotic patients with

TABLE 2. *Percentage of psychiatric patients with CPK elevations*

		Time of CPK elevation			
Diagnosis	N	Admission	Later	Anytime	Never
Nonpsychotics	19	0	5.3	5.3	94.7
All psychotics	187	47.1	60.4	75.9	24.1
Acute schizophrenic	123	50.4	61.0	78.9	21.1
Nonparanoid	67	49.3	59.7	76.1	23.9
Paranoid	56	51.8	62.5	82.1	17.9
Chronic schizophrenic	40	42.5	65.0	70.0	30.0
Nonparanoid	15	20.0	73.3	73.3	26.7
Paranoid	25	56.0	60.0	68.0	32.0
Bipolar, manic phase	12	33.3	58.3	75.0	25.0
Psychotic depression	12	41.7	41.7	66.7	33.3

increased serum CPK activity at admission had a subsequent period of increased serum CPK activity later in hospitalization as did 28% of those psychotic patients without increased serum CPK activity at admission (Table 2), so that ultimately 75% of all psychotic patients, and 66 to 82% of patients with different types of psychoses, had increased serum CPK activity at some time during the course of the study. These data demonstrate that repeated study of serum CPK activity throughout hospitalization is necessary to identify all psychotic patients with a propensity to manifest increased serum CPK activity.

All groups of psychotic patients had a significantly greater incidence of increased serum CPK activity at admission or later in hospitalization than did nonpsychotics, but there were no significant differences between groups of psychotics. Combining all schizophrenics, all affectives, or all acute schizophrenics plus all affectives revealed no trends for significant distinctions along the schizophrenic–affective or acute–chronic dimensions with regard to the incidence of increased serum CPK activity.

Magnitude and Duration of Serum CPK Increases

The magnitude of increased serum CPK activity for the acute and chronic schizophrenics and for the manic and psychotically depressed patients is given in Fig. 1. The results are expressed as multiples of the upper limit of normal for

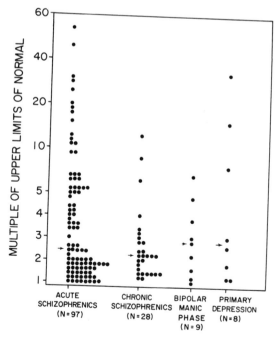

FIG. 1. Magnitude of peak increases in serum CPK activity in acutely psychotic patients as multiples of upper limit of normal for the patients' respective race–sex group.

the appropriate race-sex group of the patients. The median increase for each diagnostic group was 2.2 to 2.8 times the upper limit of normal, but in 25% of the patients the peak increase was equal to or greater than five times the 95% upper limit of normal. Of those psychotic patients with both admission and later elevations ($N = 59$), 29 had their largest serum CPK level at admission, 29 had their greatest increase later, and one had identical elevations. The median duration of the admission and late increases for the patients in this study was 4 days. In some patients the levels of serum CPK activity were still not below generally accepted limits, even at discharge.

Origin of CPK in Serum: CPK Isozymes, CSF and Other Enzymes

In all psychotic patients for whom we have studied which isozymes of CPK were present in serum, only the skeletal muscle isozyme of CPK was found (1,2,4). We have examined the cerebrospinal fluid (CSF) of numerous patients with the schizophrenic illnesses as well as the affective psychoses and have not observed any detectable CPK activity in the CSF in any of these patients (4). Of the enzymes studied, only those enzymes associated with muscle disease have been increased in the sera of psychotic patients—aldolase (1–4) and pyruvate kinase (Meltzer and Pscheidt, *unpublished observations*). Other serum enzymes such as aspartate aminotransferase, lactic dehydrogenase, malic dehydrogenase, and alkaline phosphatase have not been increased (4).

Possible Nonspecific Causes of Increased Serum CPK Levels

Because demonstration of the skeletal muscle isozyme of CPK in serum, together with the absence of CPK activity in spinal fluid, strongly suggested that the source of the increased CPK in the serum of psychotic patients was skeletal muscle, we sought to explain these increases by considering specific factors known to cause, or conceivably capable of causing, increased release of CPK from skeletal muscle. This included hypothyroidism, muscle trauma, alcoholic myopathy, psychoactive drugs (oral and parenteral), isotonic physical activity, isometric physical activity, starvation, toxic substances in the diet, sleep disturbance, stress, hereditary factors and nonspecific concomitants of acute, organic brain dysfunction. Several of these, such as hypothyroidism, muscle trauma, and alcoholic myopathy could be eliminated by careful physical examination and appropriate laboratory investigation. Most of the other factors have been considered in some detail in previous publications (2,4,8,24–27) and are not considered again here. However, there are several points we would like to make.

Because the psychotic patients with increased serum CPK activity are those most likely to receive intramuscular injections under ordinary clinical circumstances, it is most important to make a special effort to not use this route of administration if one wishes to study serum CPK levels. Second, we have found that the increases in serum CPK activity following an exhausting series of isometric exercises in psychotic patients and controls are similar and not so large as to be a major factor in the large increases found in some of our patients (Goode and Meltzer, *unpublished data*). To sum up, the nonpsychotic factors that might produce increases in serum CPK activity, which we listed at the beginning of this section, do not individually account for the increases in serum CPK activity we have noted in psychotic patients, but we cannot exclude the possibility that collectively they account for all or part of the increase in some patients.

Clinical Characteristics of Patients with Serum CPK Increases

Time of Onset of Psychotic Symptoms

A major aim of our research has been to determine if there are any clinical differences between those psychotic patients with and without increased serum CPK levels at admission or later in hospitalization. Because of the brief duration of most increases in serum CPK activity, it seemed likely that a major factor determining the presence of increased serum CPK at admission might be the interval between the onset of psychotic symptoms, the time of admission, and obtaining the first blood serum. As can be seen in Table 3, for all psychotic patients, the incidence of increased serum CPK activity at admission is significantly greater for those whose gross psychotic symptoms began 1 to 7 days prior to admission than for those whose symptoms began 8 or more days prior to admission. The differences did not reach statistical significance for the individual diagnostic groups, but were all in the expected direction.

Prognosis

The incidence of increased serum CPK levels in good prognosis and poor prognosis schizophrenic patients as determined by the Stephans–Astrup scale (17) was not significantly different [89/113 (79%) versus 36/50 (72%)].

TABLE 3. *Percentage incidence of serum-CPK elevations at admission as a function of time of onset of psychotic symptoms*

Diagnosis	Onset < 1 week	Onset > 1 week	p
All psychotic patients	58.7 (54/92)	35.8 (34/95)	< 0.005
Acute schizophrenics	58.1 (43/74)	38.8 (19/49)	< 0.10
Chronic schizophrenics	62.5 (5/8)	37.5 (12/32)	> 0.5
Bipolar, manic phase	40.0 (2/5)	28.6 (2/7)	> 0.5
Psychotic depression	80.0 (4/5)	14.3 (1/7)	< 0.10

TABLE 4. Mean peak first week behavior ratings for groups with and without serum CPK elevation at admission[a]

Item	All psychotics		Acute schizophrenics		Chronic schizophrenics		Bipolar manic phase		Psychotic depression	
	$N=88$ I	$N=99$ NI	$N=62$ I	$N=61$ NI	$N=17$ I	$N=23$ NI	$N=4$ I	$N=8$ NI	$N=5$ I	$N=7$ NI
Psychotic behavior	6.375	5.434[b]	6.532	5.787	5.706	4.478	7.250	6.000	6.000	4.857
Paranoia	4.784	4.071[b]	5.048	4.393	3.824	3.348	5.250	3.500	4.400	4.286
Effective contact with people	5.318	4.515[b]	5.758	5.131	3.941	3.217	5.000	4.625	4.800	3.286
Hyperactivity	2.932	1.949[b]	3.371	2.262[b]	1.471	1.087	4.000	2.625	1.600	1.286
Underactivity	1.568	1.576	1.387	1.623	1.235	1.087	2.500	1.375	4.200	3.000
Depression	4.818	4.727	4.855	4.787	2.294	4.217	4.750	4.250	6.200	6.429
Anger	4.523	3.879[b]	4.919	4.049[b]	3.588	3.174	5.000	4.250	2.400	4.286
Anxiety	5.750	5.455	5.887	5.754	5.353	4.565	6.000	5.750	5.200	5.429

[a] I = Increase in serum CPK admission; NI = No Increase in serum CPK at admission.
[b] Univariate analysis of variance, Scheffe comparison: $p < 0.05$.

Symptomatology

There were some significant differences in the clinical behavior of the psychotic patients with and without increased serum CPK activity. The means of the peak ratings during the first week of hospitalization for all psychotic patients combined, and for each diagnostic group divided into those with and those without increased serum CPK activity *at admission* are given in Table 4. All psychotic patients with and without increased serum CPK activity at admission differed significantly ($p < 0.05$) in peak ratings during the first week of hospitalization for five of eight items on our rating scale: Psychotic Behavior, Paranoia, Effective Contact with People, Hyperactivity, and Anger. All significant differences were in the direction of higher ratings for patients with admission serum CPK elevations. It should be noted that mean Hyperactivity ratings in both groups are under three, which is the low range of the hyperactivity spectrum and is mainly indicative of some pacing, agitation, and restlessness. On one item, Underactivity, patients without admission CPK elevation had minimally higher ratings. For the five items mentioned above, Sheffe's comparisons within diagnostic categories between patients with and without admission CPK elevation were significant in only two cases. Both were for acute schizophrenic patients, and both items—Hyperactivity and Anger—were rated higher for acute schizophrenics with admission elevations. The relatively small number of patients with affective psychoses studied so far may contribute to the lack of significant differences within this diagnostic group.

Two behavioral items from the Stephans–Astrup prognosis scale, Hallucinations and Excitement, were present significantly more often at admission in schizophrenic patients with an elevation of serum CPK activity above normal limits at any time during hospitalization than were those who never had such an elevation (Table 5).

The mean of all ratings of each item of the rating scale throughout hospitalization were determined for each psychotic subject. The mean ratings for all psychotic patients and for each diagnostic group, divided into those with and without elevated serum CPK activity at any time during hospitalization are given in Table 6. The psychotic patients with elevated serum CPK levels had

TABLE 5. *Incidence of excitement and hallucination in schizophrenics with and without elevated serum CPK activity*

	Serum CPK increased	Serum CPK not increased	χ^2	p
Excitement	58.4% (73/125)	31.6% (12/38)	7.360	<0.01
Hallucinations	56.0% (70/125)	28.9% (11/38)	7.483	<0.01

TABLE 6. Mean behavior ratings for groups with elevated serum CPK activity anytime and never elevated[a]

Item	All psychotics		Acute schizophrenics		Chronic schizophrenics		Bipolar manic phase		Primary depression	
	$N=142$ AE	$N=45$ NE	$N=97$ AE	$N=26$ NE	$N=28$ AE	$N=12$ NE	$N=9$ AE	$N=3$ NE	$N=8$ AE	$N=4$ NE
Psychotic behavior	2.803	2.267[b]	2.845	2.269	2.893	2.167	2.556	1.333	2.250	3.250
Paranoia	1.972	2.089	2.062	2.038	1.964	2.417	1.111	1.000	1.875	2.250
Effective contact with people	1.908	1.489	2.031	1.538	1.571	1.250	1.667	1.000	1.875	2.250
Hyperactivity	0.944	0.733	1.000	0.692	0.786	0.833	1.111	1.000	0.625	0.500
Underactivity	0.472	0.622	0.485	0.692	0.429	0.250	0.000	0.000	1.000	1.750
Depression	3.338	3.133	3.258	3.115	3.321	2.917	3.333	3.000	4.375	4.000
Anger	2.613	2.444	2.680	2.423	2.500	2.417	2.444	2.333	2.375	2.750
Anxiety	3.620	3.311	3.649	3.269	3.607	3.167	3.556	3.333	3.375	4.000

[a] AE = Increased serum CPK activity at anytime during hospitalization; NE = no elevation in serum CPK activity at anytime.

[b] Univariate analysis of variance, Scheffe comparison: $p < 0.05$.

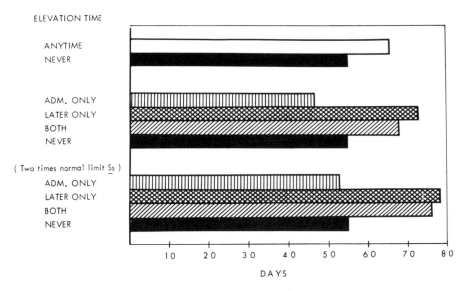

FIG. 2. Mean length of hospitalization for patients with increased serum CPK activity anytime versus never; at admission only, later only, both admission and later, or never. Lower group includes only patients with no increases and those with increases that were at least twice normal.

significantly higher ratings on Psychotic Behavior, but not on any other item. There were no significant comparisons within diagnostic groups for the psychotic behavior ratings.

Length of Hospitalization and Medication

The psychotic patients with elevated serum CPK activity at any time during hospitalization had longer periods of hospitalization than those who never had increased serum CPK levels (Fig. 2). Patients with elevations in serum CPK activity later in hospital had longer hospitalizations than those who only had elevations at admission or never had an increase. This was also true when only patients with peak serum CPK levels that were at least twice the upper limit of normal were included in the analyses. The schizophrenic patients with increased serum CPK activity also required higher doses of neuroleptic medication in chlorpromazine equivalents than did those without increased serum CPK activity (Table 7).

Serum CPK Activity in Nonpsychotic Periods as a Factor in Serum CPK Elevations

We were interested in determining whether the psychotic patients who had an elevation in serum CPK levels at any time during hospitalization had any other

TABLE 7. *Mean maximum chlorpromazine equivalent dose (milligrams) for schizophrenics with and without increased serum CPK levels at anytime by sex–race groups*

Sex–race	Increased serum CPK activity at any time			No increase in serum CPK activity at any time		
	N	Mean	SD	N	Mean	SD
Black males	36	636.9	361.5	7	514.3	279.5
White males	24	604.2	419.3	15	580.0	400.4
Black females	49	562.2	322.3	11	281.8	244.2
White females	26	409.6	322.5	7	185.7	146.4

Analysis of variance results for maximum dose

Source	df	Mean square	F	p
Sex–race	3	541,595	4.604	<0.01
Increase/No increase	1	741,779	6.306	<0.01
Interaction	3	89,568	0.761	—
Within	167	117,626	—	—

evidence for a tendency to have a relative excess of serum CPK activity. The peak serum CPK value during the last 2 days of hospitalization was used as the predischarge serum CPK level for each patient. We also calculated mean serum CPK activity for each patient based on all samples through hospitalization, excluding all samples that exceeded the 95% upper limits of normal and all

TABLE 8. *Mean predischarge serum CPK levels for all psychotics with elevated serum CPK at anytime vs no elevation by sex–race groups*

Sex–race	Increased anytime			Never elevated		
	N	Mean	SD	N	Mean	SD
Black males	38	79.9	40.6	5	54.2	21.7
White males	27	51.1	37.5	18	32.3	11.9
Black females	59	50.7	41.6	15	27.7	15.7
White females	32	30.1	25.9	15	21.9	13.2

Analysis of variance results for predischarge serum CPK activity

Source	df	Mean square	F	p
Sex–race	3	9,408	8.266	<0.01
Increase/ No increase	1	11,492	10.096	<0.01
Interaction	3	470	0.413	—
Within	201	1,138	—	—

TABLE 9. *Mean serum CPK levels for all psychotic patients with elevated serum CPK at anytime versus no elevation by sex–race groups*

Sex/race	Increase anytime			No increase in serum CPK activity at anytime		
	N	Mean	SD	N	Mean	SD
Black males	36	69.1	31.5	7	42.3	9.6
White males	29	43.5	20.2	18	32.6	10.5
Black females	59	40.6	15.1	15	25.9	11.0
White females	33	27.6	9.3	15	18.3	4.3

Analysis of variance results for mean CPK

Source	df	Mean square	F	p
Sex/race	3	6,776.920	20.787	<0.01
Increase/ No increase	1	8,640.093	26.501	<0.01
Interaction	3	567.871	1.742	—
Within	204	326.024	—	—

samples for 5 days after a muscle biopsy or 3 days after an intramuscular injection. The predischarge serum CPK levels (Table 8) and overall mean serum CPK levels (Table 9) were significantly greater for all psychotics with an elevation in serum CPK activity at anytime than for those psychotics who never had such an increase. There was also a tendency for the mean serum CPK levels of the psychotic patients with increased serum CPK activity to be greater than those of nonpsychotic patients (data not presented).

Correlation between Serum CPK Activity and Psychopathology

If increased serum CPK activity is more than a nonspecific accompaniment of the psychotic state, there should be positive correlations between the daily determinations of serum CPK activity and specific items of the daily rating scale. Therefore, we determined product-moment correlations between serum CPK activity and each of the eight independent items on our rating scale. All correlation coefficients which exceeded the 0.05 level of confidence were considered significant. Table 10 presents the percentage of significant positive and negative correlations of all psychotic patients with and without increased serum CPK activity at any time. The percentage of psychotic patients who had elevated serum CPK activity at any time who had significant positive correlations between CPK levels and behavior was generally much greater than the percentage for those who never had increased serum CPK activity; the percentage of positive correlations

TABLE 10. Percent significant positive and negative correlations between serum CPK activity and daily behavior ratings for diagnostic groups as a function of increased serum CPK levels at any time

		Diagnostic group[a]									
		All psychotics		Acute schizophrenics		Chronic schizophrenics		Bipolar manic phase		Primary depression	
Item	r	AE	NE	AE	NE	AE	NE	AE	NE	AE	NE
Depression	+	15.5	6.7	14.4	7.7	10.7	0	11.1	0	50.0	25.0
	−	8.5	2.2	7.2	0	14.3	0	11.1	33.3	0	0
Anger	+	20.4	6.7	22.7	7.7	14.3	0	22.2	0	12.5	25.0
	−	5.6	2.2	6.2	3.8	3.6	0	0	0	12.5	0
Anxiety	+	31.0	13.3	30.9	11.5	21.4	0	77.8	33.3	12.5	50.0
	−	6.3	0	5.2	0	7.1	0	11.1	0	12.5	0
Psychotic behavior	+	35.2	13.3	38.1	15.4	14.3	0	77.8	33.3	25.0	25.0
	−	4.9	4.4	3.1	7.7	10.7	0	11.1	0	0	0
Paranoia	+	28.2	8.9	32.0	7.7	14.3	0	44.4	0	12.5	50.0
	−	14.8	6.7	17.5	11.5	10.7	0	0	0	12.5	0
Hyperactivity	+	24.6	11.1	24.7	11.5	17.9	8.3	55.6	33.3	12.5	0
	−	1.4	0	2.1	0	0	0	0	0	0	0
Underactivity	+	10.6	4.4	9.3	3.8	10.7	0	11.1	0	25.0	25.0
	−	3.5	0	2.1	0	10.7	0	0	0	0	0
Effective contact with people	+	21.8	15.6	21.6	15.4	14.3	0	55.6	33.3	12.5	50.0
	−	11.3	6.7	12.4	7.7	10.7	8.3	11.1	0	0	0
Total N:		142	45	97	26	28	12	9	3	8	4

[a] AE = Increased serum CPK activity at anytime during hospitalization; NE = no elevation in serum CPK activity at anytime.

between serum CPK levels and behavior was generally much greater than the percentage of negative correlations in both groups. For all psychotic patients who had elevated serum CPK levels at any time, serum CPK activity had a significant positive correlation most frequently with Psychotic Behavior ratings. This was also true for the acute schizophrenic and manic patients. Anxiety was the most frequent significant positive correlate of serum CPK levels for chronic schizophrenic patients with elevated serum CPK levels. Hyperactivity and serum CPK activity had a significantly positive correlation in 55% of the manic patients, but only 12.5% of the depressed patients with elevated serum CPK activity. Underactivity was significantly positively correlated with serum CPK activity in 25% of depressed patients with elevated serum CPK and 11.1% of manic patients with elevated serum CPK activity. In general, serum CPK levels were least frequently correlated with specific items of the rating scale for chronic schizophrenic patients.

We are presently investigating the relationship between time of CPK elevation (admission or later) and the strength of association between CPK and behavior ratings. In addition, because of a potential lag between serum CPK activity and behavior, we are doing individual profiles on patients to better explicate the relationship between behavior and serum CPK activity.

Serum CPK Levels in First-Degree Relatives of Psychotic Patients

We have previously reported that first-degree relatives of both schizophrenic patients and patients with affective psychoses have slightly elevated serum CPK levels (2,4,5,7,8). To date, we have obtained one or more serum CPK samples from 337 first-degree relatives of 162 psychotic patients, and of these 337 individuals, 103 or 30.6% have had at least one elevation of serum CPK levels based on the norms for their respective race–sex groups. These data will be reported in detail elsewhere. The magnitude of the increases is generally 25 to 50% above the upper limit of normal, but in 10% of those with increases, serum CPK levels have been as high as two to three times normal. The increases are present in approximately the same percentage of parents, siblings, and children of psychotic patients. These increases were present in relatives of patients with all types of "functional" psychoses. We have found a significant relationship concerning serum CPK levels in these relatives and the index patients: the incidence of increased serum CPK activity in the first degree relatives of psychotic patients who themselves had increased serum CPK activity (92/256 or 35.9%) is significantly greater than the incidence in first-degree relatives of psychotic patients who did not have serum CPK elevation (11/87 or 13.6%). These incidences are significantly different at the 0.001 level of confidence ($x^2 = 13.46$).

Serum CPK Activity in Acute Brain Diseases

A series of publications has demonstrated increased serum CPK activity in patients with hemorrhagic and thrombotic cerebrovascular disease, necrotic gli-

TABLE 11. *Comparison of increased serum CPK activity in acute psychoses, acute brain diseases, polymyositis, and chronic neuromuscular diseases*

Disorder	Time after onset of 1st CPK increase (days)	Time from onset of increase to peak increase (days)	Duration of CPK increase (days)	Magnitude of CPK increase	Patients with CPK increase (%)
Acute psychoses	1–3	1–3	1–7	1^+–2^+	50
Acute brain diseases	1–3	1–3	1–7	1^+–2^+	60
Polymyositis	1	Variable	Variable	1^+–4^+	80
Chronic neuromuscular	Unknown	Unknown	Prolonged	1^+–2^+	60

omas, cerebral anoxia, status epilepticus, brain trauma (e.g., gunshot wounds), subarachnoid hemorrhages, drug-induced coma, encephalitis, and meningitis (28–36). It is skeletal muscle-type CPK that is present in the serum of patients with these various types of acute brain syndromes (30,35). Other characteristics of the serum CPK increases in acute brain syndromes and the acute psychoses are strikingly similar to each other and quite different from those in chronic neurogenic muscle disease or a myopathy such as polymyositis (Table 11). This includes the time from onset of symptoms to the first rise in serum CPK activity, the time from the onset of the CPK increase to the peak increase in CPK activity, the duration of increased CPK activity, the magnitude of increased serum CPK activity and the percentage of patients who have increased serum CPK activity.

DISCUSSION

Elevations of serum CPK activity beyond the 95% upper limit of normal are present at admission and later during hospitalization in patients with affective psychoses and in patients with schizophrenic psychoses, but not in severely disturbed nonpsychotic psychiatric patients. It is unlikely that all serum CPK increases in psychotic patients could be caused by such factors as alcoholism, muscle trauma, physical activity, drugs, stress, sleep deprivation, diet, and other nonspecific factors (2,4,8,24–27). These factors may account for some of the smaller serum CPK elevations that we have observed. The evidence suggests that the larger increases and possibly many of the smaller increases as well are not caused by any of these nonspecific factors.

The pattern of enzymes whose serum activities are increased (CPK, aldolase, pyruvate kinase), the fact that it is the skeletal muscle-type CPK that is present in the serum of psychotic patients, and the absence of CPK in the CSF of psychotic patients strongly suggests that the source of the increased enzyme activities in the serum of psychotic patients is skeletal muscle. However, recent studies indicate that rabbit-brain-type CPK is unstable under certain *in vivo* or *in vitro* conditions (37). Because of this instability, during electrophoresis, brain-type CPK may be indistinguishable from the cardiac and skeletal muscle types. We have been conducting similar studies with human brain CPK and have found that it, too, can appear like cardiac muscle CPK after *in vitro* incubation (Cho and Meltzer, *unpublished data*). No *in vivo* studies of the instability of human brain CPK have been carried out. These studies make it difficult to dismiss entirely the possibility that brain is the source of the CPK in the serum of acutely psychotic patients.

Not all acutely psychotic patients, just as not all patients with acute brain diseases, have increased serum CPK levels. It is clear that this is not simply because the increases are unique to one or another of the common functional psychoses. However, we have been able to define both clinical and biologic factors that begin to account for why some but not all acutely psychotic patients have increased serum CPK levels. We have clearly demonstrated that the shorter the interval between the onset of psychotic symptoms and obtaining a blood sample, the more likely it is that an increase in serum CPK activity will be present. When the interval is greater than 1 week, the chances of finding a serum CPK increase are slight, even if the psychotic symptoms are unabated. It may be the failure to study a high proportion of patients within the first few days of psychosis which may account for the failure to replicate some of our findings in a few studies (38,39).

In this chapter, we have demonstrated for the first time that psychotic patients with increased serum CPK levels have significantly greater psychopathology in some dimensions, e.g., Hyperactivity and Psychotic Behavior, or a higher incidence of Hallucinations and Excitement, than do patients without increased serum CPK activity. In most other parameters measured by our daily rating scale, the peak ratings were greater for patients with increased serum CPK activity, although the differences were not significant at the 0.05 level of confidence. The basic prognosis as estimated by the Stephans–Astrup scale did not differ in schizophrenic patients with and without serum CPK increases. Preliminary studies indicate that the 2-year readmission rate is not significantly different for patients with and without elevations in serum CPK activity. Hence, these findings indicate that psychotic patients with more acute and florid psychopathology during the index hospitalization are the ones who are most likely to have increased CPK levels at admission. However, the basic prognosis and medium-term outcome of the two groups do not differ significantly.

Furthermore, we demonstrated that the patients with increased serum CPK levels at any time during hospitalization had significantly higher mean ratings on some items of the daily rating scale than patients who never had such increases at any time. The schizophrenic patients with increased serum CPK levels at any time also had higher requirements for phenothiazines than those who never had increases. Furthermore, all psychotic patients with increased serum CPK levels at any time had significantly longer hospitalizations than those who never had such increases. This indicates that at least for the psychotic episode which led to the index hospitalization, patients with increased serum CPK activity have more prolonged psychotic symptomatology and are more treatment-resistant. This might imply a more profound central nervous system disturbance than that which occurs in those psychotic patients who do not have serum CPK increases.

The serum CPK increases that we have observed in the acute phase may also be related to the significantly greater mean serum CPK activity and the significantly greater serum CPK levels present in the last 2 days of hospitalization in the patients with an elevated serum CPK at any time during hospitalization. These findings suggest that at least for the period surrounding the psychotic episode, those psychotic patients who have transient periods of serum CPK elevation that exceed the upper limit of normal have persistently greater permeability of skeletal muscle. This could mean prolonged "leakiness" of skeletal muscle is a consequence of the transient elevations. Alternatively, the tendency toward excessive muscle permeability might predate the psychosis and contribute to the transient elevation. We favor the latter possibility. Further studies long after the psychotic episode is over will be needed to determine if these relative elevations in serum CPK activity, i.e., elevated mean serum CPK levels persist indefinitely.

Finally, we have presented evidence that the higher mean serum CPK levels in psychotic patients with increased serum CPK levels may occur on a genetic basis as indicated by the significantly higher incidence of first-degree relatives with slightly higher than normal serum CPK levels. We also have preliminary evidence that serum CPK activity is heritable from studies of monozygotic (Mz) and dizygotic (Dz) twins (Meltzer et al., *submitted for publication*). Thus, some of the psychotic patients who have relatively large increases in serum CPK activity when psychotic may have an inherited tendency toward more permeable skeletal muscle (or slower serum enzyme clearance) than the psychotic patients who never had such increases. No discernible pattern of familial relationship and increased serum CPK levels is apparent as yet from our studies of psychotic patients and their relatives, but further study of entire cohorts may be more informative. Another intriguing question that requires further investigation is whether the first-degree relatives with slowly increased serum CPK activity are more vulnerable to the development of psychosis than relatives without such increases.

The high percentages of positive correlations between serum CPK activity and various items of the daily rating scale in psychotic patients with increased serum CPK levels at any time is some indication that on a day-to-day basis even during the periods when serum CPK levels are fluctuating within normal limits, serum CPK levels and behavior are interrelated. It is of interest that Psychotic Behavior ratings and serum CPK activity are most frequently correlated for the entire group of psychotic patients. Acute schizophrenic patients and manic patients tended to have more significant positive correlations between specific rating scale items and serum CPK levels than did chronic schizophrenic and psychotic depressive patients. The pattern of correlates for manic and depressed patients tended to be a mirror image, e.g., CPK and Depression ratings were correlated in 11.1% of manic patients but 50% of depressed patients, whereas Hyperactivity was correlated with serum CPK activity in 55.6% of manic patients and 12.5% of depressed patients. This type of difference is virtually the only significant difference with respect to serum CPK increases in psychotic patients of different diagnostic types.

Assuming that skeletal muscle is the source of the increased CPK activity and that the excess in serum is not caused by simply nonspecific factors, how does one account for the increase, particularly in view of the presence of the increases in all types of "functional" psychoses? A possible mechanism would be diminished clearance of CPK from serum (40). Clearance is a little-understood process, and there are no methods that are readily available to assess this over time for a given subject or between subjects. Hence, diminished clearance as a cause of increased serum CPK activity in psychotic patients is a viable but untested hypothesis.

Increased efflux of enzymes from skeletal muscle as a cause of increased serum CPK activity in psychotic patients is a more likely possibility, if only because of its apparent explanation of serum CPK elevations in variety of disease states and after intense muscular activity (41,42). The most likely cause of increased CPK efflux in psychotic patients is increased cell membrane permeability rather than gross muscle damage as in polymyositis. Although it is difficult to conceptualize the process by which protein molecules exit through a viable muscle cell membrane, such an event is the most likely explanation of the massive increases in serum CPK activity which occur after administration of the psychotomimetic drug phencyclidine and restraint in rats (43). The presence of gross muscle fiber abnormalities and Z-band streaming in psychotic patients does not correlate with the presence of increased serum CPK levels (11,15,44).

Although there are basic similarities in the time course and magnitude of the serum CPK increases in acutely psychotic patients of all the common "functional" types and of patients with well-defined acute brain diseases, this does not mean that all of the increases have the same etiology. It is possible that disruption of tonic upper motoneuron influences on lower motor neurons, loss of trophic substances transported to muscle via blood or nerve, elaboration of myotoxic substances by the brain itself, changes in muscle blood flow, muscle electrolyte composition, oxygen supply or muscle contraction patterns and intensity might occur in the acute psychoses and acute brain syndromes and have an effect on muscle enzyme efflux. There are other possible causes of enzyme release that might come into play during an acute psychosis or an acute organic brain disease. Entirely different factors or variations of a similar process might account for the increased muscle enzyme release in this wide range of disorders. For example, abnormalities of catecholamines and indoleamines are being investigated in the schizophrenic psychoses (45,46), affective psychoses (47,48), acute cerebrovascular diseases (49,50), some chronic brain diseases (51,52), and Duchenne-type muscular dystrophy (53,54). Serotonin can increase serum CPK levels in rats (55), and under various conditions it can produce skeletal muscle pathology (56–58). The hallucinogenic serotonin derivative, harmaline, can increase serum CPK levels in rabbits (Meltzer, *unpublished observations*). It should be apparent from this brief discussion that (a) there are mechanisms by which central processes might influence muscle enzyme release; (b) serum CPK increases in the schizophrenic and affective psychoses indicate at least one shared pathophysiologic process (increased muscle enzyme efflux) but not necessarily a common etiology of that process; and (c) that the acute psychotic states share this pathophysiologic process with acute organic brain diseases, which might indicate the acute psychoses are a type of organic brain disease.

It is apparent from the data we have presented that determination of serum CPK levels throughout hospitalization is not of value in distinguishing among the various types of "functional" psychoses. Such determinations will help distinguish between psychotic and non-psychotic patients, but there may well be false-positives and false-negatives. Because of this, determination of serum CPK activity may have only limited usefulness in the hospital practice of psychiatry. Conceivably, other enzymes may prove superior for clinical purposes, just as determination of pyruvate kinase activity has been proposed to be superior to CPK activity for detection of the carrier state of Duchenne muscular dystrophy. The most important value of the serum enzyme studies may be to stimulate further directed investigation of the neuromuscular apparatus in psychotic patients, as exemplified by the studies of skeletal muscle fibers and subterminal motor nerves in psychotic patients, which are discussed in the next chapter, and studies of the pathophysiology underlying enzyme release from muscle.

SUMMARY

Eighty-eight of 187 (47.1%) psychotic patients had increased serum creatine phosphokinase (CPK) activity at admission. By the time of discharge, 75.9% had had an increased serum CPK activity. There was no significant difference between various groups of types of psychoses in the incidence of increased serum CPK activity. In 25% of the patients with increased serum CPK levels, the peak increase was equal to or greater than five times the upper limit of normal. Only the skeletal muscle isozyme of CPK was present in serum. The incidence of increased serum CPK activity at admission is significantly greater for those patients whose gross psychotic symptoms began 1 to 7 days prior to admission than for those whose symptoms began 8 or more days prior to admission. Some types of psychopathology were more intense or more frequently present in those patients with increased serum CPK activity at admission. Moreover, patients with increased serum CPK activity at any time during hospitalization had significantly greater mean ratings of some types of psychopathology, longer mean hospitalization and required higher doses of medication than did patients who never had such increases. Serum CPK levels were correlated with particular types of behavior for many psychotic patients. "Baseline" mean serum CPK activity of psychotic patients with increased serum CPK levels at some time during hospitalization was significantly greater than that of psychotic patients who never had increases in the hospital. One hundred and three of 337 (30.6%) first-degree relatives of psychotic patients also had slightly increased serum CPK activity. A significantly greater proportion of the relatives with slight elevation were related to patients who had elevated serum CPK activity. Many of the characteristics of increased serum CPK levels in patients with various types of major mental illnesses are similar to each other and to increases present in patients with a variety of acute brain diseases. This obviously does not mean that all these diseases have a common cause. They may, however, share a common mechanism producing increased efflux of CPK from skeletal muscle or decreased clearance of CPK from serum. Determination of serum CPK activity in newly admitted psychiatric patients may help distinguish psychotic from nonpsychotic patients, but the number of false-negatives and -positives will be considerable. The most important values of serum CPK determinations in psychotic patients may be to stimulate further investigation of the neuromuscular system.

ACKNOWLEDGMENTS

The assistance of Pamela Holy and Glenn Lucht in the analysis of research data is gratefully appreciated. The staff of the Acute Psychosis Research Program of the Illinois State Psychiatric Institute assisted immeasurably in the care and investigation of the patients in this study. This research was supported by USPHS grants 16,129 and 18,396 and State of Illinois, Department of Mental Health Grant 231-12-RD. Dr. Meltzer is recipient of USPHS Career Development Award MH-47,808.

REFERENCES

1. Meltzer, H. Y. (1968): Creatine kinase and aldolase in serum; abnormality common to acute psychoses. *Science,* 159:1368–1370.
2. Meltzer, H. Y. (1969): Muscle enzyme release in the acute psychoses. *Arch. Gen. Psychiatry,* 21:102–112.
3. Meltzer, H. Y., Elkun, L., and Moline, R. (1969): Serum enzyme changes in newly admitted psychiatric patients. *Arch. Gen. Psychiatry,* 21:731–738.
4. Meltzer, H.Y., and Moline, R. (1970): Muscle abnormalities in acute psychoses. *Arch. Gen. Psychiatry,* 23:481–491.
5. Meltzer, H. Y., Grinspoon, L., and Shader, R. (1970): Serum creatine phosphokinase and aldolase activities in acute schizophrenic patients and their relatives. *Compr. Psychiatry,* 11:552–558.
6. Meltzer, H. Y., Nankin, R., and Raftery, J. (1971): Serum creatine phosphokinase activity in newly admitted psychiatric patients. II. *Arch. Gen. Psychiatry,* 24:568–572.
7. Meltzer, H. Y. (1973): Skeletal muscle abnormalities in patients with affective disorders. *J. Psychiatr. Res.,* 10:43–57.
8. Meltzer, H. Y. (1974): Serum creatine phosphokinase and serum aldolase levels in acutely psychotic patients. In: *Enzymology in the Practice of Laboratory Medicine,* edited by P. Blume and E. F. Freier, pp. 351–379. Academic Press, New York.
9. Engel, W. K., and Meltzer, H. (1970): Histochemical abnormalities of skeletal muscle in patients with acute psychoses. I. *Science,* 168:273–276.
10. Meltzer, H. Y., and Engel, W. K. (1970): Histochemical abnormalities of skeletal muscle in patients with acute psychoses. II. *Arch. Gen. Psychiatry,* 23:492–502.
11. Fischman, D. A., Meltzer, H. Y., and Poppei, R. W. (1970): The disruption of myofibrils in the skeletal muscle of acutely psychotic patients. *Arch. Gen. Psychiatry,* 23:503–515.
12. Meltzer, H. Y. (1972): Central core fibers in an acutely psychotic patient. *Arch. Gen. Psychiatry,* 27:125–132.
13. Meltzer, H. Y., McBride, E., and Poppei, R. W. (1973): Rod (memaline) bodies in the skeletal muscle of an acute schizophrenic patient. *Neurology,* 23:769–780.
14. Meltzer, H. Y., and Crayton, J. W. (1974): Subterminal motor nerve abnormalities in psychotic patients. *Nature,* 249:373–375.
15. Meltzer, H. Y., and Crayton, J. W. (1974): Muscle abnormalities in psychotic patients. II. Serum CPK activity, fiber abnormalities and branching and sprouting of subterminal nerves. *Biol. Psychiatry,* 8:191–208.
16. Astrachan, B. M., Harrow, M., Adler, D., Brauer, L., Schwartz, A., Schwartz, C., and Tucker, G. (1972): A checklist for the diagnosis of schizophrenia. *Br. J. Psychiatry,* 121:529–539.
17. Stephens, J. H., Astrup, C., and Mangrum, J. C. (1966): Prognostic factors in recovered and deteriorated schizophrenics. *Am. J. Psychiatry,* 122:1121–1126.
18. Hargreaves, W. A. (1968): Systematic nursing observation of psychopathology. *Arch. Gen. Psychiatry,* 18:518–531.

19. Rosalki, S. B. (1967): An improved procedure for serum creatine phosphokinase determination. *J. Lab. Clin. Med.,* 69:696–705.
20. Meltzer, H. Y. (1971): Factors influencing serum creatine phosphokinase levels in the general population. The role of race, activity and age. *Clin. Chim. Acta,* 33:165–172.
21. Ellis, G., and Goldberg, D. M. (1972): Automation of a kinetic spectrophotometric assay for ATP: Creatine phosphotransferase activity suitable for human serum and muscle extracts. *Enzymologia,* 42:407–422.
22. Van Der Veen, K. J., and Willebrands, A. F. (1966): Isoenzymes of creatine phosphokinase in tissue extracts and in normal and pathological sera. *Clin. Chim. Acta,* 13:312–316.
23. Meltzer, H. Y., Mrozak, S., and Boyer, M. (1970): Effect of intramuscular injections on serum creatine phosphokinase activity. *Am. J. Med. Sci.,* 259:42–48.
24. Meltzer, H., and Moline, R. (1970): Plasma enzymatic activity after exercise: Study of psychiatric patients and their relatives. *Arch. Gen. Psychiatry,* 22:390–397.
25. Meltzer, H., Kupfer, D., Wyatt, R., and Snyder, F. (1970): Sleep disturbance and serum CPK activity in acute psychosis. *Arch. Gen. Psychiatry,* 22:398–405.
26. Balmer, S. E., and Rutishaure, I. H. E. (1968):Serum creatine kinase in malnutrition. *J. Pediatr.,* 73:783–787.
27. Bennert, H. W., and Betts, A. (1967): The serum CPK levels in postoperative patients over forty. *J. Maine Med. Assoc.,* 58:214–218.
28. Acheson, J., James, D. C., Hutchinson, E. C., and Westhead, R. (1965): Serum-creatine-kinase levels in cerebral vascular disease. *Lancet,* 1:1306–1307.
29. Langston, L., Riddoch, D., Moxan, C. P., Westherd, R. A., and Woolf, A. L. (1967): Jugular bulb creatine kinase as an indication of slight transient brain damage. *Lancet,* 2:278–281.
30. Dubo, H., Park, D. C., Pennington, R. J. T., Kalbag, R. M., and Walton, J. N. (1967): Serum creatine kinase in cases of stroke, head injury and meningitis. *Lancet,* 2:743–748.
31. Cohnen, G., and Werner, M. (1967): Serum-creatine-kinase in cerebral vascular accidents. *Lancet,* 1:389.
32. Eisen, A. A., and Sherwin, A. L. (1968): Serum creatine phosphokinase activity in cerebral infraction. *Neurologia,* 18:263–268.
33. Wolintz, A. H., Jacobs, L. D., Christoff, N., Solomon, M., and Chernik, N. (1969): Serum and cerebrospinal fluid enzymes in cerebrovascular disease. *Arch. Neurol.,* 20:54–61.
34. Hunt, D., McRae, C., and Zapf, P. (1969): Electrocardiographic and serum enzyme changes in subarachnoid hemorrhage. *Am. Heart J.,* 77:479–488.
35. Cao, A., DeVirgilis, S., Lippi, C., and Trabalza, N. (1969): Creatine kinase isoenzymes in serum of children with neurological disorders. *Clin. Chim. Acta,* 23:475–478.
36. Katz, R.M., and Liebman, W. (1970): Creatine phosphokinase activity in central nervous system disorders and infections. *Am. J. Dis. Child.,* 120:543–546.
37. Frotscher, U., Dominik, B., Richter, R., Zschaege, B., Schulte-Lippern, M., Jennett, G., Messerschnidt, W., Schnitmann, W., and Wilbrandt, R. (1973): Die Instabilitat der Kreatin-Phosphokinase-Isoenzyme im Serum. *Klin. Wochenschr.,* 51:801–805.
38. Cunningham, L. A., Rich, C. L., Woodruff, R. A., Jr., and Olney, J. W. (1974): Creatine phosphokinase and psychiatric illness. *Br. J. Psychiatry,* 124:8291.
39. Harding, T. (1974): Serum creatine kinase in acute psychosis. *Br. J. Psychiatry,* 125:280–285.
40. Posen, S. (1970): Turnover of circulating enzymes. *Clin. Chem.,* 16:71–84.
41. Thomson, W. H. S. (1964): The clinical biochemistry of the muscular dystrophies. *Adv. Clin. Chem.,* 7:137–197.
42. Fowler, W. M., Chowdhury, S. R., Pearson, C. M., Gardner, G., and Bratton, R. (1962) Changes in serum enzyme levels after exercise in trained and untrained subjects. *J. Appl. Physiol.,* 17:943–946.
43. Meltzer, H. Y. (1972): Muscle toxicity produced by phencyclidine and restraint stress. *Res. Commun. Chem. Pathol. Pharmacol.,* 3:369–382.
44. Meltzer, H. Y., and Crayton, J. W. (1975): This volume.
45. Snyder, S. H., Banerjie, S. P., Yamamura, H. I., and Greenberg, D. (1974): Drugs, neurotransmitters and schizophrenia. *Science,* 184:1243–1353.
46. Wyatt, R. J., Saavedra, J. M., Belmaker, R., Cohen, S., and Pollin, W. (1973): The dimethyltryptamine-forming enzyme in blood platelets: A study in monozygotic twins discordant for schizophrenia. *Am. J. Psychiatry,* 130:1359–1361.
47. Schildkraut, J. J. (1965): The catecholamine hypothesis of affective disorders: A review of supporting evidence. *Am. J. Psychiatry,* 122:509–522.

48. Coppen, A., Shaw, D. M., Malleson, A., Eccleston, E., and Gunding, G. (1965): Tryptamine metabolism in depression. *Br. J. Psychiatry,* 111:993–998.
49. Osterholm, J. L. (1974): Noradrenergic mediation of traumatic spinal cord autodestruction. *Life Sci.* (I), 14:1363–1384.
50. Costa, J. L., Ito, U., Spatz, M., Klatzo, I., and Demirjaian, C. (1974): 5-Hydroxytryptamine accumulation in cerebrovascular injury. *Nature,* 248:135–136.
51. Hornykiewicz, O. (1973): Parkinson's disease from brain homogenate to treatment. *Fed. Proc.,* 32:183–190.
52. Klawans, H. L., Ilahi, M. M., and Ringel, S. P. (1971): Toward an understanding of the pathophysiology of Huntington's chorea. *Confin. Neurol.,* 33:297–303.
53. Mendell, J. R., Engel, W. K., and Derrer, E. C. (1971): Duchenne muscular dystrophy: Functional ischemia reproduces its characteristic lesions. *Science,* 172:1143–1145.
54. Murphy, D. L., Mendell, J. R., and Engel, W. K. (1973): Serotonin and platelet function in Duchenne muscular dystrophy. *Arch. Neurol.,* 28:239–242.
55. Meltzer, H. Y., Margulies, P., and Cho, H. W. (1973): Release of creatine phosphokinase from muscle. II. Effect of multiple doses of polymyxin B or compound 48/80 on increases in plasma enzyme levels. *Biochem. Pharmacol.,* 22:857–863.
56. O'Steen, W. K., Barnard, J. L. Jr., and Yates, R. D. (1967): Serotonin induced changes in skeletal muscle of mice as revealed with the light and electron microscopes. *Anat. Rec.,* 157:380.
57. Parker, J. M., and Mendell, J. R. (1974): Proximal muscle necrosis induced by 5-HT-imipramine simulates Duchenne dystrophy. *Nature,* 247:103–104.
58. Meltzer, H. Y., and Rastogi, S. L. (1974): Rat skeletal muscle necrosis following amine uptake blockers or pargyline plus serotonin. *Society for Neuroscience, St. Louis, Mo., October, 1974.*

Biology of the Major Psychoses, edited by D. X.
Freedman, Res. Publ. Assoc. Res. Nerv. Ment.
Dis., Vol. 54. Raven Press, New York   1975

Neuromuscular Abnormalities in the Major Mental Illnesses. II. Muscle Fiber and Subterminal Motor Nerve Abnormalities

Herbert Y. Meltzer and John W. Crayton

Department of Psychiatry, University of Chicago and The Illinois State Psychiatric Institute,
Chicago, Illinois 60637

In the previous chapter (1), we presented evidence that suggests that there is excessive release of creatine phosphokinase (CPK) and other enzymes from skeletal muscle of most, but not all psychotic patients. There are many instances in which increased serum CPK activity is present in conditions associated with morphologic abnormalities of skeletal muscle, e.g., Duchenne-type muscular dystrophy (2), polymyositis (3), some neurogenic muscle diseases such as motoneuron disease (4), susceptibility to malignant hyperpyrexia (5), and hypothyroidism (6). On this basis, we decided that it would be important to examine skeletal muscle specimens taken by biopsy from psychotic patients, first degree relatives of psychotic patients, nonpsychotic psychiatric patients and normal controls. The results of these studies in some of our subjects have been presented previously (7–13). Here we wish to present a summary of our current data in relation to the theme of this book: a comparison of findings in the schizophrenic and affective psychoses.

METHODS

Patient Population and Normal Controls

The patients are mainly those whose serum enzyme data were reported in the previous chapter (1). Some patients refused a muscle biopsy and some specimens were inadequate for technical reasons, which reduced the number of subjects from 187 to 166. The preceding chapter may be referred to for information about methods of diagnosis, and age, sex, and race of the patients. In addition, skeletal muscle biopsies were obtained from 26 first-degree relatives of psychotic patients. Most of these relatives had no previous history of hospitalization for psychiatric illness prior to the time of biopsy. However, five of the relatives had been hospitalized in our unit, for nonpsychotic psychiatric illnesses. The relatives ranged in age from 16 to 46. Skeletal muscle biopsies were also obtained from 34 paid normal volunteers who were screened for the absence of any personal or family history of medical illness that might produce muscle abnormalities or psychiatric illness.

Muscle specimens were first obtained from the vastus lateralis muscle. When our interest broadened to include subterminal motor nerves, we biopsied the peroneus brevis muscle. Biopsies were obtained under local anesthesia usually within 4 to 6 weeks of admission when the acute symptoms had subsided and informed consent could be obtained. Premedication for the patients usually consisted of chlorpromazine (Thorazine®) 50 mg i.m.; meperidine (Demerol®) 50 mg i.m.; and promethazine (Phenergan®) 25 mg p.o. Specimens were obtained for histochemical studies, for phase and electron-microscopic examination of Araldite-embedded muscle and for examination of subterminal motor nerves with supravital staining. The methods used have been described elsewhere (7,9,13).

Skeletal Muscle Fiber Abnormalities

We have examined with histochemical and phase microscopic methods muscle specimens from the vastus lateralis or peroneus brevis muscles from 34 volunteers between the ages of 18 and 34, without any personal or family history of muscle disease and psychiatric illness or personal history of trauma (14,15).

In frozen sections, examined with histochemical methods, the most common types of deviation from normal morphology in the control subjects were central nuclei and atrophic fibers, either angular or round. Much more rare in the normal volunteers were ring fibers, necrotic fibers, splitting fibers, and fiber-type grouping. Not present in these controls were atrophic fascicles, fiber-type atrophy (16), alkaline phosphatase-positive fibers (17), targetoid (central core) fibers (18), and fibers with rod bodies (19). Specimens were considered abnormal when they exceeded the 95% confidence limits for scattered atrophic fibers, hypertrophy, central nuclei, splitting fibers, ringed fibers or fiber-type grouping. They were also considered abnormal if they had any alkaline phosphatase-positive fibers, necrotic fibers, fibers with rod bodies or cytoplasmic masses or targetoid (central core) fibers, or if extensive fiber-type atrophy was present.

In phase examination of an Araldite-embedded muscle specimen, we noted that the most common deviation from normal anatomy in patients and controls were in the Z-band, consisting of focal Z-streaming (streaming of the Z-band over an area less than three adjacent sarcomeres and three adjacent myofibrils) and extensive Z-streaming (streaming over an area more than three adjacent sarcomeres and myofibrils). Specimens were considered abnormal if they had extensive Z-streaming in more than 2.4% of the fibers examined or if central core fibers, fibers with rod bodies or necrotic fibers were present (9,15,20).

The significance of the differences in the incidences of various types of pathology in patients and controls was tested by means of the Chi-square test with Yates's correction for continuity; the criterion level for significance was the 0.05 level of confidence.

RESULTS

The overall incidence of biopsies that were abnormal by any histochemical or phase criteria in the normal volunteers, non-psychotic psychiatric patients,

TABLE 1. *Percentage of abnormal muscle biopsies in psychiatric patients and first-degree relatives*

Group	Number	% Abnormal	p
Controls	34	14.7	—
Nonpsychotic	19	5.3	NS
All psychotics	166	69.3	<0.001
Acute schizophrenics	108	69.9	<0.001
Chronic schizophrenics	36	83.3	<0.001
Biphasic, manic phase	12	66.7	<0.001
Primary depression	10	80.0	<0.001
All schizophrenics	144	68.8	<0.001
All affective psychoses	22	72.7	<0.001
Acute schizophrenics plus			
all affectives	130	65.4	<0.001
Chronic schizophrenics	36	83.3	<0.001
First-degree relatives of			
psychotics	26	50.0	<0.001

psychotic patients classified according to diagnosis and first-degree relatives is given in Table 1. Five of the 34 specimens from controls were sufficiently deviant to be considered abnormal as was one of those from the 19 nonpsychotic patients. There was no statistically significant difference in the incidence of abnormal specimens between these two groups. One hundred and fifteen of 166 psychotic patients (69.3%) had abnormal biopsies. This was significantly different from that of the controls ($\chi^2 = 42.17$, $p < 0.001$). The percentage of abnormal biopsies in the acute or chronic schizophrenic patients and the patients with affective psychoses ranged from a low of 63.9% in acute schizophrenic patients to 80% in the patients with an affective psychosis, depressed type. The incidence of abnormal muscle specimens in the different groups of psychotic patients was markedly greater than it was in the controls. None of the groups of patients with different types of psychoses was significantly different from each other with regard to the incidence of abnormal biopsies. There was a tendency that did not reach statistical significance for the incidence of abnormal muscle specimens in chronic schizophrenic patients (30/36) to be slightly greater than that in the combined group of patients with remitting psychoses (the acute schizophrenics and the patients with affective psychoses) of whom 85/130 (65.4%) had abnormal skeletal muscle ($\chi^2 = 3.47$, $p < 0.10$). The incidence of abnormal muscle specimens in paranoid schizophrenic patients (53/72) was not significantly different from that in nonparanoid schizophrenic patients (46/72) ($\chi^2 = 1.16$, p < 0.5).

Thirteen of 26 first-degree relatives of psychotic patients had abnormal muscle. This was a significantly greater incidence than that of the controls $\chi^2 = 7.14$, $p < 0.001$), and was not significantly less than that of the psychotic patients ($\chi^2 = 2.94$, $p < 0.10$). Two of the three relatives with the most abnormal biopsies were hospitalized for nonpsychotic psychiatric illnesses. One was diagnosed as borderline and the second, as having neurotic depression. The other relative with a very abnormal biopsy compared to the rest of the group was the son of two persons both of whom are manic-depressive. He has experienced moderate

TABLE 2. *Percentage of muscle biopsies abnormal by histochemical, phase or both criteria in psychiatric patients, first-degree relatives and controls*

Group	Number	Histochemical abnormal (%)	Phase abnormal (%)	Both abnormal (%)
Controls	34	8.8	5.8	0
Nonpsychotic	19	5.0	0	0
All psychotics	166	53.6	34.3	18.7
Acute schizophrenics	108	50.0	33.3	19.4
Chronic schizophrenics	36	63.9	36.1	16.7
Bipolar, manic phase	12	41.7	33.3	8.3
Psychotic depression	10	70.0	40.0	30.0
All schizophrenics	144	53.5	34.0	18.7
All affective psychoses	22	54.5	36.4	18.2
Acute schizophrenics plus				
all affectives	130	50.8	33.8	19.2
Chronic schizophrenics	36	63.9	36.1	16.7
First-degree relatives of				
psychotics	26	42.2	23.0	15.3

depressions and periodic mood swings, but has not sought psychiatric treatment.

The percentage of muscle specimens which were abnormal by histochemical or phase criteria, or both is given in Table 2. It is apparent that the histochemical abnormalities were more common than were the phase abnormalities; furthermore, the overall incidence for the various groups of psychotic patients does not differ appreciably except that the psychotically depressed patients have a higher incidence of abnormal muscle specimens by histochemical criteria. Only about one in five specimens from psychotic patients were abnormal by both histochemical and phase criteria. There was no significant trend for the histochemical and phase abnormalities to occur in specimens from the same patient. The previously noted tendency toward a higher incidence of muscle abnormalities in the chronic schizophrenic patients was mainly the result of abnormalities apparent by histochemical techniques.

The precentages of the more common types of muscle abnormalities in the various groups of subjects is given in Table 3. The most common histochemical abnormality in psychotic patients was excessive numbers of scattered atrophic fibers which were present in 32.5% of all psychotic patients and similar percentages of specific types of psychotic patients. The other histochemical abnormalities were present in less than 1% to 9% of the psychotic patients. These included alkaline phosphatase-positive fibers, excessive central nuclei, necrotic fibers, splitting fibers, and ring fibers, fibers with rod bodies, targetoid fibers, fibers with abnormalities of the intermyofibrillar network, atrophic fascicles and fiber-type atrophy. Examples of some of these types of pathology are given in Figs. 1 and 2. The incidence of each of these abnormalities in all psychotic patients was sufficiently rare that individually none of them was present significantly more commonly than in the 34 volunteers. However, if the 19 non-psychotic patients and 34 volunteers are combined into one comparison group, then the incidences

TABLE 3. *Percentage of patients and controls with specific muscle abnormalities*

Group	N	Scattered atrophy	AP+ fibers[a]	Central nuclei	Necrotic fibers	Splitting fibers	Ring fibers	Extensive Z-streaming
				Patients with abnormal specimens (%)				
Controls	34	8.8	0	0	0	0	0	0
Nonpsychotics	19	5.3	0	0	0	0	0	5.3
All psychotics	166	32.5	9.0	7.2	7.8	7.2	4.2	19.9
Acute schizophrenics	108	29.6	12.0	4.6	7.4	1.9	2.3	19.4
Chronic schizophrenics	36	38.9	5.6	13.8	8.3	16.7	5.6	16.7
Bipolar, manic phase	12	33.3	0	3.3	8.3	16.7	0	25.0
Primary depression	10	40.0	0	10.0	10.0	20.0	20.0	30.0
All schizophrenics	144	31.9	10.4	6.9	7.6	5.0	3.5	18.8
All affective psychoses	22	36.4	0	9.1	9.1	18.2	9.1	27.3
Acute schizophrenics plus all affectives	130	30.8	10.0	5.4	2.3	4.6	3.8	20.8
Chronic schizophrenics	36	38.9	5.6	16.7	5.6	16.7	5.6	16.7
First-degree relatives of psychotics	26	34.6	0	0	0	0	0	23.1

[a] AP+ = Alkaline phosphatase-positive fibers.

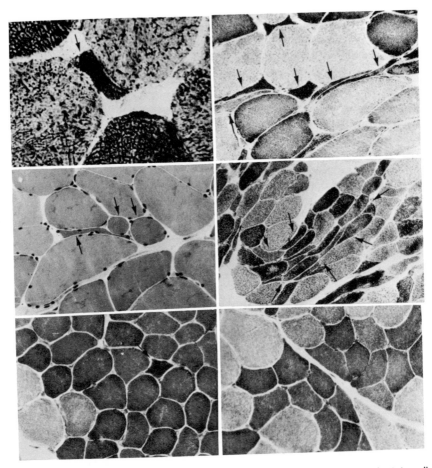

FIG. 1. **(Top left)** Arrow indicates small angular atrophic fiber, nicotinamide tetrazolium reductase reaction, NADH-TR. (x540.) **(Top right)** Arrows indicate small angular or long, thin atrophic fibers, NADH-TR. (x117.) **(Middle left)** Arrows indicate small round and long, skinny atrophic fibers. (x180.) **(Middle right)** Arrow indicates cluster of atrophic fibers, NADH-TR. (x220.) **(Bottom left)** Small group of type I fibers, arrow indicates atrophic fiber, NADH-TR. (x180.) **(Bottom right)** Type I atrophy, NADH-TR. (x180.)

of alkaline phosphatase-positive fibers or necrotic fibers, in all psychotic patients, were significantly greater than that of the comparison group. Whereas there were variations with regard to the incidences of the various types of histochemical abnormalities between groups of psychotic patients, the sizes of the groups other than the acute schizophrenic patients were so small that it is hazardous to attach any solid significance to these group differences.

The percentage of fibers that had the various types of abnormalities discussed previously varied widely. For example, we considered some biopsies abnormal because they had just one alkaline phosphatase-positive fiber; the maximum

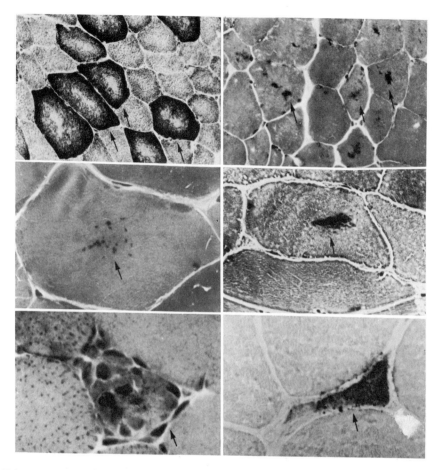

FIG. 2. **(Top left)** Type I targetoid fibers indicated by arrows, NADH-TR. (x200.) **(Top right)** Fibers with rod bodies indicated by arrows, trichrome. (x220.) **(Middle left)** Arrow indicates rods. (x580.) **(Middle right)** Fiber with cytoplasmic bodies, trichrome. (x540.) **(Bottom left)** Necrotic fiber, trichrome. (x740.) **(Bottom right)** Alkaline phosphatase-positive fiber. (x870.)

number was 17. One specimen from a manic-depressive patient had 34% type I fibers, nearly all of which were targetoid (10), whereas a specimen from a schizophrenic patient had rods in nearly 40% of the fibers (11). In the vastus lateralis specimens, the 95% upper limit of normal for scattered atrophic fibers was 3/1000. The number of scattered atrophic fibers in the patients with excessive numbers of such fibers ranged from 4/1000 to 34/1000. The 95% upper limit of normal for atrophic fibers in the peroneus brevis muscle was 12.9/1000. The number of scattered atrophic fibers in the peroneus brevis muscle of the psychotic patients ranged from 14/1000 to 58/1000. The percentages of muscle specimens that had extensive Z-band streaming for the various diagnostic groups are given in Table 3. The percentages of patients with extensive Z-streaming was about the

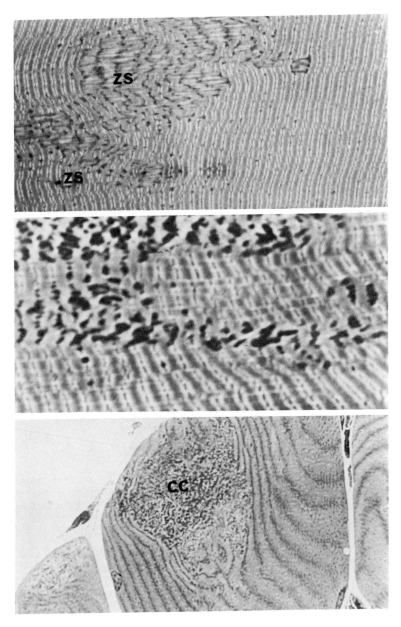

FIG. 3. **(Top)** Araldite-embedded muscle with extensive Z-band streaming **(ZS).** (x500.) **(Middle)** Araldite-embedded muscle, rod bodies. (x250.) **(Bottom)** Araldite-embedded muscle, targetoid fiber, also known as central core **(CC).** (x500.)

TABLE 4. *Percentage of abnormal muscle specimens in psychotic patients with and without increased serum CPK activity*

		Increased serum CPK activity			Normal CPK activity	
Group	N	Abnormal muscle (%)	Normal muscle (%)	N	Abnormal muscle (%)	Normal muscle (%)
All psychotics	128	71.9	28.1	38	60.5	39.5
Acute schizophrenics	86	64.0	36.0	22	63.6	36.4
Chronic schizophrenics	26	88.5	11.5	10	70.0	30.0
Bipolar, manic phase	9	77.8	22.2	3	33.3	66.7
Primary depression	7	100	0	3	33.3	66.7
All schizophrenics	112	69.6	30.4	32	65.6	34.4
All affective psychoses	16	87.5	12.5	6	33.3	66.7
Acute schizophrenics + all affectives	102	67.6	32.4	28	57.1	42.9
Chronic schizophrenics	26	88.5	11.5	10	70.0	30.0

same in all groups of psychotic patients. The percentage of muscle fibers in a given specimen with extensive Z-streaming (Fig. 3) varied from $> 2.5\%$ to 31.5%. Other abnormalities present in Araldite-embedded muscle specimens such as rods, targetoid fibers, and necrosis were even more rare (Fig. 3). No evidence of glycogen or lipid accumulation was noted.

We considered whether there was a relationship between increased serum CPK activity at any time during hospitalization and the presence of a muscle specimen abnormal by any criteria. As is apparent in Table 4, the percentage of abnormal muscle specimens was not significantly different in the entire group of psychotic patients with and without increased serum CPK activity. However, for the patients with affective psychoses, those with increased serum CPK activity had abnormal muscle specimens significantly more frequently than those without increased serum CPK activity (14/16 versus 2/6; Fischer exact probability, $p <$ 0.024). However, because of the small number of subjects, this result must be considered highly tentative.

We have not found any relationship between maximum dose of medication or total doses of medication (either neuroleptic, tricyclic antidepressants or lithium carbonate), and the incidence or extent of muscle abnormalities in psychotic patients. The first-degree relatives of psychotic patients who had abnormal biopsies had not been treated with psychotropic medication. Rats given chlorpromazine for up to 30 days, 10 mg/kg i.p. daily, did not develop any muscle abnormalities (Meltzer, *unpublished data*). This evidence suggests that the muscle fiber abnormalities are not a drug effect. Because the patients were relatively young and had no history or evidence of trauma, diabetes, vitamin deficiency, or prolonged inactivity, it is unlikely that any of these factors could account for their presence.

We found no relationship between abnormal muscle specimens in psychotic patients and age, race, sex, Stephans–Astrup prognosis, family history of hospitalized mental illness, total number of psychiatric hospitalizations, or interval between onset of current episode and biopsy.

Subterminal Motor Nerve Abnormalities in Psychotic Patients

The primary cause of the various abnormal muscle fibers found in specimens from psychotic patients could be abnormalities of the motor nerve rather than intrinsic pathology in the muscle fiber itself. The evidence for this hypothesis has been provided elsewhere (10). To initiate an investigation of whether any part of the alpha motor neuron was abnormal in psychotic patients, we decided to examine the subterminal motor axon and the subneural apparatus using the supravital staining method of Cöers and Woolf (2) as modified by Evans et al. (22). If degeneration or severe impairment of function of some motor neurons occurred at the level of the nerve cell body, axon, or subterminal region, surviving healthy nerves should branch at the level of the subterminal motor axon in order to reinnervate muscle fibers deprived of their innervation (2). Supravital staining permits visualization of such branching as well as other abnormalities of the subterminal motor nerves.

Axonal branching may lead to more than one terminal arborization (nerve ending) on one muscle fiber or in the innervation of more than one muscle fiber. A quantitative estimate of axonal branching can be obtained by calculating the terminal innervation ratio (TIR). The absolute TIR (ATIR) is defined as the average number of subterminal motor arborizations per motor axon (2). The functional TIR (FTIR) is the average number of muscle fibers innervated per subterminal nerve (2). In normal muscles, no more than 10% of subterminal motor nerves branch or innervate more than one muscle fiber. The range of the FTIR in normal controls is 1.01 to 1.20 (mean $1.10 \pm SD$ 0.05) (23). Similar values of the ATIR are found in normals (21). We have confirmed this in nine normal controls and also found similar results in three nonpsychotic patients. The data from these 12 subjects were pooled to form a comparison group (Table 5).

We found that in some psychotic patients and their first-degree relatives there is excessive branching and excessive multiple innervation of muscle fibers (Table 5). An example of a subterminal neuron with excessive branching from a psychotic patient is given in Fig. 4. The mean ATIR and FTIR of all psychotic patients was significantly greater than those of the comparison group. The ATIR and FTIR for all patients and relatives, elevated or not, were virtually identical (data not presented).

The 95% upper limit of normal for the ATIR of our comparison group is 1.25; for the FTIR, 1.24. The incidence of and percentage of specimens that exceed the 95% upper limit for the various groups is given in Table 6. Forty-four percent of all psychotic patients had increased ATIRs or FTIRs as did 63% of the first-degree relatives of psychotic patients. These proportions are not significantly different. The percentage of psychotic patients with elevated ATIR or

TABLE 5. *Absolute and functional terminal innervation ratios*

Group	N	ATIR Mean ± SD	ATIR Range	p +<	FTIR Mean ± SD	FTIR Range
Comparison group	12	1.11 ± 0.06	1.01–1.20	—	1.00 ± 0.00	1.01–1.21
Controls of Coers et al. (28)	56	—	—	—	1.11 ± 0.05	1.00–1.20
All psychotics	68	1.30 ± 0.37	1.00–3.12	—	1.33 ± 0.34	1.00–3.00
Acute schizophrenics	40	1.36 ± 0.21	1.00–0.92	—	1.27 ± 0.35	1.00–1.72
Chronic schizophrenics	15	1.51 ± 0.59	1.08–3.12	—	1.45 ± 0.55	1.07–3.00
Bipolar, manic phase	5	1.56 ± 0.35	1.16–1.54	—	1.52 ± 0.31	1.11–1.87
Primary depression	8	1.44 ± 0.35	1.04–1.93	—	1.37 ± 0.30	1.03–1.82
All schizophrenics	55	1.33 ± 0.37	1.00–3.12	0.05	1.29 ± 0.32	1.00–3.00
All affectives	13	1.49 ± 0.34	1.04–1.96	0.05	1.42 ± 0.31	1.03–1.87
Acute schizophrenics plus all affectives	57	1.32 ± 0.26	1.00–1.96	—	1.27 ± 0.23	1.00–1.07
Chronic schizophrenics	13	1.51 ± 0.59	1.08–3.12	—	1.45 ± 0.52	1.07–3.00
First-degree relatives	9	1.41 ± 0.28	1.07–1.80	—	1.36 ± 0.24	1.07–1.80

ANOVA tables

Source of variance	df	Mean Square	F	p<
ATIR				
Between diagnosis	5	0.330	3.135	0.05
Within subjects	82	0.105		
FTIR				
Between diagnosis	5	0.211	2.259	N.S.
Within subjects	82	0.093		

FTIR that we are now reporting is less than that previously observed in a smaller group of psychotic patients (16/24, 67%) (13). This is partly because we are now utilizing more conservative upper limits of normal (e.g., FTIR > 1.25 rather than 1.16). The more conservative limits are based on data from 12 rather than six subjects and on a more conservative means of calculating the confidence limit for a single sample (24). The percentage of psychotic patients with abnormal ATIRs ranged from a low of 35% for acute schizophrenics ($N = 46$) to a high of 80% for bipolar, manic-phase patients ($N = 5$), but we do not attribute much significance to this difference because of the small size of the group of manic patients.

In addition to branching, large number of sprouts (branches without terminal arborizations) were seen in patients but not the controls (13). The terminal arborizations of the psychotic patients also tended to be more fragmented and dispersed than those of the controls. These results will be presented elsewhere.

In a smaller group of these patients for whom data analysis was completed, we found no relationship between age, sex, race, prognosis, the number of psychotic episodes a patient had had, the interval between the onset of the

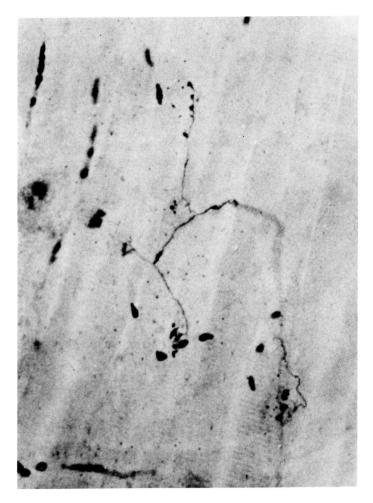

FIG. 4. Subterminal motor nerve with five terminal arborizations on four different muscle fibers, methylene blue. (x360.)

psychotic symptoms of this psychotic episode and the time at which the biopsy was performed, or peak dose of phenothiazines and the ATIR or FTIR (13).

There was also no relationship between the presence of elevated serum CPK activity at any time during hospitalization and either an abnormal ATIR or FTIR. However, patients whose biopsies were abnormal by either histochemical or phase criteria had significantly higher incidence of elevated ATIRs (29/53) than those whose muscle specimens were normal by both criteria (2/13, $\chi^2 = 5.001$, $p < 0.02$). The relationship between the FTIR and abnormal muscle fibers just failed to reach statistical significance ($\chi^2 = 3.565$, $p < 0.10$).

Of the 66 psychotic patients for whom there was complete serum CPK activity,

TABLE 6. Incidence of abnormal ATIRs and FTIRs

Group	ATIR	% Abnormal	FTIR	% Abnormal
Comparison[a]	0/12	0	0/12	0
All psychotics	30/68	44	30/68	44
Acute schizophrenics*	14/40	35	15/50	38
Chronic schizophrenics*	8/15	53	7/15	47
Bipolar, manic phase*	4/5	80	4/5	80
Primary depression*	4/8	63	4/8	50
All schizophrenics	22/55	40	22/55	40
All affectives	8/13	62	8/13	62
Acute schizophrenics + affectives	22/53	42	30/57	38
Chronic schizophrenics	8/15	53	8/12	47
First-degree relatives*	5/8	63	6/9	63

[a] The incidences of abnormal ATIR and FTIR in the six groups marked by an asterisk (*) were significantly different using 2×6 χ^2 analyses (ATIR: $\chi^2 = 14.909$, $p < 0.02$; FTIR: $\chi^2 = 13.761$, $p < 0.02$).

histochemical, phase and TIR data, 64 (94%) had either increased serum CPK activity at some time during hospitalization, abnormal skeletal muscle specimens or significantly elevated TIRs.

DISCUSSION

The studies reported here suggest that some psychotic patients of all common diagnostic types have excessive abnormal muscle fibers and abnormalities of the subterminal motor nerves. However, as we shall indicate, because of the nature and extent of such pathology, and the possibility of nonspecific causes, interpretation of these findings must be cautious. There were many different types of abnormal muscle fibers observed in the frozen sections and Araldite-embedded muscle specimens. Only excessive numbers of scattered atrophic fibers and a greater than normal percentage of fibers with extensive Z-band streaming were present in nearly 20% or more of the specimens from all psychotic patients. The other deviations from normal occurred relatively infrequently over the entire sample, e.g., 1 to 9% of patients had alkaline phosphatase-positive fibers, excessive numbers of ring fibers, rod bodies, targetoid fibers, and other types of pathology previously cited. There were relatively large amounts of pathology in 15 patients: two cases of rod bodies, one of targetoid fibers, two of alkaline phosphatase-positive fibers, two of fiber type atrophy, four of scattered atrophic fibers, and four of extensive Z-band streaming. In all the other 102 patients with abnormal muscle specimens, by our criteria, the amount of a given type of pathology that we have observed in the 34 specimens was actually only slightly to moderately more than in the age-matched controls.

The paradigm of this type of specimen is one with only one alkaline phosphatase-positive fiber. In our controls and in the hundred examined by Engel and

Cunningham (17) and Engel *(personal communication)* not one alkaline phosphatase-positive fiber has ever been present in a muscle specimen. By these standards, the patient's biopsy is abnormal. It is clear that by the criteria of absolute amount of pathology, the muscle specimens from these psychotic patients are not impressively abnormal. Nevertheless, there is an apparent continuum of pathology within the entire series, which makes it difficult to dismiss the findings of slight pathology as meaningless. The relatively small amount of pathology in the psychotic patients may be due to only selective vulnerability of some motor nerves or muscle fibers or regeneration of the majority of nerves and muscles. It is also possible that had we obtained specimens from different muscles or at different times that more extensive pathology might have been present. The absence of any detectable muscle weakness in all but one psychotic patient (a patient with fiber-type atrophy) is consistent with this small amount of pathology. No weakness was detectable in the patients with extensive muscle pathology.

The diversity of muscle pathology in our patient group may not be surprising in light of the relative nonspecificity of muscle pathology. The same pathologic changes in muscle may be found in a multiplicity of diseases and variations in the type of pathology can frequently be found in different patients with the same disease (25–27). Because of this, it is hazardous to speculate about common or unique causes for the various pathologic changes found in patients with different types of the major mental illnesses. However, all of the types of pathology that we have found in psychotic patients have been attributed by experienced muscle pathologists to abnormalities of the muscle innervation rather than to primary muscle disease (10). A similar hypothesis for the etiology of the muscle abnormalities in psychotic patients is attractive because it allows for the possibility of a link between the muscle fiber abnormalities and any neuronal abnormalities of the CNS that may underlie psychosis. Abnormalities of motor neurons have also been proposed as the primary cause of skeletal muscle abnormalities in Duchenne and murine muscular dystrophy (28–30), myotonic dystrophy (31), and myasthenia gravis (32).

The nature of the muscle fiber abnormalities in psychotic patients led us to initiate studies of the subterminal motor nerves in psychotic patients. Thirty of 68 patients with all types of major mental illnesses had abnormalities of the subterminal motor nerves as indicated by elevated ATIRs or FTIRs. We found elevated ATIR and FTIR in comparable percentages of patients with the various major psychoses. We cannot attribute the increased ATIRs or FTIRs in some psychotic patients or relatives as compared to controls to differences in age, sex, race, activity pattern, trauma, or medication. We found no relationship between the degree of subterminal motor nerve pathology and either the severity of illness, the duration of illness, or the type of psychosis.

Abnormalities of the TIRs were also present in first-degree relatives of psychotic patients. Whereas none of the relatives had gross psychotic episodes, a few had other types of psychopathology. Degeneration or loss of function of the subterminal motor neurons would have to occur at times prior to the development of the florid psychotic symptoms to account for these data. It also suggests but does not prove, that the phase of florid psychotic symptoms does not lead to more extensive motor nerve degeneration. This conclusion is also supported by the lack of a difference in muscle fiber abnormalities and TIRs in patients with just a single or multiple psychotic episodes. It is not yet apparent to us what are the relevant factors which determine why some, but not all psychotic patients, have abnormalities of the TIRs. Not all patients with muscle diseases that definitely affect the subterminal nerves have elevated TIRs (33). Conceivably, the sampling problem partially explains this—sampling different areas of the same muscle or other muscle might produce more uniform results. We have not yet ascertained if type or intensity of psychopathology correlates with the presence of abnormal TIRs. It is possible that there is a difference in the incidence of elevated TIRs in patients with a strong genetic component to their illness, i.e., those patients with multiple first-degree relatives with psychotic illnesses. Such analyses are in progress.

The chronicity of the motor nerve and muscle fiber pathology would help to explain the lack of correlation between increased serum CPK activity and either of the ratios or the number of scattered atrophic fibers. The release of CPK from skeletal muscle is greatest during the acute phase of the psychosis and may be the result of transient neurochemical events which are common to a variety of acute brain diseases (1).

Branching is a common response of nerve tissue to a variety of toxic and metabolic insults, so there is little indication from the present work as to the nature of the offending process. However, it is noteworthy that the pattern of branching is much more characteristic of a primary neuronal disease than of a primary muscular disease. This conclusion arises from the observation that both the ATIR and FTIR were increased in our patients and they were virtually identical. This pattern occurs when most of the new branches innervate previously denervated muscle fibers rather than increase the number of end plates on already innervated muscle fibers. In primary muscle disease, the death and removal of pathologic muscle fibers usually leads to the FTIR being close to unity. The most common exception to this rule is in myositis where branching may increase both the ATIR and FTIR (21). There were no signs of myositis in our patients. Therefore the elevation of ATIRs and FTIRs together with a variety of changes in skeletal muscle fiber morphology which could be neurogenic in etiology is highly suggestive of the existence of neurogenic muscle disease in some psychotic patients (10).

The finding that a significantly greater proportion of muscle specimens which had abnormal ATIRs were from patients who had abnormalities of their muscle fibers as well, also suggest an important relationship between the pathology of the subterminal motor nerves and muscle fibers. This possibility is underscored by the fact that different aliquots of muscle were used for the determination of the TIRs, the histochemical and the phase-microscopic studies, and that all specimens were examined entirely independently.

If, as our data suggest, psychotic patients have an abnormality of motor neurons, a variety of pathophysiologic mechanisms could be involved. Possible causes of α-motor neuron pathology in the psychotic patients which it seems possible to dismiss include vitamin deficiency and diabetes mellitus. Routine laboratory workup and physical examination revealed no evidence of abnormalities consistent with these diseases. Nerve compression does not lead to sprouting (21). It is possible that the motor nerve abnormalities in some psychotic patients are caused by (a) intrinsic alpha-motor neuron pathology such as that seen in a variety of degenerative spinal cord diseases such as syringomyelia or Werdnig-Hoffman disease; or (b) alpha-motor neuron dysfunction secondary to some suprasegmental defect as might occur in the so-called "central atrophy" (34), the atrophy of skeletal muscle consequent to gross lesions in the CNS, particularly the parietal lobe, caused by neoplasms or cerebrovascular disease. Edstrom has found skeletal muscle fiber abnormalities in patients with upper motor neuron lesions secondary to cerebrovascular accidents and Parkinson's disease (35). McComas et al. (36) and Sica et al. (37) have found neurophysiologic evidence of dysfunction of the alpha-motor neuron in patients with cerebrovascular accidents and Parkinson's disease. Schwartzman and Dimanescu reported that unilateral lesions of the primary or secondary sensory cortical area in rhesus monkeys produces atrophy of type I fibers in the biceps and quadriceps muscles (38). The most widely accepted explanation of the abnormalities of skeletal muscle following upper motor neuron lesions is the loss of trophic influence(s) of motor neurons upon the skeletal muscle fibers (39). A neuropathologic study of the spinal cord from deceased psychotic patients would be necessary to establish whether or not psychotic patients have morphologic abnormalities of alpha-motor neuron cell bodies. The possibility of suprasegmental causes of the alpha-motor neuron (and skeletal muscle fiber) abnormalities in psychotic patients will require a greater understanding of transsynaptic degeneration, neurotrophism, and further investigation of neuropathology in psychotic patients. Given the large number of possible causes of α-motor neuron abnormalities in psychotic patients, it should be clear that the fact that increased TIRs are found in some patients with the schizophrenic and affective psychoses does not require that they have a common etiology.

The significance, if any, of these abnormalities of the motor nerves for motor performance in psychotic patients is an intriguing question. Impaired psychomotor performance in schizophrenics was demonstrated as early as the 1930s (40). Holzman has argued "motor functioning and coordination of various movements is a crucial aspect of the process of organization and control of psychological processes (40)." Conceivably the abnormalities of motor nerves reported here might affect a number of critical fine motor processes such as eye movements, larynx, and finger dexterity such that they contributed to the psychotic patients' difficulties in adaption. Holzman et al. have recently reported abnormalities of the eye movements in most schizophrenic patients, and their first-degree relatives, with a lower incidence in manic-depressive patients (41). Shagass et al. have found a similar incidence in patients with affective and schizophrenic psychoses (42). These might be functional correlates in the eye muscle of denervation and branching found in the peroneus brevis muscle.

It is of interest to point out that the multibranched subterminal neuron (see Fig. 4), although it is abnormal, is an attempt to maintain function, just as is a hypertrophied muscle fiber. Although significant branching of the subterminal motor nerves of eye muscles could interfere with fine motor control, this is presumably less of a problem than is atrophy of the muscle fibers, which might occur without branching. It is tempting to speculate that excessive neuronal branching might occur to a significant extent in the CNS of an individual with schizophrenic of affective psychoses. The extent of disability might depend on what type of new connections were made. It seems improbable that there should be denervation and reinnervation in the peripheral motor nerves of psychotic patients without comparable abnormalities or attempts at restoration of function in the CNS.

ACKNOWLEDGMENTS

The technical assistance of Jane Click, Judith Ellison, and Sneh Rastogi is gratefully appreciated. The assistance of Pamela Holy and Glenn Lucht in the analysis of research data is gratefully appreciated. The staff of the Acute Psychosis Research Program of the Illinois State Psychiatric Institute assisted immeasurably in the care and investigation of the patients in this study. This research was supported by USPHS grants 16,129 and 18,396 and the State of Illinois, Department of mental health Grant 231–12–RD. Dr. Meltzer is recipient of USPHS Career Development Award MH 47,808. Dr. Crayton is recipient of USPHS Career Development Award MH 70,896.

REFERENCES

1. Meltzer, H. Y. (1975): This volume.
2. Okinaka, S., Kumagai, H., Ebashi, S., Sugita, H., Momoi, H., Toyokura, Y., and Fujie, Y. (1961): Serum creatine phosphokinase. *Arch. Neurol.*, 4:520–525.
3. Brownlow, K., and Elevitch, F. R. (1974): Serum creatine phosphokinase isoenzyme (CPK$_2$) in myositis. *J. Am. Med. Assoc.*, 230:1141–1144.
4. Achari, A. N., and Anderson, M. S. (1974): Serum creatine phosphokinase in amyotrophic lateral sclerosis. *Neurology (Minneap.)*, 26:834–837.
5. Denborough, M. A., Hudson, M. C., Forster, J. F. A., Carter, N. G., and Zapf, P. (1970): Biochemical changes in malignant hyperpyrexia. *Lancet*, 1:1137–1138.
6. Graig, F. A., and Smith, J. C. (1965): Serum creatine phosphokinase activity in altered thyroid states. *J. Clin. Endocrinol.*, 25:723–731.
7. Engel, W. K., and Meltzer, H. (1970): Histochemical abnormalities of skeletal muscle in patients with acute psychoses. I. *Science*, 168:273–276.
8. Meltzer, H. Y., and Engel, W. K. (1970): Histochemical abnormalities of skeletal muscle in patients with acute psychoses. II. *Arch. Gen. Psychiatry*, 23:492–502.
9. Fischman, D. A., Meltzer, H. Y., and Poppei, R. W. (1970): The disruption of myofibrils in the skeletal muscle of acutely psychotic patients. *Arch. Gen. Psychiatry*, 23:503–515.
10. Meltzer, H. Y. (1972): Central core fibers in an acutely psychotic patient. *Arch. Gen. Psychiatry*, 27:125–132.

11. Meltzer, H. Y., McBride, E., and Poppei, R. W. (1973): Rod (nemaline) bodies in the skeletal muscle of an acute schizophrenic patient. *Neurology (Minneap.)*, 23:769–780.
12. Meltzer, H. Y. (1973): Skeletal muscle abnormalities in patients with affective disorders. *J. Psychiat. Res.*, 10:43–57.
13. Meltzer, H. Y., and Crayton, J. W. (1974): Muscle abnormalities in psychotic patients. II. Serum CPK activity, fiber abnormalities and branching and sprouting of subterminal nerves. *Biol. Psychiatry*, 8:191–208.
14. Meltzer, H. Y., and Kuncl, R. W. (1975): Incidence of Z-band streaming and myofibrillar disruptions in normal human skeletal muscle. *(Submitted for publication.)*
15. Meltzer, H. Y., and Rastogi, S. (1975): Quantitative histochemical evaluation of normal human muscle. *(Submitted for publication.)*
16. Mendell, J. R., and Engel, W. K. (1971): The fine structure of type II muscle fiber atrophy. *Neurology (Minneap.)*, 21:358–365.
17. Engel, W. K., and Cunningham, G. G. (1970): Alkaline phosphatase-positive abnormal fibers of humans. *J. Histochem. Cytochem.*, 18:56–57.
18. Shy, G. M., Engel, W. K., Somer, J. E., and Wanko, T. (1963): Myopathy. A new congenital myopathy. *Brain*, 86:793–810.
19. Shy, G. M., and Magee, K. R. (1956): A new congenital non-progressive myopathy. *Brain*, 610–621.
20. Fischman, D. A., Meltzer, H. Y., and Poppei, R. W. (1973): The ultrastructure of human skeletal muscle: Variations from archetypal morphology. In: *The Striated Muscle*, edited by C. M. Pearson, pp. 58–76. Williams & Wilkins, Baltimore, Maryland.
21. Coers, C., and Woolf, A. L. (1959): *The Innervation of Muscle*, pp. 1–42. Blackwell Scientific Publications, Oxford.
22. Evans, R. H., Haynes, J., Morris, C. J., and Woolf, A. L. (1970): *In vitro* staining of intramuscular nerve endings. *J. Neurol. Neurosurg. Psychiatry*, 33:783–785.
23. Coers, C., Telerman-Toppet, N., and Gerard, J-M. (1973): Terminal innervation ratio in neuromuscular disease. I. Methods and controls. *Arch. Neurol.*, 29:210–214.
24. Hays, W. L., and Winkler, R. L. (1971): *Statistics: Probability, Inference and Decision*, pp. 338–339. Holt, New York.
25. Engel, W. K. (1966): The multiplicity of pathologic reactions of human skeletal muscle. In: *Proceedings of the 5th International Congress of Neuropathology, Zurich, 1965*, pp. 613–624. Excerpta Medica Foundation, Amsterdam.
26. Engel, A. G. (1967): Pathological reactions of the Z disk. In: *Exploratory Concepts in Muscular Dystrophy and Related Disorders*, edited by A. T. Milhorat, pp. 398–412. Excerpta Medica Foundation, Amsterdam.
27. Dastur, D. K., and Razzak, Z. A. (1973): Possible neurogenic factor in muscular dystrophy: its similarity to denervation atrophy. *J. Neurol. Neurosurg. Psychiatry*, 36:399–410.
28. McComas, A. J., Sica, R. E. P., and Currie, S. (1970): Muscular dystrophy: Evidence for a neural factor. *Nature*, 226:1263–1263.
29. Harris, J., and Wilson, P. (1971): Denervation in murine dystrophy. *Nature*, 229:61–62.
30. Gallup, B., and Dubowitz, V. (1973): Failure of "Dystrophic" neurones to support functional regeneration of normal or dystrophic muscle in culture. *Nature*, 243:287–289.
31. McComas, A. J., Campbell, M. J., and Sica, R. E. P. (1971): Electrophysiological study of dystrophia myotonica. *J. Neurol. Neurosurg. Psychiat.*, 34:132–139.
32. Brownell, B., Oppenheimer, D. R., and Spalding, J. M. K. (1972): Neurogenic muscle atrophy in mysthenia gravis. *J. Neurol. Neurosurg., Psychiatry*, 35:311–322.
33. Coers, C., Telerman-Toppet, N., and Gerard, J-M. (1973): II. Disorders of lower motor neuron, peripheral nerve and muscle. *Arch. Neurol*, 19:215–222.
34. Fenichel, G. M., Daroff, R. B., and Glaser, G. H. (1964): Hemiplegic atrophy: Histological and etiologic considerations. *Neurology (Minneap.)*, 14:883–890.
35. Edstrom, L. (1968): Histochemical changes in upper motor lesions, Parkinsonism and disuse. Differential effects on white and red muscle. *Experientia*, 24:916–917.
36. McComas, A. J., Sica, R. E. P., Upton, A. R. M., and Anguilera, N. (1973): Functional changes in motoneurons of hemiparetic patients. *J. Neurol. Neurosurg. Psychiatry*, 36:183–193.
37. Sica, R. E. P., Herskovits, E., Aguilera, N., and Poch, G. (1973): An electrophysiological investigation of skeletal muscle in Parkinson's disease. *J. Neurol. Sci.*, 18:411–420.

38. Schwartzman, R. J., and Dimancescu, M. D. (1974): Suprasegmental influence on muscle fiber type in the rhesus monkey. *Neurology (Minneap.)*, 24:397–398.
39. Guth, L. (1968): "Trophic" influence of nerve on muscle. *Physiol. Rev.*, 48:645–687.
40. Holzman, P. S. (1972): Assessment of perceptual functioning in schizophrenia. *Psychopharmacologia (Berl.)*, 24:29–41.
41. Holzman, P. S., Proctor, L. R., Levy, D. L., Yasillo, N. J., Meltzer, H. Y. and Hurt, S. W. (1974): Eye-tracking dysfunctions in schizophrenic patients and their relatives. *Arch. Gen. Psychiatry*, 31:143–154.
42. Shagass, C., Amadeo, M., and Overton, D. A. (1974): Eye-tracking performance in psychiatric patients. *Biol. Psychiatry*, 9:245–260.

Biology of the Major Psychoses, edited by D. X.
Freedman, Res. Publ. Assoc. Res. Nerv. Ment.
Dis., Vol. 54. Raven Press, New York   1975

CPK in Neuropsychiatric Diseases

Lewis P. Rowland

Department of Neurology, College of Physicians and Surgeons, Columbia University,
New York, New York 10032

It is almost 10 years since increased serum creatine phosphokinase (SCPK) activity was first reported in schizophrenia. For the greater part of this decade, Dr. Meltzer has been industriously and carefully attempting to discern the significance of this observation. It was my original belief, one that I cannot yet dispel, that there would be some mundane explanation, that it would prove to be related to intramuscular injections, to the vigorous exercise associated with struggle against restraint, or some other aspect of the behavior or treatment of these patients. Yet Dr. Meltzer has considered these possibilities, one after the other, and finds no such explanation. He attributes the serum enzyme changes to some neuropathic or myopathic disorder more directly related to the cerebral abnormality that causes psychotic behavior. He has not, however, provided a ready explanation for the enzyme abnormalities.

This lack of explanation is perhaps not surprising as there are numerous other unanswered questions related to serum enzyme activity in neuromuscular disorders.

1. We do not know why any enzyme activity is detected in normal serum. Presumably, serum activity reflects a balance between ingress and disposal, but we know little about the normal regulatory mechanisms at either end of the process. Nor do we know why some enzymes appear in the serum and others do not.

2. In considering the activities of different enzymes, SCPK itself is an instructive example, especially pertinent here because it is the specific abnormality that started Dr. Meltzer on his quest. We do not know why the behavior of this enzyme differs from other sarcoplasmic enzymes. Since the first report by Ebashi and his colleagues (1) in 1959, this enzyme has been regarded as the most "sensitive" and most "specific" indicator of myopathic disease (2). It is true that SCPK activity is increased in most muscle diseases, even when other sarcoplasmic enzymes are not. In the detection of asymptomatic carriers of X-linked diseases, SCPK is also abnormal much more often than any other indicator (2). But it is also abnormally increased, unlike the other enzymes, in clearly neurogenic disorders (3,4). The belief that abnormal SCPK activity must reflect a myopathic disorder is so strong that attempts to explain this anomaly rest upon the appearance of what are called "myopathic" changes in the muscle biopsy of these neurogenic diseases (3). There must be other mechanisms involved, however, for

it has been repeatedly shown by Dr. Meltzer and others (5) that SCPK is higher in men than in women for reasons that are not clear, and in athletes (6). Some individuals are more susceptible than others to the same stress (7).

Moreover, exercise in normal individuals induces rises of SCPK when other enzymes do not change. Sometimes this may be related to physical tearing or other damage of muscle. Hypoxia has been adduced because the intensity of effort related to maximal voluntary O_2 intake seems to be proportionate to the rise in SCPK on exercise (8,9). This would also explain why the enzyme increases after exercise in untrained individuals much more than in athletes. But even the activities of daily life may affect the serum activity of CPK (10–12); the reason is not known.

3. This "sensitivity" of SCPK can lead to diagnostic problems. In coronary care units, changes in this enzyme activity are taken as evidence of myocardial infarction (13,14), perhaps related to the size of the infarct (15). Therefore, it is of some importance when the SCPK is increased in persons who ultimately prove not to have myocardial infarction in circumstances that originally made this a reasonable diagnostic possibility. Exercise, drug injections, hypokalemia, and other circumstances explain some of these cases, but not all, and we are left with a residue of totally unexplained cases (16,17). Analysis of CPK isozymes may not resolve the issue (18,19). This kind of problem may arise in other circumstances:

A boy had learning problems in school. He was examined several times in childhood and no motor disorder was found. At age 16, in a screening battery of blood tests, the SGOT was 150 units/liter (normal to 45). Subsequent studies showed high LDH (270) and SCPKs of 1260, 192, 192, and 410 (normal to 50) on different occasions. Electromyography (EMG) and muscle biopsy showed minor abnormalities thought to be compatible with myopathy. The patient's 10-year-old brother was therefore examined and was found to have similar abnormalities. Because two brothers were apparently affected, the family was told that this was an X-linked dystrophy. Yet neither brother was weak in any way, and repeat EMGs were normal. Therefore it would be more appropriate to call this "high serum enzymes, cause undetermined."

4. Duchenne dystrophy is the prototype disease characterized by persistently high serum enzymes. It was the recognition of increased aldolase activity in this disease by Sibley and Lehninger in 1949 (20) and by the seminal report of Dreyfuss and the Schapiras in 1953 (21), which may be said to be the origin of modern diagnostic enzymology. Twenty years later, however, we still do not understand why serum enzymes are increased in this condition. The most facile explanation, and probably the one most widely accepted, relates serum enzyme changes to necrotic muscle fibers, which may be seen with the light microscope. There is, however, another explanation, which seems more likely, that there is an abnormality of the process that regulates the intracellular concentration of enzyme protein, one that involves a "leaky" membrane, a phrase that implies more complex processes. This would explain why there is no clear relationship between the magnitude of serum enzyme abnormality, most severe in the first year of life of a child with the disease, and the number of necrotic fibers seen

at biopsy. It would explain why the serum enzyme abnormality is so much more marked in Duchenne dystrophy than in other, genetically distinct, dystrophies. It would explain why enzyme activity occurs in asymptomatic carriers of the disease who have infrequent necrotic fibers. It would explain why treatment with diethylstilbesterol (22) or thyroid hormones (23,24) might reduce serum enzyme activities without altering strength. [In polymyositis, too, corticosteroid therapy may influence serum enzymes without clinical improvement (25).]

5. There are clues to some of the mechanisms that cause release of sarcoplasmic enzymes from muscle. These come from cases of myoglobinuria, a condition resulting from diverse causes with common denominators—direct damage to muscle (crush injury, ischemia, or toxins that attack muscle membranes) or a variety of conditions that interfere with cellular metabolism and the production of ATP (26). The role of ATP in preventing leakage of cellular enzymes has been studied experimentally in isolated muscle (27,28), leukocytes (29), and erythrocytes (30). It seems unlikely, however, that the drastic changes of muscle metabolism in these conditions explain changes in CPK in chronic disorders that are not characterized by myoglobinuria, or in acute psychoses.

6. Dr. Meltzer has suggested an analogy between the transient rises in SCPK in acute psychoses and those in cerebral diseases, such as stroke or encephalitis. But the basis for the increased SCPK in cerebral disease is also unexplained, and, whatever the explanation, it seems unlikely that we will gain information about the basic mechanisms of stroke or encephalitis by studying SCPK. We might, however, learn more about serum enzymes.

Finally, a word about Dr. Meltzer's histologic studies. As in everything else he has done, he has been meticulous in using controls and in seeking quantitative expression of results, so one cannot quibble with the observations. It is the meaning that bothers me. If there really is a myopathy or a neuropathy, as suggested by these histologic studies, why do we never see this clinically? In some other conditions, there is a continuum. For instance, in thyrotoxicosis "myopathy" is rare if severe symptomatic weakness is taken as the criterion, more common if some weakness on examination is the measure, and almost universal if electromyographic (but not histologic) evidence is taken. The same reasoning applies to the neuropathy of uremia, diabetes mellitus, or Charcot-Marie-Tooth disease; in these conditions neuropathy is much more common if nerve conduction velocity is studied than if weakness is taken as the expression. But in both thyrotoxicosis and in neuropathies we can accept "subclinical" cases because we know that there are clinical examples. The lack of clinical evidence, however, makes me skeptical about the recent theory that diseases traditionally regarded as myopathy are really caused by sick motor neurons, and makes me similarly skeptical about the existence of neuropathy or myopathy in acute psychoses.

The increase in SCPK that Dr. Meltzer has reported in acute psychoses is an unanswered problem, but this is merely one more in a long list of unanswered questions relating to serum enzyme activity in health and disease. The crucial question is whether further attempts to explain this abnormality will actually be relevant to the search for the basic mechanisms of schizophrenia or depression. In the meantime, Dr. Meltzer has served both psychiatry and neurology in his diligent studies.

Two questions: Would Dr. Meltzer comment about the lack of correlation of the SCPK abnormality and any diagnostic classification? And about the lack of correlation, in individual patients, between histologic abnormality and SCPK abnormality?

REFERENCES

1. Ebashi, S., Toyokura, Y., Momoi, H., and Sugita, H. (1959): Creatine phosphokinase activity of sera of progressive muscular dystrophy patients. *J. Biochem. (Tokyo)*, 46:103.
2. Munsat, T. L., Baloh, R., Pearson, C. M., and Fowler, W. Jr. (1973): Serum enzyme alterations in neuromuscular disorders. *JAMA*, 228:1395–1396.
3. Achari, A. N., and Anderson, M. S. (1974): Serum creatine phosphokinase in amyotrophic lateral sclerosis. *Neurology*, 24:834–837.
4. Hetnarska, L., Prot, J., and Sawicka, E. (1968): Creatine phosphokinase activity in spinal muscular atrophy. *J. Neurol. Sci.*, 6:261–267.
5. Hughes, B. P. (1962): A method for the estimation of serum creatine kinase and its use in comparing creatine kinase and aldolase activity in normal and pathological sera. *Clin. Chim. Acta*, 7:597–603.
6. Garcia, W. (1974): Elevated creatine phosphokinase levels associated with large muscle mass. *JAMA*, 228:1395–1396.
7. Rawie, J., and Knight, J. A. (1971): Elevated CPK in blood donors. *Am. J. Clin. Pathol.*, 56:253–254.
8. Ledwich, J. R. (1973): Changes in serum creatine phosphokinase during submaximal exercise testing, *CMA J.*, 109:273–278.
9. Shapiro, Y., Magazanik, A., Sohar, E., and Reich, C. G. (1973): Serum enzyme changes in untrained subjects following a prolonged march. *Can. J. Physiol. Pharmacol.*, 51:271–276.
10. Paterson, Y., and Lawrence, E. F. (1972): Factors affecting serum creatine phosphokinase activity in normal adult females. *Clin. Chim. Acta*, 42:131–139.
11. Perry, T. B., and Fraser, F. C. (1973): Variability of serum creatine phosphokinase activity in normal women and carriers of the gene for Duchenne muscular dystrophy. *Neurology*, 23:1316–1323.
12. Griffiths, P. D. (1966): Serum levels of ATP: Creatine phosphotransferase (creatine kinase): Normal range and effect of muscular activity. *Clin. Chim. Acta*, 13:413–420.
13. Konttinen, A., and Somer, H. (1972): Determination of serum creatine kinase isoenzymes in myocardinal infarction. *Am. J. Cardiol.*, 20:817–820.
14. Goto, I. (1974): Serum creatine phosphokinase isozymes in hypothyroidism, convulsion, myocardial infarction and other diseases. *Clin. Chim. Acta*, 52:27–30.
15. Sobel, B. E., Bresnahan, G. F., Shell, W. E., and Yoder, R. D. (1972): Estimation of infarct size in man and its relation to prognosis. *Circulation*, 46:640–648.
16. Nevins, M. A., Saran, M., Bright, M., and Lyon, L. J. (1973): Pitfalls in interpreting serum creatine phosphokinase activity. *JAMA*, 224:1382–1387.
17. Galen, R. S., Reiffel, J. A., and Gambino, S. R. (1974): Enzymes in infarction. *JAMA*, 228:1229.
18. Konttinen, A., Somer, H., and Auvineu, S. (1974): Serum enzymes and isozymes. Extrapulmonary sources in acute pulmonary embolism. *Arch. Int. Med.*, 133:243–246.
19. Frotscher, U., Dominik, B., Richter, R., Zschaege, B., Schulte-Lippern, M., Jennett, G., Messerschmidt, W., Schmidtmann, W., and Wilbrandt, R. (1973): Die Instabilität der Kreatin-Phosphokinase-Isoenzyme in Serum. *Klin. Wochenschr.*, 51:801–805.
20. Sibley, J. A., and Lehninger, A. L. (1949): Aldolase in the serum and tissues of tumor-bearing animals. *J. Natl. Cancer Inst.*, 9:303–309.
21. Schapira, G., Dreyfus, J. C., and Schapira, F. (1953): L'élévation du taux de l'aldolase serique, test biochimique des myopathies. *Sem. Hop. Paris*, 29:1917–1920.

22. Cohen, L., Morgan, J., and Schulman, S. (1972): Serum enzyme lowering and other aspects of diethylstilbesterol in Duchenne dystrophy. *Proc. Soc. Exp. Biol. Med.,* 140:830–835.

23. Danowski, T. S., Vester, J. W., Sabeh, G., Sullivan, W. A., and Sarver, M. E. (1964): Thyroid therapy, serum CPK, and other indices in muscular dystrophy. *Metabolism,* 13:1393–1401.

24. Danowski, T. S., Sabeh, G., and Vester, J. W. (1969): Serum creatine phosphokinase in muscular dystrophy during iodinated amino acid therapy. *Metabolism,* 18:1–15.

25. Thomson, W. H. S. (1971): Serum enzyme studies in acquired disease of skeletal muscle. *Clin. Chim. Acta,* 35:193–199.

26. Rowland, L. P., and Penn, A. S. (1972): Myoglobinuria. *Med. Clin. North Am.,* 56:1233–1256.

27. Zierler, K. (1958): Muscle membrane as a dynamic structure and its permeability to aldolase. *Ann. NY Acad. Sci.,* 75:227–234.

28. Zierler, K. (1961): Potassium flux and further observations on aldolase flux in dystrophic mouse muscle. *John Hopkins Med. J.,* 108:208–215.

29. Wilkinson, J. H., and Robinson, J. M. (1974): Effect of ATP on release of intracellular enzymes from damaged cells. *Nature,* 249:663–664.

30. Sweetin, J. C., and Thomson, W. H. S. (1973): Enzyme efflux and clearance. *Clin. Chim. Acta,* 48:403–411.

Discussion

Dr. Meltzer: Dr. Rowland's second question is why there was no relationship between increased serum CPK activity and the muscle fiber abnormalities in psychotic patients. The answer lies, I think, in the point he emphasized in his discussion—that we know very little about the mechanism of enzyme release from skeletal muscle, and about the process of enzyme clearance from blood.

Some studies we did awhile ago may illustrate this point in a way that is particularly relevant to psychotic patients. In a study of the effect of serotonin and histamine on enzyme release from skeletal muscle, we administered polymyxin-B and other mast cell depletors to rats (H. Y. Meltzer, and P. Margulies: *Biochem. Pharmacol.,* 20:3501, 1971). We found that these drugs produced massive necrosis of skeletal muscle, but only relatively modest (four- or fivefold) increases in serum CPK activity.

This should be compared with the effects of phencyclidine in the restrained rat, which produces relatively subtle changes in myofibrillar structure but almost no necrosis, and yet serum CPK increases average 100 times normal (H. Y. Meltzer: *Res. Commun. Chem. Pathol. Pharmacol.,* 3:369, 1972). Tenotomy and denervation in the rat also produce no increases in plasma CPK activity, but extensive muscle fiber morphologic change (H. Y. Meltzer: *Exp. Neurol.,* 40:547, 1973).

The conclusion that I reach from these and other studies is that the morphologic abnormalities that lead to enzyme release are not the kind of dramatic fiber changes that are manifest in such pathology as necrotic fibers, central core fibers, atrophic fibers, fibers with rods, fibers with Z-streaming, etc. It is more likely that subtle changes in the muscle cell membrane, which may be undetectable morphologically with current techniques, underlie increased serum muscle enzyme activity.

The answer to the first question that Dr. Rowland raised, "Why aren't these muscle abnormalities more disease specific?," is in fact the theme of these presentations. I don't know the answer. I can only suggest that there is some process or state that is common to these disorders which may have some effect on the process of enzyme release from muscle or clearance from serum. It is also well established that morphologic changes in muscle disease are rarely specific for any disease.

I would also add that the data that I presented on mean or baseline serum CPK activity in psychotic patients and the significant proportion of relatives with increased serum CPK activity suggest that a certain proportion of patients and their first-degree relatives in *each* of the categories of the major mental illnesses have either greater release of CPK from muscle or a slower clearance rate from serum. This suggests a biologic diathesis that predisposes to increased serum CPK activity at the time of an acute episode in some patients with all types of the major psychoses.

Biology of the Major Psychoses, edited by D. X.
Freedman, Res. Publ. Assoc. Res. Nerv. Ment.
Dis., Vol. 54. Raven Press, New York 1975.

Smooth-Pursuit Eye Movements in Schizophrenia: Recent Findings

Philip S. Holzman

Department of Psychiatry, University of Chicago, Chicago, Illinois 60637

Although our work began as a broad-gauged investigation of perceptual aspects of schizophrenic pathology, my colleagues Leonard Proctor and Deborah Levy and I have begun to center our work on the unexpected but robust discovery that smooth-pursuit eye movements are disordered in most schizophrenic patients and in a large number of their first-degree relatives. This discovery occurred during the course of our studies of vestibular and proprioceptive functioning. In this chapter, some of the major findings from our eye-tracking studies are reviewed and new data in three areas are presented. These new findings illuminate the question of the specificity of the phenomenon for schizophrenia, the genetic issues raised by the family data, and the question of drug effects.

A person fixates on a moving target by activating two independent visual mechanisms: the saccadic system, which centers the target on the fovea, and the pursuit system, which maintains the target image on the fovea. The saccadic system consists of high-velocity eye movements, sometimes as high as 600°/sec. Pursuit movements, on the other hand, are considerably slower in that they coordinate eyeball velocity to that of the target. Both systems usually operate cybernetically during normal viewing of a moving object, but it is the pursuit system, operating with the most delicate neuromuscular coordination, that continuously samples and thereby follows the position of a moving target. A common clinical test uses a pendulum to study eye movements. In normal eye tracking, the eye reproduces the sinusoidal motion of the pendulum within a critical oscillation frequency range. Most normal persons can accurately track a pendulum for a target excursion of 20 deg of visual angle the oscillation frequency of which does not exceed about 0.8 Hz. Examples of normal and deviant eye-tracking patterns are given in our previous publications, and other examples may be found in Benitez (1) and Corvera et al. (2). Deviations from normal tracking are associated with various kinds of vestibular and central nervous system disease.

Our rather simple procedure calls for the subject to be seated in front of the moving pendulum, which oscillates at a frequency of 0.4 Hz. Electronystagmographic recordings are made of eye movements in the horizontal plane. Channel 1 of our recorder displays actual eye movements, and channels 2 and 3 yield the derivative of the eye-movement signal as velocity in the right and left directions.

We have employed two different kinds of scoring for our data. One is a qualitative examination of the curve, which permits us to classify it as either

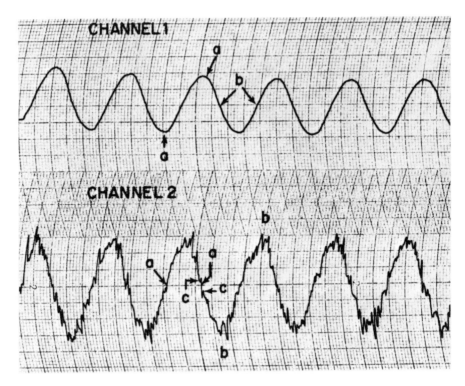

FIG. 1. Eye-tracking record of a normal subject. Channel 1 records direct eye movement. Channel 2 records the velocity of the eyes in the right (up) and left (down) directions. Calibration: 10 mm of pen deflection corresponds to 10° of eye movement.

disordered or ordered. We believe that this qualitative score is generally an accurate one. The second score, which we devised, is a quantitative index of the degree to which the sinusoidal wave departs from the target motion. We score the number of times the eye stops moving when it should indeed be following the target. We call this score "velocity arrest." This is an arbitrary score, but one that approximately represents an aspect of the tracking behavior. In our previous publications (3,4) we reported that the repeat reliability of this score ranged from 0.52 to 0.79 and correlations with the qualitative score of "good" or "bad" tracking patterns were 0.76 and 0.61.

In our earlier work, we established that velocity arrests are not under voluntary control; we concluded that if a person is watching the pendulum, velocity arrests were a fairly good but imperfect measure of the integrity of the pursuit system. Figure 1 illustrates these aspects of our scoring system.

Figure 2 is part of the record of a 46-year-old woman whose condition was diagnosed as "psychotic depression." The tracing in channel 1 represents fairly good pursuit movements, and the number of velocity arrests is rather low at 7.4 per cycle. In contrast, a portion of the record of a woman of approximately the

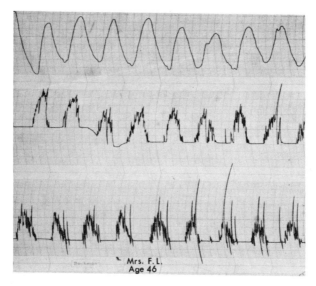

FIG. 2. Eye movement record of a psychotically depressed patient. In this record channels 2 and 3 show the velocity of the eyes in the right (channel 2) and left (channel 3) directions.

same age as the previous patient whose condition was diagnosed as schizophrenic is shown in Fig. 3. Here the qualitative pattern is noticeably disrupted and the number of velocity arrests is relatively high, 13.2 per cycle.

In our previous study, we reported on the eye-tracking of 46 recent schizo-

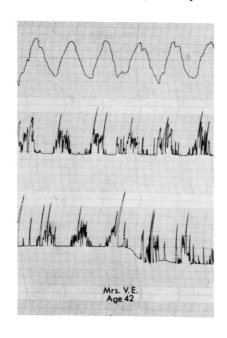

FIG. 3. Eye movement record of a patient whose condition was diagnosed as schizophrenic.

phrenics, nine manic-depressive, 19 non-psychotic psychiatric patients, 29 chronic schizophrenics, and 72 normal controls. We determined that 69% of the schizophrenic patients showed bad eye tracking. In contrast, 22% of the manic-depressives, 21% of the non-psychotic patients, and 8% of the normal subjects showed poor eye tracking. The number of velocity arrests also discriminated between the schizophrenic group and the other patients and controls.

A startling and entirely unexpected finding was that 44% of the relatives of the schizophrenic subjects, compared with only 10% of the relatives of the nonschizophrenic patients, also showed poor eye tracking. Within the schizophrenic group, moreover, there were no differences between patients with poor premorbid and good premorbid histories, patients with one or more hospitalizations, or patients classified as paranoid or non-paranoid.

When we used the specific criterion of thought disorder to classify the patients, a criterion that distinguishes manic flightiness, clanginess, and pressure from the schizophrenic bizarre and contaminated thinking, our results were somewhat improved over those that used only hospital diagnosis. Seventy-five percent of all schizophrenic subjects showed deviant eye tracking, as compared with 17% of the nonschizophrenic psychotic patients, and 5% of the non-psychotic psychiatric patients. About half of the first-degree relatives of the schizophrenics also showed poor eye tracking. Likewise, the number of velocity arrests significantly distinguished the schizophrenic groups—including the relatives—from all other patient groups and from the normal controls. Figure 4 is a graphic representation of these results.

Our interpretation of these results was quite tentative. We stated that both psychologic and neurophysiologic factors are probably involved in the dysfunction of smooth-pursuit movements. The psychologic dysfunction seemingly involves a core attentional process which appears as an impairment in the centering of attention—but it does not reflect impaired motivation or "inattention." The neurophysiologic factors are probably manifested in some as yet unspecified problem in neural transmission. We are pursuing this work from several directions. At this point I should like to present three new sources of data.

The first set of new data concerns the specificity of our findings. Do most psychotic patients show the eye-tracking dysfunction or is it specific for schizophrenia? We know that similar eye-tracking impairments occur in persons with arteriosclerosis, Parkinson's disease, brainstem lesions, hemispheric lesions, and other organic conditions. Hence, there is no specificity of the disorder for schizophrenia. We cannot, for example, distinguish smooth-pursuit dysfunctions that are referrable to organic lesions from those that occur in our schizophrenic patients—at least with our present technology. Furthermore it is a question as to whether smooth-pursuit dysfunctions occur in nonschizophrenic psychiatric patients. This question of specificity is surely a problem in studying an acute population from a large mental hospital. In the absence of organic lesions, our data favor specificity. But there are sufficient ambiguities with respect to diagnosis, particularly when employing the clinical diagnosis, to keep the issue of

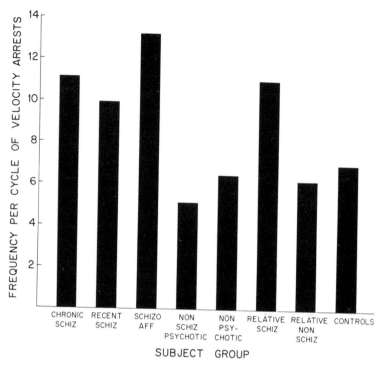

FIG. 4. Comparison of subject groups on velocity arrest score. Subjects are classified here by psychological test diagnosis (4).

specificity as an open one. When psychologic test diagnosis was used, however, relying only on the special kind of thought disorder that distinguishes schizophrenic thinking from other psychotic thought disruption, the nonschizophrenic psychotic patients were (a) significantly different from the schizophrenic patients, and (b) not significantly different from normals with respect to both the qualitative eye-tracking patterns and the number of velocity arrests. Although we are reasonably certain of the specificity of eye-tracking dysfunctions for schizophrenic patients, because we have seen the majority of manic patients we have tested track with great accuracy, there is doubt raised not only by our results but by a recent study by Shagass, Amadeo, and Overton (5). Shagass reports generally confirmatory results, but finds poor eye tracking, not only in his schizophrenic patients, but also in his depressed psychotic patients, particularly when this group included four depressed schizo-affective persons. The results for the five manic patients were equivocal, however.

We are convinced that more data must be gathered, particularly because the differential diagnosis between schizophrenia and nonschizophrenic psychosis during an acute state is a very difficult task when one has to rely only on the clinical interview and on ward observations. We have consequently been testing many more patients and we have instituted a follow-up study in which we are monitoring both the eye-tracking dysfunctions and the clinical state of patients at periodic intervals over several years. I should like to report on 36 additional patients—23 schizophrenics, four non-schizophrenic psychotic patients, and nine non-psychotic patients, as diagnosed by hospital psychiatrists. Sixteen of the schizophrenics (70%) showed impaired eye tracking by the qualitative index. This compares with the prevalence figure of 69% that we obtained in our previous study. Two of the four non-schizophrenic psychotics (50%), and two of the nine nonpsychotic patients (22%) showed poor eye tracking by the qualitative index. The mean velocity arrest score for the schizophrenic group was 13.45 arrests per cycle, compared with 9.63 velocity arrests per cycle for the non-schizophrenic psychotic patients. This is a significant difference and is quite similar to the results that we had reported for earlier groups.

The area of specificity is clearly one that needs the most careful consideration. It is an empirical issue, of course, and the data reported here are "interim data," that were released in the course of an ongoing study. Sensitive, expert, independent diagnostic studies are of the utmost importance here and the place of follow-up information for clarifying the issues cannot be overestimated. The clinical course of patients whose diagnosis is in doubt is crucial. Most clinicians are aware of the mercurial appearance of patients' symptoms on subsequent admissions to the same hospital. At times the patient may appear to be clearly suffering from a manic excitement, and on a subsequent admission he may appear to be schizophrenic. Although our experience, both from clinical sources and from psychological test data, leans toward the specificity of the findings for schizophrenia, we believe it is prudent to reserve judgment on the issue of specificity until more data are gathered.

As to the genetic implications of our findings, you recall that about 45% of the first-degree relatives of the schizophrenic patients, compared with 10% of the first-degree relatives of the nonschizophrenic patients, showed poor pursuit movements. The number of velocity arrests per cycle of these relatives was equal to that of the schizophrenic patients themselves. These findings suggest a genetic basis for the association. Because our sample was inadequate from the vantage point of a genetic study, we did not draw any further conclusions about these data. We are now beginning two studies that could illuminate this important issue. The first is undertaken in collaboration with Dr. Einar Kringlen in Norway. A decade ago, Kringlen (6) studied 55 pairs of monozygotic (Mz) twins and 90 pairs of dizygotic (Dz) same-sex twins, where one twin had been hospitalized for schizophrenia or schizophreniform psychosis. Using strict diagnostic criteria, Kringlen determined that 25% of the Mz twins and 7% of the Dz twins were concordant. By less stringent criteria, which includes borderline cases, 38% of the Mz and 10% of the Dz cases were concordant. Kringlen's population seemed to us to be an excellent one for determining concordance for eye tracking. If the eye-tracking dysfunction represents a genetic marker, we should expect considerably higher concordance for eye tracking than for clinical schizophrenia. Dr.

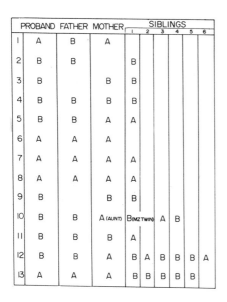

PROBAND	FATHER	MOTHER	SIBLINGS 1	2	3	4	5	6
1	A	B	A					
2	B	B		B				
3	B		B	B				
4	B	B	B	B				
5	B	B	A	A				
6	A	A	A					
7	A	A	A	A				
8	A	A	A	A				
9	B		B	B				
10	B	B	A (AUNT)	B(MZ TWIN)	A	B		
11	B	B	B	A				
12	B	B	A	B	A	B	B	B	A
13	A	A	A	B	B	B	B	B

FIG. 5. Congruence of good (A) and poor (B) eye tracking among schizophrenic probands and their first-degree relatives.

Kringlen and our group will be joining as a team to gather data on his twin sample and this study will be completed by the end of 1975.

A second study for which we have begun pilot work calls for collecting eye-tracking records from the first-degree families of schizophrenic patients. We are trying to get intact families in order to test mothers, fathers, and as many siblings as possible. This is difficult because there are large numbers of broken families among these patients. We do at this time have data on 13 families. With the collaboration of Dr. Shelby Haberman of our Department of Statistics, we are trying to fit the data to a model of genetic transmission. Figure 5 shows these interim data. Note that in every case in which the proband has impaired eye tracking, at least one parent also shows impaired eye tracking. Subject 10 has an Mz twin who is not clinically schizophrenic, and this twin shows impaired eye tracking. Occasionally, a relative will refuse to come in for testing after we had made the arrangements, as in cases 3 and 9. These fragmentary data are consistent with a hypothesized single gene, possibly a simple dominant. These data will help us piece together some of the genetic puzzle of schizophrenia. Although I believe a genetic factor has been demonstrated with respect to the potential for becoming schizophrenic, we have as yet no methods for deciding the mode of transmission. We await the use of an endophenotype—to use the term introduced by John and Lewis and referred to by Gottesman and Shields (7)—an internal phenotype the presence of which is recognizable only with the aid of an instrument, to help solve the puzzle of transmission mode. The eye-tracking dysfunction may be such an endophenotypic phenomenon and as such it may help us to fit a statistical model to the data.

Finally, I wish to report some drug studies that Proctor, Levy, and I have performed with the collaboration of Drs. Uhlenhuth, Schuster, and Freedman (8).

Although the data from our previous studies strongly supported our hunch that neuroleptic drugs did not produce the effects we saw—since relatives not on drugs showed the eye-tracking dysfunction, a number of schizophrenics taken off medications still showed the eye-tracking dysfunctions, and some non-schizophrenic patients who were on high doses of phenothiazines did not show the eye-tracking dysfunctions, as well as the report by Shagass et al. (5) that he could determine no specific drug effects—we nevertheless did not systematically observe the effects on smooth-pursuit movements of single and chronic dosages of specific drugs. We are currently studying the effects of chronic dosages of a variety of drugs on rhesus monkeys who are trained to follow a pendulum. Those data are reported later. We have tested the effects of single doses of chlorpromazine, diazepam, and secobarbital (Seconal®) on normal human volunteers and I can report those results here. We administered three weight-adjusted doses of diazepam, corresponding to about 5, 10, and 20 mg to four subjects. We tested the subjects pre- and postdrug. Testing occurred 1 hr and 45 min after drug administration; we used that point as the best estimate of maximum drug effect.

Chlorpromazine was administered in weight-adjusted dosages of approximately 50 and 100 mg. Subjects were tested 1 hr and 45 min after ingestion of chlorpromazine. One hundred mg of secobarbital was also administered to these subjects. Testing postsecobarbital occurred in 10 min intervals up to 80 min. The three drug experiments were separated by one week.

There were no differences between pre- and postdrug performances for diazepam or chlorpromazine. But secobarbital did produce a highly significant effect. Figure 6 shows one subject's chlorpromazine trials before and after drug ingestion. The eye tracking is unimpaired. These qualitative cruves were typical for all subjects. In contrast, Fig. 7 shows the secobarbital curves for all four subjects. Qualitative effects are obvious in two subjects, but differences are apparent in the remaining two subjects as well. All subjects experienced marked drowsiness and lethargy, particularly after both dosages of chlorpromazine, after the secobarbital, and after the 10 and 20 mg of diazepam (Valium®). Subjects were so sleepy that they would nap between testing sessions and they had to be awakened to perform the tasks. Thus, the effect of secobarbital on eye tracking does not seem referable to the sedative component or to attentional and motivational interferences with task efficiency, because other drugs produced those effects as well, but did not significantly disrupt eye tracking.

One subject, the one who showed the least disruption of pursuit movements under 100 mg of secobarbital, returned for serial testing on the three drugs. We administered to him 1.334 mg/kg of chlorpromazine, 0.284 mg/kg of diazepam, and 130 mg of secobarbital. Testing of these three drugs was carried out on successive weeks. Figure 8 shows that the secobarbital trials produced a disruption of smooth-pursuit eye tracking very quickly after administration, and after

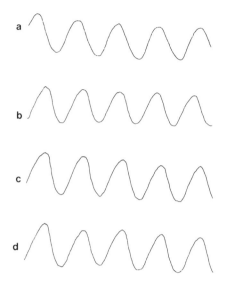

FIG. 6. One subject's eye-tracking record on CPZ trials. **(a)** Before: 0.667 mg/kg, **(b)** after: 0.667 mg/kg, **(c)** before: 1.334 mg/kg, **(d)** after: 1.334 mg/kg.

a maximum effect at 30 min, when a quantity of velocity arrests greater than those of the schizophrenic population occurred, dropped to a level that was still statistically elevated above predrug levels. This elevation remained at that clinically significant level even 24 hr after administration of this short-acting barbiturate.

The trials of diazepam and chlorpromazine are interesting in their own right. Although the rise in velocity arrests remained essentially within the normal clinical limits—and the qualitative scores are also normal—there is an initial rise of diazepam at 30 min and for chlorpromazine at 90 min. The number of velocity arrests ebbs and then at 6 hr shows a clear increase after which it falls again and at 24 hr returns to predrug levels. This initial rising, ebbing, and subsequent rise

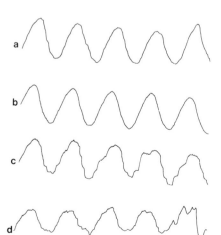

FIG. 7. Eye-tracking records of four subjects 60 min after ingestion of 100 mg Seconal®.

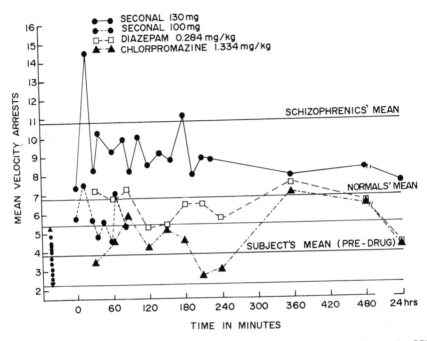

FIG. 8. Repeated eye-tracking trials for one subject after administration of 1.334 mg/kg CPZ, 0.284 mg/kg diazepam, and 100 and 130 mg of secobarbital (Seconal®). The mean velocity arrest scores of the schizophrenic subjects and the normal subjects from Holzman et al. (4) are presented for comparison. The subject's own predrug scores of 10 trials is also shown, as is ±2 σ from his own mean.

claim special attention. Baird and Hailey (9,10) had reported an increase in plasma levels of diazepam up to 90 min followed by a quick disappearance from circulating blood, but the drug then reappeared with a second peak at about 6 hr after administration. Those authors suggested a process of initial storage and later release into circulation. The diazepam curve we obtained for velocity arrests is congruent with the Baird and Hailey curves for plasma concentrations. Furthermore, because our chlorpromazine curve shows the same peaking at 6 hr, it appears likely that a similar pharmacokinetic process of storage and later release of CPZ is involved, although no one has yet demonstrated that process for chlorpromazine. These drug data suggest that in addition to their usefulness for exploring the process of smooth-pursuit movements and their impairments, they may demonstrate usefulness of the eye-tracking procedure as a method for pharmacokinetic studies.

COMMENTS

It is noteworthy that deviant smooth-pursuit eye movements are not correlated with severity of psychosis. Some patients in remission showed the poorest eye tracking, some of the most regressed and disturbed patients showed only mildly impaired records, and a few deteriorated schizophrenics even showed unimpaired eye tracking. Shagass (5) reports similar data. Furthermore, many of the relatives of schizophrenic patients—persons who themselves had never been hospitalized for a psychotic condition and who were functioning well socially, occupationally, and intellectually—showed eye tracking that was as deviant as that shown by many schizophrenic patients. Our early follow-up data, too, showed that poor eye tracking seems to be relatively stable over time, even in the presence of improved clinical state. In this regard, we found a zero correlation between eye-tracking performance and peak level of creatine phosphokinase (CPK) in several of Dr. Herbert Meltzer's patients (11).

These facts strongly suggest that eye-tracking patterns reflect a more enduring characteristic of the person than does psychotic state. Eye-tracking integrity may be a manifestation of a quasi-stable quality—a trait—whereas psychosis is a transitory, temporary state. Meltzer's data on peak CPK levels reflect relationships between serum enzymes and a phase of the psychotic state and therefore we should not expect serum enzyme levels to be correlated with a more enduring phenomenon like eye-tracking patterns.

Schizophrenic psychosis may thus be an exacerbation of a generally subclinical and lifelong organismic disequilibrium. This general organismic instability may be only a predisposition—like Meehl's schizotype—which never progresses toward decompensation into psychosis. But the predisposition may show itself in some disequilibrated processes, like smooth-pursuit eye movements, which implicate the most exquisite proprioceptive processes.

Such a view is consistent with the findings of those genetic studies that report more or less subtle forms of psychopathology in the biologic relatives of schizophrenics. This set of pathologic conditions has been called "the schizophrenic spectrum" (12). Although the schizophrenic spectrum is not well defined, it seems to reflect mildly disequilibrated adaptive behaviors. The genetic mapping of the transmission of schizophrenia has been hampered by the absence of a useable genetic marker or endophenotype. Clinical examinations for genetic studies are very time consuming and are subject to much subjective bias. Should the deviant eye tracking studied by our group prove to be a genetic marker, we can expect considerable progress not only in understanding the transmission for the potential for becoming schizophrenic, but in probing some of the underlying processes involved in this disorder.

A final word on the behavioral effects of deviant eye tracking is in order. Our first publication alluded to the obvious relationship between smooth-pursuit movements and visual perception. We suggested that impaired eye tracking in schizophrenic patients "may be associated with the impaired and idiosyncratic reality appraisal typical of these patients, inasmuch as visual perception, a central factor in reality contact, involves the organization of the entire perceptual system and requires effective motor response in feedback for its adaptive task" (ref. 3, p. 181). It seems to me that we may have made too far a leap from one level of data—the physiologic—to another—the experiential. It is an error to assume a one-to-one relationship between these two levels of discourse, even though the connection is a tempting one to make. The fact that the eye-tracking dysfunctions do not seem to improve with amelioration of clinical status and the fact that they occur among about half of the first-degree relatives who are not themselves clinically disturbed, should caution us against assuming an isomorphism between the eye-tracking dysfunction and phenomenal experience.

The issues must be more complex than simple isomorphism. Deviant eye tracking involves a considerable number of velocity arrests and a large number of saccadic movements are therefore required for the eye to catch up to the target. During saccadic movements there is a suppression of visual stimulation. Consequently, it would appear that those persons with poor eye tracking—and hence a greater number of saccades—are receiving a poorer sampling of the visual world than are those whose pursuit movements are not interrupted by velocity arrests and subsequent saccades. Yet it is probable that such decreased perceptual stimulation can be offset or neutralized by compensatory fixations. It is further possible that in some subjects there is an accompanying failure of saccadic suppression of stimulation. Because saccadic suppression is adaptively necessary for maintaining constancy of both object position and movement, failure of saccadic suppression may result in perceived instabilities in the visual world. These comments are, of course, speculative. They do indicate directions for further research, both into the process and the effects of the dysfunction we have been describing.

This work was supported in part by USPHS grant MH–19477, and by a grant from the Benevolent Foundation of the Scottish Rite, Northern Masonic Jurisdiction.

REFERENCES

1. Benitez, J. T. (1970): Eye-tracking and optokinetic tests: Diagnostic significance in peripheral and central vestibular disorders. *Laryngoscope,* 80:834–848.
2. Corvera, J., Lombardo, L., and Torres-Courtney, G. (1966): Alteraciones nistagmograficas en lesiones del tallo cerebral. *Neurol. Neurocir. Psiquiatr.,* 7:77–86.
3. Holzman, P. S., Proctor, L. R., and Hughes, D. W. (1973): Eye-tracking patterns in schizophrenia. *Science,* 181:179–181.
4. Holzman, P. S., Proctor, L. R., Levy, D. L., Yasillo, N., Meltzer, H. Y., and Hurt, S. W. (1974): Eye-tracking dysfunctions in schizophrenic patients and their relatives. *Arch. Gen. Psychiatry,* 31:143–151.
5. Shagass, C., Amadeo, M., and Overton, D. A. (1974): Eye-tracking performance in psychiatric patients. *Biol. Psychiatry,* 9:245–260.
6. Kringlen, E. (1967): *Heredity and Environment in the Functional Psychoses. Norwegian Monographs on Medical Science.* Universitetsforlaget, Oslo.
7. Gottesman, I. I., and Sheilds, J. (1972): *Schizophrenia and Genetics. A Twin Study Vantage Point.* Academic Press, New York.
8. Holzman, P. S., Levy, D. L., Uhlenhuth, E. H., Proctor, L. R., and Freedman, D. X. Smooth-pursuit eye movements and diazepam, CPZ, and secobarbital. *(Submitted for publication.)*
9. Baird, E. S., and Hailey, D. M. (1972): Delayed recovery from a sedative: Correlation of the plasma levels of diazepam with clinical effects after oral and intravenous administration. *Br. J. Anaesth.,* 44:803–808.
10. Baird, E. S., and Hailey, D. M. (1973): Plasma levels of diazepam and its major metabolite following intramuscular administration. *Br. J. Anaesth.,* 45:546–547.
11. Meltzer, H. Y., Elkun, L., and Moline, R. (1969): Serum enzyme changes in newly admitted psychiatric patients. *Arch. Gen. Psychiatry,* 21:731–738.
12. Kety, S. S., Rosenthal, D., Wender, P. H., and Schulsinger, F. (1968): The types and prevalence of mental illness in the biological and adoptive families of adopted schizophrenics. In: *The Transmission of Schizophrenia,* edited by D. Rosenthal and S. S. Kety. Pergamon, Oxford.

Discussion

Spitzer: The terminological quandaries we encounter in all these discussions are problems that the Committee on Revising DSMII into DSMIII has been wrestling with and are worth highlighting as we assess the research findings.

First there is the use of the terms psychosis and psychotic. We have the problem that manic-depressive psychosis is seen as a psychosis in Europe, but in America the DSMII Committee decided to refer to the condition as manic-depressive illness in recognition of the fact that many patients with this disorder are never psychotic at any stage in their illness.

And that, of course, is the second use of the term psychotic, which refers to a level of functioning. Here we do not have agreement on what we mean by the level of functioning that is psychotic.

DSMII introduced the concept of psychotic as a failure to meet the everyday demands of life, which might include many of us who don't like to think of ourselves as psychotic. They did this because of the problem of so-called psychotic depressive reaction, which includes many individuals who are not psychotic in the sense of having delusions or hallucinations.

I'm not sure as to whether all the patients who were referred to as psychotic in some of the studies just presented were psychotic in the sense of delusions or hallucinations. We're evidently dealing with a continuum, and it's hard to know where to establish the dichotomy.

We have the problem of the use of the term "acute," as in "acute schizophrenia." Does that mean recent and sudden onset? Does it mean that the duration has not gone on beyond a certain period of time? If someone shows an insidious development of a chronic, eccentric, schizoid personality and then suddenly has a flare-up, of overt schizophrenic illness, is that acute schizophrenia? I believe Dr. Kety would say that such a condition is not acute schizophrenia, but many in this country use the category acute schizophrenia episode to include those individuals who had a poor premorbid history, if this is the first onset of schizophrenia. So we have a real problem as to how to subtype these conditions and how to agree on the terms that we're using.

One solution to this problem of terminology that is being considered by our committee is to subtype schizophrenia along two axes: the first being the course of the illness, the second being the clinical phenomenology of a particular episode. The course of the illness would be divided into acute, subacute, subchronic, and chronic. The acute course would be defined as sudden onset (less than three months from first signs of increasing psychopathology to any of the core symptom), short course (continuously ill for less than three months), and full recovery from any previous episode. Chronic schizophrenia would be defined as significant signs of schizophrenia more or less continuously present for at least the last two years. The subacute and subchronic types would be intermediate. The second axis would involve the traditional subtypes of paranoid, catatonic, hebephrenic, and schizoaffective, as well as some other recognizable clinical subtypes.

Holzman: I have been asked to comment on the data suggesting abnormalities in rotationally induced nystagmus in schizophrenia.

Rotationally induced nystagmus, as many of you know, is a less precise way of measuring vestibular functioning than is caloric irrigation. That is, with this method we cannot assess each side separately as we can in caloric studies. Furthermore, if the subject is tested with opportunity for fixation, there is the possibility of inducing an optokinetic nystagmus, which would counteract the vestibularly induced nystagmus with no means of assessing either one. The abnormalities that have been demonstrated in the literature have not controlled for fixation opportunities and alerting opportunities. And the results that have been demonstrated have been on catatonic schizophrenics generally in a stupor or quite psychotic, and who therefore are not alert and who stare, both of which will tend to inhibit nystagmus. And therefore, I think, just as with the caloric studies, the results are suspect.

In addition, the measures of response that have been used seem to me to be less appropriate than others that might be employed. They typically use latency of response and duration of response, and at least in caloric irrigation these measures have less to do with the integrity of the vestibular system than with the conductivity of the temporal bone.

I have also been asked whether the ability to fixate on an object and track it is affected by vestibular dysfunction? As far as I know, it is affected by the vestibular dysfunction, and this is one of the tests otolaryngologists use.

I have also been asked about correlations of eye-tracking dysfunction, perceptual disorders, and thought disorders. When we first discovered the eye-tracking dysfunctions, I did think that there might be a connection between them and the perceptual abnormalities in schizophrenia. We did allude to that connection in a paper Proctor, Hughes, and I published in *Science* in 1973. But the connection is not simple, that is, I do not believe it accounts for the perceptual disturbances of schizophrenics, since so many nonschizophrenics—such as relatives of the schizophrenics—show the dysfunction. Its connection to perceptual abnormalities is rather indirect and complex. The issue of saccadic inhibition is probably relevant, but further careful study is needed. All I can say now with confidence is that there is a relationship between poor eye tracking and schizophrenia and that this is a stable relationship.

The issue of thought disorder and the eye-tracking abnormalities is an intriguing one, however. As you saw from our data, the correlations are increased a good deal when one uses a specific criterion of thought disorder rather than relying only on the hospital diagnosis of schizophrenia. And I think that this is important when one talks about specific aspects of the illness rather than the global syndrome of schizophrenia, whatever that might be.

If we are talking about thought disorder and if we define that phenomenon rather carefully, then everybody will know what we're talking about. And if we have a quantitative index of the thought disorder, we should get further than if we just talk about "schizophrenia," as there are many, many ambiguities in the use of that diagnostic category, particularly in acute populations.

If we had to be pinned down, I would say that the correlation that we see between eye tracking and psychopathology is between eye tracking and a certain specific kind of thought disorder. And there I think it is rather a firm correlation. It is possible that whatever produces the disordered thinking may also be producing the disordered eye tracking.

Kety: I don't have any questions, but I can't repress a comment. I think the two presentations by Dr. Meltzer and Dr. Holzman, both, by coincidence, from the University of Chicago, are illustrative of a trend that has taken place in biologic psychiatry largely in the past decade. Positive biologic findings, in schizophrenia especially, but also in the affective disorders, have not been difficult to obtain. In fact, we have seen positive biologic findings for the past 25 or 50 years, most of which have been explicable in terms of very trivial variables which were not controlled. Both of these papers illustrate a new approach by scientists interested in testing their hypotheses by what testing hypotheses means, that is, trying to disprove them. The careful, systematic way in which these investigators have been examining their findings is impressive. Neither has drawn sweeping conclusions or implications as to etiology or pathogenesis. They have been mainly concerned with the findings themselves and with ruling out a number of nondisease variables and alternative hypotheses. The significance of the findings can come later.

Callaway: I agree that recent research has been elegant and marked by sound scientific strategy, but we still would do well to attend to "Zubin's law." Dr. Joseph Zubin has reminded us that to find something that will really tell you about schizophrenia you need to find something that schizophrenics do better than a normal!

These findings are still, unfortunately, nonspecific. I don't mean to denigrate their importance, but to point up the problem that we still have.

Freedman: I thought a severe schizophrenic hallucinated a lot better than most normals.

Callaway: So, according to Zubin's law, efficiency of hallucination would be a better measure than inefficiency of eye tracking.

Freedman: I suppose the definition of efficiency may become the issue, unfortunately, since efficiency experts in the recent past have succeeded in not advancing any field of our inquiries!

Meltzer: Zuben's law is indeed challenging—maybe the biologic data which I demonstrated fulfill it, in fact. Although subterminal motor nerves which branch are not found frequently in normal individuals (less than 10% of subterminal motor nerves), they are not really true pathology. They are attempts at adaptation. Current theory as to why the subterminal motor nerves branch is that they do so as a response to the degeneration or dysfunction of other subterminal nerves. This produces denervated muscle fibers. The body attempts to restitute normal innervation to them. The healthy, surviving nerves in the same region branch and take over the innervation of the denervated muscle fibers. There may be a comparable process in the CNS. After a psychotic episode, the neurons in the CNS may branch and make connections to other neurons. This could lead to good or bad connections and might relate to good or poor remission of the psychosis.

Thus branching in the peripheral nervous systems such as we have demonstrated may be an example of an attempt of neurons in psychotic patients to restore function. And perhaps the psychotic patients do it better than normals. If they didn't do it better than normals, I might be able to answer Dr. Rowland's criticism as to why psychotic patients don't show some functional loss: They may not show loss of function because their subterminal motor nerves can branch and restore function!

Biology of the Major Psychoses, edited by D. X.
Freedman, Res. Publ. Assoc. Res. Nerv. Ment.
Dis., Vol. 54. Raven Press, New York   1975

Effects of Neuroleptics on the Nigroneostriatal and Mesocortical Dopaminergic Systems

J. Glowinski

Groupe de Neuropharmacologie Biochimique, Laboratoire de Neurophysiologie, Collège de France, Paris, France

Amphetamine in high doses induces a psychotic syndrome in man, which, in certain respects, has been compared to schizophrenia (1). This amphetamine effect is prevented by neuroleptics, drugs widely used in the treatment of schizophrenic patients. Clinical observations have stimulated numerous studies during the past decade. Indeed, the discovery of the various sites of action of psychotropic drugs in the brain and of their biochemical effects should be critical for the understanding of some of their behavioral effects. Indirectly, this could also contribute to the determination of some of the biochemical abnormalities that occur in schizophrenia.

In the earlier studies it was found that both dopaminergic and noradrenergic (NA) transmission were affected by amphetamine (2) and by neuroleptics (3,4). Subsequently, comparative analysis of the biochemical effects of various classes of neuroleptics revealed that potent antipsychotic agents with weak sedative activities were acting particularly on dopaminergic neuronal systems (5,6). Various *in vivo* release studies have indicated that amphetamine enhances the quantities of dopamine (7–9) and norepinephrine (NE) (10) at catecholaminergic synapses. This effect results from the direct action of the drug on catecholaminergic nerve endings. In contrast to amphetamine, all known neuroleptics block DA transmission; they are potent antagonists of DA receptors (3,11).

For various reasons, the biochemical and pharmacologic effects of amphetamine and neuroleptics have been examined mainly in connection with the nigroneostriatal DA system. Its anatomic localization is well established in various species, and the caudate nucleus is densely innervated by DA terminals. Some of the neuronal systems connected with the DA system have been found (Fig. 1). Moreover, this DA pathway is involved in extrapyramidal processes, which has stimulated many workers to design original experimental animal models allowing a quantitative evaluation of pharmacologic effects. Although we cannot review all the studies of the effects of amphetamine and neuroleptics upon the nigroneostriatal DA system in this chapter, some recent data obtained by our group or by other laboratories in particular, are summarized and discussed. The data illustrate some interesting new aspects of the mechanisms of action of these drugs upon the nigroneostriatal dopamine system.

For many years it was thought that only three dopaminergic systems were

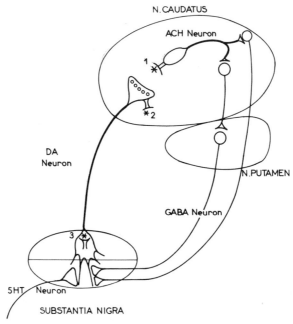

FIG 1. Schematic representation of the various neuronal systems involved in the control of the activity of the nigroneostriatal dopaminergic pathway. Numbers 1,2,3 refer to the localization of the various dopaminergic receptors identified by electrophysiologic, pharmacologic, or biochemical methods.

present in the brain. Besides the nigroneostriatal DA pathway, histochemical studies had revealed the existence of a tuberoinfundibular system and of a mesolimbic DA system (12). The tuberoinfundibular dopaminergic system is involved in various neuroendocrine regulations. The mesolimbic DA pathway that projects mainly to the tubercule olfactorium and the nucleus accumbens, appears to originate in cells lying closely adjacent to those of the nigroneostriatal DA pathway, but its functions are little understood. It has been suggested that the antipsychotic effects of neuroleptics could be related particularly to their action on this pathway (13,14). However, this is still a working hypothesis. Unfortunately, real experimental evidence to support this statement is lacking.

Using lesions and biochemical techniques, we recently discovered the existence of a complex mesocortical dopaminergic system projecting into various specific areas of the cerebral cortex in the rat. As in the mesolimbic DA system, this mesocortical DA pathway might represent a critical site for the pharmacologic effects of amphetamine and neuroleptics. I will summarize most of the available information on the various properties of this recently characterized mesocortical DA system.

EFFECTS OF AMPHETAMINE AND NEUROLEPTICS UPON THE NIGRONEOSTRIATAL DOPAMINERGIC SYSTEM

Various approaches improved our knowledge of the modes of action of amphetamine and neuroleptics upon the nigroneostriatal DA neurons. (a) Biochemical experiments carried out *in vivo* or *in vitro* have suggested the occurrence of presynaptic DA receptors. They are involved in the control of the release and synthesis of the transmitter. (b) By neurophysiologic methods, the fluctuations of the activity of the DA neurons have been measured directly under various pharmacologic situations. (c) Sensitive techniques have been developed to study *in vivo* the release of dopamine from the caudate nucleus. (d) A dopamine-sensitive adenylate cyclase likely closely associated to the postsynaptic dopamine receptor has been characterized in striatal tissue. (e) Simultaneous studies performed in different laboratories indicate the occurrence of a close link between DA terminals and cholinergic interneurons within the cat caudate nucleus or the rat striatum. (f) Finally, the effects of repeated injections of neuroleptics upon the nigroneostriatal dopaminergic system have been examined and compared to those induced by acute injections of these drugs.

The Presynaptic Dopaminergic Receptors

Injected acutely, various types of neuroleptics rapidly activate the synthesis and turnover of DA in striatal dopaminergic terminals (4,13–16). For many years this effect has been attributed mainly to an interneuronal activation of the DA neurons triggered by the blockade of postsynaptic DA receptors (3,5,17). In contrast to neuroleptics, apomorphine—an agonist of these receptors—reduces the rate of synthesis and turnover of dopamine (18). Recordings of the activity of DA cells in the substantia nigra indicate that receptor blockade and increased dopamine turnover are associated with an increase in the rate of nerve-impulse flow, whereas receptor stimulation and decreased synthesis are associated with decreased impulse flow (19,20).

Recent findings suggest that neuroleptics also directly affect dopamine metabolism in nerve terminals by blocking presynaptic dopamine receptors. Some of the evidence that supports this mode of action can be summarized briefly. First, it was found that the effect of electrical-field stimulation upon DA release from striatal slices was enhanced in the presence of neuroleptics and was inhibited by apomorphine (21). The release of DA is blocked immediately after the interruption of firing in DA neurons induced by transection of the dopaminergic pathway (22) or by injection of γ-hydroxybutyrate, a potent general anesthetic (23). In the rat, this latter effect is associated with a transient activation of dopamine synthesis (18,24,25). The change in synthesis is very likely triggered by the reduction of available DA at presynaptic DA receptor sites. Following the interruption of firing, apomorphine can still reduce DA synthesis in nerve terminals;

this effect is blocked by neuroleptics (18,24). These various results provide strong argument to support the existence of presynaptic DA receptors. Moreover, they suggest that neuroleptics may partially activate DA synthesis by acting directly upon DA neurons. The protective effect of neuroleptics on the inhibitory action of apomorphine on DA synthesis was also demonstrated recently *in vitro* in a striatal synaptosomal preparation (26). The occurrence of DA receptors directly on nigral DA cell bodies has been postulated on the basis of microiontophoretic neurophysiologic studies. This may also represent a critical site for a direct action of neuroleptics on DA neurons (27).

In Vivo Estimation of DA Release from the Caudate Nucleus

During the last few years, we have studied in our laboratory the effects of various pharmacologic treatments on the release of DA from the surface of the cat caudate nucleus. For this purpose a cup technique was used, and the release of [^{3}H] DA continuously synthesized from L-3,5-[^{3}H] tyrosine was estimated in superfusates. The direct introduction of thioproperazine into the cup induces only a slight increase in the spontaneous release of the newly synthesized transmitter. A progressive and much more important stimulation of [^{3}H]DA release is observed following the intravenous injection of this potent antipsychotic agent. This effect is immediately blocked by the transection of the nigroneostriatal DA pathway, another indication that nerve activity is required to detect the neuroleptic action on the release process (28,29).

An important question should be resolved with this approach: What is the relative importance of the effects of the neuroleptics on presynaptic and postsynaptic DA receptor sites in the changes in DA release and synthesis detected in *in vivo* situation? It will not be surprising to find that they may vary from one species to another. Indeed, in contrast to observations in the rat (25), until now we have failed to detect a transient increase in DA synthesis following the immediate interruption of the DA pathway in the cat (22). This suggests that the presynaptic DA receptors may be less efficient in the control of DA synthesis in the cat than in the rat. However, new experiments are required to confirm this hypothesis.

The addition of amphetamine to the cup immediately induces a significant release of DA (8,28). A similar effect is detected when the drug is injected intravenously. According to other workers, the amphetamine effect is partly dependent upon nerve activity, but it can also be seen following interruption of firing (9). This is not surprising because amphetamine, in contrast to thioproperazine, markedly enhances the release of [^{3}H]DA previously synthesized from labeled tyrosine in the isolated rat striatum (30). In all studies performed *in vivo* or *in vitro*, we observed that the effect of amphetamine upon DA release was associated with an inhibition of the transmitter synthesis (15,31). Two mechanisms may be involved in this situation. The inhibition of the transmitter synthesis may be the result of a stimulation of presynaptic DA receptors by the large quantities of the amine released in the synapse. The interneuronal inhibition of the activity of DA neurons triggered by the stimulation of postsynaptic DA receptor may occur *in vivo* situations. Indeed, the firing of DA nigral cells is inhibited following the injection of amphetamine, and this effect is reversed by neuroleptics (19).

The Dopamine-Sensitive Adenylate Cyclase

The identification by Kebabian et al. (32) of a DA-sensitive adenylate cyclase in homogenates of striatal tissue has stimulated various researches upon the *in vitro* potency of various DA agonists and antagonists on this system. Indeed, this membranous enzymatic system is probably closely coupled to the postsynaptic DA receptor. This biochemical model has already been used to define some of the structural requirements for the agonists (33,34) and antagonists (33,35) of the DA receptor. Although less effective than DA, apomorphine stimulates the formation of cyclic AMP, and this effect is blocked by neuroleptics. The effects of various classes of neuroleptics have been examined. All of them are potent inhibitors of the DA-stimulating effect on the adenylate cyclase.

However, curiously the butyrophenone derivatives, which are particularly active in clinical therapy, were *less* effective than most of the phenothiazine derivatives exhibiting antipsychotic properties (35). The activity of the DA-sensitive adenylate cyclase has been measured in striatal homogenates following degeneration of the nigroneostriatal DA pathway. Some authors have even detected a supersensitivity to DA in this situation (36).

Relationships between Dopaminergic and Cholinergic Neurons

On the basis of clinical and pharmacologic observations, the concept of a balance between dopaminergic and cholinergic systems within the striatopallidonigral complex has emerged in various laboratories. Recently, the relationship between the nigroneostriatal DA system and the striatal cholinergic interneurons were clarified. The original findings of Dr Bartholini's group (37) have stimulated studies on this problem. Measuring the release of ACh in the absence of cholinesterase inhibitor with a push–pull cannula inserted deeply in the cat caudate nucleus, these authors observed that neuroleptics enhanced ACh release, whereas apomorphine induced an opposite effect. These changes in ACh release elicited by antagonists and an agonist of postsynaptic DA receptors were only detected in the caudate nucleus and not in other structures innervated by cholinergic neurons (14).

In our own study on the rat (38,39), changes in ACh utilization were estimated by measuring the transmitter levels in tissues. Indeed, it is well established that ACh levels increase when the utilization of the transmitter is reduced and vice versa. Interesting information was obtained. Various neuroleptics enhanced the utilization of ACh in the striatum but not in other structures such as the cerebral cortex or the hippocampus—structures rich in cholinergic terminals. The acute injection of chlorpromazine reverses the inhibiting effect of apomorphine upon ACh utilization in the striatum. The effects of apomorphine as well as those of neuroleptics could still be detected following complete degeneration of the nigroneostriatal DA pathway (38).

This suggests that the drugs act directly upon cholinergic interneurons through their effects on postsynaptic DA receptors. From these results, it may be suspected that the DA receptors are localized on the cholinergic interneurons. The persistence of the effects of neuroleptics on ACh utilization in the absence of dopaminergic transmission is puzzling. A change in the conformation of the receptors directly induced by the drug could be involved in this effect. Such an action could affect the membrane permeability to ions and trigger the activation of cholinergic interneurons. The rate of ACh utilization was also affected by the direct manipulation of the DA neuronal system (39). Indeed, immediately following the blockade of DA release induced by the transection of the nigroneostriatal DA pathway, the utilization of ACh was accelerated in the striatum. With the opposite procedure, the stimulation of DA release elicited by amphetamine inhibited the activity of cholinergic interneurons. This effect was no longer detected following complete degeneration of the nigroneostriatal DA pathway, confirmation that amphetamine acts directly upon DA neurons.

From all these results, it can be concluded that the nigroneostriatal DA system tonically inhibits the activity of cholinergic interneurons within the striatum. Consequently, facilitation or interruption of DA transmission respectively induced by drugs such as amphetamine or neuroleptics are associated with deep changes in the activity of the cholinergic neurons. Although the relationship between dopaminergic and cholinergic neurons within the basal ganglia may be much more complex, the present results explain in great part how anticholinergic agents reverse some of the extrapyramidal disorders observed following treatment with neuroleptics.

Effects of Long-Term Administration of Neuroleptics on Dopaminergic Neurons

In most cases, the antipsychotic properties of neuroleptics are observed in patients following long-term treatments. This can be applied as well to their extrapyramidal side effects. Therefore, changes in activity of dopaminergic or cholinergic neurons must be studied in the brains of animals treated repeatedly with neuroleptics. Interesting results on the effects of various long-term treatments with neuroleptics on the activity of the nigroneostriatal DA system have been obtained in the rat (40). As previously mentioned, the acute injection of neuroleptics markedly activates DA synthesis within a short period (3 to 5 hr). This effect is of short duration and 24 hr later the rate of synthesis of transmitter is identical to control values. A completely different picture is observed following the last injection of repeated treatments (12 days, one injection each day) made with classic neuroleptics such as thioproperazine, haloperidol or pipothiazine. Three hr later, DA synthesis is still accelerated but at a much lesser degree than following a single acute injection of these drugs. Surprisingly the transmitter synthesis is always reduced 24 hr after the last injection as compared to that observed in animals injected once with these drugs. This reduction in striatal DA synthesis, which is associated with a decrease in the amine turnover, corresponds very likely to a sustained decrease in the basal activity of the nigroneostriatal DA pathway. This complex effect of neuroleptics upon the nigroneostriatal DA pathway was also detected following a single injection of a long-acting neuroleptic—the palmitic ester of pipotiazine (40). In this case, after an initial 8-to-10-day period during which DA synthesis was accelerated, the rate of formation of the transmitter and its turnover were reduced significantly for several weeks. A similar long-term decrease in the activity of the dopaminergic pathway is seen in young animals treated repeatedly with classic neuroleptics immediately after birth (41). We already know that this curious effect can only be detected only in the nigroneostriatal DA pathway and not in the mesolimbic and the mesocortical DA systems.

Two questions may be asked: What are the mechanisms involved in the long-term inhibition of the basal activity of the nigroneostriatal DA pathway seen after constant impregnation of cerebral tissues by small concentrations of neuroleptics? What is the pharmacologic significance of this phenomenon? Various hypotheses have been considered in an attempt to answer the first question and have been discussed extensively elsewhere (40). One hypothesis, based on electrophysiologic data, is particularly attractive. Some cells in the caudate nucleus are inhibited by DA (42); as discussed previously, it is very likely that they correspond to the cholinergic interneurons. The blockade of the DA effect upon these neurons by high doses of neuroleptics is probably responsible for the activation of a "positive" interneuronal feedback loop, and consequently for the enhanced activity of DA neurons seen after a single injection of neuroleptics or shortly following each daily injection in repeated treatments. Other cells within the caudate nucleus are stimulated by DA (42). The identity of these cells is still unknown. The blockade of the postsynaptic DA receptors localized on these cells could trigger a "negative" interneuronal feedback loop distinct from that described previously. The latter effect could be responsible for the long-term inhibition of the activity of DA neurons observed following long-term treatment with neuroleptics. According to this hypothesis the postsynaptic DA receptors localized on the neurons stimulated by DA should be particularly sensitive to low concentrations of neuroleptics. No definite answer can be provided for the second question. The sustained decrease in DA transmission induced by long-term neuroleptic treatments could be directly responsible for some extrapyramidal disorders. However, this may just be a secondary effect, the main factor involved in the pharmacologic action being the blockade of the postsynaptic DA receptors by the neuroleptics.

THE MESOCORTICAL DOPAMINERGIC SYSTEM—ANOTHER SITE OF ACTION OF NEUROLEPTICS

For many years, mainly on the basis of histochemical data, it was assumed that the cerebral cortex was innervated by NE but not by DA neurons. In a study in which the effects of thioproperazine on the rate of catecholamine turnover were examined in the cerebral cortex of the rat, we were surprised to see that the concentration of dopamine was only slightly lower than that of NE (43). In contrast, the cerebellum, another structure innervated by NA terminals but devoid of DA terminals, could not provide measurement of DA by available spectrofluorimetric methods. This initial observation led us to postulate that the cerebral cortex of the rat was not only innervated by NE but also by DA terminals. This hypothesis was confirmed rapidly by a series of experiments.

Discovery of the Mescortical Dopaminergic System

The main steps that were involved in the discovery of the occurrence of cortical DA terminals can be briefly summarized. First, DA was easily estimated in the cerebral cortex of rats in which NA neurons projecting to the cerebral cortex were previously destroyed using various procedures. This was shown in adult rats, following electrolytic lesions of the locus coeruleus, and after localized microinjections of 6-OH-DA, which specifically destroyed the ascending ventral and dorsal NA pathways (44,45). Similar observations were made in young rats (40 days old) injected intraperitoneally with low doses of 6-OH-DA *intra utero* or immediately after birth (46). This latter procedure affects only central NA neurons, and is without effect on DA systems. Second, the synthesis of [³H] DA from [³H] tyrosine was demonstrated in synaptosomes prepared from cerebral cortical tissues of rats in which the cortical NA terminals were previously destroyed (45). Moreover, a specific DA uptake process, sensitive to benzotropine and unsensitive to desmethylimipramine could be demonstrated in cortical synaptosomes of such lesioned rats (47). Finally, the DA terminals were visualized directly using histochemical fluorescent methods in these "NA lesioned" rats (48) as well as in normal animals (49). The DA terminals can be distinguished from the NA terminals by their appearance and by their localization. Whereas the NA terminals are scattered throughout various parts of the cerebral cortex, particularly in the superficial layers, the DA terminals are found in deeper layers and only in certain areas. They are concentrated mainly in the frontal, the entorhinal, and the cingular cortex (Fig. 2). Recently, with a new sensitive radioenzymatic assay, DA could be detected in relatively high concentration in these various areas (50,52).

The precise localization of the cell bodies of the DA neurons is not yet well established. But lesions made in the A10 and A9 areas induced a rather significant degeneration of the cortical DA terminals. This was demonstrated by histochemical (51,52) as well as biochemical methods (Tassin, Blanc, and Thierry, *unpub-*

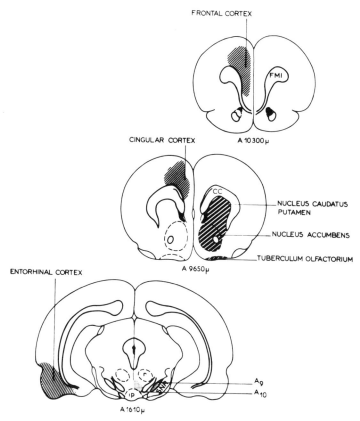

FIG. 2. Schematic representation of the localization of the cell bodies and terminals of the various ascending dopaminergic systems in the rat. A9 cell bodies of the nigroneostriatal pathway projecting in the nucleus caudatus putamen: A10 cell bodies of the mesolimbic pathway projecting in the nucleus accumbens and the tuberculum olfactorium. A10 and possibly A9 correspond also to the cell bodies of the mesocortical dopaminergic systems projecting in the frontal, cingular, and entorhinal cortex.

lished observations). The concentrated distribution in the ventral tegmental area of the cell bodies of the various DA systems (mesocortical, mesolimbic, and nigroneostriatal) is particularly striking. It is quite possible that some of the neurons projecting to the various limbic structures are also damaged in parkinsonian patients.

Some information about the postsynaptic DA receptors of the mesocortical DA neurons have already been obtained. An adenylate cyclase sensitive to DA has been detected in homogenates of cerebral cortex in the rat. The stimulating effect of DA can be blocked by neuroleptics (53). Recently in our laboratory, similar observations have been made in discrete areas of the frontal cortex particularly rich in DA terminals (Bockaert, Premont, Tassin, and Thierry, *unpublished observations).* However, the receptor cells are still unidentified. As previously mentioned, there are some indications that these receptor cells are not cholinergic neurons in contrast to that observed in the caudate nucleus.

Characteristics of the Mesocortical Dopaminergic Neurons

Some of the properties of the mesocortical DA system are already established. A partial degeneration of the system induced by an intracisternal injection of 6-OH-DA, made shortly after birth led to an hyperactivity of the remaining intact dopaminergic neurons (46). This phenomenon is similar to that observed previously in the nigroneostriatal DA system (54). As suggested by the marked increase in DA levels seen in the cerebral cortex, following the injection of γ-hydroxybutyrate (Tassin et al., *unpublished observations*), this drug may block the nerve impulse flow in the mesocortical DA system as in other DA neurons. The mesocortical DA system is also sensitive to various neuroleptics, but some interesting differences in its reactivity to these drugs can be seen. As expected, acute injections of neuroleptics stimulate the synthesis of DA in the cerebral cortex (55). This was observed not only in control animals, but also in lesioned rats devoid of cortical NA innervation. Apomorphine, the agonist of DA receptors, inhibits the transmitter synthesis. Interestingly enough, the doses of neuroleptics required to produce a 50% increase in DA synthesis in the cerebral cortex were much higher than those eliciting a similar effect in the nigroneostriatal DA pathway (55,56). This may be related to a different interneuronal regulation of the mesocortical DA pathway. Moreover, the synthesis of DA was always much more stimulated following repeated treatment with neuroleptics than after a single injection of the drugs. This could be seen even 24 hr following the last injection of the neuroleptic (Scatton, Glowinski, and Julou, *unpublished observations*). Thus, this pattern of reactivity of the mesocortical DA neurons under these treatments, which mimic in some way those used in patients, is different to that observed in nigroneostriatal DA neurons. This critical observation may have an important pharmacologic significance.

Little is yet known about the cerebral cortical DA innervation in species other than the rat. Evidence have been obtained for the presence of DA terminals in the cerebral cortex of the cat (57). The knowledge of their distribution in man will be of particular interest and should be provided some working hypothesis in order to elucidate some of the functional characteristics of the corresponding DA pathways.

CONCLUSION

The wide distribution of DA terminals and DA receptors in the brain is now well established. The nigroneostriatal, the mesolimbic and the mesocortical DA systems are involved in different functions. Changes in DA transmission in the various structures innervated by these neurons induced by neuroleptics or by amphetamine may thus have various pharmacologic and clinical consequences.

What is (or what are) the critical site(s) contributing to the psychotic syndrome observed following administration of high doses of amphetamine is still an open question. Intensive studies of the role of the mesolimbic and the mesocortical DA systems are necessary in order to clarify the problem.

Various working hypotheses can be used to explain some of the beneficial clinical effects of neuroleptics. In schizophrenic patients, disturbances in the intra- or interneuronal regulatory processes could lead to sustained hyperactivity of some DA neurons. Some of the postsynaptic DA receptors could be supersensitive to DA. Owing to restricted degeneration of some neuronal systems or to biochemical abnormalities in their functional capacity, some DA neurons closely located may develop abnormal connections. These new connections may be responsible for the appearance of new behavioral patterns. For many of us, these hypotheses could appear too simple or too naive to explain the complexity of the behavior changes seen in schizophrenic patients. Nevertheless, it will be already of great interest if some of these phenomenona could be demonstrated in experimental animal models.

REFERENCES

1. Snyder, S. H., Banerjee, S. P., Yamamura, H. I., and Greenberg, D. (1974): Drugs, neurotransmitters and schizophrenia. *Science,* 184:1243–1253.
2. Glowinski, J. (1970): Effects of amphetamine on various aspects of catecholamine metabolism in the central nervous system of the rat. In: *Proceedings of the Mario Negri,* edited by E. Costa and S. Garattini, pp. 301–316. Raven Press, New York.
3. Carlsson, A., and Lindqvist, M. (1963): Effect of chlorpromazine or haloperidol on formation of 3-methoxytyramine and normetanephrine in mouse brain. *Acta Pharmacol. Toxicol. (Kbh),* 20:140–144.
4. Corrodi, H., Fuxe, K., and Hökfelt, T. (1967): The effect of neuroleptics on the activity of central catecholamine neurones. *Life Sci.* (I), 6:767–774.
5. Anden, N. E., Butcher, S. G., Corrodi, H., Fuxe, K., and Ungerstedt, U. (1970): Receptor activity and turnover of dopamine and noradrenaline after neuroleptics. *Eur. J. Pharmacol.,* 11:303–314.
6. Nybäck, H., and Sedvall, G. (1970): Further studies on the accumulation and disappearance of catecholamines formed from tyrosin-^{14}C in mouse brain. Effect of some phenothiazine analogues. *Eur. J. Pharmacol.,* 10:193–205.
7. McKenzie, G. M., and Szerb, J. C. (1968): The effect of dihydroxyphenylalanine pheniprazine and D-amphetamine on the *in vivo* release of dopamine from the caudate nucleus. *J. Pharmacol. Exp. Ther.,* 162:302–308.
8. Besson, M. J., Cheramy, A., Feltz, P., and Glowinski, J. (1971b); Dopamine: Spontaneous and drug induced release from the caudate nucleus in the cat. *Brain Res.,* 32:407–424.
9. Von Voigtlander, P. F., and Moore, K. E. (1973): Involvement of nigrostriatal neurons in the *in vivo* release of dopamine by amphetamine, amantadine and tyramine. *J. Pharmacol. Exp. Ther.,* 184:542–552.
10. Philippu, A., Glowinski, J., and Besson, M. J. (1974): *In vivo* release of newly synthesized catecholamines from the hypothalamus by amphetamine. *Arch. Pharmacol.,* 282:1–8.
11. Ungerstedt, U. (1971): Postsynaptic supersensitivity after 6-hydroxydopamine induced degeneration of the nigro-striatal dopamine system. *Acta Physiol. Scand.* (Suppl.) 367: 69–93.
12. Fuxe, K., Hökfelt, T., and Ungerstedt, U. (1970): Morphological and functional aspects of central monoamine neurons. *Int. Rev. Neurobiol.,* 13:93–126.
13. Anden, N. E. (1972): Dopamine turnover in the corpus striatum and the limbic system after treatment with neuroleptic and anti-acetylcholine drugs. *J. Pharm. Pharmacol.,* 24:905–906.
14. Lloyd, K. G., Stadler, H., and Bartholini, G. (1973): Dopamine and acetylcholine neurons in

striatal and limbic structures: Effect of neuroleptic drugs. In: *Frontiers in Catecholamine Research,* edited by E. Usdin and S. Snyder, pp. 777–779. Pergamon, London.

15. Besson, M. J., Cheramy, A., and Glowinski, J. (1971): Effects of some psychotropic drugs on dopamine synthesis in the rat striatum. *J. Pharmacol. Exp. Ther.,* 177:196–205.

16. Nybäck, H., and Sedvall, G. (1969): Regional accumulation of catecholamines formed from tyrosine-^{14}C in rat brain: Effect of chlorpromazine. *Eur. J. Pharmacol.,* 5:245–252.

17. Cheramy, A., Besson, M. J., and Glowinski, J. (1970): Increased release of dopamine from striatal dopaminergic terminals in the rat after treatment with a neuroleptic: Thioproperazine. *Eur. J. Pharmacol.,* 10:206–214.

18. Kehr, W., Carlsson, A., and Lindqvist, M. (1975): Biochemical aspects of dopamine agonists. In: *Advances in Neurology,* edited by B. Calne, T. N. Chase, and A. Barbeau, Vol. 9, pp. 185–195. Raven Press, New York.

19. Bunney, B. S., Walters, H. R., Roth, R. H., and Aghajanian, G. K. (1973): Dopaminergic neurons: Effect of antipsychotic drugs and amphetamine on single cell activity. *J. Pharmacol. Exp. Ther.,* 185:560–571.

20. Bunney, B. S., Aghajanian, G. K., and Roth, R. H. (1973): Comparison of effects of L-DOPA, amphetamine and apomorphine on firing rate of rat dopaminergic neurons. *Nature (New Biol.),* 245:123–125.

21. Farnebo, L. O., and Hamberger, B. (1971): Drug induced changes in the release of ^{3}H-monoamines from field-stimulated rat brain slices. *Acta Physiol. Scand. (Suppl.)* 371:35–44.

22. Besson, M. J., Cheramy, A., Gauchy, C., and Glowinski, J. (1973): In vivo continuous estimation of ^{3}H–DA synthesis and release in the cat caudate nucleus: Effects of a-Mpt and of transection of the nigro-neostriatal pathway. *Arch. Pharmacol,* 278:101–105.

23. Walters, J. R., Roth, R. H., and Aghajanian, G. K. (1973): Dopaminergic neurons: Similar biochemical and histochemical effect of gammahydroxybutyrate and acute lesions of the nigro-neostriatal pathway. *J. Pharmacol. Exp. Ther.,* 186:630–639.

24. Kehr, W., Carlsson, A., Lindqvist, M., Magnusson, T., and Atack, C. (1972): Evidence for a receptor mediated feedback control of striatal tyrosine hydroxylase activity. *J. Pharm. Pharmacol.,* 24:244–247.

25. Agid, Y., Javoy, F., and Glowinski, J. (1974): Chemical or electrolytic lesion of the substantia nigra: Early effects on neostriatal dopamine metabolism. *Brain Res.,* 74:41–49.

26. Christiansen, J., and Squires, R. F. (1974): Antagonistic effects of apomorphine and haloperidol on rat striatal synaptosomal tyrosine hydroxylase. *J. Pharm. Pharmacol.,* 26:367–369.

27. Aghajanian, G. K., and Bunney, B. S. (1974): Dopaminergic and non-dopaminergic neurons of the substantia nigra: Differential responses to putative transmitters. In: *Pharmacology and Biochemistry of the Nigro-striatal System. Dopaminergic and Non-dopaminergic Systems.* CINP Symposium, Paris.

28. Besson, M. J., Cheramy, A., Gauchy, C., and Glowinski, J. (1973) In vivo spontaneous and evoked release of newly synthesized dopamine in the cat caudate nucleus. In: *Advances in Neurology,* edited by F. H. McDowell and A. Barbeau, Vol. 5, pp. 69–79. Raven Press, New York.

29. Cheramy, A., Besson, M. J., Gauchy, C. Javoy, F., Agid, Y., Guyenet, P., and Glowinski, J. (1974): In vivo techniques for the analysis of biochemical effects of antipsychotic drugs. Edited G. Sedvall. In: *Antipsychotic Drugs, Pharmacodynamics and Pharmacokinetics,* International Symposium: Karolinska Institutet and Wenner Grenn Center, Suède. (in press).

30. Besson, M. J., Cheramy, A., Feltz, P., and Glowinski, J. (1969): Release of newly synthesized dopamine from dopamine-containing terminals in the striatum of the rat. *PNAS,* 62:741–748.

31. Javoy, F., Hamon, M., and Glowinski, J. (1970): Disposition of newly synthesized amines in cell bodies and terminals of central catecholaminergic neurons. I. Effect of amphetamine and thioproperazine on the metabolism of CA in the caudate nucleus, the substantia nigra and the ventro-medial nucleus of the hypothalamus. *Eur. J. Pharmacol.,* 10:178–188.

32. Kebabian, J. W., Petzold, G. L., and Greengard, P. (1972): Dopamine-sensitive adenylate cyclase in caudate nucleus of rat brain and its similarity to the "dopamine receptor." *RNAS,* 69: 2145–2149.

33. Kebabian, J. W., Clement Cormier, Y. C., Petzold, G. L., and Greengard, P. (1975): Chemistry of dopamine receptors. In: *Advances in Neurology,* edited by B. Calne, T. N. Chase, and A. Barbeau, Vol. 9, pp. 1–11. Raven Press, New York.

34. Iversen, L. L., Horn, A. S., and Miller, R. J. (1975): Action of dopaminergic agonists on cyclic

AMP production in rat brain homogenates. In: *Advances in Neurology,* edited B. Calne, T. N. Chase, and A. Barbeau, Vol. 9, pp. 197–212. Raven Press, New York.

35. Miller, R., and Hiley, R. (1975): Antimuscarinic actions of neuroleptic drugs. In; *Advances in Neurology,* edited B. Calne, T. N. Chase, and A. Barbeau, Vol. 9, pp. 141–154. Raven Press, New York.

36. Mishra, M. K., Garder, E. L., Katzman, R., and Makman, M. H. (1974): Enhancement of dopamine-stimulated adenylate cyclase activity in rat caudate after lesions in substantia nigra: Evidence for denervation supersensitivity. *PNAS,* 10:3883–3887.

37. Stadler, H., Lloyd, K. E., Gadea-Ciria, M., and Bartholini, G. (1973): Enhanced striatal ACh release by chlorpromazine and its reversal by apomorphine. *Brain Res.,* 55:476–480.

38. Guyenet, P., Agid, Y., Javoy, F., Beaujouan, J. C., Rosier, J., and Glowinski, J. (1975): Effects of dopaminergic receptor agonists and antagonists on the activity of the neostriatal cholinergic system. *Brain Res.,* 84:227–244.

39. Agid, Y., Guyenet, P., Glowinski, J., Beaujouan, J. C., and Javoy, F. (1975): Inhibitory influence of the nigrostriatal dopamine system on the striatal cholinergic neurons in the rat. *Brain Res.,* 86:408–482.

40. Scatton, B., Garret, C., Glowinski, J., and Julou, L. (1975): Effect of a long-acting injectable neuroleptic, the palmitic ester of pipotiazine, on dopamine metabolism in the rat neostriatum. In: *Pharmacology and Biochemistry of Nigro-striatal system. Dopaminergic and Non-dopaminergic Systems.* CINP Symposium, Paris.

41. Velley, L., Blanc, G., Tassin, J. P., Thierry, A. M., and Glowinski, J. (1975): Inhibition of striatal dopamine synthesis in rats injected chronically with neuroleptics in their early life. *Naunyn Schmiedebergs Arch. Pharmacol.,* 228:97–102.

42. York, D. H. (1967): The inhibitory action of dopamine on neurons of the caudate nucleus. *Brain Res.,* 5:263–266.

43. Thierry, A. M., Blanc, G. and Glowinski, J. (1971): Dopamine–norepinephrine: Another regulatory step of norepinephrine synthesis in central noradrenergic neurons. *Eur. J. Pharmacol.,* 14:303–307.

44. Thierry, A. M., Stinus, L., Blanc, G., and Glowinski, J. (1973): Some evidence for the existence of dopaminergic neurons in the rat cortex. *Brain Res.,* 50:230–234.

45. Thierry, A. M., Blanc, G., Sobel, A., Stinus, L., and Glowinski, J. (1973): Dopaminergic terminals in the rat cortex. *Science,* 182:495–501.

46. Tassin, J. P., Velley, L., Stinus, L., Blanc, G., Glowinski, J., and Thierry, A. M. (1975): Development of cortical and nigroneostriatal dopaminergic systems after destruction of central noradrenergic neurons in foetal or neonatal rats. *Brain Res.,* 83:93–106.

47. Tassin, J. P., Thierry, A. M., Blanc, G., and Glowinski, J. (1974): Evidence for a specific uptake of dopamine by dopaminergic terminals of the rat cerebral cortex. *Arch. Pharmacol.,* 282:239–244.

48. Berger, G., Tassin, J. P., Blanc, G., Moyne, M. A., and Thierry, A. M. (1974): Histochemical confirmation of dopaminergic innervation of the rat cerebral cortex after destruction of the noradrenergic ascending pathways. *Brain Res.,* 81:332–337.

49. Hökfelt, T., Fuxe, K., Johansson, O., and Ljungdahl, A. (1974): Pharmaco-histochemical evidence of the existence of dopamine nerve terminals in the limbic cortex. *Eur. J. Pharmacol.,* 25:108–112.

50. Browstein, M., Saavedra, J. P., and Palkovits, M. (1974): Norepinephrine and dopamine in the limbic system of the rat. *Brain Res.,* 79:431–437.

51. Lindvall, O., Björklund, A., More, Y., and Stenevi, U. (1974): Mesencephalic dopamine neurons projecting to neocortex. *Brain Res.,* 81:325–331.

52. Fuxe, K., Hökfelt, T., Johansson, O., Jonsson, G., Lidbrink, P., and Ljungdahl, A. (1974): The origin of the dopamine nerve terminals in limbic and frontal cortex. Evidence for mesocortico dopamine neurons. *Brain Res.,* 82:349–355.

53. Hungen, K. von and Roberts, S. (1973): Adenylate-cyclase receptors for adrenergic neurotransmitter in rat cerebral cortex. *Eur. J. Biochem.,* 36:391–401.

54. Agid, Y., Javoy, F., and Glowinski, J. (1973): Hyperactivity of the remaining dopaminergic neurons after partial destruction in the nigrostriatal dopaminergic system in the rat. *Nature,* 245:150–151.

55. Scatton, B., Thierry, A. M., Glowinski, J., and Julou, L. (1975): Effects of thioproperazine and

apomorphine on dopamine synthesis in the mesocortical dopaminergic systems. *Brain Res.,* 88:389–393.

56. Scatton, B., Glowinski, J., and Julou, L. (1975): Neuroleptics: Effects on dopamine synthesis in the nigro-neostriatal mesolimbic and mesocortical dopaminergic systems. In: *Antipsychotic Drugs, Pharmacodynamics and Pharmacokinetics,* edited by G. Sedvall. International Symposium, Karolinska Institutet and Wenner Grenn Center.

57. Thierry, A. M., Hirsch, J., Tassin, J. P., Blanc, G., and Glowinski, J. (1974): Presence of dopaminergic terminals and absence of dopaminergic cell bodies in the cerebral cortex of the cat. *Brain Res.,* 79:77–88.

Biology of the Major Psychoses, edited by D. X. Freedman, Res. Publ. Assoc. Res. Nerv. Ment. Dis., Vol. 54. Raven Press, New York 1975

Psychotropic Drugs and Dopamine Uptake Inhibition

Angelos E. Halaris and Daniel X. Freedman

Department of Psychiatry, University of Chicago, Chicago, Illinois 60637

For more than a decade a growing body of evidence has linked brain amines to both affective disorders and schizophrenia. The majority of studies and hypotheses about affective disorders have emphasized the role of norepinephrine and serotonin. Dopamine, on the other hand, has been linked primarily to schizophrenia. The association of brain dopamine with schizophrenia has been deduced mainly from the clinical efficacy of neuroleptics and from animal data indicating that neuroleptics block the dopamine receptor. Amphetamine, related initially to hypotheses of depression, has received recent attention because of links (e.g., stereotypy in animals and paranoid behavior in man) which are attributed to a dopamine agonist action of the drug owing to release and inhibition of reuptake of dopamine.

Reuptake blockade of norepinephrine (and to a lesser extent of serotonin) and a consequent shift in amine metabolites have been key for inferring the therapeutic mode of action of antidepressants and, by extension, the underlying pathophysiology of affective disorders. Thus, a recent series of investigations in man have been aimed at ascertaining a preexisting deficit in norepinephrine and serotonin in the brain of depressed patients largely inferred from measures of metabolites. The possibility that dopamine may play some role in depression has not, however, been as systematically pursued as has the study of norepinephrine; further, the role of dopamine in the mode of action of antidepressants has received little attention.

We recently reported (1) that a number of antidepressants currently in clinical use affect the uptake of dopamine into rat brain synaptosomal suspensions. We now call attention to evidence that, in fact, blockade of dopamine uptake is produced by a series of structurally unrelated compounds that in man act as antidepressants, neuroleptics, or stimulants. The ultimate and as yet unresolved question is: Does this uptake inhibition play any differentiating role in either the mechanism of action or the therapeutic and side effects of these compounds?

RESULTS

Using nuclei-free homogenates from rat whole brain, we tested a number of psychotropic drugs to ascertain their ability to inhibit the uptake of tritiated dopamine. Representatives from the group of antidepressants, neuroleptics, and stimulants were included in the study. We used the method of Snyder and Coyle (2) with minor modifications. Data expressing the variation of uptake of tritiated dopamine with increasing substrate concentrations, when graphed, revealed the existence of two consecutive saturable systems. The substrate concentration used in the present experiments was chosen to fall within the range of the high-affinity uptake system.

Data expressed as the inhibitory concentration that produced 50% inhibition of uptake (IC_{50}) are summarized in Table 1. Uptake inhibition is a common property of all drugs tested. The stimulants by far exceed in potency both the antidepressants and the neuroleptics. On the whole, neuroleptics are somewhat more potent than antidepressants in inhibiting the uptake of dopamine; nevertheless, neuroleptics and antidepressants show overlap.

We have recently begun regional studies of these drugs. Effects of chlorimipramine, chlorpromazine, and pimozide on dopamine uptake in nuclei-free homogenates from rat cortex, striatum, hypothalamus, and midbrain were investigated following kinetic analysis of the uptake systems in these regions. Preliminary data indicate that chlorimipramine is more potent in hypothalamus and midbrain (IC_{50} 1 to 3 μM). Chlorpromazine is also more potent in the hypothalamus (IC_{50} 0.1 μM). Both drugs have a weaker action in cortical and striatal synaptosomal preparations (IC_{50} 7 to 9 μM). Pimozide, the most potent inhibitor of dopamine uptake among the compounds tested, also shows high potency in striatum and cortex (IC_{50} 0.3 to 0.9 μM) but is somewhat weaker in hypothalamus and midbrain (IC_{50} 1 to 3 μM).

TABLE 1. Effect of psychotropic compounds on ^{3}H-dopamine uptake[a]

Drug	IC_{50} (μM)	Drug	IC_{50}(μM)
Antidepressants		Neuroleptics	
Nortriptyline	8.1	Pimozide	1.1
Protriptyline	8.3	Haloperidol	4.4
Chlorimipramine	8.5	Perphenazine	4.8
Amitriptiline	9.7	Thioridazine	5.8
Maprotiline	14.9	Trifluoperazine	10.4
Iprindole	25.2	Chlorpromazine	10.6
Desipramine	25.4	Fluphenazine	11.4
Imipramine	27.0	Other drugs	
Doxepin	35.5	Fenfluramine	39.5
Stimulants		Apomorphine	44.2
d-Amphetamine	0.4	Amantadine	292.0
Methylphenidate	0.5		
Cocaine	1.6		
l-Amphetamine	2.2		

[a] These results were obtained using nuclei-free homogenates from rat whole brain; regional data are mentioned in the text.

In another series of experiments, animals pretreated with chlorimipramine or chlorpromazine were sacrificed at various time intervals following injections of the drug. Nuclei-free homogenates from the brains of these animals showed inhibition of uptake comparable to the effects observed following *in vitro* testing of the investigative compound. Thus there may be physiologic relevance to the observations of dopamine uptake blockade reported here.

DISCUSSION

The striking feature of the present data is that a number of structurally unrelated compounds produce *in vitro* inhibition of dopamine uptake. Table 1 shows, to our knowledge, the most extensive list of antidepressants and neuroleptics reported, and these findings are in accord with scattered data in the literature indicating that representatives of these compound classes affect the uptake of dopamine (3–7).

Inhibition of dopamine uptake is a common property shared by antidepressants, neuroleptics, and stimulants, and there are differences in potency among drugs and drug classes. These differences in potency within or between classes of drugs cannot yet be systematically explained on the basis of molecular structure or side-chain substituents or even pharmacologic class; there are exceptions and overlaps.

Thus in the group of antidepressants it is not possible to detect differences in potency between secondary and tertiary amines. Among the antidepressants tested, the secondary (nortriptyline and protriptyline) and the tertiary (chlorimipramine and amitriptyline) amines are the most potent in inhibiting dopamine uptake; the tetracyclic maprotiline follows in the rank order; iprindole, the secondary desipramine, and the tertiary imipramine are equipotent but weaker, and the tertiary amine doxepin is the weakest of all. The absence of a methyl group at the side chain of the secondary amines does not appear to be a crucial factor. The fact that maprotiline, a tetracyclic compound, also inhibits uptake suggests that the three-ring structure may not be the essential prerequisite.

Amphetamine and amphetamine analogues are among the most potent inhibitors of dopamine uptake; therefore, we would have thought that high potency in dopamine-uptake blockade might classify a drug as a stimulant. Further, for the major depressive disorders, stimulants have not been found to be of therapeutic utility (8); perhaps potency in inhibition of dopamine uptake would be a disadvantage. When compared to the stimulants, antidepressants as a group are indeed weaker in inhibiting dopamine uptake. For example, chlorimipramine is 20 and 5 times weaker than *d*-amphetamine and cocaine, respectively. However, a recent report (6) states that a new antidepressant, nomifensine, is a more potent blocker of dopamine uptake in striatal synaptosomes than is amphetamine. Nomifensine is not classified as a stimulant and, if sustained, the data would at the least cast some doubt on the view of a unique property of stimulants. Indeed, our own data show that pimozide which is not a stimulant but is a specific dopamine-receptor blocker (9) is as potent as amphetamine in inhibiting dopamine uptake.

Among the neuroleptics tested, we find no clear basis to account for differences in potency. Regional data may be important since similar concentrations of both chlorpromazine and haloperidol were shown to inhibit dopamine uptake in striatal synaptosomes of the rat (7), although we find haloperidol more potent in whole brain.

When neuroleptics are compared to antidepressants, haloperidol, one of the most potent dopamine-uptake blockers of the neuroleptics on our list, is only twice as potent as the most potent of the antidepressants tested; chlorpromazine is as potent as amitriptyline. Similar results were reported by Ahtee et al. (10) who tested the effect of a number of phenothiazines and tricyclic antidepressants on dopamine uptake by rabbit platelets. In that system, thioridazine and chlorimipramine were the most potent compounds, followed by amitriptyline and chlorpromazine which were equipotent. Imipramine was the weakest of the tricyclic antidepressants. Interestingly, cocaine was 100 times weaker than thioridazine. These authors concluded that neither the ring structure nor the side-chain substituents seemed to influence the ability of these drugs to inhibit dopamine uptake by platelets.

These results and our own data are in accord with those reported by Horn et al. (3) who could not find any major difference in potency between chlorpromazine and amitriptyline as inhibitors of dopamine uptake by striatal synaptosomes in the rat. Thus potency in dopamine-uptake inhibition is not particularly useful in differentiating the two main groups of therapeutic agents used in the major mental illnesses; nor does this property correlate with any of the known subgroups of these drug classes.

Since structurally unrelated neuroleptics can produce both dopamine-receptor blockade and dopamine-uptake inhibition, we did look at the possibility that *specificity* in receptor blockade might account for the rank order in potency of uptake inhibition within the group of neuroleptics. We therefore tested pimozide, a neuroleptic (toxic in man) which is not a tricyclic and yet is considered to be the most potent and specific dopamine-receptor blocker, as assessed in functional tests (9). Surprisingly, pimozide is the most potent dopamine-uptake inhibitor of the neuroleptics, whether nerve endings from whole brain or from brain regions such as cortex, striatum, hypothalamus, or midbrain are used. It inhibits uptake at concentrations as low as 10^{-7} M, and the IC_{50} values are comparable to those obtained for the stimulants. Other specific dopamine receptor antagonists (e.g., butaclamol, clozapine) should be tested. Specificity in dopamine-receptor blockade, however, does not appear to correlate strictly with potency in dopamine-uptake inhibition; for example, thioridazine in the functional tests was rated equally effective on norepinephrine and dopamine receptors (9), but in our system is about as effective as the fairly specific dopamine receptor antagonist haloperidol.

In searching for any other relevant variable with which dopamine uptake inhibition would correlate, we thought it of interest to examine where pimozide ranks in its ability to inhibit the dopamine-stimulated adenylate cyclase, an enzyme which is closely associated with the dopamine receptor (11). However, pimozide and the butyrophenones are less potent than the phenothiazines in this system (12,13). Pimozide is only about 2.5 times more potent than the tricyclic antidepressants (12,13) which have also been shown to be effective in inhibiting the adenylate cyclase (14), but haloperidol—less potent than pimozide in our system—is approximately 14 times more potent than the antidepressants on the adenylate cyclase (12,13). Thus there is no systematic correlation of uptake inhibition with either receptor-blockade specificity or adenylate cyclase activity.

In the search for a common accountable factor for the effect of structurally unrelated compounds of dopamine uptake, anticholinergic action might be considered. Several investigators have shown that neuroleptics exhibit a wide range of antimuscarinic properties (15–19). Although this property may make important contributions to the pharmacologic profile of these drugs (in particular with regard to the appearance of parkinson-like side effects), it shows no correlation with the rank order of potency in inhibiting dopamine uptake. Whereas thioridazine and clozapine are the most potent anticholinergic compounds, pimozide, chlorpromazine, trifluoperazine, haloperidol, and fluphenazine are weak anticholinergics although they are potent antidopaminergic agents (20). Similarly, in the group of antidepressants, the anticholinergic potency is quite variable and the new antidepressant nomifensine has been reported (6) to possess minimal anticholinergic activity. This drug is of further interest because it is reportedly more active than either amphetamine or benztropine as a dopamine-uptake blocker (6). Finally, these effects are in accord with the work of Horn et al. (3) who concluded that several centrally active anticholinergic agents (e.g., atropine and scopolamine) have a relatively weak action on striatal dopamine uptake. The ability of a number of compounds which are apparently structurally unrelated to produce a similar pharmacologic effect may have to be understood on a submolecular level in relation to the steric configuration, as described by Maxwell et al. (21,22) and Horn et al. (3).

The question arises as to whether or not this difficulty in correlating potency of uptake blockade in the case of dopamine does, in fact, characterize the situation with norepinephrine and serotonin. In reviewing the literature, it is clear not only that different methods for assessing amine-uptake blockade have been used but also that even with the same method the neuroleptics and antidepressants show variable potencies (23–27). The comparison of potency has not yet been systematically reviewed.

Tables 2 and 3 were prepared in an initial attempt to compare potency based on IC_{50} values. The few studies in which potency is expressed differently (e.g., K_i values) have not been tabulated. It is perfectly clear in these tables that one can find neuroleptics and antidepressants that affect the uptake of all three aminergic systems but, for a given drug with high potency, a single amine stands out, e.g., chlorimipramine and serotonin or desipramine and norepinephrine.

TABLE 2. *Inhibition of norepinephrine uptake by psychotropic drugs in brain tissue*

Drug	IC_{50} (μM)	Substrate concentration (μM)	Tissue preparation	Reference
Desipramine	0.05	0.1	hypothalamic	Horn et al.
Amitriptyline	0.05	0.1	synaptosomes,	(3)[a]
Chlorpromazine	0.5	0.1	rat	
Doxepin	0.65	0.1		
Imipramine	1.0	0.1		
Nortriptyline	1.3	0.1		
Trifluoperazine	9.0	0.1		
Protriptyline	10.0	0.1		
Imipramine	0.08	0.1	midbrain slices,	Ross et al.
Iprindole	9.0	0.1	mouse	(23)
Chlorimipramine	0.8	0.1	midbrain slices, mouse	Ross et al. (24)
Nortriptyline	0.027	0.02	cortical slices,	Hamberger and
Chlorimipramine	0.16	0.02	rat	Tuck (25)

[a] Data expressed as "relative potency" were converted into IC_{50} values as described by the authors.

TABLE 3. *Inhibition of serotonin uptake by psychotropic drugs in brain tissue*

Drug	IC_{50} (μM)	Substrate concentration (μM)	Tissue preparation	Reference
Imipramine	0.6	0.1	midbrain slices,	Ross and
Amitriptyline	2.0	0.1	mouse	Renyi (26)
Cocaine	3.0	0.1		
Desipramine	4.0	0.1		
Nortriptyline	5.0	0.1		
Amphetamine	>5.0	0.1		
Imipramine	0.2	0.1	midbrain slices,	Ross et al.
Iprindole	50.0	0.1	mouse	(23)
Chlorimipramine	0.07	0.1	midbrain slices, mouse	Ross et al. (24)
Chlorimipramine	0.013	0.002	cortical slices,	Hamberger and
Chlorimipramine	0.03	0.02	rat	Tuck (25)
Amitriptyline	0.38	0.002		
Imipramine	0.58	0.002		
Imipramine	0.69	0.02		
Nortriptyline	1.9	0.002		
Chlorpromazine	3.8	0.002		

The most interesting findings are with respect to the secondary tricyclics which have generally been considered the most potent compounds in inhibiting the uptake of norepinephrine (see Table 2). However, there is clear overlap with tertiary amines, as in the case of imipramine. This drug is only 2.5 times less potent than desipramine in an *in vitro* system (23). Differences of this order of magnitude in uptake blockade potency are not too impressive in differentiating drugs. Further, Horn et al. (3) reported that in the hypothalamus the secondary amine nortriptyline is 24 times less potent than the tertiary parent amine amitriptyline. Clearly, it should not be generally accepted that demethylation of the tertiary amine results in high potency in inhibition of norepinephrine uptake. In the same report (3), the secondary amine protriptyline was the weakest of the tricyclics in clinical use in inhibiting hypothalamic uptake of norepinephrine. If the *in vitro* effects reported by these investigators correlate with physiologic activity, then we agree with their comment that "the greater antidepressant efficacy in animal tests of nortriptyline as compared to amitriptyline is unrelated to more potent inhibition of norepinephrine uptake." In further support of the questionable absolute correlation between antidepressant activity and high potency in norepinephrine uptake inhibition are data on iprindole, an active tricyclic antidepressant with only weak inhibitory action on uptake of both norepinephrine and serotonin (23). However, this compound significantly potentiated the awakening effect of L-DOPA in reserpinized mice, as did chlorimipramine (23), a tertiary amine generally associated with high potency on serotonergic neurons.

In the case of serotonin-uptake blockade, the data to date are perhaps the strongest in this particular comparison and show somewhat more consistency in that high potency is linked to tertiary amines. Thus chlorimipramine is the most potent serotonin-uptake inhibitor, although it is not specific to this transmitter (the drug is also effective in inhibiting norepinephrine uptake). Imipramine and amitriptyline follow in the rank order of potency and are equipotent, but they also lack selectivity. Regional analyses, however, as initially undertaken by Horn et al. (3), have not been reported with the tertiary amines; it is conceivable that exceptions—such as the case of nortriptyline mentioned above—may occur.

The effects on dopamine uptake of both neuroleptics and antidepressants warrant further investigation. A systematic regional analysis of the same drug and all major amines is required. This is exemplified by the case of nortriptyline, the effects of which may vary significantly depending on the brain region under investigation (see Table 2). Our own unpublished data indicate that, although chlorimipramine and chlorpromazine are almost equipotent in inhibiting dopamine uptake in striatal and cortical synaptosomes, chlorpromazine is 10 times more potent than chlorimipramine in hypothalamic synaptosomes. Similar experimental conditions, especially of the substrate concentration, are also required. Variation in concentration may cause apparent differences in potency and thus render inaccurate comparative assessments from different laboratories (see Table 3).

We repeated the *in vitro* studies using synaptosomes from animals pretreated with chlorimipramine or chlorpromazine and found that drugs reached active sites and that amine uptake was blocked. Since we had previously correlated reuptake blockade of serotonin by chlorimipramine with increases in serotonin and decreases in 5-hydroxyindoleacetic acid (28), we measured brain dopamine 30 to 60 min following chlorimipramine. A 30% increase of dopamine observed in whole brain was further localized primarily to the diencephalon. Interestingly, the drug's potency in uptake blockade was also greater in the hypothalamus than in other regions.

CONCLUSIONS

Thus a number of antidepressant and neuroleptic drugs can inhibit dopamine uptake and some are moderately potent. Neuroleptics appear to be slightly more potent than antidepressants but the two drug classes show overlap and both are weaker than stimulants. Potency differences are therefore not useful in differentiating the two major drug classes and there may be nonstimulant drugs that are as potent as stimulants. In the search for a common accountable factor for potency differences we found no systematic correlation with properties such as inhibition of the dopamine-sensitive adenylate cyclase or anticholinergic activity. High specificity in dopamine-receptor blockade might correlate with potency in dopamine uptake inhibition in the case of neuroleptics. Regional analysis is clearly critical for a more precise characterization of the uptake inhibition property of drugs since chlorpromazine was 10 times more active than chlorimipramine in inhibiting hypothalamic uptake of dopamine, although both drugs were equipotent in whole brain preparations.

The *in vivo* relevance of these findings is indicated by increased levels of dopamine after parenteral chlorimipramine; this was greatest in the hypothalamus where chlorimipramine-induced inhibition was highest after both *in vivo* administration and *in vitro* addition. A similar parallelism of *in vitro* and *in vivo* results was obtained in whole brain after parenteral chlorpromazine.

In reviewing the drug-induced uptake inhibition of norepinephrine and serotonin, as determined *in vitro* in synaptosomal preparations, we find—perhaps surprisingly—a similar pattern as with dopamine. Drugs of a particular class show no uniformity in affecting a particular amine; there are wide differences in potencies, and systematic regional analyses—where interesting differences do appear —as well as studies of species other than rodents are generally lacking. Without systematic studies of several representatives of each drug class, generalizations about the role of a particular amine for a particular drug class or disease are indeed hazardous.

To relate uptake blockade to mode of drug action requires a number of measures that can serve, in effect, as indices of relevance. Thus with an excess of amine, such as dopamine, at a receptor there should be changes in the pattern of metabolites, in storage and release, perhaps in synthesis either mediated directly or by feedback, as well as effects on neuronal firing, on other aminergic systems, and on specific behaviors of animal or man. The latter approach is perhaps best illustrated by Snyder's attempt to relate the effects of amphetamine on uptake blockade to dopamine-mediated stereotypy and norepinephrine-mediated locomotor activity.

In attempts to infer the significance of uptake blockade by comparing drug potencies, we are cautioned by the obvious fact that usually we have to cite naked numbers! Meaningful differences in potency could be easily over- or under-estimated without empirical tests of the specific consequences of uptake blockade. Thus the "tolerance" in the nigroneostriatal system after chronic neuroleptic dosage poses an experiment with respect to uptake blockade; if blockade persisted, then the expected effect of reduced synthesis and firing would become dominant and a physiologic role for the blockade mechanism would be identified. Indeed, theoretically, were the neuroleptics not receptor blockers, they, as dopamine agonists, might enhance schizophrenic symptomatology *(vide infra)* and be potent antidepressants! The challenge, in any event, is to ultimately understand mode of drug action and criteria determining antidepressant or neuroleptic effect or effects common to the two drug classes.

While such future research is of fundamental importance, there may be some practical value in utilizing uptake blockade as a tool to determine whether an antidepressant, for example, has a selective advantage for the treatment of sub-classes of affective disorders. If the prior state of a depressed subgroup was characterized by low MHPG levels, one might predict that the potency of imipra-mine in norepinephrine blockade would be selectively advantageous as compared with the secondary amine nortriptyline. And, indeed, this has been suggested by clinical data. If low levels of 5-HIAA preexisted, it is possible that chlorimipra-mine might have selective advantage. The point is that, while there is wide variability among the antidepressants, one drug may be found with special high potency for one or another amine.

Thus there may be depressive disorders "requiring" more dopamine at certain (unknown) receptors. Whether this "need" might be reflected in lower HVA is discussed by Goodwin and Post in *this volume.* If chlorimipramine is a model, we could anticipate that regional potencies of other antidepressants can be in a range that warrants serious discussion of the role of dopamine in depression, just as the early studies of drugs such as desipramine enhanced interest in the role of norepinephrine.

Accordingly, antidepressants can potentiate excitation induced by L-DOPA and dopamine receptor agonists (29–32). It is possible that catalepsy produced by neuroleptics is mediated by dopamine. It can, in any event, be antagonized by antidepressants (33), as can the narcoleptic cataplexy (34). The precise role of the mediating amines in the above test systems should be experimentally stipulated. While the success of L-DOPA in parkinsonism is more impressive than reports of L-DOPA therapy in depression, it is apparently variable in both disorders, in part dependent on heterogeneity of patient populations. It is interesting that antidepressants have been used with success in parkinsonism (35–41) and the question now is if this is related to the effect on dopamine uptake blockade. The parkinsonian symptoms of psychomotor retardation and inertia had earlier been linked by Mettler and Crandell (42) to striatal lesions. It is these symptoms that Mandell et al. (39) noted were the first to improve during treatment of parkinsonians with tricyclics. There is recent evidence linking dopamine deficiency to psychomotor retardation (43,44). The effect of tricyclics on these behavioral dimensions in depression merits further study, even though analysis of psychiatric illness does not yield as readily as neurologic disease to the identification of component responses that are amine-contingent.

Whatever the role of dopamine in disease, the antidepressant and dopamine agonists can overcome neuroleptic receptor blockade in animals and in schizophrenic man where symptomatology is enhanced. This observation not only implicates an action of antidepressants on dopamine but speaks for the state-dependence of drug action and the importance of prior state. For example, schizophrenic symptomatology is not readily induced in recovered schizophrenics by dopamine agonists and in normals antidepressants tend to produce a sedative effect. In essence, this means that we intervene with drugs to establish—or permit the organism to establish—a new equilibrium that can be viewed as either a correction or a compensation for the maladaptive dysfunction (presumably of amine mechanisms) during a psychotic state. What genetic, biological, or experiential factors may predispose or trigger the altered amine status in psychosis are still unknown. Over a decade ago (45,46) it was clear that the amines may normally have a "buffer" function, modulating stimuli that induce an intense central activation. Further, manipulations that alter normal regulatory mechanisms governing metabolism, binding, and release could inhibit or enhance the effects of stress or chemicals (e.g., methionine and MAO inhibition, or reserpine and LSD).

The lack of modulated, flexible behavior that characterizes psychosis and the ungoverned intensity of thoughts and activity (changes in their rates—rapid or retarded—and their organization control) are common to being psychotic. The amines are strikingly implicated in both major mental illnesses—perhaps commonly related to the intensity of being psychotic—but exactly how they are differentially related to being schizophrenically or depressively psychotic still eludes us.

ACKNOWLEDGMENT

This research was supported by U.S. Public Health Service research grants MH-13,186 and DA-00250 and research grant 506–03 from the Illinois Department of Mental Health.

REFERENCES

1. Halaris, A. E., Belendiuk, K. T., and Freedman, D. X. (1975): Antidepressant drugs affect dopamine uptake. *Biochem. Pharmacol. (in press).*

2. Snyder, S. H., and Coyle, J. T. (1969): Regional differences in H³-norepinephrine and H³-dopamine uptake into rat brain homogenates. *J. Pharmacol. Exp. Ther.,* 165:78–86.
3. Horn, A. S., Coyle, J. T., and Snyder, S. H. (1971): Catecholamine uptake by synaptosomes from rat brain. Structure-activity relationships of drugs with differential effects on dopamine and norepinephrine neurons. *Mol. Pharmacol.,* 7:66–80.
4. Kafoe, W. F., and Leonard, B. E. (1973): The effect of a new tetracyclic antidepressant compound, Org GB 94, on the turnover of dopamine, noradrenaline and serotonin in the brain. *Arch. Int. Pharmacodyn.,* 206:389–391.
5. Leonard, B. E. (1974): Some effects of a new tetracyclic antidepressant compound, Org GB 94, on the metabolism of monoamines in the rat brain. *Psychopharmacologia,* 36:221–236.
6. Hunt, P., Kannengiesser, M.-H., and Raynaud, J.-P. (1974): Nomifensine: A new potent inhibitor of dopamine uptake into synaptosomes from rat brain corpus striatum. *J. Pharm. Pharmacol.,* 26:370–371.
7. Seeman, P., and Lee, T. (1974): The dopamine-releasing actions of neuroleptics and ethanol. *J. Pharmacol. Exp. Ther.,* 190:131–140.
8. Fawcett, J., Maas, J. W., and Dekirmenjian, H. (1972): Depression and MHPG excretion. Response to dextroamphetamine and tricyclic antidepressants. *Arch. Gen. Psychiatry,* 26:246–251.
9. Andén, N.-E., Butcher, S. G., Corrodi, H., Fuxe, K., and Ungerstedt, U. (1970): Receptor activity and turnover of dopamine and noradrenaline after neuroleptics. *Eur. J. Pharmacol.,* 11:303–314.
10. Ahtee, L., Boullin, D. J., Saarnivaara, L., and Paasonen, M. K. (1974): The inhibition of the uptake of monoamines by blood platelets by phenothiazines and other drugs. In: *The Phenothiazines and Structurally Related Drugs,* edited by I. S. Forrest, C. J. Carr, and E. Usdin, pp. 379–388. Raven Press, New York.
11. Kebabian, J. W., Petzold, G. L., and Greengard, P. (1972): Dopamine-sensitive adenylate cyclase in caudate nucleus of rat brain and its similarity to the 'dopamine receptor.' *Proc. Natl. Acad. Sci. USA,* 69:2145–2149.
12. Clement-Cormier, Y. C., Kebabian, J. W., Petzold, G. L., and Greengard, P. (1974): Dopamine-sensitive adenylate cyclase in mammalian brain: A possible site of action of antipsychotic drugs. *Proc. Natl. Acad. Sci. USA,* 71:1113–1117.
13. Krueger, B. K., Forn, J., and Greengard, P. (1975): Dopamine-sensitive adenylate cyclase and protein phosphorylation in the rat caudate nucleus. In: *Pre- and Postsynaptic Receptors,* edited by E. Usdin and W. E. Bunney, pp. 123–147. Dekker, New York.
14. Karobath, M. E. (1975): Tricyclic antidepressive drugs and dopamine-sensitive adenylate cyclase from rat brain striatum. *Eur. J. Pharmacol.,* 30:159–163.
15. Andén, N.-E., and Bedard, P. (1971): Influences of cholinergic mechanisms on the function and turnover of brain dopamine. *J. Pharm. Pharmacol.,* 23:460–462.
16. Andén, N.-E. (1972): Dopamine turnover in the corpus striatum and the limbic system after treatment with neuroleptic and anti-acetylcholine drugs. *J. Pharm. Pharmacol.,* 24:905–906.
17. Andén, N.-E. (1973): Effect of clozapine on the turnover of dopamine in the corpus striatum and in the limbic system. *J. Pharm. Pharmacol.,* 25:346–348.
18. Miller, R. J., and Hiley, C. R. (1974): Anti-muscarinic properties of neuroleptics and drug-induced Parkinsonism. *Nature,* 248:596–597.
19. Snyder, S. H., Greenberg, D., and Yamamura, H. (1974): Antischizophrenic drugs and brain cholinergic receptors. *Arch. Gen. Psychiatry,* 31:58–61.
20. Iversen, L. L., Horn, A. S., and Miller, R. J. (1975): Structure-activity relationships for agonist and antagonist drugs at pre- and postsynaptic dopamine receptor sites in rat brain. In: *Pre-and Postsynaptic Receptors,* edited by E. Usdin and W. E. Bunney, pp. 207–243. Dekker, New York.
21. Maxwell, R. A., Kennan, P. D., Chaplin, E., Roth, B., and Eckhardt, S. B. (1969): Molecular features affecting the potency of tricyclic antidepressants and structurally related compounds as inhibititors of the uptake of tritiated norepinephrine by rabbit aortic strips. *J. Pharmacol. Exp. Ther.,* 166:320–329.
22. Maxwell, R. A., Ferris, R. M., Burcsu, J., Woodward, E. C., Tang, D., and Williard, K. (1974): The phenyl rings of tricyclic antidepressants and related compounds as determinants of the potency of inhibition of the amine pumps in adrenergic neurons of the rabbit aorta and in rat cortical synaptosomes. *J. Pharmacol. Exp. Ther.,* 191:418–430.
23. Ross, S. B., Renyi, A. L., and Ögren, S.-O. (1971): A comparison of the inhibitory activities of

iprindole and imipramine on the uptake of 5-hydroxytryptamine and noradrenaline in brain slices. *Life Sci.,* 10:1267–1277.

24. Ross, S. B., Renyi, A. L., and Ögren, S.-O. (1972): Inhibition of the uptake of noradrenaline and 5-hydroxytryptamine by chlorphentermine and chlorimipramine. *Eur. J. Pharmacol.,* 17:107–112.

25. Hamberger, B., and Tuck, J. R. (1973): Effect of tricyclic antidepressants on the uptake of noradrenaline and 5-hydroxytryptamine by rat brain slices incubated in buffer or human plasma. *Eur. J. Clin. Pharmacol.,* 5:1–7.

26. Ross, S. B., and Renyi, A. L. (1969): Inhibition of the uptake of tritiated 5-hydroxytryptamine in brain tissue. *Eur. J. Pharmacol.,* 7:270–277.

27. Alpers, H. S., and Himwich, H. E. (1969): An *in vitro* study of the effects of tricyclic antidepressant drugs on the accumulation of C^{14}-serotonin by rabbit brain. *Biol. Psychiatry,* 1:81–85.

28. Halaris, A. E., Lovell, R. A., and Freedman, D. X. (1973): Effect of chlorimipramine on the metabolism of 5-hydroxytryptamine in the rat brain. *Biochem. Pharmacol.,* 22:2200–2202.

29. McGrath, W., and Ketteler, H. (1963): Potentiation of the anti-reserpine effects of dihydroxyphenylalanine by antidepressants and stimulants. *Nature,* 199:917–918.

30. Everett, G. (1967): The dopa response potentiation test and its use in screening for antidepressant drugs. In: *Antidepressant Drugs,* edited by S. Garattini and M. Dukes, pp. 164–167. Excerpta Medica, International Congress Series No. 122, Amsterdam.

31. Friedman, E., and Gershon, S. (1972): L-DOPA and imipramine: Biochemical and behavioral interaction. *Eur. J. Pharmacol.,* 18:183–188.

32. Pedersen, V. (1967): Potentiation of apomorphine effect (compulsive gnawing behavior) in mice. *Acta Pharmacol. Toxicol. (Suppl. 4),* 25:63.

33. Morselli, P., Rizzo, M., Zaccala, M., and Garattini, S. (1970): Haloperidol-desipramine interaction in mice, rats and man. *Chem. Biol. Interact.,* 2:160–164.

34. Guilleminault, C., Wilson, R. A., and Dement, W. C. (1974): A study on cataplexy. *Arch. Neurol.,* 31:255–261.

35. Sigwald, J., Bouttier, D., Raymondeaud, O., Marquez, M., and Gal, J.-C. (1959): Etude de l'action sur l'akinesie parkinsonienne de deux derivés de l'iminodibenzyle. *La Presse Med.,* 67:1697–1698.

36. Gal, J.-C. (1960): Etude de l'action de l'imipramine sur l'akinesie parkinsonienne. *Gaz. Med. Fr.,* 67:1821–1824.

37. Denmark, J. C., David, J. D., and McComb, S. G. (1961): Imipramine hydrochloride (Tofranil) in parkinsonism. *Br. J. Clin. Pract.,* 15:523–524.

38. Gillhespy, R. O., and Mustard, D. M. (1963): The evaluation of imipramine in the treatment of Parkinson's disease. *Br. J. Clin. Pract.,* 17:205–208.

39. Mandell, A. J., Markham, C., and Fowler, W. (1961): Parkinson's syndrome, depression and imipramine. *Calif. Med.,* 95:12–14.

40. Pohlmeier, H., and Matussek, N. (1965): Untersuchungen über den Einfluss von desmethyl-imipramin = Pertofran auf den Parkinsonismus beim Menschen. *Arch. Psychiatr. Nervenkr.,* 207:174–184.

41. Laitinen, L. (1969): Desipramine in treatment of Parkinson's disease. *Acta Neurol. Scand.,* 45:109–113.

42. Mettler, F. A., and Crandell, A. (1959): Relation between parkinsonism and psychiatric disorder. *J. Nerv. Ment. Dis.,* 129:551–563.

43. Papeschi, R., and McClure, D. J. (1971): Homovanillic and 5-hydroxyindoleacetic acid in cerebrospinal fluid of depressed patients. *Arch. Gen. Psychiatry,* 25:354–358.

44. McClure, D. J. (1973): The role of dopamine in depression. *Can. Psychiatr. Assoc. J.,* 18:309–312.

45. Freedman, D. X., and Giarman, N. J. (1963): Brain amines, electrical activity, and behavior. In: *EEG and Behavior,* edited by G. H. Glaser, pp. 198–243. Basic Books, New York.

46. Freedman, D. X. (1966): Aspects of the biochemical pharmacology of psychotropic drugs. In: *Psychiatric Drugs,* edited by Solomon, pp. 32–57. Grune & Stratton, New York.

Biology of the Major Psychoses, edited by D. X.
Freedman, Res. Publ. Assoc. Res. Nerv. Ment.
Dis., Vol. 54. Raven Press, New York   1975.

Amine Precursors in Neurologic Disorders and the Psychoses

Harold L. Klawans

Division of Neurology, Michael Reese Hospital and Medical Center, and Department of Medicine, University of Chicago, Pritzker School of Medicine, Chicago, Illinois 60616

Despite the fact that the precursor load strategy was first applied in the treatment of psychiatric disorders (1), the use of amine precursors in human disease states has been investigated most extensively in extrapyramidal movement disorders. Many of the observations that have resulted from these studies of the biochemistry and pharmacology of extrapyramidal disorders have direct implications for the biology of the major psychoses. The purpose of this chapter is to review the pharmacology of these neurologic disorders, emphasizing both the theoretical role that various neurotransmitters may play in each and the direct implications for the role of the same neurotransmitters in the functional psychoses.

THE PHARMACOLOGY OF PARKINSONISM

The use of L-DOPA in the treatment of parkinsonism is the precursor amine strategy that has been most thoroughly studied. Two basic premises underlie the presently accepted theory of the pharmacology of parkinsonism. (a) Acetylcholine and dopamine have antagonistic effects on the neurons of the striatum and that normal striatal function depends upon the balance between these two neurotransmitters. (b) A shift of this balance away from dopamine tends to produce the symptoms of parkinsonism. As numerous reviews of the evidence supporting these concepts have already appeared (2–5), these aspects are only briefly outlined here.

Belladonna alkaloids were used in the treatment of parkinsonism for almost 75 years before Feldberg (6) suggested that the usefulness of atropine in the treatment of parkinsonism was based upon the central anticholinergic effect of this drug. By 1962, it was generally accepted that virtually all the drugs useful in the long-term treatment of parkinsonism derived their therapeutic effect from central acetylcholine antagonism (7). This mechanism seemed to explain the antiparkinson activity of both the naturally occurring and synthetic alkaloids and the various antihistamines and phenothiazines used in the treatment of this syndrome. Any theory that proposes that antagonism of acetylcholine within the central nervous system (CNS) improves the signs and symptoms of parkinsonism must presuppose some altered or increased effect of acetylcholine in such patients.

At that time there was no reasonable explanation as to why the effect of acetylcholine was altered in these patients.

Research completed in the last 15 years may have supplied an answer to this question. It appears that the physiologically significant lesion in parkinsonism is destruction of the nigrostriatal dopaminergic neuronal system (2,3). Prior to the development of a histochemical fluorescent technique for the demonstration of serotonin and catecholamines within tissue slices, this pathway was not clearly established. The striatum is rich in dopamine, which is located within a dense meshwork of fine nerve terminals. The cell bodies of these axons are the neurons of the substantia nigra. Destruction of the substantia nigra results in loss of dopamine from the ipsilateral striatum. The nigrostriatal pathway has its cells of origin in the substantia nigra and its termination in the striatum. These neurons contain dopamine, which they apparently release upon the neurons of the striatum in order to influence the activity of these striatal neurons.

The nigrostriatal pathway is of great significance in the pathophysiology of parkinsonism, because the most conspicuous site of pathology in both idiopathic and postencephalitic parkinsonism is the substantia nigra (8,9). If these cells are affected, the dopamine content of the striatum should be decreased. Hornykiewicz (2) has clearly shown this to be true. The striatal neurons themselves are relatively preserved in parkinsonism, and the loss of dopamine is a reflection of the degeneration of the nigrostriatal dopaminergic endings. The loss of dopamine within the striatum is considered to be related to the development of the signs and symptoms of parkinsonism.

CEREBROSPINAL FLUID HOMOVANILLIC ACID IN PARKINSONISM

Because parkinsonism is related to loss of dopamine within the nigrostriatal system (which contains the majority of all the dopamine within the human CNS), it is important to determine whether or not this proven "deficiency" of dopamine is reflected by examination of spinal fluid metabolites. The metabolite that has been studied most extensively is the major catabolite of dopamine metabolism, homovanillic acid (HVA). The results of a number of the largest series of spinal fluid HVA in parkinsonism are summarized in Table 1. Table 1 documents that there is a marked decrease in concentration of HVA in the lumbar spinal fluid of patients with parkinsonism. It can be seen that the cerebrospinal fluid HVA is greatly decreased in all studies. Although it is possible that akinesia may itself account for some of this decrease (10), akinesia is unlikely to be the major factor that produces this change.

A closely related problem is whether cerebrospinal fluid HVA is related to severity of parkinsonism. Table 2 compiles the findings of some of the larger studies that examined this question. Although we found no correlation in our initial study (11), more recent studies (12,13) including our recent study (14) have found a negative correlation between the cerebrospinal fluid concentration of HVA and the severity of parkinsonism. In other words, lower levels of cerebrospi-

TABLE 1. *Cerebrospinal fluid HVA in parkinsonism*

Parkinsonian patients		Controls		
CSF HVA level (ng/cm³)	N	CSF HVA level (ng/cm³)	N	Source
15 ± 8	19	—	—	Weiner et al. (11)
8.8 ± 3.8	12	—	—	Bertler et al. (34)
11 ± 1.6	23	36 ± 4	25	Chase and Ng (12)
14 ± 9	26	40 ± 14	11	Gumpert et al. (17)
14.8 ± 6	60	38 ± 8	45	Weiner and Klawans (14)
15.8 ± 1.1	125	34.4 ± 1.9	64	Rinne et al. (19)

TABLE 2. *Relationship of pretreatment cerebrospinal fluid HVA and severity of parkinsonism*

N	Correlation	Source
19	No correlation	Weiner et al. (11)
23	Negative correlation*	Chase and Ng ( )
60	Slight negative correlation	Weiner and Klawans (14)
157	Negative correlation	Rinne and Sonninen (13)

* Cerebrospinal fluid was collected following probenecid administration.

nal fluid HVA are correlated with increased parkinsonian deficit (primarily akinesia). This is also seen in the scattergram of the relationship between disability as measured by the Northwestern disability scale (15) and cerebrospinal fluid HVA (see Fig. 1).

From a therapeutic standpoint the more intriguing question is whether there is any correlation between pretreatment cerebrospinal fluid HVA and subsequent response to L-DOPA. A number of studies have examined this question and the findings of these studies are summarized in Table 3.

Three early studies consisting of limited numbers of patients (16–18) all suggested that patients with higher HVA levels prior to L-DOPA therapy show less clinical improvement when placed on L-DOPA. Larger studies have failed to show any correlation at all (14,19).

PARKINSONISM IN DISEASES OF THE STRIATUM

If parkinsonism reflects altered striatal dopaminergic response, such dysfunction could occur as a result of either of one or two separate physiologic alterations: (a) loss of dopaminergic input (presynaptic dopamine deficiency) or (b) loss of striatal responsiveness to dopamine (postsynaptic receptor site dysfunction). The first process would be expected to result in decreased cerebrospinal fluid HVA, whereas the second need not be associated with any alteration in cerebrospinal fluid HVA. If parkinsonism in such patients is caused by loss of striatal response

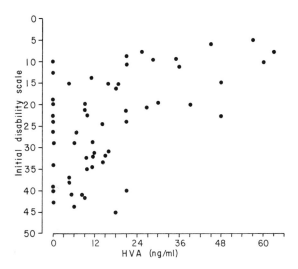

FIG. 1. Relationships between control raw Northwestern disability score and initial cerebrospinal fluid homovanillic acid concentration expressed in nanograms per milliliter (14).

TABLE 3. *Relationship between pretreatment cerebrospinal fluid HVA and subsequent response to L-DOPA*

N	Response	Source
16	Four of 5 patients without response had normal pretreatment HVA levels	Godwin-Austen et al. (16)
26	Patients with higher pretreatment HVA levels tended to be relatively resistant	Gumpert et al. (17)
21	The mean HVA in CSF in 11 patients who were most responsive to L-DOPA was significantly lower than the mean HVA in 10 poorly responsive patients*	Jequier and Dufresne (18)
14	No correlation	Weiner and Klawans (14)
151	No correlation	Rinne et al. (19)

* Cerebrospinal fluid was obtained by suboccipital puncture.

to dopamine the efficacy of L-DOPA may be quite limited. This raises the possibility that at least some of the patients reported by Godwin-Austen et al. (16), Gumpert et al. (17), and Jequier and Dufresne (18) may have had postsynaptic striatal dysfunction which could produce clinical parkinsonism not associated with altered cerebrospinal fluid HVA and unresponsive to L-DOPA.

It is becoming clear that several such states do exist. The first of these is striatonigral degeneration. This is a disorder that is characterized clinically by parkinsonism and pathologically by degeneration of both the substantia nigra and the putamen. The results of clinical trials of L-DOPA in 10 patients (20–25) with pathologically proven striatonigral degeneration are shown in Table 4. Six of the

TABLE 4. *Efficacy of L-DOPA in striatonigral degeneration*

N	Response to L-DOPA		Source
1	No improvement	1	Andrews et al. (20)
3	No improvement	1	Fahn and Greenberg (21)
—	Significant but transient improvement	2	
2	No improvement	2	Inzumi et al. (22)
2	No improvement	2	Rajput et al. (23)
1	Transient response	1	Sharpe et al. (24)
1	Transient response	1	Trotter (25)
Total: 10	No improvement	6	
	Transient response	4	

10 patients showed no response at all to L-DOPA, whereas four showed only transient improvement. This is clearly inferior to the expected response in classic parkinsonism. Although there are no studies of cerebrospinal fluid HVA in such patients, it is clear that such patients do not respond as well to chronic L-DOPA therapy as do patients with parkinsonism per se.

Postsynaptic striatal dysfunction also results in parkinsonism in the so-called rigid or akinetic form of Huntington's disease (26). Although the akinetic form of Huntington's disease usually occurs before the age of 20 the clinical manifestations include parkinsonian-like akinesia and rigidity. The parkinsonian-like manifestations of the akinetic form of Huntington's disease is felt to be related to degeneration of striatal neurons and loss of response to dopamine (26,27). If the parkinsonian features of this form of Huntington's disease are related to a decreased effect of dopamine, it is reasonable to use L-DOPA in an attempt to increase the activity of dopamine within the striatum. The results of L-DOPA trials in such patients are summarized in Table 5. Barbeau (28) gave L-DOPA to two such patients, one of whom improved significantly. Bird and Paulson (29) reported significant but transient improvement in one patient. Low et al. (30) have recently reported another case of a patient who was unresponsive to L-DOPA.

TABLE 5. *Efficacy of L-DOPA in the rigid form of Huntington's disease*

N	Response		Source
2	Significant improvement	1	Barbeau (28)
—	No improvement	1	
1	Transient improvement	1	Bird and Paulson (29)
5	Transient improvement	2	Klawans (*unpublished observations*)
	No improvement	3	
1	No improvement	1	Low et al. (30)
Total: 9	No improvement	5	
—	Transient improvement	3	
—	Significant improvement	1	

We have given L-DOPA to five such patients and observed a transient response in two and no improvement in the other three. In three of these patients the cerebrospinal fluid HVA was normal. It appears that akinetic Huntington's disease is associated with normal cerebrospinal fluid HVA and a limited response to L-DOPA.

A third state in which parkinsonism is related to postsynaptic striatal pathology is the Shy–Drager syndrone. The results of the few clinical trials of L-DOPA in this disorder are summarized in Table 6. Here again the response to L-DOPA therapy is poor. None of the eight patients showed any significant improvement when treated with L-DOPA (31).

These various observations have several possible implications for the study of the biochemistry and pharmacology of psychoses.

1. Presynaptic deficiency and postsynaptic dysfunction in relation to the same amine system can result in identical clinical pictures.
2. Only the presynaptic deficiency state is associated with detectable alterations in amine metabolites in the cerebrospinal fluid.
3. Although there is some correlation between severity of the clinical state and decrease in cerebrospinal metabolites in the presynaptic deficiency state, there is no correlation between decrease in cerebrospinal fluid metabolites and response to amine precursor therapy.
4. The two states may differ in the response to amine precursors.

L-DOPA AND CEREBROSPINAL FLUID HOMOVANILLIC ACID

The L-DOPA-induced improvement in parkinsonism is felt to be caused by increased activity of dopamine within the striatum (26,32). This concept derives much of its support from the postmortem studies of Hornykiewicz (33) who has shown that chronic L-DOPA therapy does result in increased levels of dopamine within the striatum.

If L-DOPA-induced improvement in parkinsonism is related to increased dopamine activity within the striatum, it is important to know whether this increase is reflected by changes in cerebrospinal fluid HVA and whether there is any correlation between L-DOPA-induced increases in cerebrospinal fluid HVA and L-DOPA efficacy. The results of the larger studies (12,14,19,34,35,36) of the relationship between L-DOPA-induced increases in cerebrospinal fluid HVA and clinical response to L-DOPA are summarized in Table 7. Although there is a

TABLE 6. *Efficacy of L-Dopa in Shy-Drager syndrome* (8 patients)

N	Response	Source
5	No improvement 5	Aminoff et al. (31)
3	No improvement 3	Klawans (*unpublished observations*)

TABLE 7. *Relationship between L-DOPA-induced increase in cerebrospinal fluid HVA and efficacy of L-DOPA*

N	Correlation	Source
12	No correlation[a]	Bertler et al. (34)
16	Five patients with greatest increase showed little or no improvement	Godwin-Austen et al. (16)
23	No correlation[a]	Chase and Ng (12)
47	No correlation[a]	Mones et al. (36)
60	No correlation[a]	Weiner and Klawans (14)
151	No correlation[a]	Rinne et al. (19)

[a] Increase was correlated with dose of L-DOPA.

correlation between the daily dose of L-DOPA and cerebrospinal fluid HVA, there appears to be no correlation at all between clinical response to L-DOPA and increase in cerebrospinal fluid HVA.

How can we explain this lack of correlation? It appears that all of the HVA found in the cerebrospinal fluid of patients receiving L-DOPA is not synthesized by the brain itself, as a result of which the cerebrospinal fluid HVA level in a patient receiving L-DOPA is not a reflection of brain dopamine metabolism. Based on studies in rabbits receiving L-DOPA and a selective peripheral DOPA decarboxylase inhibitor, Bartholini et al. (37) suggested that some of the HVA found in the cerebrospinal fluid originates in the walls of brain capillaries. Rinne et al. (19) studied cerebrospinal fluid HVA in patients receiving L-DOPA alone and L-DOPA with various doses of a peripheral decarboxylase inhibitor, and demonstrated that increased decarboxylase inhibition is associated with lower degrees of increased HVA. It is most probable that the increasing doses of decarboxylase inhibitor block the formation of HVA by various peripheral sites including the brain capillaries more efficiently and that much of the HVA increase in the cerebrospinal fluid of patients on L-DOPA alone comes from such peripheral sources.

Patients on L-DOPA and a DOPA decarboxylase inhibitor still have significantly increased levels of HVA, but the increase is not as marked as those receiving L-DOPA alone. This has been shown by both Chase (38) and Rinne et al. (19). Whether there is any correlation between L-DOPA-induced increase in HVA and clinical efficacy in patients with maximal peripheral decarboxylase inhibition is not known.

EFFECTS OF L-DOPA OR SEROTONIN

It appears that long-term L-DOPA therapy affects more than just central dopamine metabolism. Chase (38) has shown that L-DOPA therapy is associated with decreased cerebrospinal fluid concentrations of 5-hydroxyindoleacetic acid (5-HIAA), the major catabolite of serotonin. L-DOPA therapy of depressed patients results in a similar decrease in cerebrospinal fluid 5-HIAA (35).

The exact mechanism of this L-DOPA effect on cerebrospinal fluid 5-HIAA is not known. L-DOPA has been shown to decrease the absorption of tryptophan (39). L-DOPA inhibits synthesis of 5-hydroxytryptamine from tryptophan in brain slices (40). L-DOPA competes with other aromatic amino acids for transport into the CNS (41), and it is felt that L-DOPA enters serotonergic terminals where it displaces serotonin from its storage granules (42).

It has been suggested that the entrance of L-DOPA into serotonergic nerve terminals and the subsequent formation of dopamine within these serotonin terminals may play a role in the therapeutic effect of L-DOPA (42). Whether or not this mechanism plays a role in the beneficial effect of L-DOPA, evidence is accumulating that L-DOPA-induced alterations in brain serotonin activity may play a role in production of some of the side effects of L-DOPA.

Lehmann (39) demonstrated decreased levels of serum tryptophan in patients receiving L-DOPA and noted mental changes in cases with extremely low serum tryptophan levels. These mental disturbances included toxic confusion, decreased intellectual function, and depression, and were presumed to be caused by insufficient serotonin synthesis within the brain. In two patients therapy with tryptophan was associated with considerable improvement in mental function. Birkmayer et al. (43) have also described mental changes consisting of both confusional and nonconfusional psychotic states in patients on L-DOPA, who responded to therapy with L-tryptophan. These investigators feel that the psychotic states induced by chronic L-DOPA therapy are the result of serotonin deficiency and respond to treatment with tryptophan.

Our recent studies on 5-hydroxytryptophan (5-HTP)-induced myoclonus is of interest in relation to the effect of L-DOPA on serotonin activity within the brain. 5-HTP given to guinea pigs produces generalized myoclonic activity, which is correlated with increased brain serotonin concentration and is specifically blocked by the serotonin antagonist, methysergide (44). Similar myoclonic jerks are seen during long-term L-DOPA therapy (45). These are not related to the other forms of L-DOPA-induced dyskinesias and unlike the latter are specifically antagonized by methysergide. This suggests that long-term L-DOPA therapy does not simply decrease serotonin turnover but that its effect on serotonin is much more complex and may best be described as altered regulation.

The effect of chronic L-DOPA therapy on brain serotonin activity in patients with parkinsonism also has implications for the biology of the functional psychoses. Therapy of any disorder with amine precursors may alter the activity of other amine systems within the brain, and such alteration may have deleterious behavior effects.

L-DOPA-INDUCED PSYCHIATRIC DISORDERS

The incidence and pathogenesis of L-DOPA-induced psychiatric disorders are not known. In our experience the most common psychiatric manifestations are hallucinations and paranoid psychoses. The hallucinations are almost invariably visual, frequently nocturnal, often appearing when the patient goes from darkness into light, and tend to recur nightly, to be stereotyped in the individual patient, and, usually after the first few appearances, to be nonthreatening to the patient who recognizes them as hallucinations. The prevalence of these hallucinations increases with duration of therapy so that the incidence during the third and fourth years is between 15% and 20% (Klawans, *unpublished observations*). Less common but more significant for the patient is the occurrence of a paranoid psychosis usually superimposed on a clear sensorium. These reactions can be seen at the initiation of L-DOPA therapy, but like the hallucinations are more common as the duration of L-DOPA therapy increases.

Hallucinations and paranoid reactions are not the only side effect the incidence of which is related to the duration of L-DOPA therapy. This is also true of the L-DOPA-induced dyskinesias as shown in Fig. 2.

The observation that prolonged L-DOPA therapy is associated with an increasing incidence of side effects that are less common during acute therapy raises the possibility that such prolonged therapy may itself alter the subsequent response of the brain and its dopamine receptors to dopamine. This possibility is supported by another set of clinical observations in a different group of patients taking a different dopamine agonist—amphetamine abusers. These individuals are again taking high doses of a dopamine agonist chronically and this chronic agonism is associated with a paranoid psychosis (incidence unknown) and lingual–facial–buccal dyskinesias and chorea (incidence unknown) (46).

We have used amphetamine-induced stereotyped behavior as a model of the effect of dopamine at striatal dopamine receptors to study the effect of chronic agonism on subsequent receptor site response. Amphetamine-induced stereotyped behavior, like L-DOPA-induced dyskinesias, are caused by action of dopamine at striatal dopamine receptors.

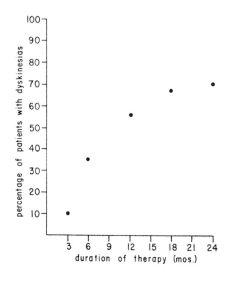

FIG. 2. Prevalence of L-DOPA-induced dyskinesias (57).

In our first experiment animals were given the same subthreshold doses of amphetamine daily and developed a progressively altered response that was characterized by both increased behavioral response and a decreased latency. This is shown in Fig. 3, which demonstrates the successive development of increased behavioral effect and decreased latency.

In subsequent studies a group of guinea pigs were given amphetamine daily for 3 weeks; their subsequent responses to amphetamine and apomorphine were studied. This response was again characterized by increased sensitivity (decreased threshold), increased intensity, and decreased latency to either amphetamine or apomorphine, which persisted for up to 5 weeks. The possible mechanisms underlying this chronic agonist hypersensitivity may conceivably involve changes in the metabolism, distribution, storage, or release of dopamine agonists or changes in the sensitivity of the neuronal membrane itself. The observation of hypersensitivity as reflected in changes in amphetamine-induced stereotyped behavior does not reveal which of these mechanisms is involved, as amphetamine is an indirect dopamine agonist. Apomorphine, however, is believed to be a direct dopamine agonist exerting its predominant effect at the postsynaptic dopamine receptor site (47). The fact that amphetamine pretreatment produces a supersensitivity to apomorphine-induced stereotyped behavior suggests that a postsynaptic mechanism is involved in the production of this supersensitivity.

It has been demonstrated that brain catecholamine levels are decreased after chronic amphetamine administration in rats (48) and guinea pigs (49). Moreover, the patterns of urinary amphetamine metabolites have been found not to change with chronic amphetamine administration in rats (48). These observations together with the data presented here suggest that functional or structural alterations or both in the dopamine receptor site, rather than changes in the metabolism of amphetamine or endogenous catecholamines, are responsible for dopaminergic supersensitivity, which occurs following chronic amphetamine administration. This drug-induced alteration could consist of a direct modification of the dopamine receptors themselves or of a suppression of some other neuronal mechanism that normally antagonizes stereotyped behavior. Whichever mechanism is operat-

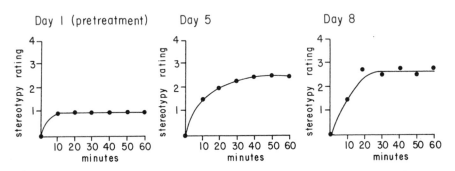

FIG. 3. Time course of amphetamine-induced stereotyped behavior in guinea pigs (47).

ing, the response of the cells upon which dopamine acts to elicit stereotypy is increased (supersensitive).

If chronic amphetamine administration to guinea pigs can elicit altered hypersensitive behavior response, similar mechanism could play a role in the pathogenesis of (a) L-DOPA-induced dyskinesias, (b) amphetamine-induced dyskinesias, (c) L-DOPA-induced psychosis, and (d) amphetamine-induced psychosis.

THE PHARMACOLOGY OF CHOREA

The possibility that increased receptor site responsiveness may play a role in the pathophysiology of these human disorders gains support from pharmacologic studies of Huntington's disease and other choreatic diseases. The choreatic movements seen in Huntington's disease appear to reflect striatal dysfunction. On the basis of pharmacologic observations in patients with Huntington's disease it has been proposed that the pathophysiology of Huntington's disease involves increased response of striatal neurons to dopamine (26,50).

The theory of receptor site hypersensitivity in Huntington's disease has a number of clinical implications. Huntington's disease is inherited according to an autosomal dominant pattern but usually does not become manifest until middle age. The defective genotype remains undetected, and most patients are asymptomatic until after the age of 30, after their offspring are conceived. If the primary defect of Huntington's disease involves an abnormally sensitive response of neurons of the striatum to dopamine, exogenous stimulation of these presumably hypersensitive receptor sites with L-DOPA in the asymptomatic persons carrying the gene of Huntington's disease might induce chorea and allow one to identify the persons in whom Huntington's disease is destined to develop. Klawans et al. (51) have pursued this problem, examining 28 subjects genetically at risk for the disease. Administering small doses of L-DOPA, they isolated two groups. One group showed no effects from the L-DOPA stimulation, and the second group developed choreatic movements. A control group of normal subjects developed no movements when given a similar regimen. These results suggest that some subjects at risk for Huntington's disease have an abnormal hypersensitive response to L-DOPA stimulation that normal individuals and other patients at risk tolerated with no effect. It is suggested that the patients in whom choreatic movements developed during L-DOPA exposure will later develop overt chorea. These data can also be interpreted to suggest that the functional hypersensitivity of striatal dopamine receptors to dopamine (as L-DOPA) in these patients predated the appearance of naturally occurring choreatic movements in at least some subjects with Huntington's disease.

The concept that altered dopamine response plays a role in the pathogenesis of choreatic movements is further supported by the observation that (a) L-DOPA worsens choreatic movements in Huntington's disease (51), (b) amphetamine worsens choreatic movements in Huntington's disease (53), (c) amphetamine worsens choreatic movements in Sydenham's chorea (53), (d) amphetamine can

.elicit choreatic movements in patients with a past history of Sydenham's chorea but no overt chorea (53), and (e) the same doses of amphetamine have no effects on normal subjects (52). It is most intriguing that in the few patients studied, L-DOPA elicits severe chorea in subjects at risk for Huntington's disease presenting as schizophrenia without chorea (26).

The sensitivity of patients with chorea to dopamine agonists is similar to the sensitivity of patients with schizophrenia to dopamine agonists, and raises the possibility that receptor site hypersensitivity may play a role in the pathophysiology of these states.

NEUROTRANSMITTER BALANCE

Clinical studies of the pharmacology of extrapyramidal movement disorders also have implications for the concept of the role of neurotransmitter balance in the major psychoses. Parkinsonism as reviewed above is felt to be the result of a decreased effect of dopamine at striatal dopamine receptors. Centrally acting cholinergic agents worsen parkinsonism, whereas anticholinergic agents improve parkinsonism, suggesting that a balance of dopamine and acetylcholine plays a role in parkinsonism (3,53). The choreatic movements in Huntington's disease are felt to be related to an increased effect of dopamine at striatal dopamine receptors (26). Centrally active cholinergic agents improve chorea in this disease, whereas anticholinergic agents worsen the movements suggesting that cholinergic–dopaminergic balance plays a role in Huntington's disease (54). The abnormal movements seen in tardive dyskinesias are usually choreatic in nature and are felt to be related to increased activity of dopamine at striatal dopamine receptors. As in Huntington's disease, centrally active cholinergic agents improve the dyskinesias and anticholinergic agents worsen the dyskinesias (55). This suggests that dopaminergic–cholinergic balance also plays a role in the pathophysiology of tardive dyskinesias.

Although these data may suggest that catecholamine–acetylcholine balance plays a role in many other physiologic states including the major psychoses, there are certain limitations that should be kept in mind. These include the following:

a. Dopamine–acetylcholine antagonism has only been demonstrated at the striatal end of the dopaminergic nigrostriatal system. The role of balance in the mesolimbic or mesocortical systems is unclear.

b. Dopamine and acetylcholine are not equal partners in striatal function. Dopaminergic activity plays a much more important role in the pathophysiology of extrapyramidal movements than cholinergic activity.

c. Other neurotransmitters, especially γ-aminobutyric acid and perhaps serotonin, play a role in striatal function.

ACKNOWLEDGMENTS

This work was supported by grants from the United Parkinson Foundation, the Boothroyd Foundation, and the Michael Reese Medical Research Institute, Chicago, Illinois.

REFERENCES

1. Pare, C. M. B., and Sandler, M. J. (1959): A clinical and biochemical study of a trial of ipioniazid in the treatment of depression. *J. Neurol. Neurosurg. Psychiatry,* 22:247–251.
2. Hornykiewicz, O. (1966): Dopamine (3-hydroxytyramine) and brain function. *Pharmacol. Rev.,* 18:925–964.
3. Klawans, H. L. (1968): The pharmacology of parkinsonism. *Dis. Nerv. Syst.,* 29:805–816.
4. Barbeau, A. (1969): L-dopa therapy in Parkinson's disease: A critical review of nine years experience. *Can. Med. Assoc. J.,* 101:59–68.
5. Klawans, H. L., Ilahi, M. M., and Shenker, D. (1970): Theoretic implications of the use of L-dopa in parkinsonism. *Acta Neurol. Scand.,* 46:409–441.
6. Feldberg, W. (1945): Present views on the mode of action of acetylcholine in the central nervous system. *Physiol. Rev.,* 25:496.
7. Ahmed, A., and Marshall, P. B. (1962): Relationship between anti-acetylcholine and anti-tremor activity in anti-parkinsonian and related drugs. *J. Pharmacol.,* 18:274–282.
8. Greenfield, J. G., and Bosanquet, F. D. (1953): The brain-stem lesion in parkinsonism. *J. Neurol. Neurosurg. Psychiatry,* 16:213–226.
9. Forno, L. S. (1966): Pathology of parkinsonism. *J. Neurosurg.,* 24:266–271.
10. Post, R. M., Kotin, J., Goodwin, F. K., and Gordon, E. K. (1973): Psychomotor activity and cerebrospinal fluid amine metabolites in affective illness. *Am. J. Psychiatry,* 130:67–72.
11. Weiner, W. J., Harrison, W. H., and Klawans, H. L. (1969): L-dopa and cerebrospinal fluid homovanillic acid in parkinsonism. *Life Sci.,* 8:971–976.
12. Chase, T. N., and Ng, L. K. Y. (1972): Central monoamine metabolism in Parkinson's disease. *Arch. Neurol.,* 27:486–491.
13. Rinne, U. K., and Sonninen, V. (1972): Acid monoamine metabolites in the cerebrospinal fluid of patients with Parkinson's disease. *Neurology (Minneap.),* 22:62–67.
14. Weiner, W. J., and Klawans, H. L. (1973): Failure of cerebrospinal fluid homovanillic acid to predict levodopa response in Parkinson's disease. *J. Neurol. Neurosurg. Psychiatry,* 36:747–752.
15. Canter, G. J., deLaTorre, R., and Mier, M. (1961): A method for evaluating disability in patients with Parkinson's disease. *J. Nerv. Ment. Dis.* 122:143–147.
16. Godwin-Austen, R. B., Kantamarreni, B. D., and Curzon, G. (1971): Comparison of benefit from L-dopa in parkinsonism with increase of amine metabolites in the CSF. *J. Neurol. Neurosurg. Psychiatry,* 34:219–223.
17. Gumpert, J., Sharpe, D., and Curzon, G. (1973): Amine metabolites in the cerebrospinal fluid in Parkinson's disease and the response to levodopa. *J. Neurol. Sci.,* 19:1–12.
18. Jequier, E., and Dufresne, J. J. (1972): Biochemical investigations in patients with Parkinson's disease treated with L-dopa. *Neurology (Minneap.),* 22:15–21.
19. Rinne, U. K., Sonninen, V., and Sürtola, T. (1973): Acid monoamine metabolites in the cerebrospinal fluid of parkinson patients treated with levodopa alone or combined with a decarboxylase inhibitor. *Eur. Neurol.,* 9:349–362.
20. Andrews, J. M., Terry, R. D., and Spataro, J. (1970): Striatonigral degeneration. *Arch. Neurol.,* 23:319–327.
21. Fahn, S., and Greenberg, J. (1972): Striatonigral degeneration. *Trans. Am. Neurol. Assoc.,* 97:275–277.
22. Izumi, K., Inoue, N., Shirabe, T., Miyazaki, T., and Kuroiwa, Y. (1971): Failed levodopa therapy in striatonigral degeneration. *Lancet,* 1:1355.
23. Rajput, A., Kazi, K. A., and Rozdilsky, B. (1972): Striatonigral degeneration: Response to levodopa therapy. *J. Neurol. Sci.,* 16:331–341.
24. Sharpe, J. A., Rewcastle, N. B., Lloyd, K. G., Hornykiewicz, O., Hill, M., and Tasker, R. R. (1973): Striatonigral degeneration. *J. Neurol. Sci.,* 20:275–286.
25. Trotter, J. L. (1973): Striatonigral degeneration, Alzheimer's disease and inflammatory changes. *Neurology (Minneap.),* 23:1211–1216.
26. Klawans, H. L. (1973): *The Pharmacology of Extrapyramidal Movement Disorders.* Karger, Basel.
27. Klawans, H. L., Ilahi, M. M., and Ringel, S. P. (1971): Toward an understanding of the patho-physiology of Huntington's chorea. *Confin. Neurol.,* 33:297–303.
28. Barbeau, A. (1969): L-dopa and juvenile Huntington's disease. *Lancet,* 2:1066.
29. Bird, M. T., and Paulson, G. W. (1970): Early onset rigid Huntington's chorea. *Neurology (Minneap.),* 20:400.
30. Low, P. A., Allsop, J. L., and Halmagyi, G. M. (1974): Huntington's chorea: The rigid form treated with levodopa. *Med. J. Aust.,* 1974 (1):393–394.

31. Aminoff, M. J., Wilcox, C. S., Woakes, M. M., and Kremer, M. (1973): Levodopa therapy for parkinsonism in the Shy-Drager syndrome. *J. Neurol. Neurosurg. Psychiatry,* 36:350–353.
32. Hornykiewicz, O. (1974): The mechanism of action of L-dopa in Parkinson's disease. *Life Sci.,* 15:1249–1259.
33. Hornykiewicz, O. (1973): Parkinson's disease: From brain homogenate to treatment. *Fed. Proc.,* 32:183–190.
34. Bertler, A., Jeppsson, P. G., Nordgren, L., and Rosengren, E. (1971): Serial determinations of homovanillic acid in the cerebrospinal fluid of parkinson patients treated with L-dopa. *Acta Neurol. Scand.,* 47:393–402.
35. Goodwin, F. R., Dunner, D. L., and Gershon, E. S. (1971): Effect of L-dopa treatment on brain serotonin metabolism in depressed patients. *Life Sci. (I),* 10:751–759.
36. Mones, R. J., Wilk, S., Green, J., and Jutkowitz, R. (1972): A study of spinal fluid homovanillic acid in patients with disease of the nervous system. *Mt. Sinai J. Med. NY,* 39:478–485.
37. Bartholini, G., Tossot, R., and Pletscher, A. (1971): Brain capillaries as a source of homovanillic acid in cerebrospinal fluid. *Brain Res.,* 27:163–168.
38. Chase, T. N. (1970): Cerebrospinal fluid monoamine metabolites and peripheral decarboxylase inhibitors in parkinsonism. *Neurology (Minneap.),* 20:36–40.
39. Lehmann, J. (1973): Tryptophan malabsorption in levodopa-treated parkinsonian patients. *Acta Med. Scand.,* 194:181–189.
40. Goldstein, M., and Frenkel, R. (1971): Inhibition of serotonin synthesis by Dopa and other catechols. *Nature (New Biol.),* 233:179–180.
41. Bartholini, G., DaPrada, M., and Pletscher, A. (1968): Decrease of cerebral 4-hydroxytryptamine by 3,4-dihydroxyphenylalanine after inhibition of extracerebral decarboxylase. *J. Pharm. Pharmacol.,* 20:228–229.
42. Ng, L. K. Y., Chase, T. N., Colburn, R. W., and Kopin, I. J. (1972): L-dopa in parkinsonism. *Neurology (Minneap.),* 22:688–696.
43. Birkmayer, W., Daniekzyk, W., Neumayer, E., Riederer, P. (1972): The balance of biogenic amines as condition for normal behavior. *J. Neural Transm.,* 33:163–178.
44. Klawans, H. L., Goetz, C., and Weiner, W. J. (1973): 5-Hydroxytryptophan-induced myoclonus in guinea pigs and the possible role of serotonin in infantile myoclonus. *Neurology (Minneap.),* 23:1234–1240.
45. Klawans, H. L., Goetz, C., and Bergen, D. (1975): L-dopa-induced myoclonus. *Arch. Neurol.,* 32:331–334.
46. Klawans, H. L., and Margolin, D. I. (1975): Amphetamine-induced hypersensitivity in guinea pigs: Implications in psychosis and human movement disorders. *Arch. Gen. Psychiatry, (In press.)*
47. Ernst, A. M. (1967): Mode of action of apomorphine on dextroamphetamine gnawing compulsion in rats. *Psychopharmacologia,* 10:316–323.
48. Lewander, T. (1968): Urinary excretion and tissue levels of catecholamines during chronic amphetamine intoxication. *Psychopharmacologia,* 13:894–907.
49. Lewander, T. (1971): Effects of acute and chronic amphetamine intoxication on brain catecholamines in the guinea pig. *Acta Pharmacol. Toxicol. (Kbh),* 39:209–225.
50. Klawans, H. L. (1970): A pharmacologic analysis of Huntington's chorea. *Eur. Neurol.,* 4:148–163.
51. Klawans, H. L., Paulson, G. W., Ringel, S. P., and Barbeau, A. (1972): Use of L-dopa in the detection of presymptomatic Huntington's chorea. *N. Engl. J. Med.,* 286:1332–1334.
52. Klawans, H. L., and Weiner, W. J. (1974): The effect of d-amphetamine on choreiform disorders. *Neurology (Minneap.),* 24:312–318.
53. Duvoisin, R. C. (1967): Cholinergic–anticholinergic antagonism in parkinsonism. *Arch. Neurol.,* 17:124–136.
54. Klawans, H. L., and Rubovits, R. (1972): Central cholinergic–anticholinergic antagonism in Huntington's chorea. *Neurology (Minneap.),* 22:107–116.
55. Klawans, H. L., and Rubovits, R. (1974): The effect of cholinergic and anticholinergic agents on tardive dyskinesia. *J. Neurol. Neurosurg. Psychiatry,* 37:941–947.
56. Klawans, H. L., Crosset, P., and Dana, N. (1975): The effect of chronic amphetamine exposure on stereotyped behavior: Implications for the pathogenesis of levodopa-induced dyskinesias. *Adv. Neurol.,* 9:105–112.

Discussion

Snyder: I'd like to emphasize the one point that Drs. Glowinski and Klawans touched on, which has to do with the feedback system in the dopamine neuronal system. In the case of dopamine receptor blockers such as the phenothiazine drugs, the postsynaptic receptor, after being blocked by the phenothiazine, says, "I don't have enough dopamine, please turn on the dopamine machine." And so you get an increase in dopamine synthesis, the increase in the firing rate of the dopamine neurons, increase of amine metabolites (HVA). These biochemical and neurophysiologic tools have been the major measurements that indirectly enable us to make all these important inferences about what is going on at the dopamine synapse.

Now, one thing that Dr. Glowinski didn't have time to make clear is that reasonably well established, recent evidence points to two kinds of feedback. One is the interneuronal feedback. In the case of the nigrostriatal dopamine pathway, there is some kind of neuronal feedback system from the striatum back to the substantia nigra.

In addition there seems to be a feedback system right across the synapse. After dopamine has been released and done its job at the postsynaptic receptor, the dopamine acts back on the presynaptic nerve ending receptors saying, "Stop releasing dopamine." These kinds of receptors have now been demonstrated for most neurotransmitters in the brain.

In the nigrostriatal system a certain proportion of the metabolic changes after receptor blockade are caused by the interneuronal feedback and some are caused by the synaptic feedback.

These feedbacks are important. Dr. Glowinski described how with chronic phenothiazine treatment dopamine synthesis returned to normal after an initial increase. And yesterday Dr. Freedman remarked that Dr. Goodwin has data showing that the spinal fluid of patients treated with phenothiazines initially shows an elevated HVA; but treated for a period long enough to be therapeutic, the elevation is not seen. How do you explain that with a therapeutic regimen of a phenothiazine you don't have the metabolic alterations which are presumably associated with the therapeutic effects?

I don't know exactly what's going on, but one possibility would be that there is a sort of habituation—a tolerance develops to the acute acceleration of synthesis accelerated.

One last point in all these data about synapses and chemicals—we seem to be getting to a point at which we have an actual real-life brain circuit in which many of the synapses are identified with respect to their transmitter. One can actually explain therapeutic effects of drugs and disease states in terms of changes in specific brain circuits with identified neurotransmitters.

Nauta: Since such a large part of the clinicopharmacologic accounts discussed in these presentations revolves around dopamine, I am tempted to comment on the anatomic ramifications of the dopamine system. It seems reasonable to assume that the dopaminergic nigrostriatal system exerts its enormously important influence upon somatic motor mechanisms by affecting the first link in a neural chain that leads from the striatum to the globus pallidus and from there by way of the ansa lenticularis to the subthalamic nucleus, to thalamomotocortical neurons, and to certain cell groups in the mesencephalic tegmentum. This enumeration of structures likely to be affected by the substantia nigra by no means explains the symptomatology of Parkinson's disease, but it at least includes neural organizations that are known to be part of the skeletomuscular effect or system.

The gulf between symptomatology and substrate identification seems much wider still when we consider the mental disorders that now seem attributable to a transmittor imbalance involving the dopamine system. We can only speculate on the neural substratum of the human thought process and hence cannot specify the sites at which dopamine could affect that process. However, in this predicament it seems only natural to think of the less massive but more widely distributed mesolimbic system described by Ungerstedt in the rat (Stereotaxic mapping of the monoamine pathways in the rat brain. *Acta Physiol. Scand. (Suppl.)* 367: 1–48, 1971) as a system of dopamine fibers originating in cell group A10 medial to the substantia nigra proper and distributed to the amygdala and in larger number to the complex formed by the olfactory tubercle and the nucleus accumbens. More recently, additional distributions of this dopamine system to the entorhinal area (T. Hökfelt, Å. Hjungdahl, K. Fuxe, and Johansson, O.: Dopamine nerve terminals in the rat limbic cortex: Aspects of the dopamine hypothesis of schizophrenia. *Science,* 184:177–179, 1974. and to the medial cortex anterior to the corpus callosum (O. Lindvall, A. Björklund, R. Y. Moore, and Stenevi, U.: Mesencephalic dopamine neurons projecting to neocortex. *Brain Res.,* 81:325–331, 1974) have been described. Ungerstedt's term, mesolimbic system, seems very appropriate, for all of the structures receiving these projections from cell group A10 are in one way or another implicated in the circuitry of the limbic system. The mesolimbic system could be regarded as being laid out in parallel to the nigrostriatal connection, but further comparison of the two dopaminergic pathways requires some qualification: whereas the nigrostriatal system is reciprocated by the massive striatonigral projection, in the mesolimbic system no direct return loop to cell group A10 is known. It would therefore seem possible that the mesolimbic system is not equipped with a direct feedback loop (I suspect that in view of his earlier remarks, Dr. Snyder would want to call it a postsynaptic feedback loop) of the sort that has been identified in the association between the substantia nigra and the striatum.

Meltzer: I have a question for Dr. Iversen. Spiroperidol, which is more potent an antipsychotic than the phenothiazines, was much less potent than some of the phenothiazines in inhibiting cyclic AMP formation by the dopamine-stimulated adenylcyclase. In addition, chlorimipramine, a tricyclic antidepressant, which is not an antipsychotic and may induce exacerbations of psychosis in some schizophrenics, was also a potent inhibitor of adenylcyclase. Do these data not detract from the possibility that the effects of dopamine on this enzyme are the basis of the neuroleptic effect of the antipsychotic drugs?

Iversen: Dr. Glowinski's slide was from our work on the effects of neuroleptic drugs as inhibitors of dopamine-sensitive adenylatecyclase (R. J. Miller, A. S. Horn, and L. L. Iversen: *Molecular Pharmacology,* Vol. 10, p. 759, 1974). The butyrophenones represent the only class of neuroleptic drugs that do not fit well in this model in terms of a good correlation between *in vivo* potency and the ability of the drugs to inhibit the dopamine induced stimulation of cyclic AMP formation in striatal homogenates. That is a paradox which is still unresolved.

But I would point out that with the other major neuroleptics, particularly the phenothiazines, such correlations are good. For example, between a very potent phenothiazine such as fluphenazine, and a virtually inert phenothiazine such as promazine or promethazine, there is more than a 10,000-fold difference in potency as inhibitors of dopamine in this biochemical test system.

This sort of correlation also holds for the thioxanthenes, where active "alpha" and inactive "beta" isomers of the drugs exist. It holds also for the new neuroleptic drug butaclamol which possesses stereoisomers. Only the (+) form of the drug is effective on the dopamine-sensitive adenylatecyclase, and it is only this form of the drug which has a neuroleptic profile in conventional animal tests.

So I think there are good grounds for believing that this is the best biochemical model that we have available at the moment for CNS dopamine receptors.

Freedman: Drs. Post and Goodwin just happen to have a slide relating to Dr. Glowinski's finding of a biphasic effect on dopamine turnover of long-term phenothiazine treatment. They are raising the question of what was the schedule of neuroleptic administration when demonstrating the biphasic effect.

Post: We have data in a mixed group of manic-depressive and schizophrenic patients which show findings similar to those that Dr. Glowinski reported in the rat. By measuring the probenecid-induced accumulations of HVA in cerebrospinal fluid we demonstrated significant increases in dopamine turnover in patients studied earlier in phenothiazine treatment, but after more extended phenothiazine treatment (greater than three weeks) dopamine turnover is no longer increased.

As Dr. Snyder suggested there are a number of interpretations for this finding, including a tolerance effect. A possible explanation is that there is an attenuation in the initial increase in HVA; that increase may represent compensatory increases in presynaptic synthesis of dopamine secondary to postsynaptic receptor blockade; but the receptor blockade endures and the dopamine system is then maximally tuned down; not only are postsynaptic receptors blocked, but the presynaptic dopamine synthesis is no longer increased.

Dr. Malcolm Bowers has shown in the rabbit (*J. Pharmacol.,* 26:743, 1974) that tolerance to the effects of phenothiazines might be specific to the neostriatal area and that tolerance did *not* occur in mesolimbic areas and hypothalamus. Because the HVA in lumbar CSF is coming mostly from striatal system, that might be one explanation of the finding of reduced HVA accumulations with chronic phenothiazine treatment, whereas the antipsychotic effects (more related to other systems) persist.

Another possibility—a distressing one at that—is that since there is tolerance to the HVA increases with chronic phenothiazine treatment and there is no tolerance to the clinical antipsychotic effects, the clinical effects may not be mediated by the dopamine system.

Glowinski: In this presentation, I did not have enough time to discuss the problem of the differences in sensitivity to neuroleptics of various dopaminergic systems. We have seen that neuroleptics enhance dopamine turnover in the nigroneostriatal dopamine pathway by blocking the postsynaptic dopamine receptors as well as actions on the presynaptic dopamine receptors. This has been nicely summarized by Dr. Snyder.

In our studies, we measured the addition of both effects. It is quite possible that the relative changes in dopamine synthesis and turnover induced directly (presynaptic receptors) or indirectly (postsynaptic receptors) may vary from one system to another. As an example, we already know that the doses of neuroleptics (such as haloperidol, thioproperazine) required to increase dopamine synthesis in the striatum by 50%, are much *lower* than those required to induce a similar effect in the mesolimbic or mesocortical dopaminergic terminals.

These differences could be related to variations in the sensitivity of presynaptic receptors to neuroleptics. However, more probably they are related to variations in the interneuronal regulatory processes. As extensively discussed by Dr. Nauta, it seems reasonable to admit on the basis of anatomic studies that the neuronal pathways controlling the activity of the nigroneostriatal dopamine neurons and the mesolimbic dopamine neurons are *not* of similar nature; their organization may differ in many ways. Therefore, the changes in dopamine synthesis induced by the blockade of postsynaptic dopamine receptors, which reflect compensatory processes, will not be identical.

Various hypotheses can be offered to explain the reduction in dopamine synthesis detected in dopamine terminals of the nigroneostriatal pathway 24 hours following the last injection of repeated treatments with neuroleptics. It has been suggested that this could be attributed to the development of tolerance. This may be one possibility. There is some information suggesting that the postsynaptic dopamine receptors become super-sensitive following repeated injections of neuroleptics. This could explain a compensatory reduction in the activity of the dopamine pathway following the disappearance of the neuroleptic at the receptor site. However, in the study by Scatton and Julou (described in my report) concerning the effect of a long-acting neuroleptic on dopamine synthesis, it appears that the inhibition of dopamine synthesis is detected *while* the neuroleptic is still present in tissues. This observation may indicate that the mechanism involved is not obligatorily related to the supersensitivity of dopamine receptors. Moreover, it could be shown that a single injection of a classic neuroleptic a few weeks after the administration of the long acting neuroleptic (when the basal activity of the dopamine pathway was reduced) could *still* induce a marked transient activation of dopamine synthesis.

This led us to postulate that neuroleptics could affect two types of dopamine receptors localized on different cells in the caudate nucleus; these cells being the first elements of two distinct interneuronal regulatory systems involved in the control of the dopamine pathway. Such an hypothesis discussed in my report, could explain the dual effects of neuroleptics on the nigroneostriatal dopamine pathway.

Friedhoff: Dr. Klawans showed that there was not a very strong relationship between HVA in spinal fluid and severity of the parkinsonian syndrome. I wonder if he looked at specific aspects of this syndrome because L-DOPA is more effective against rigidity than against tremor. Could he comment on whether there might be a stronger relationship to one or another part of the syndrome?

Klawans: The data we have relate spinal fluid HVA concentration with severity of parkinsonism estimated by a disability scale which is based primarily on akinesia. We could find no correlation with tremor or rigidity. This is essentially in agreement with other studies in the literature which have been able to find some relationship between decrease in spinal HVA and akinesia, but none with any of the other symptoms of parkinsonism.

Biology of the Major Psychoses, edited by D. X.
Freedman, Res. Publ. Assoc. Res. Nerv. Ment.
Dis., Vol. 54. Raven Press, New York   1975.

Neurotransmitter-Related Enzymes in the Major Psychiatric Disorders: I. Catechol-O-Methyl Transferase, Monoamine Oxidase in the Affective Disorders, and Factors Affecting Some Behaviorally Correlated Enzyme Activities

Dennis L. Murphy and Richard J. Wyatt

Laboratory of Clinical Science and Laboratory of Clinical Psychopharmacology, National
Institute of Mental Health, Bethesda, Maryland

Many medical and neurologic disorders result from or are reflected in enzyme activity differences. However, it has only been recently that studies of enzyme activity in tissues from patients with psychiatric disorders have been initiated. The recent marked increase in enzyme studies in psychiatry seems related to three developments: (a) The evolution of a series of hypotheses relating behavior, behavioral disorders, and the therapeutic effects of psychoactive drugs to the function of biogenic amines and other brain neurotransmitters; (b) the development and refinement of specific and sensitive assays for biogenic amine- and other neurotransmitter-related enzymes found in human blood and blood cells; and (c) the increasing awareness that measurements of biogenic amine metabolites in urine and other fluids often represent the final summation of many different metabolic processes and may not provide sufficiently precise measurements for the assessment of neurotransmitter-related functions in man (1).

The measurement of neurotransmitter-related enzymes in man is still a frontier. There are many unresolved questions which limit the implications of apparent associations between enzyme activity differences and the major psychiatric disorders. In particular, the question of whether any of the neurotransmitter-related enzymes found in plasma, platelets, or erythrocytes is identical to those found in brain or other tissues has not been verified. In addition, the question of whether factors other than those operative in the nervous system or other tissues may affect these blood enzymes has only begun to be assessed. A number of factors which may affect the activity of enzymes measured in plasma, platelets, or erythrocytes are summarized in Table 1.

This chapter and the subsequent one will survey the rapidly increasing body of information on neurotransmitter-related enzymes of possible relevance to psychiatric disorders. The greatest number of studies have focused on erythrocyte catechol-O-methyl transferase (COMT), plasma dopamine B-hydroxylase (DBH) and platelet monoamine oxidase (MAO). These enzymes have also been the subject of a few studies using brain samples obtained at autopsy. Some investigations of plasma MAO have also been accomplished in patients with psychiatric

TABLE 1. *Possible non-specific factors influencing human blood cell enzyme activity measurements*

Characteristics	Factors
Individual	Age, sex, hormonal state (e.g., menstrual cycle), stress, activity, diet, drugs, disease state
Cellular	Age and turnover of cells, storage effects, anticoagulant agents, contamination from other blood constituents, other factors as listed above
Enzyme assay conditions	Substrate and cofactor concentrations, endogenous inhibitors, pH, ionic concentration, temperature

disorders, but because the results in several of these studies may be compromised by contamination by the platelet MAO (2), these studies will not be reviewed at this time. Some other enzymes of potential relevance to the psychiatric disorders have been identified, but have not yet been extensively investigated. These include (a) an apparent indoleamine-*N*-methyl transferase in human platelets (3), which has subsequently been identified as a tryptoline-forming enzyme (4); (b) an adenyl cyclase system in human platelets which apparently functions as part of a catecholamine receptor (5–9); (c) Mg and Na–K–Mg adenosine triphosphatases, which function in the transport and storage of biogenic amines in platelets (10,11) and in cation transport in erythrocytes (12–14); and (d) histamine-*N*-methyl transferase and a methanol-forming enzyme (15). In addition, a non-neurotransmitter-related enzyme, serum creatine phosphokinase (CPK), has been the subject of an extensive series of careful studies in psychiatric patients, which are reviewed in the chapter by Meltzer *(this volume).*

Although the focus of this volume is the major psychoses, it is not possible to consider the enzyme findings in the psychiatric disorders out of the context of other factors, some of which are illness-related, which contribute to individual differences in the activity of these enzymes. This chapter begins with an examination of some of these factors. It also considers the evidence relating erythrocyte catechol-*O*-methyl transferase to the major psychoses and platelet monoamine oxidase to the affective disorders. The subsequent chapter will review monoamine oxidase in relation to acute and chronic schizophrenia and also the studies of dopamine β-hydroxylase in patients with psychosis.

FACTORS AFFECTING SOME NEUROTRANSMITTER-RELATED ENZYMES STUDIED IN HUMAN PLASMA, ERYTHROCYTES, AND PLATELETS

A summary of the various factors influencing human enzyme activities in plasma or blood cells is presented in Table 2. As indicated, in addition to changes

TABLE 2. *Factors affecting some blood enzyme characteristics in man*

Characteristic	Platelet monoamine oxidase	Plasma monoamine oxidase	Erythrocyte catechol-O-methyl transferase	Plasma dopamine β-hydroxylase	Serum creatine phospho-kinase
Genetic influences	+++	++	+	+++	+
Sex differences	+ (F > M)	+ (F > M)	+ (M > F)	0	+ (M > F)
Age differences	++	++	0	++	+
Hormone influences (including menstrual cycle)	+	?	+	+	?
Activity/Stress differences	0	?	0	+	+
Diet, nutritional effects	±	?	?	?	+
Drug effects	++	++	(0)	+	++
Changes in medical, neurologic, or psychiatric disorders	++	++	±	++	+++

+++ represents several studies definitely demonstrating an effect of large magnitude, ++ and + smaller effects, ± contradictory studies, 0 studies indicating no effect, and ? inadequately studied factors.

associated with psychiatric disorders and other illnesses, a variety of genetic and nongenetic factors can influence the measured activity of MAO, COMT, DBH, and CPK in different individuals. These factors must be studied or controlled for in comparing psychiatric patients to "normal controls."

Genetic Factors

Monozygotic–dizygotic twin comparisons have been accomplished for platelet MAO (1,16) plasma MAO (16) and plasma DBH activity (17). In addition, siblings have been compared with age and sex-matched controls for platelet MAO (1), plasma DBH (18) and erythrocyte COMT (19). All of these studies have indicated fairly marked genetic contributions to the MAO, DBH, and COMT activity differences found among individuals. Less complete data also indicate that platelet MAO activity differences in patients with schizophrenia and possibly also bipolar affective disorder are influenced by genetic factors (1,20). The large contribution of genetic factors indicates that these measures may have great potential in studies of patients should relationships be established among MAO, DBH, and COMT activity differences in blood and in the CNS and, of course, between the CNS enzymes and neurotransmitter function and behavior.

Sex Differences

Small, incompletely-defined sex differences in the activity of MAO, COMT but not DBH have been observed. In normals, platelet and plasma MAO activities were slightly higher for females across all age decades in one study (21), but not in another of platelet MAO activity (22). Significantly higher erythrocyte COMT levels in male controls were observed in one study (19), but not in three others (14, 23,24). Plasma DBH levels did not appear to be different in the data reported by Weinshilboum et al. (18).

Possible sex differences in these enzymes are of interest because there are well-known differences in the occurrence of unipolar affective disorders (which are more prevalent in women) (25) and in the age of onset of schizophrenia (which is earlier in men than women) (26). It is not clear whether bipolar affective disorders occur in equal frequency in both sexes (27) or in higher frequency in females (25).

Age Differences

Moderately increased activity with increasing age has been observed in some studies of platelet MAO (21), plasma MAO (21), serum DBH (28) but not erythrocyte COMT activity (15). The changes in MAO activity are quite minimal in adult midlife, but increase more steeply after age 50 (21,29). Serum DBH activity correlations with age are especially marked during childhood and adolescence (28).

Psychiatric disorders first occur at different ages, with schizophrenia most often being observed in late adolesence and the early midadult years (26). The average age of onset for bipolar affective disorder is in the mid-20s (25,27,30), whereas the average age of onset of unipolar affective disorder is in the mid-40s (25,27). In addition, some subgroups of patients with unipolar affective disorders have been partially delineated on the basis of different ages of onset (31).

Hormone Activity, Stress, and Nutritional Influences

Menstrual-cycle-related changes in platelet MAO and serum DBH activities have been observed (32,33). Peak-to-trough alterations averaged approximately 20 to 25% for both enzymes. Platelet MAO activity was not altered by food ingestion (33), but detailed studies of the effects of short- and long-term nutritional changes have not yet been accomplished in man. On the basis of animal data, it would be expected that alterations in the intake of vitamin and trace-metal co-factors for these enzymes as well as changes in protein synthesis might also affect the activity of these enzymes in man. Marked clinical changes accompanied by alterations in physical activity and psychologic "stress" do not appear to be associated with changes in erythrocyte COMT activity (23) or platelet MAO activity (Murphy et al., *in preparation*). Although immobilization stress and other procedures elevate serum **DBH** activity in animals (34), only modest and variable changes in human **DBH** have been observed with physical exercise and experimental stress procedures (35,36).

ERYTHROCYTE CATECHOL-*O*-METHYL TRANSFERASE ACTIVITY IN THE AFFECTIVE DISORDERS AND SCHIZOPHRENIA

Catechol-*O*-methyl transferase is a major degradatory enzyme for norepinephrine, epinephrine, dopamine, and their deaminated metabolites. It catalyzes the transfer of a methyl group from *S*-adenosylmethionine to the 3-hydroxy *(m)* site on the catecholamine ring. COMT activity has been identified in human erythrocytes and leukocytes (37,38). The erythrocyte COMT appears to have some similar properties (e.g., in pH optimum and substrate affinities) to the COMT activity studied in other tissues (15,38).

COMT and the Affective Disorders

In the first investigation of erythrocyte COMT in patients with depression, Cohn, Dunner, and Axelrod (15) reported reduced COMT activity in 36 female patients compared to 19 female controls (Table 3). In contrast, 19 men with primary affective disorders had COMT levels no different from 21 male controls. The differences in activity between the female depressed patients and the controls

TABLE 3. *Erythrocyte catechol-O-methyl-transferase (COMT) activity in the affective disorders*

Subjects	N	COMT Activity (% controls)	Reference
Female unipolar depressed patients	19	57% ($<$0.001)	Cohn et al. (15); Dunner et al. (23)
Female bipolar depressed patients	29	76% ($<$0.05)	(15, 23)
		Total 67% ($<$0.001)	
Male unipolar and bipolar depressed patients	19	96% (NS)	(15, 23)
Male depressed patients	10	102% (NS)	(15, 23)
Female depressed patients	12	67% ($<$0.001)	Briggs and Briggs (24)
Female and male unipolar and bipolar depressed patients	53	129% (F), 106% (M) ($p<$0.05)	Gershon and Jonas (personal communication)

were not explained by any differences in Km (Michaelis constant), pH optimum nor the presence of a dialyzable inhibitor.

In these studies, COMT measurements of several individuals over a 6-month period revealed consistent values that varied only 10% or less, suggesting that the enzyme activity represented a stable characteristic of the individual. COMT activity was also described as not affected by tricyclic antidepressants, phenothiazines, lithium carbonate, α-methyl-p-tyrosine, p-chlorophenylalanine, L-DOPA or electroconvulsive therapy. Recovery from depression or the development of mania was not associated with any change in enzyme activity, and patients with primary affective disorders from several different hospitals and from outpatient groups all showed similarly reduced COMT activity.

In a subsequent study by the same investigators (23), patients with primary affective disorders were subdivided into bipolar patients (with a history of mania and depression) and unipolar patients (depression only). Both groups had significantly reduced erythrocyte COMT levels; the enzyme activity in the unipolar patients was significantly less than that in the bipolar patients. Again, none of the male patients with affective disorders or antisocial personalities were different from the controls.

Briggs and Briggs (24) used the same assay for erythrocyte COMT and also found a similar magnitude of reduction in enzyme activity in 12 women with depression compared to 36 controls. COMT activity in depressed men was no different from that in the controls. However, women receiving oral contraceptives, oral estrogen, or oral progestogen and pregnant women were all found to have reduced COMT levels. Oral corticosteroids in women and oral androgen treatment in men had no effect on COMT activity.

In contrast to these two studies, Gershon and Jonas (19, and *personal communication*) recently studied 53 patients with primary affective disorders and found significantly increased erythrocyte COMT activity when both female and male patients were combined; the females had the greatest per cent difference from controls. There were no differences between unipolar and bipolar depressed patients. Also in contrast to the other studies, male controls had higher enzyme levels than did females. A different COMT assay from that used in the previously cited studies (15, 23, 24) was used in this investigation. Whether this difference in assay methods or a patient population difference is responsible for these discrepant results is not yet known.

COMT and Schizophrenia

Neither of the studies by the Dunner, Cohn, and Axelrod group (15,23) nor that by Briggs and Briggs (24) revealed any differences in erythrocyte COMT in schizophrenic patients of either sex compared to controls. Matthysse and Baldessarini (39), however, observed a somewhat elevated mean COMT activity level in 20 male chronic schizophrenic patients compared to controls, although the difference was not quite statistically significant ($0.05 < p < 0.10$) (Table 4).

TABLE 4. *Erythrocyte catechol-O-methyl-transferase (COMT) activity in schizophrenia*

Subjects	N	COMT activity (% of controls)	Reference
Chronic schizophrenia (male, female)	13, 5	108%, 107% (NS)	Cohn et al. (15); Dunner et al. (23)
Chronic schizophrenia (male)	20	130% ($<$ 0.1)	Matthysse and Baldessarini (39)
Schizophrenia (male, female)	11, 12	101%, 100% (NS)	Briggs and Briggs (24)

No association between COMT activity and drug treatment or age was observed in their patients.

COMT activity has recently been measured in autopsy brain samples from a small number of chronic schizophrenic patients and normal controls. Wise et al. (40) and Wyatt et al. (41) both found an approximate 30% reduction in COMT activity in the patients, although the difference from controls were not statistically significant except for one of the four brain areas studied by Wise et al. (40)—the diencephalon.

MONOAMINE OXIDASE ACTIVITY IN PATIENTS WITH AFFECTIVE DISORDERS

Human platelet monoamine oxidase is a mitochondrial enzyme that catalyses the oxidative deamination of many biogenic amines. It has many characteristics which differentiate it and other mitochondrial MAOs from the soluble MAO found in human plasma (2,42). Its substrate affinities and responses to inhibitors indicate that it is a "B" form of enzyme. In animals, most other tissues including brain and liver contain both "B and "A" forms of the enzyme (43,44), although problems related to the localization of the enzyme in the outer wall of mitochondria have made purification of the enzyme difficult, and it is incompletely characterized. In some studies, up to five different forms of the brain and liver enzyme have been identified by electrophoresis (45,46), although antibody studies revealed only two forms in beef brain (47).

Human platelet MAO is markedly inhibited by drugs used clinically as antidepressants, including tranylcypromine, isocarboxazid, phenelzine, and pargyline (48). As mentioned previously, the higher activity of platelet MAO and brain MAO in normal females and with increasing age has been suggested to be of possible relevance to the higher incidence of depression in females and in middle age (29). However, the one study of human brain samples obtained at autopsy which included individuals with affective disorders did not reveal any differences from controls in total MAO activity (49).

Platelet monoamine oxidase has been investigated in two groups of depressed patients. Preliminary data from a study of 202 depressed patients revealed that mean platelet MAO activity measured with benzylamine as the substrate was significantly higher than in normals at each decade (50) (Table 5). An estimation of a later graphical presentation of this data indicated that the patients averaged approximately 17% higher than the controls (51). This patient group was composed of both outpatients and inpatients, and included 26 bipolar depressed patients.

In our study of a selected population of patients hospitalized for primary affective disorders, no significant overall difference in platelet MAO activity measured using tryptamine as the substrate was found between 57 depressed patients and 52 controls (22). However, when patients were divided into unipolar and bipolar subtypes on the basis of the presence or absence of a history of mania severe enough to require hospitalization, the unipolar patients were found to have slightly, but nonsignificantly, increased MAO activity (11% over the mean of the controls). In contrast, the bipolar patients had significantly reduced platelet MAO activities in comparison to both the controls and the unipolar depressed patients (22).

Age or sex differences did not appear to contribute to the reduced platelet MAO activity observed in the bipolar patients. Although most individual patients had closely similar MAO activity values when studied at regular intervals over the period of hospitalization, a small number of patients (15 to 20%) had definite evidence of changes in MAO activity. These changes did not, however, correlate with either clinical improvement in depression or with the presence or absence of mania. The lack of change in relation to clinical state is clearly exemplified in the case of a recently studied patient who experienced 15 episodes of depression and mania with no change in MAO activity (Table 6). As expected (17), this patient did have regular elevations in CPK activity during her manic periods.

Other factors known to affect MAO activity were also studied in these patients with primary affective disorders. With the exception of the MAO-inhibiting antidepressent phenelzine, which markedly reduced platelet MAO levels (49,53),

TABLE 5. *Platelet monoamine oxidase (MAO) activity in the affective disorders*

Subjects	N	MAO activity (% of controls)	Reference
Depressed outpatients and inpatients (including 26 bipolar patients)	202	"Significantly higher than normals at each decade" (117% estimated)	Nies et al. (50, 51)
Unipolar depressed patients	34	111% (NS)	Murphy and Weiss (22)
Bipolar depressed patients	23	58% (<0.001)	(22)

TABLE 6. Blood enzyme measurements over an 18-month period in a bipolar patient with 40-day cycles of mania and depression[a]

Affective episode number	Platelet MAO (nM/mg protein/hr) (N = 25)[b]		Serum creatine phosphokinase (U/L) (N = 55)[c]	
	Depression	Mania	Depression	Mania
1	3.61 (3)	–	31 (3)	–
2	–	3.23 (2)	–	94 (3)
3	3.94 (2)	–	23 (4)	–
4	–	3.76 (2)	–	80 (3)
5	2.93 (1)	–	27 (8)	–
6	–	–	–	138 (2)
7	3.36 (2)	–	57 (8)	–
8	–	3.48 (2)	–	99 (3)
9	3.79 (2)	–	70 (2)	–
10	–	4.06 (1)	–	270 (2)
11	3.65 (2)	–	39 (3)	–
12	–	3.36 (2)	–	134 (2)
13	3.88 (2)	–	38 (6)	–
14	–	3.85 (2)	–	91 (3)
15	–	–	62 (2)	–
	3.59 ± 0.13	3.62 ± 0.14	43 ± 6	129 ± 25

[a] Numbers in parentheses are the samples evaluated during each affective episode.
[b] p = NS.
[c] p = 0.01.

other drugs including phenothiazines, lithium carbonate, L-DOPA and L-tryptophan had only slight and nonsignificant effects on the measured enzyme activity. Menstrual cycle changes were associated with a small but statistically significant decline in MAO activity during the postovulatory period which was of a similar magnitude to that observed in normal controls (33). Platelet counts, hematocrits, serum iron levels and plasma thyroxine and triidothyronine levels measured in the bipolar and unipolar patients were all within the normal control ranges.

Whether platelet MAO values may have predictive value in regard to the differential responsivity of bipolar versus unipolar patients to treatment with lithium carbonate (54, 55), L-DOPA (56) or L-tryptophan (56) is currently under study. One correlate of the unipolar–bipolar subgroup differentiation, cortical average evoked response (AER) differences (57), was demonstrated to correlate at a low but significant level ($r = -0.32$; $p < 0.05$) with platelet MAO activity in 63 patients with primary affective disorders (58). In this study, the 22 unipolar patients had the greatest individual differences in both MAO activity and AER slope and also demonstrated the highest MAO–AER correlation ($r = -0.60$, $p < 0.01$). Of additional interest is the possibility suggested by Buchsbaum (this volume) that the interrelationship between AER and MAO may be of use in patient subgroup identification.

CONCLUSION

Although some reports of altered cerebrospinal fluid or urinary levels of biogenic amine metabolites and of physiologic functions subserved by the biogenic amines, such as sleep, might be interpreted as congruent with some of the MAO and COMT blood enzyme findings, others are not, and it seems premature to attempt to cross-correlate these bodies of data until more complete studies of the enzyme activity findings are available. At present, the few studies of COMT and MAO available do not provide adequate confirmation of a general alteration in the activity of COMT in patients with affective disorder or schizophrenia, or MAO in patients with affective disorders, including affective disorder subtypes.

Whereas there are no specific COMT inhibitors that have been used clinically, it is of note that there are many behavioral and psychological consequences of treatment with drugs that are MAO inhibitors. These include both therapeutic effects in some individuals and adverse behavioral consequences in others—with some differences relatable to the different MAO inhibiting drugs used. Treatment with MAO inhibitors affects the function of the different central neurotransmitter amines by several mechanisms, some of which have been demonstrated to have behavioral correlates (59). More study is required on the clinical, biochemical, and animal behavioral levels, however, before further speculation is warranted on the relationships between measured blood enzyme levels and the clinical psychiatric disorders.

REFERENCES

1. Murphy, D. L. (1973): Technical strategies for the study of catecholamines in man. In: *Frontiers in Catecholamine Research,* edited by E. Usdin and S. Snyder, pp. 1077–1082. Pergamon, Oxford.
2. Murphy, D. L., and Donnelly, C. H. (1974): Monoamine oxidase in man: Enzyme characteristics in platelets, plasma and other human tissues. In: *Neuropsychopharmacology of Monoamines and Their Regulatory Enzymes,* edited by E. Usdin, pp. 71–85. Raven Press, New York.
3. Wyatt, R. J., Saavedra, J. M., and Axelrod, J. (1973): A dimethyltryptamine-forming enzyme in human blood. *Am. J. Psychiatry,* 130:754–760.
4. Barchas, J. D., Elliott, G. R., DoAmaral, J., Erdelyi, E., O'Connor, S., Bowden, M., Brodie, H. K. H., Berger, P. A., Renson, J., and Wyatt, R. J. (1974): Triptolines: Formation from tryptamines and 5-MTHF by human platelets. *Arch. Gen. Psychiatry,* 31:1:862–867.
5. Moskowitz, J., Harwood, J. P., Reid, W. D., and Krishna, G. (1971): The interaction of norepinephrine and prostaglandin E1 on the adenyl cyclase system of human and rabbit blood platelets. *Biochim. Biophys. Acta,* 230:279–285.
6. Murphy, D. L., Donnelly, C., and Moskowitz, J. (1973): Inhibition by lithium of prostaglandin E1 and norepinephrine effects on cyclic adenosine monophosphate production in human platelets. *Clin. Pharmacol. Ther.,* 14:810–814.
7. Wang, Y.-C., Pandey, G. N., Mendels, J., and Frazer, A., (1973): Effect of lithium on prostaglandin E1-stimulated adenylate cyclase activity of human platelets. *Biochem. Pharmacol.,* 23:845–855.
8. Wang, Y.-C., Pandey, G. N., Mendels, J., and Frazer, A. (1974): Platelet adenylate cyclase responses in depression: Implications for a receptor defect. *Psychopharmacologia,* 36:291–300.
9. Murphy, D. L., Donnelly, C. H., and Moskowitz, J. (1974): Catecholamine receptor function in depressed patients. *Am. J. Psychiatry,* 131:1389–1391.
10. Murphy, D. L., and Kopin, I. J. (1972): The transport of biogenic amines. In: *Metabolic Pathways, Vol. VI: Metabolic Transport,* edited by L. E. Hokin, pp. 503–542. Academic Press, New York.
11. Murphy, D. L., Colburn, R. W., Davis, J. M., and Bunney, W. E., Jr. (1970): Imipramine and

lithium effects on biogenic amine transport in depressed and manic-depressed patients. *Am. J. Psychiatry,* 127:339–345.

12. Skou, J. C. (1965): Enzymatic basis for active transport of Na+ and K+ across cell membrane. *Physiol. Rev.,* 45:596.

13. Hokin-Neaverson, M., Spiegel, D. A., and Lewis, W. C. (1974): Deficiency of erythrocyte sodium pump activity in bipolar manic-depressive psychosis. *Life Sci.,* 15:1739–1748.

14. Cho, H. W., and Meltzer, H. Y. (1974): Mg++-Dependent adenosine triphosphatase activity in erythrocyte ghosts of schizophrenic patients. *Biol. Psychiatry,* 9:109–116.

15. Cohn, C. K., Dunner, D. L., and Axelrod, J. (1970): Reduced Catechol-*O*-methyltransferase activity in red blood cells of women with primary affective disorder. *Science,* 170:1323–1324.

16. Nies, A., Robinson, D. S., Lamborn, K. R., and Lampert, R. P. (1973): Genetic control of platelet and plasma monoamine oxidase activity. *Arch. Gen. Psychiatry,* 28:834–838.

17. Lamprecht, F., Matta, R. J., Little, B., and Zahn, T. (1974): Plasma dopamine-beta-hydroxylase (DBH) activity during the menstrual cycle. *Psychosom. Med.,* 36(4):304–310.

18. Weinschilboum, R. N., Raymond, F. A., Elveback, L. R., and Weidman, W. H., (1973): Serum dopamine-B-hydroxylase activity: Sibling-sibling correlation. *Science,* 181:942.

19. Gershon, E. S., and Jonas, W. Z. (1975): A clinical and genetic study of erythrocyte catechol-*O*-methyl transferase activity in primary affective disorder. *(In press.)*

20. Wyatt, R. J., Murphy, D. L., Belmaker, R., Cohen, S., Donnelly, C. H., and Pollin, W. (1973): Reduced monoamine oxidase activity in platelets: A possible genetic marker for vulnerability to schizophrenia. *Science,* 179:916–918.

21. Robinson, D. S., Davis, J. M., Nies, A., Ravaris, C. L., and Sylwester, D. (1971): Relation of sex and aging to monoamine oxidase activity of human brain, plasma, and platelets. *Arch. Gen. Psychiatry,* 24:536–539.

22. Murphy, D. L., and Weiss, R. (1972): Reduced monoamine oxidase activity in blood platelets from bipolar depressed patients. *Am. J. Psychiatry,* 128:1351–1357.

23. Dunner, D. L., Cohn, C. K., Gershon, E. S., and Goodwin, F. K. (1971): Differential catechol-O-methyltransferase activity in unipolar and bipolar affective illness. *Arch. Gen. Psychiatry,* 25: 348–353.

24. Briggs, M. H., and Briggs, M. (1973): Hormonal influences on erythrocyte catechol-*O*-methyl transferase activity in humans. *Experientia,* 29:279–280.

25. Winokur, G., Clayton, P. J., Reich, T. (1969): *Manic-Depressive Illness.* Mosby, St. Louis, Missouri.

26. Rosenthal, D. (1970): *Genetic Theory and Abnormal Behavior.* McGraw-Hill, New York.

27. Perris, C. (1966): A study of bipolar (manic-depressive) and unipolar recurrent depressive psychoses. *Acta Psychiatr. Scand.* (Suppl.) 42:194.

28. Goldstein, M. (1973): Changes in human serum dopamine-B-hydroxylase in various physiological and pathological states. In: *Frontiers in Catecholamine Research,* edited by E. Usdin and S. Snyder, pp. 1109–1114. Pergamon, Oxford.

29. Robinson, D. S., Davis, J. M., Nies, A., Colburn, R. W., Davis, J. N., Bourne, H. R., Bunney, W. E., Shaw, S. M., and Coppen, A. J. (1972): Ageing monoamines, and monoamine-oxidase levels. *Lancet,* 1:290–291.

30. Angst. J. (1966): Zur Ätiologie und Nosologie endogener depressiver Psychosen. *Monogr. Neurol. Psychiatrie,* 11:1–118.

31. Winokur, G., Cadoret, R., Dorzab, J., and Baker, M. (1971): Depressive disease. *Arch. Gen. Psychiatry,* 24:135.

32. Belmaker, R. H., Murphy, D. L., Wyatt, R. J., and Loriaux, D. L. (1974): Human platelet monoamine oxidase changes during the menstrual cycle. *Arch. Gen. Psychiatry,* 31:553–556.

33. Lamprecht, F., Matta, R. J., Little, B., and Zahn, T. (1974): Plasma dopamine-beta-hydroxylase (DBH) activity during the menstrual cycle. *Psychosom. Med.,* 36(4):304–310.

34. Weinshilboum, R. M., Kvetnansky, R., Axelrod, J., and Kopin, I. J. (1971): Elevation of serum dopamine-B-hydroxylase activity with forced immobilization. *Nature (New Biol.),* 230:287–288.

35. Wooten, G. F., and Cardon, P. (1973): Plasma dopamine-B-hydroxylase activity. *Arch. Neurol.,* 28:103–106.

36. Planz, G., and Palm, D. (1973): Acute enhancement of dopamine-B-hydroxylase activity in human plasma after maximum work load. *Eur. J. Clin. Pharmacol.,* 5:255–258.

37. Baldessarini, R. J., and Bell, W. R. (1966): Methionine-activating enzyme and catechol-*O*-methyl transferase activity in normal and leukemic white blood cells. *Nature,* 209:78–79.

38. Axelrod, J., and Cohn, C. K. (1971): Methyltransferase enzymes in red blood cells. *J. Pharmacol. Exp. Ther.,* 176:650–654.

39. Matthysse, S., and Baldessarini, J. (1972): *S*-adenosylmethionine and catechol-*O*-methyltransferase in schizophrenia. *Am. J. Psychiatry,* 128:10.

40. Wise, C. D., Baden, M. M., and Stein, L. (1975): Postmorten measurement of enzymes in human brain: Evidence of a central noradrenergic deficit in schizophrenia. *J. Psychiat. Res.,* 11:185–198.

41. Wyatt, R. J., Erdelyi, E., Barkhas, J., and Schwartz, M. A. *(In preparation.)*

42. McEwen, C. M., Jr., (1972): The soluble monoamine oxidase of human plasma and sera. In: *Advances in Biochemical Psychopharmacology,* Vol. 5, edited by E. Costa and P. Greengard, pp. 151–165. Raven Press, New York.

43. Johnston, J. P. (1968): Some observations upon a new inhibitor of monoamine oxidase in brain tissue. *Biochem. Pharmacol.* 17:1285–1297.

44. Neff, N. Y., and Goridis, C. (1972): Neuronal monoamine oxidase: Specific enzyme types and their rates of formation. In: *Advances in Biochemical Psychopharmacology,* edited by E. Costa and P. Greengard, pp. 307-323. Raven Press, New York.

45. Youdim, M. B. H. (1972): Multiple forms of monoamine oxidase and their properties. In: *Advances in Biochemical Psychopharmacology,* Vol. 5, edited by E. Costa and P. Greengard. Raven Press, New York.

46. Sandler, M., and Youdim, M. B. H. (1972): Multiple forms of monoamine oxidase: Functional significance. *Pharmacol. Rev.* 24:331–348.

47. Hartman, B. K., and Udenfriend, S. (1972): The use of immunological techniques for the characterization of bovine monoamine oxidase from liver and brain. In: *Advances in Biochemical Psychopharmacology.* Vol. 5, edited by E. Costa and P. Greengard, pp. 119–128. Raven Press, New York.

48. Robinson, D. S., Lovenberg, W., Keiser, H., and Sjoerdsma, J. (1968): Effects of drugs on human blood platelet and plasma amine oxidase activity *in vitro* and *in vivo. Biochem. Pharmacol.,* 17:109–119.

49. Grote, S. S., Moses, S. G., Robins, E., Hudgens, R. W., and Croninger, A. B. (1974): A study of selected catecholamine metabolizing enzymes: A comparison of depressive suicides and alcoholic suicides with controls. *J. Neurochem.,* 23:791–802.

50. Nies, A., Robinson, D. S., Ravaris, C. L., and Davis, J. M. (1971): Amines and monoamine oxidase in relation to aging and depression in man. *Psychosom. Med.,* 33:470.

51. Nies, A., Robinson, D. S., Harris, L. S., and Lamborn, K. R. (1974): Comparison of monoamine oxidase substrate activities in twins, schizophrenics, depressives and controls. *Adv. Biochem. Psychopharmacol.,* 12:59–70.

52. Murphy, D. L., Brand, E., Baker, M., van Kammen, D., and Gordon, E. (1974): Phenelzine effects in hospitalized unipolar and bipolar depressed patients: Behavioral and biochemical relationships. *J. Pharmacologie (Suppl.),* 5:102–103.

53. Goodwin, F. K., Murphy, D. L., Dunner, D. L., and Bunney, W. E., Jr. (1972): Lithium response in unipolar versus bipolar depression. *Am. J. Psychiatry,* 129:44–47.

54. Prien, R. F., Klett, C. J., and Caffey, E. M., Jr. (1974): Lithium prophylaxis in recurrent affective illness. *Am. J. Psychiatry,* 131:2:198–203.

55. Murphy, D. L., Goodwin, F. K., Brodie, H. K. H., and Bunney, W. E., Jr., (1973): L-DOPA, dopamine, and hypomania. *Am. J. Psychiat.,* 130:79–82.

56. Murphy, D. L., Baker, M., Kotin, J., and Bunney, W. E., Jr. (1973): Behavioral and metabolic effects of L-tryptophan in unipolar depressed patient. In: *Serotonin and Behavior,* edited by I. J. Barchas and E. Usdin, pp. 529–537. Academic Press, New York.

57. Buchsbaum, M., Landau, D., Murphy, D. L., and Goodwin, F. (1973): Average evoked response in bipolar and unipolar affective disorders: Relationship to sex, age of onset, and monoamine oxidase. *Biol. Psychiatry,* 7:199–212.

58. Buchsbaum, M., Landau, S., Murphy, D., and Goodwin, F. (1973): Average evoked response in bipolar and unipolar affective disorders: Relationship to sex, age of onset, and monoamine oxidase. *Biol. Psychiatry,* 7:3:199–212.

59. Murphy, D. L., Belmaker, R., and Wyatt, R. J. (1975): Monoamine oxidase in schizophrenia and other behavioral disorders. *J. Psychiatr. Res.,* 11:221–248.

Biology of the Major Psychoses, edited by D. X. Freedman, *Res. Publ. Assoc. Res. Nerv. Ment. Dis.,* Vol. 54. Raven Press, New York © 1975.

Neurotransmitter-Related Enzymes in the Major Psychiatric Disorders: II. MAO and DBH in Schizophrenia

Richard J. Wyatt and Dennis L. Murphy

Laboratory of Clinical Psychopharmacology and Laboratory of Clinical Science, National Institute of Mental Health, Bethesda, Maryland 20014

This chapter surveys the information on several neurotransmitter-related enzymes of possible relevance to schizophrenia. The enzymes monoamine oxidase (MAO) and dopamine-B-hydroxylase (DBH) have attracted considerable attention in the last few years with significant findings being claimed for both.

MAO

The Platelet

Chronic Schizophrenics

Sixty-eight chronic schizophrenics (1) with evidence of illness for at least 2 years, hospitalization for at least 1 year, and evidence of thought disorder while in our care were studied for platelet MAO activity. Their mean ± SEM MAO activity was 2.86 ± 0.25, whereas the value for 181 normals (ages 18 to 40) was 5.24 ± 0.20 (Table 1). This difference was statistically significant ($p < .001$) using a two-tailed t-test. The mean for the 53 male chronic schizophrenics was 2.91 ± 0.30 whereas that for 79 normal males was 5.12 ± 0.32 ($p < .001$). The mean for the 15 female chronic schizophrenics was 2.72 ± 0.49, whereas that for 102 normals was 5.34 ± 0.26 ($p < .001$). To date we have not been able to find a systematic relationship between platelet MAO activity and length of illness, hospitalization, or chronic schizophrenic subtypes. Further investigations to determine whether psychosocial factors may be different in the normal and low platelet MAO schizophrenic patients are under way.

Acute versus Chronic Schizophrenics

To determine whether acute schizophrenics have a reduction in platelet MAO similar to that in the chronic schizophrenics, platelet MAO activity was studied in 27 acute undifferentiated schizophrenics who were free from all drugs for a period of at least 2 weeks. These patients were housed on a special research ward at the National Institute of Mental Health in Bethesda, supervised by Dr. William Carpenter et al. (2). The acute schizophrenics (ages 16 to 30) had a mean platelet

TABLE 1. *Mean MAO activity (in nanomoles) of tryptamine converted per milligram of platelet protein per hour*

Patient group	N	Mean
Normals	308	5.07
Unipolar	43	4.98
Bipolar I	34	3.61
Acute schizophrenics	27	5.48
Chronic schizophrenics	68	2.87

MAO activity of 5.4 ± 0.44, which was no different from that for 181 age-matched normals (5.24 ± 0.70). The 11 male acute patients had a mean of 4.56 ± 0.45, which was no different from that for 79 normal males (5.12 ± 0.30). The 16 female acute schizophrenics had a mean of 6.11 ± 0.64, which was no different from that of 102 normal females (5.34 ± 0.27). There did not appear to be any subgrouping differences amongst the acute schizophrenics. Carbon-14-tryptamine was used as the substrate for MAO in these studies of acute and chronic schizophrenics.

Confirmation

Meltzer and Stahl (3) using tryptamine and octopamine as substrates, studied 15 normal controls, 10 acute schizophrenics, and 12 chronic schizophrenics. They found low platelet MAO activity only in the chronic schizophrenics. However, using *m*-iodobenzylamine and tyramine, both the acute and chronic patients were found to have low platelet MAO activity. Our own studies using tyramine as a substrate in 10 chronic schizophrenic patients produced mean activities in picomoles per milligram protein per hour of 17.8 ± 1.95. The activity for 16 acute schizophrenics was 36.2 ± 3.86, whereas that for 19 normal controls was 37.5 ± 4.95. The difference between the chronic schizophrenics and controls was highly significant ($p < 0.01$).

Nies, Robinson, Harris, and Lamborn (4) reported on 12 schizophrenic subjects who had at least two unequivocal episodes of schizophrenic illness resulting in hospitalization for no longer than 4 months in any one year and had not been hospitalized for more than 1 year during the last 5 years. When not hospitalized the patients generally were able to go about their normal activities. These subjects might be called relapsing schizophrenics because at the time of the study they certainly had not demonstrated the chronic signs that our patients had. When platelet MAO activity was examined for these patients, using both benzylamine and tryptamine, it was found to be decreased.

Specificity with Regard to Other Illness

Acute schizophrenics and unipolar depressives do not differ in platelet MAO activity from normals. Chronic schizophrenics have mean platelet MAO activity

TABLE 2. *Percent of subjects studied with platelet MAO activities under two units*

Patient group	%
Normals	10
Unipolar	2
Bipolar I	20
Acute schizophrenics	0
Chronic schizophrenics	40

lower than these groups. Bipolar I[1] affective disorder patients were also lower than the other groups, but the difference was not as large as that for the chronic schizophrenics. If two MAO units are used as an arbitrary cutoff point, a point under which 40% ($\chi^2 = 33.46$; $df = 1$; $p > 0.001$) of the chronic schizophrenics fit, (Table 2), we find seven of 34 bipolar patients. This is about 20%, which is not significantly different from that for controls ($\chi^2 = 2.69$; $df = 1$; $p > 0.1$). There was no significant difference ($\chi^2 = 2.47$; $df = 1$; $p > 0.1$) between the chronic schizophrenics and the bipolar I patients. Therefore, even though the bipolar I patients have a mean MAO that is low (using the arbitrary cutoff of two MAO units), it is not yet clear whether they represent a separate group as far as platelet MAO activity is concerned.

Twins Discordant for Schizophrenia

To decrease the likelihood that the low platelet MAO activity seen in the chronic schizophrenics was caused by nongenetic as opposed to genetic factors, we studied monozygotic (Mz) twins discordant for schizophrenia (5). If the low platelet MAO activity resulted from some factor secondary to schizophrenia, low platelet MAO should only be present in the schizophrenic twin. Thirteen schizophrenic index twins, all of whom had been hospitalized at least once for schizophrenia and had been extensively studied by Dr. William Pollin and his associates, were examined along with their nonschizophrenic co-twins. At the time of the study, one patient resided within a hospital while 5 were in remission. Four of the patients had had acute forms of schizophrenia and six patients were not receiving any antipsychotic medication. The nonschizophrenic co-twins had never been hospitalized for a behavioral disorder and were functioning well within their families and communities, except for one individual with borderline psychosocial adjustment.

Only two twin pairs were living in the same household and nine of the co-twins were living in different cities. It was therefore necessary to obtain and prepare

---

[1] Bipolar depressed patients were differentiated from unipolar depressed patients on the basis of the occurrence of mania severe enough to require hospitalization or specific treatment in the bipolar patients.

the blood samples at various facilities throughout the country. Because of this, samples from normal controls were obtained at the same time as those from the twins. They were coded and shipped to the laboratory. All samples were batched together before assay. (In all studies samples are run in a manner so that their origins are unknown to all investigators until the final calculations are made.)

The MAO activity of the 23 normal controls was the same as that obtained for previous controls (6.4 ± 0.562).[2] The schizophrenic twins (3.9 ± 0.638; $p < 0.005$), and nonschizophrenic twins (4.7 ± 0.804; $p < 0.05$) were significantly lower than the normals, but there was no difference between the twin groups. There was a significant Pearson correlation ($r = 0.67$; $p < 0.01$) between the MAO activities in the schizophrenic and nonschizophrenic twins.

There were four pairs of twins whose MAO activities were below two units. The indexes of all four of these twin pairs were chronic schizophrenics, whereas the more acute patients had MAO activities closer to normal. The severity of impairment (based upon number and duration of hospitalizations) was rated on a five-point scale for the schizophrenic twins by an investigator with no knowledge of the platelet assay. A forced rank order was then made between the numerical ratings, with the highest number given to the patients who were most ill. Using this order, and comparing it to the MAO activities, a Spearman rank-order correlation of -0.54 ($p < 0.05$) was found.

Platelet MAO activity was also examined in nine Mz and 10 Dz normal twins (6). The intraclass correlation coefficient was 0.88 for the monozygotic and 0.45 for the dizygotic twins. The correlations were significantly different from one another (Mann-Whitney U test, $p < 0.001$). Same-sex siblings matched for age and sex were about the same as the dizygotic twins, whereas unrelated pairs were not significantly correlated with each other (6). These results are similar to those reported by Nies, Robinson, Lamborn, and Lampert (7) for normal Mz and Dz twins, who used benzylamine instead of tryptamine as a substrate.

Taken together these data indicate that platelet MAO activity is in a large part determined by genetic factors and that the low platelet MAO activity seen in the chronic schizophrenics is not secondary to being ill, but is genetically related to the liability to be schizophrenic.

The Brain

Brain MAO activity has been examined in six studies (8–13). Except for the first study (8) in which a small difference in MAO activity was found, these studies have failed to find a difference in brain enzyme activity between schizophrenics and controls in spite of the fact that MAO seems to be very stable in autopsied brains. Whereas normal MAO activity may represent the true state of affairs in the brain of chronic schizophrenics, it is recognized that glial cells

---

[2] Normal values have varied over the 4 years we have been performing these studies, with a general downward trend, related, in part, to some minor variations in assay procedures.

greatly outnumber neurons, and if a difference were to exist in neuronal MAO it would be washed out by normal glial MAO activity.

DBH

Stein and Wise (14) postulated that there might be a deficit in dopamine-B-hydroxylase (DBH), the enzyme that converts dopamine to norepinephrine, in schizophrenic patients. Several studies (15–17) prior to and following the promulgation of this hypothesis demonstrated that plasma DBH activity of schizophrenics was no different than that for normal controls or patients with affective disorders, and what evidence there is suggests that the enzymes in the plasma and brain are the same (18). The plasma enzyme has been shown to be under considerable genetic control (19,20) in normals and Mz twins discordant for schizophrenia, and although under certain circumstances [such as exercise or stress (21)] DBH activity may be greatly altered, resting plasma enzyme activities seem to represent the genotype.

In spite of this, Wise et al. (11) tested their hypothesis by collecting the brains of 18 chronic schizophrenics who had died in a state hospital and 12 persons without a history of psychiatric illness who had died suddenly as a result of a heart attack or accident. The schizophrenics had decreased DBH activity ranging from 49% in the hippocampus, 58% in the diencephalon, and 70% in pons-medulla. All of these differences were statistically significant at $p < 0.05$. Because of these dramatic differences in the predicted direction, Wise et al. (11) made a number of attempts to control for artifacts. After considering all of these sources of artifacts, the significant differences between schizophrenic and normal DBH activity remained.

In an attempt to replicate their study (22) we obtained specimens of autopsied brains from five chronic schizophrenic patients with the aid of the neuropathologist at St. Elizabeth's Hospital, Washington, D.C. Brain specimens from four chronic schizophrenics and nine controls were obtained by a similar arrangement with the D.C. Medical Examiners Office. Information about the subjects was obtained by interviewing with family members, and by consulting hospital and police records. The control brains were obtained from persons without evidence of a psychiatric history, although one was from an individual with a police record and two were from heavy drinkers. The schizophrenics (seven males; two females) had a mean age of 49.2 ± 6.3. Four died suddenly after traumatic suicides (in our experience suicide is common among chronic schizophrenics), three from cardiac arrests, one from pulmonary aspiration, and one suddenly from pulmonary edema. The controls (all male) had a mean age of 42.3 ± 4.5. Six died suddenly of trauma and three of cardiac arrests.

The periaqueductal pons–mesencephalon, hypothalamus, and hippocampus were removed at autopsy and immediately placed on dry ice and subsequently stored at $-80°C$ for up to 1 year. Wise et al. (11) found DBH activity stable for 1 year at $-15°C$. There was no difference in mean storage time for the schizo-

TABLE 3. *DBH activity in postmortem specimens from nine schizophrenic patients and nine controls[a]*

Region	Control		Schizophrenic activity
	Activity	Activity (minus long D to M subject)	
Pons–mesencephalon	77.3 ± 19.5	84.8 ± 20.4	65.0 ± 14.3
Hypothalamus	140.8 ± 26.8	152.4 ± 7.4	123.4 ± 23.5
Hippocampus	38.8 ± 2.72	41.2 ± 2.66	35.5 ± 2.31

[a] Enzyme activity is expressed as nanomoles of octopamine formed per gram of tissue per hour. Values are expressed as means ± SEM. Because one of the controls (who had the lowest DBH activity) also had the longest (27 hr) death to morgue time, control means and *t*-tests are reported with and without this value.

phrenics and controls. All DBH assays were performed by a staff member who was unaware of whether the samples were from schizophrenics or controls.

There was no significant difference in DBH activity in any area between the two groups (Table 3). Although the differences were not statistically different, the DBH activity mean for the schizophrenic groups ranged between 77 and 89% of controls. Although seven of nine of our patients were taking phenothiazines at the time of death, Wise et al. (11) indicate that this is probably not a cause of their DBH differences. Rats who had been given chlorpromazine (20 mg/kg/24 hr) for 12 weeks had a small increase in DBH activity. Although the patients in our study were taking a number of non-neuroleptic drugs, there were significant ($p < 0.05$) negative correlations between the daily dosage of chlorpromazine or chlorpromazine equivalent and the DBH activity in the hypothalamus ($r = -0.60$) and pons ($r = -0.65$). This could mean that in the brains of schizophrenics, neuroleptics do decrease DBH activity, or possibly that there is a negative correlation between clinical pathology (as determined by the need for higher drug dosages) and DBH activity.

Wise et al. (11) also attempted to determine the effects of postmortem intervals on brain DBH activity (after a person dies, it may take several hours for that person to reach the morgue). Simulating this situation rats that were killed and allowed to remain 3 hr at room temperature prior to assay had DBH activity reduced by 27%. In a similar experiment performed in our laboratory over a 6-hr period there was a 15% decrease in activity. Because Wise et al. (11) human brain postmortem intervals were "several hours" and ours a mean of 4.2 for the controls and 3.0 hr for the schizophrenics, this does not appear to be an important factor, except possibly for one control who was not brought to the morgue for 27 hr. As he had the lowest DBH activity of any of the subjects, the DBH activities were examined for the controls with and without this subject's values. The exclusion of this value did not change the failure to reach statistical significance. Two subjects with death-to-morgue times (D to M) of 7 and 11 hr had DBH activities above their group means. One subject with a 3.5-hr time lag was low. All other subjects had intervals of about 1 hr.

Wise et al. (11) also compared the effects on brain DBH activity of the time from which the subject reached the morgue to the time of autopsy. They did this by storage of rat brains at 4°C for up to 3 days and found a decrease in DBH activity of 18%. Their subjects' brains, however, ranged from 1 day to 8 days at this temperature. Because of this, they matched time intervals for controls and schizophrenics and still found the DBH activity of the schizophrenics lower. Our controls were in the morgue for a mean of 9.7 ± 1.9 hr, while the patients were there for 35.6 ± 7.9 hr, which is statistically significant ($t = 2.73$; $p < 0.02$). Furthermore, there are significant negative correlations between time in the morgue to autopsy and DBH activity in the hippocampus ($r = -0.53$; $p < 0.05$) and hypothalamus ($r = -0.49$; $p < 0.05$), whereas that for the pons ($r = -0.46$) was not significant. This suggests that the uneven distribution between the two groups in morgue time may be responsible for the small nonsignificant differences in DBH activity in our samples. As the Wise, Baden, and Stein brains came from two sources, it is possible that some of their group differences may have resulted from different storage techniques.

CONCLUSION

Mindful of the many sources of error discussed in the companion to this chapter, there seems to be little doubt that platelet MAO activity as currently measured is low in some chronic schizophrenic patients, although it appears to be normal in the autopsied brains of chronic schizophrenics. What is more, platelet MAO activity seems to be under genetic control in normals as well as the schizophrenics, suggesting that the MAO deficits we are seeing may not be caused by something associated with the disease state such as chronic usage of neuroleptic drugs. Many efforts, however, in our laboratory and others are rigorously attempting to rule out such sources of artifact. It is therefore premature to draw any conclusions regarding low platelet MAO and chronic schizophrenia or to spend much time postulating a relationship to the cause of the disease.

With regard to DBH two studies have now found low DBH in the autopsied brains of schizophrenics. The first study found very large statistically significant decreases, and the second study found small statistically nonsignificant decreases, which possibly could be explained by drugs and differential autolysis. Further studies are necessary to explain the reason for the apparently discrepant results.

REFERENCES

1. Wyatt, R. J., Belmaker, R., and Murphy, D. (1975): Low platelet monoamine oxidase and vulnerability to schizophrenia. *Neuropsychopharmacologia. (In press.)*
2. Carpenter, W. T., Jr., Murphy, D. L., and Wyatt, R. J. (1975): Platelet monoamine oxidase activity in acute schizophrenics. *Am. J. Psychiatry. (In press.)*
3. Meltzer, H. Y., and Stahl, S. M. (1974): Platelet monoamine oxidase activity and substrate preferences in schizophrenic patients. *Res. Common Chem. Pathol. Pharmacol.,* 7:419–431.

4. Nies, A., Robinson, D. S., Harris, L. S., and Lamborn, K. R. (1974): Comparison of monoamine oxidase substrate activities in twins, schizophrenics, depressives, and controls. In: *Neuropsychopharmacology of Monoamines and Their Regulatory Enzymes,* edited by E. Usdin. Raven Press, New York.

5. Wyatt, R. J., Murphy, D. L., Belmaker, R., Cohen, S., Donnelly, C. H., and Pollin, W. (1973): Reduced monoamine oxidase in platelets: A possible marker for vulnerability to schizophrenia. *Science,* 179:916–918.

6. Murphy, D. L., Belmaker, R., and Wyatt, R. J. (1974): Monoamine oxidase in schizophrenia. *J. Psychiatr. Res.,* 11:221–247.

7. Nies, A., Robinson, D. S., Lamborn, K. R., and Lampert, R. P. (1973): Genetic control of platelet and plasma monoamine oxidase activity. *Arch. Gen. Psychiatry,* 28:834–838.

8. Birkhäuser, V. H. (1940): Cholinesterase und mono-aminoxydase im zentralen nervensystem. *Schweiz. Med. Wochenschr.,* 22:750–752.

9. Utena, H., Kanamura, H., Suda, S., Nakamura, R., Machiyama, Y., and Takahashi, R. (1968): Studies on the regional distribution of the monoamine oxidase activity in the brains of schizophrenic patients. *Proc. Jap. Acad.,* 44:1078–1083.

10. Domino, E. F., Krause, R. R., and Bowers, J. (1973): Various enzymes involved with putative transmitters. *Arch. Gen. Psychiatry,* 29:195–201.

11. Wise, C. D., Baden, M. H., and Stein, L. (1974): Postmortem measurements of enzymes in human brain: Evidence of a central noradrenergic deficit in schizophrenia. *J. Psychiatr. Res.,* 11:185–198.

12. Schwartz, M., Aikens, A. M., and Wyatt, R. J. (1974): Monoamine oxidase in brains from schizophrenic and mentally normal individuals. *Psychopharmacologia,* 38:319–328.

13. Schwartz, M. A., Wyatt, R. J., Yang, H. Y. T., and Neff, N. (1974): Multiple forms of monoamine oxidase in brain: A comparison of enzymatic activity in mentally normal and chronic schizophrenic individuals. *Arch. Gen. Psychiatry,* 31:557–560.

14. Stein, L., and Wise, C. D. (1971): Possible etiology of schizophrenia: Progressive damage to the noradrenergic reward system by 6-hydroxydopamine. *Science,* 171:1032–1036.

15. Dunner, D. L., Cohn, C. K., Weinshilboum, R. M., and Wyatt, R. J. (1973): The activity of dopamine-beta-hydroxylase and methionine activating enzymes in blood of schizophrenic patients. *Biol. Psychiatry,* 6:215–220.

16. Wetterberg, L., Åberg, H., Ross, S. B., and Fröden, Ö. (1972): Plasma dopamine-B-hydroxylase activity in hypertension and various neuropsychiatric disorders. *Scand. J. Clin. Lab. Invest.,* 30:283–289.

17. Shopsin, B., Freedman, L. S., Goldstein, M., and Gershon, S. (1972): Serum dopamine-B-hydroxylase (DBH) in affective states. *Psychopharmacologia,* 27:11–16.

18. Goldstein, M., Freedman, L. S., Ebstein, R. P., Park, D. H., and Kashimoto, T. (1974): Human serum dopamine-B-hydroxylase: Relationship to sympathetic activity in physiological and pathological states. In: *Neuropsychopharmacology of Monoamines and Their Regulatory Systems,* edited by E. Usdin. Raven Press, New York.

19. Lamprecht, F., Wyatt, R. J., Belmaker, R., Murphy, D. L., and Pollin, W. (1973): Plasma dopamine beta hydroxylase in identical twins discordant for schizophrenia. In: *Frontiers in Catecholamine Research,* edited by E. Usdin and S. H. Snyder. Pergamon, New York.

20. Weinschilboum, R. N., Raymond, F. A., Elveback, L. R., and Weidman, W. H. (1973): Serum dopamine-B-hydroxylase activity: Sibling–sibling correlation. *Science,* 181:943–945.

21. Wooten, F. G., and Cardon, P. V. (1973): Plasma dopamine-B-hydroxylase activity: Elevation in man during cold pressor test and exercise. *Arch. Neurol.,* 28:103–110.

22. Wyatt, R. J., Schwartz, M. A., Erdelyi, E., and Barchas, J. (1975): Normal dopamine-beta-hydroxylase activity in the brains of chronic schizophrenic patients. *Science.,* 187:368–370.

23. Wise, D. C., and Stein, L. (1975): Dopamine-β-hydroxylase activity in the brains of chronic schizophrenic patients. Reply to Wyatt, Schwartz, Erdelyi, and Barchas. *Science. (In press.)*

Discussion

Iversen: I was very interested in what Dr. Wyatt said about measurements of the dopamine-sensitive adenylate cyclase system in postmortem brain material. Could I ask exactly how this is done?

We have done some preliminary work in this direction which shows that you can indeed demonstrate this system to exist in postmortem human material from caudate putaman; Greengard and his colleagues have also indicated that this is possible. But may I ask how many patients you looked at? Was the tissue fresh or frozen?

Wyatt: You've obviously caught us in a problem. From rat brain experiments we believe there is a postmortem drop-off of dopamine-sensitive adenylate cyclase activity of about two-thirds. The human caudate activity is about one-third of the fresh rat activity, which is consistent with this notion.

There is one interesting thing. We've just completed these data and there is an inverse correlation in the schizophrenic brains. They're small numbers—we're dealing with a total of only 14 brains.

There is a fairly high inverse correlation between the baseline activity and the ability to stimulate the brains. And we partial out for the amount of drug that we think was present in the people—that correlation drops just very slightly. But because we're using a partial statistic, a statistic that partials out for that, we lose our significance. So where we have a significance of correlation it's around 0.85, which, when we partial out it comes down to 0.79. But just because of our losses of degrees of freedom we lose our significance.

Really what we're saying is it is probably an inadequate study and needs to be repeated with a larger sample. I don't know that we could get fresher material though.

Friedhoff: Dr. Wyatt, the data you have on identical twins are certainly convincing. There is strongly convincing evidence that there is—that MAO is under genetic control. But I wonder if this completely rules out the possibility that the low MAO in schizophrenics might not be drug-related. And the reason I say this is that presuming that there is—that twins, schizophrenic twins, that have low MAO will have a co-twin who has low MAO; it follows that if the administration of phenothiazines over a long period of time produced a further decrement in the MAO level, you wouldn't substantially disrupt the correlation between the two twins or between patients who are getting phenothiazine.

And I think you, yourself, suggest the possible mechanism by which drugs might produce that decrement in MAO; that is, phenothiazines and other antipsychotic drugs have very potent hormonal effects. And when they're administered over a number of years, these affects might well persist and continue to affect the MAO level. Could you comment on that?

Wyatt: I certainly think that a part of the deficit that we are seeing could be the result of the drugs. To date, however, we have no evidence for this and what evidence there is suggests that this is not the case. But it's impossible for me to explain the four co-twins who are clearly not schizophrenic, who never received drugs, who had exactly the same mean level. And with that correlation, you just can't explain that on the basis of drugs. It's conceivable that we have picked out somehow from the population those who have low MAO and just happen to be schizophrenic. But I think that's a very unlikely statistical basis, and I don't think that explains the data.

Biology of the Major Psychoses, edited by D. X.
Freedman, Res. Publ. Assoc. Res. Nerv. Ment.
Dis., Vol. 54. Raven Press, New York   1975

Studies of Amine Metabolites in Affective Illness and in Schizophrenia: A Comparative Analysis

Frederick K. Goodwin and Robert M. Post

Section on Psychiatry, LCS/NIMH, Bethesda, Maryland 20014 and Section on
Psychobiology, Adult Psychiatry Branch, National Institute of Mental Health,
Bethesda, Maryland 20014

The purpose of this chapter is to review the major studies of amine metabolites in affective illness and schizophrenia, including the effects of various pharmacologic treatments on these metabolites. A large body of evidence from animal studies indicates that the biogenic amines, norepinephrine, dopamine, and serotonin act as CNS neurotransmitters, particularly in critical integrative neuropathways. Hypotheses that functional abnormalities in one or more of these neurotransmitter amines may be involved in human psychiatric states have been based largely on indirect evidence from pharmacologic studies in animals (1–4). For example, drugs that increase the functional levels of biogenic amines in the brain of experimental animals can alleviate some depressions in man, while many drugs that block central dopamine receptors have potent tranquilizing properties, and are quite useful in the treatment of the acute psychoses of mania and of schizophrenia (5). Because of problems inherent in the interpretation of indirect data from animal studies, several groups have attempted to more directly evaluate central amine function in psychiatric patients by measuring levels of amine metabolites in available tissues or body fluids. This chapter reviews these efforts, focusing on important methodologic and conceptual issues in this rapidly advancing field.

The report of "abnormal" metabolites in bodily fluids particularly in schizophrenic patients constitute a special topic area that is not covered here; the reader reader is referred to recent critical reviews on this subject (3,6,7). In the discussion of urinary amine metabolites we have left out a large number of earlier studies, either because the questionable specificity of the assays or because the reports concern metabolites now known to originate exclusively or predominantly from peripheral sources.

STUDIES OF AMINE METABOLITES IN HUMAN BRAIN TISSUE

The most direct attempts to evaluate the hypothesis of altered amine function in the mental illnesses have involved the use of autopsy material for the measurement of amines of their metabolites in postmortem brain specimens from mental patients as compared to various control groups (8–13). Virtually all of the studies in this area have concerned suicide victims and are outlined in Table 1. Although

TABLE 1. *Amines and metabolites in the brains of suicide victims[a]*

Study	Brain areas	Finding
Shaw et al. (8)	Lower brainstem	5-HT *low*
Bourne et al. (9)	Lower brainstem	5-HT normal
		5-HIAA *low*
		NE normal
Pare et al. (10)	Lower brainstem	5-HT *low*
		NE normal
		DA normal
Lloyd et al. (11)	Various brain regions including six raphe nuclei	5-HT *Low* in Nuc-dorsalis⎫ Raphe Cent-inferior⎭
Gottfries et al. (12)	Various brain areas	5-HT normal
		5-HIAA normal
		NE normal

[a] 5-HT = 5-Hydroxytryptamine (serotonin); 5-HIAA = 5-hydroxyindoleacetic acid; NE = norepinephrine; and DA = dopamine.

this approach has the advantage of directness, and in some cases, even regional localization, the methodologic problems (as reviewed elsewhere in this volume by Wyatt and Murphy) are considerable, and ultimately limit the interpretability of these kinds of data. Nevertheless, Table 1 shows that in spite of the limitations, there is a pattern of findings clustering around some deficiency in serotonin or its metabolite in brains taken from suicide victims compared to various control groups. However, because these studies present very little data on other amines or metabolites, the question of whether the decreased serotonin or 5-hydroxyindoleacetic acid (5-HIAA) has any specific meaning is still very much open.

To our knowledge the only available data concerning biogenic amines in autopsy material from schizophrenics exist in an unpublished study (13) in which a nonsignificant trend toward lower levels of norepinephrine was noted in the diencephalon of the schizophrenics as compared to the controls with no differences in serotonin; however, the investigators are very cautious about the interpretation of these data because of the very long storage time of the frozen samples. A recent autopsy study involving four chronic schizophrenics (14), using specific histofluorescent staining techniques (15), found no difference between the patients and controls in the intensity of catecholamine staining (predominantly norepinephrine) in slices for various brain regions. Although these results are only semiquantitative, the authors conclude that no substantial differences in numbers of viable noradrenergic nerve endings exist between the patients and the controls.

STUDIES OF URINARY AMINE METABOLITES

General Methodologic Issues

5-Hydroxyindoleacetic acid (5-HIAA) is the major metabolite of serotonin, both centrally and peripherally (16); however, brain serotonin metabolism cannot be studied in the urine because of the very large peripheral contribution to urinary 5-HIAA. Dopamine is metabolized principally to 3-*methoxy*-4-hydroxyphenyla-cetic (HVA), and to a lesser extent, to dihydroxyphenylacetic acid (DOPAC) (17). The question as to what proportion of urinary dopamine metabolites origi-nate in brain is unsettled; however, in parkinsonism, a disease in which dopamine deficiency is known to exist centrally, urinary HVA has been reported as not different from controls (18–21). For this reason alone, and until further informa-tion is available, one is skeptical about the use of urinary HVA as a reflection of brain dopamine metabolism in man.

On the other hand, studies of norepinephrine metabolites in the urine offer considerable promise, although the urinary amine itself (as with serotonin and dopamine) is of peripheral origin. The major metabolites of norepinephrine in the urine are 3-*methoxy*-4-hydroxymandelic acid (VMA) and 3-*methoxy*-4-hy-droxyphenylglycol (MHPG) (22). Attempts to evaluate the relative peripheral versus central origins of these metabolites have varied in their approach. Enzyme studies in animal species indicate that aldehyde reductase predominates over aldehyde dehydrogenase in the brain, whereas the converse is true in peripheral tissues (23). From these data it would be expected that the aldehydes of norepi-nephrine follow a predominately reductive pathway (to the glycol) in the central nervous system and an oxidative pathway (to the acid) in peripheral tissues. Several studies in different species have provided data that suggest that from 25 to 60% of the urinary MHPG has its origins in the metabolism of norepinephrine in the brain (24–26). Recent work from this laboratory (27) using [C^{14}] dopamine infusions in patients and in normal controls suggest that the majority of urinary MHPG in man has its origins in brain pools of norepinephrine, whereas virtually all of the urinary VMA results from metabolism of peripheral norepinephrine.

Studies of Urinary MHPG in Affective Illness

It has been reported that daily excretion of urinary MHPG is low in patients with endogenous depressions as compared to controls (28), that urinary MHPG levels in depressed patients increase after recovery (29), and that MHPG excre-tion is higher in patients in the manic phase than in the same or other patients in the depressed phase of bipolar affective illness (29–31). In recent longitudinal studies of two regularly cycling manic depressive patients (32–33) we have con-firmed these earlier reports that urinary MHPG is significantly elevated in the manic compared to the depressed phase. However, a significant increase in MHPG *prior to* the switch into mania, as reported by Jones et al. (31), was not found.

Figure 1 illustrates the overall results of the recent NIMH studies of urinary MHPG in a large group of hospitalized depressed patients compared to normal controls (34). All patients met the criteria for major primary, affective disorder as described by the research diagnostic criteria of Feighner et al. (35) as revised by Spitzer et al. (36). In addition, five patients who met the research diagnostic criteria for schizoaffective-depressed were included. The depressed patients were

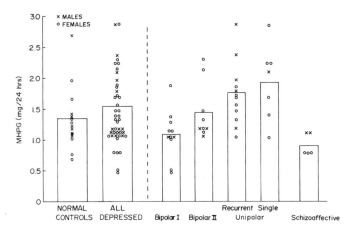

FIG. 1. Urinary MHPG in subgroups of depressed patients and controls. Significant differences between subgroups are as follows: (1) Bipolar I versus controls ($p < 0.05$); (2) Unipolar (single episode) versus controls ($p < 0.05$); (3) Schizoaffective versus controls ($p < 0.01$); (4) Unipolar (single + recurrent) versus bipolar I ($p < 0.001$); (5) Schizoaffective versus unipolar (single + recurrent) ($p < 0.001$); (6) Bipolar II versus unipolar (single + recurrent) ($p < 0.01$, males only).

further subdivided according to whether they had a prior history of hospitalization or definitive treatment for mania (bipolar I) or depressions interspersed with some definitive hypomania (bipolar II), or a history of depressions with neither mania nor hypomania (unipolar); our criteria for these designations are described in more detail elsewhere (37). The age of the NIMH patient group ranged from 22 to 72 with a mean of 46.4. At the time of the study the depressed patients evidence moderate to severe symptoms, including psychomotor retardation, or agitation, or both, depressed mood, anorexia, weight loss, sleep disturbance, and depressive thought content including, at times, depressive delusions. Age and sex-matched healthy, normal volunteers were selected on the basis of absence of any history of psychiatric or medical illness as determined by a full psychiatric and medical workup, and were admitted to the unit. Dietary, activity, and drug controls are as described below for the CSF studies. Details of our urine collection system have been described elsewhere (38).

Overall, the urinary excretion of MHPG was not significantly different in the total group of depressed patients compared to the normal controls, nor was there any difference between the depressed patients and the normal controls when the males and females were examined separately. However, when the depressed patients were subdivided according to the unipolar–bipolar dichotomy, it can be noted from the figure that the bipolar I group excreted about 30% less MHPG than the controls. The small group of schizoaffective depressed patients had the lowest mean MHPG excretion. Within the depressed population, clear unipolar–bipolar differences in urinary MHPG excretion are apparent, as summarized in the legend to the figure. Although within the overall depressed group modest correlations were noted between urinary MHPG and global ratings of anxiety, factoring out the anxiety contribution to the MHPG data by a discriminant function analysis did not alter the supgroup differences noted above.

The NIMH data appear to be similar to the recent findings of Maas et al. (39) who noted among a group of 32 hospitalized depressed females a subgroup of five bipolar patients who had urinary MHPG excretion levels significantly lower than controls, whereas those classified as unipolar did not. However, Maas's subsequent analyses, removing 11 patients from the unipolar group because they did not fit stringent criteria for primary affective disorder, reduced the unipolar–bipolar differences. Schildkraut et al. (40) reported that patients with "manic-depressive" depressions had significantly lower urinary MHPG than patients with "chronic characterologic depressions." The relationship of this finding to the unipolar–bipolar distinction is unclear at present. It should be noted that the majority of the NIMH unipolar patients had recurrent rather than chronic depressions, and characteristically the depressions were more "endogenous" than "characterologic"; however, the mean MHPG excretion for our bipolar I group was very close to that reported by Schildkraut et al. for manic-depressive illness, and to the five bipolar depressions reported by Maas et al. (39). All three studies essentially agree about MHPG excretion in the bipolar group—a situation not unrelated to the fact that clinically this is the most definable form of major affective disorder. Unfortunately, in both the study of Maas et al. and the NIMH study the research diagnostic criteria for primary affective disorder were applied retrospectively using recorded material in the chart.

Interpretations about mania and depression based on urinary MHPG data must be made with caution not only because of questions about relative contribution from brain versus periphery, but also because of evidence suggesting that non-specific factors such as physical activity (41) and stress (42) can alter the urinary excretion of this metabolite in depressed patients. In this regard it should be noted that we found no significant correlation between MHPG excretion and ratings of agitation, or retardation, or both, in agreement with the observations of Schildkraut (43) and of Maas et al. (39). However, the known difficulty in the assessment of these behavioral phenomena, and the previously mentioned activity data (41) suggest that the possible contribution of psychomotor activity state to urinary MHPG in affective disorder is still an open question.

To our knowledge there are no comprehensive studies of urinary MHPG in schizophrenic syndromes.

STUDIES OF CEREBROSPINAL FLUID AMINE METABOLITES

General Methodologic Considerations

Studies of the cerebrospinal fluid (CSF) have represented a major avenue for direct investigation of the hypothesized dysfunctions in amine systems in various mental illnesses. Before reviewing the results of these studies, we should discuss some of the general potentials and limitations of these approaches. First, it should be asked what is the evidence that 5-HIAA, HVA, and MHPG do in fact represent the major CSF metabolites of brain serotonin, dopamine, and norepinephrine, respectively. In the case of serotonin, there is clear evidence that 5-HIAA is by far the major metabolite, as noted previously. The question is somewhat less clear for dopamine; in addition to HVA, DOPAC may be an important CSF metabolite of dopamine; for example, it has been suggested that under certain circumstances DOPAC may provide a better reflection of the firing rate of dopamine neurons than HVA (44). Recent advances in the development of mass spectroscopy now make it possible to simultaneously study DOPAC and HVA in human CSF and studies of this metabolite are underway in our lab and elsewhere (45). MHPG has been found to be the major metabolite of norepinephrine in brain in a variety of animal species (24,25,46–49); this is also apparently true for man as well, as recent studies from this laboratory indicate that in CSF the concentration of MHPG is approximately 10 times that of VMA (50).

A basic question concerns the relative proportions of brain amine metabolites which are removed by the CSF system in comparison with the amounts removed directly into the blood. With regard to serotonin metabolism, there are ample data to suggest that a substantial portion of the 5-HIAA never enters the CSF and is removed directly via the blood (51); nevertheless, the periventricular location of some important serotonin nuclei and terminals, such as the median raphe nuclei and hypothalamus, suggests that they may be more substantially reflected in CSF than the whole-brain studies indicate. To our knowledge, no data are available that bear directly on the question of non-CSF routes for removal of either HVA or MHPG from the brain.

Even though the CSF may account for only a portion of the amine metabolites found in brain tissue it has been demonstrated by a variety of techniques that changes in amine metabolism in the brain are reliably reflected in parallel changes in CSF metabolites; these studies are outlined in Table 2. A further methodologic question in the interpretation of human CSF data is to what extent the lumbar CSF reflects the ventricular CSF; particularly, what is the proportion of the amine metabolites contributed by the spinal cord itself? Table 3 reviews the information relevant to this question, which has been reviewed in detail elsewhere (57). It

TABLE 2. *CSF Amine metabolites as a reflection of brain amines*

1. Does 5-HIAA in CSF reflect brain serotonin metabolism?
   a. 5-HIAA ↓ in cisternal CSF following raphe lesions (52)
   b. 5-HIAA ↑ in cisternal CSF following raphe stimulation (53)
   c. Drug-induced changes in cisternal 5-HIAA parallel 5-HIAA changes in brain tissue (54)
   d. 10 to 15% of total brain 5-HIAA removed by CSF (51)

2 Does HVA in CSF reflect brain dopamine metabolism?
   a. ↓ cisternal HVA following striatal lesions (55)
   b. ↑ cisternal HVA following striatal stimulation (56)
   c. Drug-induced changes in cisternal HVA parallel HVA changes in brain tissue (54)
   d. Some dopamine metabolized to DOPAC?

TABLE 3. *Studies on the relationship between ventricular and lumbar CSF*

---

1. Does 5-HIAA in lumbar CSF reflect ventricular 5-HIAA?
   a. Serotonin neurons present in spinal cord
   b. ↓ Lumbar 5-HIAA with spinal fluid block (58) or clinical lesion in brain stem (59)
   c. 4-hr lag in lumbar 5-HIAA ↑ following tryptophan infusion (60) or probenecid (61)
   d. 25 to 40% estimate of cord contribution based on HVA–5-HIAA gradient differences (62)
   e. 50% cord contribution to lumbar 5-HIAA in cats, estimated from isotope infusion data (63)
   f. 5-HIAA in lumbar CSF lower in noncommunicating compared to communicating hydrocephalus (64)

2. Does HVA in lumbar CSF reflect ventricular HVA?
   a. Little or no dopamine in spinal cord (65)
   b. Virtual absence of lumbar HVA with spinal fluid block (58,66)

3. Does MHPG in lumbar CSF reflect ventricular MHPG?
   a. NE neurons present in cord (67)
   b. No ventricular–lumbar gradient for MHPG (68)

---

would seem reasonable to conclude from these studies that for HVA there is little or no contribution from the cord, whereas 50% or more of the 5-HIAA under baseline conditions may represent cord contribution; for MHPG there is clearly a contribution from the cord (66), although the central proportions cannot be estimated at this time. Moreover the lack of a rostral–caudal gradient for MHPG suggests that the CSF may not act like a "sink" for this metabolite as it does for 5-HIAA and HVA.

A recent and particularly fruitful elaboration of the CSF technology has involved the development of the probenecid technique. The rationale for this technique, which by measuring a dynamic event ("turnover") provides a more valid assessment of central amine function that baseline metabolite levels alone, is based on the observation that probenecid can inhibit the transport systems responsible for the removal of 5-HIAA and HVA (54). Thus in animal studies the rate of metabolite accumulation in brain or CSF following probenecid is proportional to the turnover rate of the parent amine as measured directly (69). Furthermore, we have recently demonstrated in psychiatric patients that MHPG increases only about twofold in the CSF following probenecid (70). Unlike the probenecid-induced increases in MHPG reported in rat brain (71), this increase occurs in the free rather than the conjugated fraction, and thus may not reflect transport inhibition. Clinical studies from this laboratory indicate that the MHPG increase on probenecid parallels and amplifies baseline MHPG levels, but may not provide an index of norepinephrine turnover (72).

Some direct evidence for the validity of the probenecid technique in the estimation of CNS amine turnover was obtained by a study of the alterations in the probenecid-induced accumulations of 5-HIAA and HVA produced by amine precursors and synthesis inhibitors. As indicated in Fig. 2, two specific precursors of serotonin and dopamine (L-tryptophan and L-DOPA, respectively) increase the appropriate amine metabolite accumulation, while relatively specific inhibi-

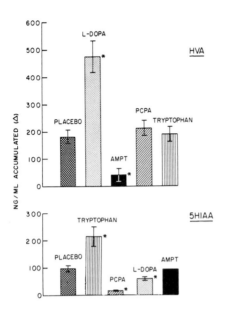

FIG. 2. Probenecid-induced increase in amine metabolites—effects of drugs. AMPT:HVA significantly different from placebo $p < 0.01$ (paired t-test). L-DOPA:HVA significantly different from placebo $p < 0.05$ (paired t-test). PCPA: 5-HIAA significantly different from placebo $p < 0.01$ (paired t-test). Tryptophan:5-HIAA significantly different from placebo $p < 0.05$ (paired t-test). L-DOPA:5-HIAA significantly different from placebo $p < 0.001$ (grouped t-test).

tors of synthesis (parachlorophenylalanine and α-*methyl-p*-tyrosine) decrease amine metabolite accumulation. In addition to providing a measure of a dynamic function, probenecid administration attenuates the steep downhill ventricular-lumbar gradients (gradients that are normally maintained by the acid metabolite removal system) which in effect makes lumbar CSF a better reflection of ventricular CSF and reduces the relative importance of the cord contribution (73). It has been shown that brain serotonin synthesis is partly a function of available tryptophan (74); thus the observation that plasma tryptophan decreased in patients on probenecid (75) raised a question about the validity of the probenecid technique as a measure of brain serotonin turnover. However, CSF tryptophan is unchanged in patients on probenecid (76), and in rats large doses of probenecid have only slight and transient effects on brain serotonin synthesis (76).

Studies of CSF Amine Metabolites in Affective Illness, Baseline Levels

The individual studies of baseline levels of amine metabolites in the CSF are outlined in Table 4. Five of the ten studies have found a decreased level of 5-HIAA in depression compared to various "control" groups (77,78,80,83,85), whereas the other half do not find a significant difference (79,81,82,84,86). In the case of HVA, four of the six studies report a deficit of HVA in depression as compared to controls (81,84,88,89). In manic patients 5-HIAA has been reported as not different than controls in four studies (77,81,82,86), although not all studies agree (78,80). HVA has been found to be higher in manics than in depressed patients or controls in three out of five studies (81,87,89). Two of the three studies of MHPG in the CSF of depressed patients report no difference from controls

TABLE 4. CSF amine metabolites in affective illness

	Control		Depression		Mania	
Study	N	Mean ± SD	N	Mean ± SD	N	Mean ± SD
			CSF 5-HIAA (ng/ml)			
Ashcroft (77)	21	19.1 ± 4.4	24	11.1 ± 3.9	4	18.7 ± 5.4
Dencker (78)	34	30 (median)	14	10 (median)	6	10 (median)
Fotherby (79)	11	11.5 ± 4.1	11	12.2 ± 8.2		
			6	16.6 ± 9.4		
Coppen (80)	20	42.3 ± 14	31	19.8 ± 8.5	18	19.7 ± 6.8
Roos (81)	26	29 ± 7	17	31 ± 8	19	36 ± 9
Bowers (82)	18	43.5 ± 16.8	8	34.0 ± 11.5	8	42.0 ± 10.3
van Praag (83)	11	40 ± 24	14	17 ± 17		
Papeschi (84)[a]	10	28 ± 3	12	22 ± 2		
McLeod (85)	12	32.6 ± 11.4	25	20.5 ± 12.1		
Goodwin (86)	29	27.3 ± 1.6	85	25.5 ± 1.3	40	28.7 ± 2.5
			CSF HVA (ng/ml)			
Roos (81)	7	44 ± 31	6	29 ± 7	7	41 ± 23
Roos (87)[a]	39	34 ± 3	37	34 ± 4	42	59 ± 6
Bowers (82)			8	22.7 ± 14.1	7	22.2 ± 16.3
Papeschi (84)[a]	18	50 ± 6	17	19 ± 4		
van Praag (88)	12	42 ± 16	20	39 ± 16		
Goodwin and Post (89)	28	22.4 ± 2.4	80	15.2 ± 2.1	40	25.7 ± 4.3
			MHPG (ng/ml)			
Wilk (90)[a]	24	16 ± 4.2	8	17.6 ± 1.2	11	31.6 ± 5.8
Post (91)[a]	44	15.1 ± 3.6	55	10.2 ± 2.4	26	15.4 ± 5.5
Shaw (92)[a]	13	10.8 ± 2.8	22	11.9 ± 2.6		

[a] Data are presented as mean ± SEM.

(90,92), and the largest study (in which activity and time of L.P. were carefully controlled), reports a significant deficit of MHPG compared to normal and neurologic controls (91). Inspection of Table 4 shows that for all three metabolites much of the discrepancy in the results between investigators is related to the large differences in the values for the various "control" groups, presumably reflecting variability both in the composition of the groups, or in the methods for obtaining the CSF, or both; unfortunately, most of the studies provide little or no description of the control groups. The NIMH controls were made up of two separate groups: (a) age-matched normals who were parents of children admitted for neurologic evaluation and (b) neurologic patients with syndromes known not to involve central amine metabolism.[1] Differences in the patient population may also contribute to the variability in baseline studies (and also in the probenecid studies to be described below). Although all of the CSF studies involve patients hospitalized for depression or mania, some give essentially no further description while others provide more details including subdivisions such as retarded versus agi-

---

[1] The control groups were studied in collaboration with T. N. Chase.

tated and unipolar versus bipolar. In the NIMH studies all patients met the
criteria for major, primary affective disorder and diagnostic details have been
described in the preceding section on urinary amine metabolite studies. In addition, the CSF studies included some manic patients, both those with moderate
"hypomanic" symptoms as well as those with more severe florid mania as described in detail elsewhere (93).

In order to systematically evaluate the potential role of activity in contributing
to the variability in CSF amine metabolite data, we studied hospitalized depressed
patients after complete bedrest for 9 hr prior to the' L.P., after normal activity,
and after some had artificially increased their activity level for 4 hr prior to the
L.P. The effect of these various procedures on CSF MHPG is illustrated in Fig.
3. These studies, decribed in more detail elsewhere (94), strongly suggest that
level of physical activity is an important variable contributing to the baseline level
of amine metabolites in the CSF, as summarized in Table 4, and thus should be
controlled in studies of this kind. In the NIMH studies we attempted to minimize
the potential contribution of extraneous variables in several ways. (a) The patients
and the control groups were kept on similar clinical research units, providing an
opportunity to monitor stress and control activity, and reduce the chance that
any drugs such as aspirin or sedatives would be inadvertently ingested; (b) L.P.s
in both the patients and in the control groups were done at 9 A.M. after 9 hr of
bedrest, and all assays were done in the same laboratory. Preliminary studies in
our depressed patients indicate that there may be some diurnal variation in CSF
amine metabolites, with higher 5-HIAA levels in the morning as compared to
the afternoon. Because normal diurnal patterns in some biologic systems are
known to be altered in depression (95), a more sophisticated study of CSF amine
metabolites should involve comparisons of depressed patients versus normal controls at various times of the day. It is quite conceivable that a depression-versus-
normal difference in a given amine metabolite might be found at one time of the
day, and not at another. Unfortunately in many of the CSF studies in the literature specific information on the procedure is lacking particularly in regard to

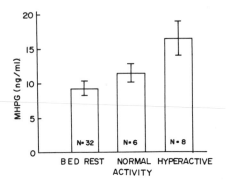

FIG. 3. Effect of activity on spinal fluid MHPG
in depressed patients.

controls for activity and extraneous drugs, time of the day of sampling, and so forth.

Amine Metabolites in Affective Illness, Probenecid Studies

Because of the potential artifacts and methodologic limitations inherent in studies of baseline CSF amine metabolites, several research groups have recently focused on the probenecid methodology (see above) as an approach to the study of CSF amine metabolites in affective illness. The results of these studies are outlined in Table 5. Variations among the studies in the absolute amount of acid metabolite accumulated on probenecid (related to variations in probenecid dose and duration of administration) make it necessary to express the data as percent of controls. Although it is not our purpose here to review each of these studies in detail, some general observations should be made. In relation to 5-HIAA, the two European studies (96,97) report a significant deficit in accumulation in depressed patients compared to controls, whereas Bowers (98) notes no differences in his overall group but does find a 5-HIAA deficit in a subgroup of bipolar patients. In the NIMH study we noted a trend towards a low 5-HIAA accumulation in depressed patients compared to controls; in this study our control data were obtained at 9 hr of probenecid administration, and there were only a limited number of depressed patients for that particular time comparison. In relation to HVA, our findings are clearly in agreement with the two European studies (96,99) and with the data of Bowers for his bipolar patients (98) in that the depressed patients are significantly lower than the controls when both are compared at the 9-hr point. The fact that Bower's results for the *overall* group of depressed patients are different, particularly in regard to HVA, may be related to the fact that his depressed population included a large number of agitated and atypical patients. Both Sjöstrom (100) and van Praag (101) have been able to show that

TABLE 5. *5-HIAA and HVA following probenecid in depressed patients*

	Accumulations in depressed patients as percent of controls			
	5-HIAA	N	HVA	N
Sjostrom and Roos, 1972 (96)	41%*	(24)	40%*	(10)
Bowers, 1974 (98)	109%	(11)	138%	(10)
Goodwin et al., 1973 (61)	78%	(6)**	47%*	(6)**
van Praag and Korf, 1973 (97,99)	69%*	(28)	75%*	(28)
Sjostrom, 1974 (100)	low*	(22)	low*	(22)

Reference numbers are in parentheses.
* Significant, $p < 0.05$
** Only the depressed patients studied under conditions identical to that of the controls are included. The total number of depressed patients studied with probenecid is 54.

the metabolite differences between depressed patients and controls can not be attributed to differences in a level of probenecid found in the CSF.

Intrarelationships Between the Metabolites of Norepinephrine, Dopamine, and Serotonin in Depressed Patients

The correlations among the three metabolites in the NIMH data are illustrated in Fig. 4. The significant correlation between the probenecid-induced accumulation of HVA and that of 5-HIAA is in agreement with the other clinical probenecid studies (100–102). This relatively high correlation in the absence of a correlation between either acid and MHPG, suggests that transport differences might play some role; at the dose of probenecid employed in the NIMH study (100 mg/kg) one group has reported that no correlation exists between CSF probenecid levels and metabolite accumulation (103), whereas Bowers has reported a correlation between 5-HIAA accumulation and CSF probenecid even at this dose level (102). The correlation between the acid metabolites is found in the baseline as well as in the probenecid data, further suggesting that it is not simply a function of intragroup differences in CSF probenecid level. The scattergram of the probenecid 5-HIAA-versus-baseline MHPG (Fig. 4c) illustrates that there are some

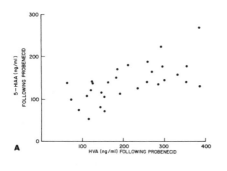

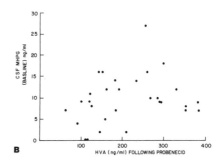

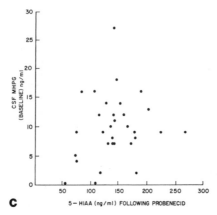

FIG. 4. Correlation between CSF 5-HIAA and HVA in depressed patients. **(A)** $N = 30$; $r = 0.64$; $p = 0.001$. Correlation between CSF HVA and MHPG in depressed patients. **(B)** $N = 30$; $r = 0.14$. **(C)** Correlation between CSF 5-HIAA and MHPG in depressed patients. $N = 31$; $r = 0.18$.

patients who are very low in both metabolites; although no single clinical characteristic adequately defines them as a subgroup, it is of interest that each of them is among the most severely ill of our depressed population, including some severely agitated female patients with involutional depression.

Metabolite Differences in Subgroups of Depressed Patients

One of the striking features of amine metabolite studies in affective illness is the biochemical variability within a group of depressed patients who are apparently relatively homogeneous clinically. This variability (as illustrated in our MHPG data—Fig. 5) suggests the possibility of biologically identifiable subgroups of patients. Several attempts have been made to explore metabolite differences in independently derived clinical subgroups of depressed patients. The unipolar–bipolar dichotomy by which patients with major depressive illness can be subdivided according to the presence or absence respectively of a prior history of mania, has revealed significant differences between these subgroups in a wide variety of parameters including family history, age of onset, course, clinical features of the depression, biologic measures, and therapeutic responses to specific drugs (reviewed in ref. 3). Ashcroft et al. (104) report that unipolar depressed patients have low baseline levels of both 5-HIAA and HVA, while bipolars are not different from controls. On the other hand, van Praag et al. (101) report no unipolar–bipolar differences in baseline metabolites but do report that a considerably larger proportion of subnormal 5-HIAA (but not HVA) responses to probenecid occur among bipolar compared to unipolar depressed patients; as noted previously, Bowers also finds lower accumulations of both 5-HIAA and HVA in bipolar compared to unipolar depressed patients (98). Table 6 shows the mean levels of the three metabolites (baseline and after probenecid) among the NIMH

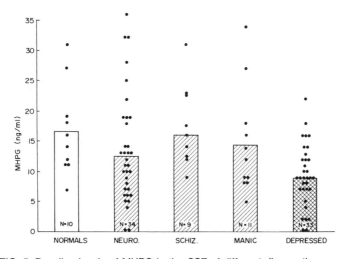

FIG. 5. Baseline levels of MHPG in the CSF of different diagnostic groups.

TABLE 6. *CSF amine metabolites in subgroups of affective illness*

	5-HIAA		HVA		MHPG	
	Baseline	Probenecid	Baseline	Probenecid	Baseline	Probenecid
Unipolar	26 ± 2.1	159 ± 16	22 ± 3.6	211 ± 22	11 ± 1.6	15 ± 2.3
	(36)	(19)	(33)	(19)	(19)	(16)
Bipolar II	26 ± 2.7	136 ± 12	24 ± 6.0	208 ± 22	9 ± 2.2	15 ± 2.5
	(20)	(12)	(19)	(12)	(10)	(7)
Bipolar I	25 ± 2.7	134 ± 10	17 ± 3.2	216 ± 22	11 ± 0.9	17 ± 1.5
	(27)	(23)	(24)	(22)	(18)	(22)

Number of patients in parentheses.

group of depressed patients subdivided according to the unipolar–bipolar dichotomy; no unipolar–bipolar differences in CSF amine metabolites were found. Although some tendency for the bipolar I group to have lower 5-HIAA (on probenecid) and HVA (baseline) is suggested.

The question of whether the predominance of agitation or retardation contributes to metabolite differences within a group of depressed patients is of importance, particularly in light of the activity data noted above. van Praag has reported an association between low HVA in depressed patients (both baseline and after probenecid) and psychomotor retardation; he reports no relationship between psychomotor state and 5-HIAA (101). Weiss et al. (105) studying hospitalized unipolar depressed patients found no significant correlation between baseline 5-HIAA or HVA and telemetrically measured activity; however, these CSF studies were done following bedrest, conditions under which no activity correlation would be expected.[2] In the NIMH study there are no significant correlations between nurse ratings of agitation or retardation and CSF amine metabolites, although there is a trend toward a positive correlation between the ratio of agitation–retardation ratings and the baseline levels of all three metabolites, particularly HVA. The difficulty in reliably rating agitation and retardation, which may be admixed in the same patient, suggest caution in the interpretation of all studies of this type.

In another approach to clinical subtyping we examined correlations between amine metabolites and the individual scores for the 34 items taken from the NIMH Intramural Research Affective Illness Rating Scale. It is of interest that a *positive* correlation was found between 5-HIAA and many of the individual items, particularly those relevant to subjective distress. This suggests a paradox in which 5-HIAA appears to be higher in association with higher levels of subjective distress and yet the depressed population as a whole tends to have low accumulation of 5-HIAA compared to controls. In dealing with this paradox it might be important to distinguish the relative contribution of the illness per se as opposed to a symptom or group of symptoms. Related to this is the question

---

[2] The activity measures were obtained 1 to 3 days prior to the L.P.

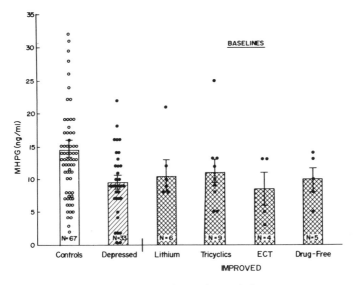

FIG. 6 CSF MHPG during depression and after recovery.

of whether a metabolite abnormality presumed to exist in depression is state dependent or not; in fact there is some evidence that the mean MHPG in our depressed patients (which is significantly lower than controls) does not change following recovery from the depressive episode. This data is illustrated in Fig. 6.

Attempts have also been made to correlate CSF amine metabolite levels with another biologically meaningful independent parameter, that is, subsequent response to specific psychotrophic drugs. Some of these data are illustrated in Table 7. When a group of the NIMH depressed patients were subdivided according to their subsequent response to tricyclic antidepressants or to lithium, significant differences were found in the metabolites of serotonin and dopamine. That is, subsequent tricyclic responders have higher pretreatment accumulations of 5-HIAA and HVA on probenecid compared to those who do not respond; for the lithium-treated depressed patients, HVA is significantly lower in the nonresponders, and there is a similar but nonsignificant trend for 5-HIAA. MHPG in the CSF was not predictive of differential response to these drugs. The fact that both 5-HIAA and HVA are in the same direction in the responders and nonresponders suggest that some factor common to both metabolites might be operating, such as level of monoamine oxidase (MAO) activity or differences in transport mechanisms, or probenecid sensitivity, or both. Asberg and her colleagues (106) reported that depressed patients with normal baseline levels of 5-HIAA were more likely to be good responders to nortriptyline than those with low levels; they do not report HVA data. van Praag and his colleagues, found a favorable response to a serotonin precursor (L-5-HTP) in a small group of

TABLE 7. *Probenecid-induced accumulation of 5-HIAA and HVA in the CSF: Relationship to antidepressant response to lithium and to tricyclics*

Drug category	N	5-HIAA	HVA
Lithium			
Responders	18	132.8 ± 12.4	193.7 ± 16.4
		↕ N.S.	↕ $p < 0.04$
nonresponders	14	154.2 ± 9.8	258.4 ± 26.0
Tricyclics			
(Imipramine and Amitriptyline)			
Responders	12	203.8 ± 31.6	299.5 ± 33.4
		↕ $p < 0.03$	↕ $p < 0.01$
Nonresponders	10	120.6 ± 12.0	176.4 ± 24.7

CSF data expressed as ng/ml ± SEM.

depressed patients distinguishable by a low pretreatment 5-HIAA on probenecid (107).

Effects of Treatments on CSF Amine Metabolites in Depressed Patients

Because theories that the pathophysiology of affective illness involved alterations in central amines initially were based on the known effects of specific mood altering drugs on brain amine systems in animals, it became quite important to ascertain whether these drugs when administered to patients could be shown to produce specific changes in amine systems as reflected in amine metabolite changes. Table 8 summarizes the data from the literature concerning the affects of the major classes of psychoactive drugs (and ECT) on the probenecid-induced accumulation of 5-HIAA and HVA in the CSF of depressed patients. Results of the NIMH studies are as follows: the tricyclic antidepressants, imipramine and amitriptyline reduced 5-HIAA accumulations on probenecid by 35% ($p < 0.01$) after 3 to 4 weeks of treatment at 150 to 300 mg per day as compared to the same patients studied while drug free (108). There were no differences in the effect of imipramine compared with amitriptyline on the patterns of CSF amine metabolites. The effects of tricyclics on 5-HIAA is in agreement with an independent study of amitriptyline treated patients (109). The decreases in probenecid-induced levels of 5-HIAA did not appear clearly related to clinical improvement with a marginal correlation ($r = +0.33$) between decrease in 5-HIAA and decrease in depression ratings. There was no effect on HVA. Tricyclic treatment was associated with a slight increase in MHPG among the responders and a significant

TABLE 8. *Relationship of antidepressant efficacy to decreased CSF 5-HIAA accumulation following probenecid*

| | Antidepressant efficacy | Probenecid-induced accumulations | | Reference |
		5-HIAA	HVA	
Antidepressants				
Electroshock Therapy	++++	Decrease?	No change	(110)
Tricyclics-Tertiary Amines				
Amitriptyline	+++	Decrease	No change	(108,109)
Imipramine	+++	Decrease	No change	(108)
Monoamine Oxidase Inhibitors				
Phenelzine	+++	Decrease?	Decrease	(111)
Lithium	++	Decrease	Decrease	(110)
p-Chlormethamphetamine	+	Decrease*	—	(112)
Phenothiazines				
Trifluoperazine and				
Chlorpromazine	±	No change	Increase	(113,114)
Butyrophenones				
Methylperiodol	±	Increase	No change	(115)
Haloperidol	+	No change	Increase	(116)
Narcotics				
Methadone	±	Decrease	Decrease	(117)
Psychotomimetic**				
Lysergic acid diethyla-				
mine (LSD)	±	Decrease	No change	(113)

* Data available only on probenecid-induced accumulation of 5-HIAA in the brains of mice.
** Patients studied only while psychotic after a presumptive ingestion of LSD.

decrease among the nonresponders. The responder/nonresponder difference in tricyclic effect on MHPG was significant ($p < 0.001$).

Lithium was administered to a group of 17 depressed patients. Following 2 to 4 weeks on lithium, with plasma levels between 0.8 and 1.2 mEq/liter, probenecid-induced accumulation of 5-HIAA was low compared to the prelithium period ($p < 0.05$); there was a nonsignificant decrease in HVA accumulation, and no change in MHPG (110). The effect of ECT on amine metabolites was also evaluated longitudinally in eight depressed patients all of whom responded to the procedure with a remission. There was a significant decrease in probenecid-induced accumulation of 5-HIAA: there was no significant effect on HVA or on MHPG (110). In a related study, Bowers demonstrated that patients receiving a MAO inhibitor had a significant decrease in accumulations of both 5-HIAA and HVA on probenecid (111). As reviewed in Table 8 it has been shown that neuroleptic drugs do not alter 5-HIAA in the CSF. Thus, widely diverse treatments effective in depressions, i. e., tricyclics, lithium, MAO inhibitors, and ECT, all result in a eventual decrease in 5-HIAA accumulation in the CSF.[3]

---

[3] All drugs of the studies reviewed above deal with the effect of chronic treatment of drugs or ECT, that is, the CSF changes were evaluated after 2 to 3 weeks of treatment.

Studies of CSF Amine Metabolites in Schizophrenia

As summarized in Table 9 except for two early studies of small numbers of patients (77,82), baseline levels of 5-HIAA, HVA, and MHPG have not been reported as significantly different in patients with a variety of schizophrenic diagnoses compared to controls (79,118–121). Using the probenecid methodology, similar negative findings are reported for 5-HIAA accumulations in schizophrenic patients compared to controls (121–124). However, the story is more suggestive for HVA accumulations. Bowers' initial study reported that HVA was lower in Schneiderian positive schizophrenics than those without these specific symptoms (122). His more recent study (123) showed that HVA accumulations were low in schizophrenics compared with an affectively ill population; moreover HVA accumulations were lowest in patients with poor prognosis schizophrenia as evaluated on the Stephens-Astrup scale. Although the recent NIMH study of hospitalized acute schizophrenic patients (121) (Table 10) showed no statistically significant decrease in HVA relative to psychiatric controls, the results are not inconsistent with those of Bowers et al. (123), as only good prognosis patients were included in the NIMH study[4] and a significant negative correlation was demonstrated between HVA accumulations and Schneiderian symptomatology (121).

When the NIMH acute schizophrenic patients recovered, both with or without the aid of neuroleptic medication, reassessment of cerebrospinal fluid amine metabolites during a drug-free interval of at least 2 weeks demonstrated significantly lower HVA accumulations (Fig. 7). This evidence for reduced dopamine turnover in patients recovered from acute schizophrenic episodes could represent an underlying biologic change predisposing to the illness. Thus there is some consensus in the CSF data suggesting alterations in dopamine metabolism may occur in acute schizophrenia.

The Effects of Drug Treatments on CSF Amine Metabolites in Schizophrenia

As reviewed above, the most consistent finding in the studies of CSF amine metabolites in schizophrenia is an alteration in HVA, the dopamine metabolite. In light of this it is of considerable interest to note that the major pharmacologic treatments of schizophrenia (the neuroleptics) have been found to have a relatively selective effect on HVA in the CSF. Thus baseline levels of HVA have been reported as increased following the therapeutic administration of phenothiazines and butyrophenones (82,114,126,127); similarly, increased HVA accumulation following probenecid administration has been demonstrated to occur following acute or subacute treatment with various neuroleptics including chlorpromazine (113,122,123,129), thioridazine (128,129), haloperidol (114,116), and pimozide

---

[4] The NIMH patients met World Health Organization criteria for acute schizophrenia; these criteria are described in detail elsewhere (125).

TABLE 9. CSF amine metabolites in schizophrenic patients compared to various control groups

5-HIAA	HVA	MHPG	Diagnosis	Controls	Comments	Source
N.S. (11)			AS	Psy		Fotherby et al. (79)
Low (7)	N.S. (4)		AS,CS	Psy,Neurol	Only AS low	Ashcroft et al. (77)
N.S. (40)	N.S. (6)		CS	Psy,Norm	Pts. on neuroleptics	Persson and Roos (118)
Low (7)	N.S. (30)		U	Psy,Norm		Bowers (82)
N.S. (22)		N.S. (26)	AS	Psy	Higher HVA in paranoid	Rimon et al. (119)
		N.S. (17)	AS	Psy,Norm		Shopsin et al. (120)
N.S. (18)	N.S. (17)		AS	Psy,Norm,Neurol		Post et al. (121)
				CSF studies employing probenecid accumulations		
N.S. (18)	N.S. (18)		AS,CS	Psy,Norm Inmates	Low HVA in Schneiderian +	Bowers (122)
N.S. (17)	Low (17)		AS,CS	Psy	Lowest HVA in poor prognosis	Bowers (123)
N.S. (9)	N.S. (9)		Autism	Psy,Neurol	Autistic children intermediate between atypical and seizure patients	Cohen et al. (124)
N.S. (18)	N.S. (20)	N.S. (17)	AS	Psy	Good prognosis pts. only, HVA lower on recovery	Post et al. (121)

Number of subjects in parentheses.
Abbreviations: N.S. = not statistically significant; AS = acute schizophrenics; CS = chronic schizophrenics; U = unavailable diagnosis; Psy = psychiatric nonschizophrenic controls.

TABLE 10. CSF amine metabolites in acute schizophrenic patients and controls

Diagnosis	Baseline			Probenecid		
	5-HIAA	HVA	MHPG	5-HIAA	HVA	MHPG
Control groups Normal and neurologic	27.3 ± 2.2 (29)	22.4 ± 2.4 (28)	14.6 ± 1.4 (36)			
Depressed	26.1 ± 1.3 (77)	20.4 ± 2.3 (69)	10.6 ± 0.9* (38)	142.5 ± 7.6 (50)	214.7 ± 14.0 (48)	15.5 ± 1.3 (41)
Manic	28.7 ± 2.4 (21)	19.6 ± 3.8 (22)	15.3 ± 2.1 (15)	145.1 ± 9.1 (16)	219.7 ± 20.2 (15)	18.5 ± 3.2 (13)
Acute Schizophrenic	27.1 ± 2.6 (18)	21.4 ± 2.5 (20)	15.8 ± 1.6 (17)	150.8 ± 11.7 (18)	242.9 ± 23.6 (17)	21.8 ± 2.1 (15)

* $p < 0.02$ compared to all other groups.
Data are presented as mean ± SEM.
From ref. 121.

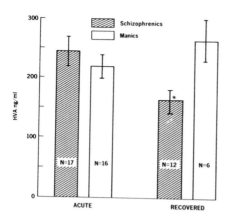

FIG. 7. Differences in HVA accumulation in recovered schizophrenics and manics on probenecid, from ref. 121.

(130). These HVA changes following neuroleptic treatment are consistent with a substantial body of animal data indicating that these drugs increase brain dopamine turnover.

However, we have recently demonstrated a differential effect of neuroleptic treatment of CSF HVA in psychotic patients, the magnitude of the effect apparently depending on the duration of drug administration. Thus following acute treatment (less than 3 weeks) with either chlorpromazine or thioridazine, a substantial increase in the probenecid-induced accumulation of HVA was observed, whereas after more chronic administration of these drugs a difference from baseline was no longer demonstrable (129). Ongoing studies with another neuroleptic, pimozide, suggests that there may be individual differences in the relationship between duration of treatment and HVA change, with some patients maintaining a substantial HVA effect even after more than 3 weeks of drug administration (130).

It is premature to assume that the CSF data support the conclusion that the effects neuroleptics have on brain amines in patients are limited to dopamine systems. Although there is considerable data indicating that neuroleptic treatment does not alter 5-HIAA in the CSF (122,128,130), there is a paucity of data on the effects of these drugs on CSF MHPG. In the NIMH study no effect of neuroleptics on MHPG was noted; on the other hand, clozapine, a dibenzodiazepine neuroleptic has been reported to decrease CSF MHPG (131).

DISCUSSION

General Considerations

It is first important to ask ourselves whether we can reliably and validly measure neurochemical events in man using the methods described in this chapter. Within the limitations outlined earlier, we feel the answer is a qualified affirmative. However, the time frame and neuroanatomic loci that one is considering needs to be specified. For example, with studies of the CSF, it is likely that we have the potential to assess the global, tonic state of amine metabolism or function, including phasic shifts, but not the more rapid, discretely localized changes in brain amine systems that are demonstrable *in vitro*. Thus it is understandable why it is easier to reliably demonstrate alterations in amine metabolism with different pharmacologic treatments (which have global effects on CNS systems) than in the major psychoses which may be related to discrete and localized abnormalities. On the other hand, to the extent that the major psychoses involve more generalized, tonic alterations in amine metabolism, the CSF and urinary metabolite techniques described here are well suited to the establishment of biochemical–behavioral relationships.

A closely related and critical issue in the interpretation of biologic data in psychiatric disorders involves the phase of the illness in which the data are obtained. It would be ideal to study a patient longitudinally throughout the illness; that is, during the early acute phase, during the stable and waning phases and following recovery. This would allow a more clear separation of state-dependent from state-independent variables. Variables established as state-dependent could be examined for potential relationships to external precipitating factors (i.e., stress), to internal processes relating to the illness itself, or to more non-specific secondary concomitants of the illness (such as hyperactivity, poor appetite, anxiety, and the like). On the other hand, state-independent variables are more likely to reflect either relevant underlying predispositions, or irrelevant characteristics of the population. For example, preliminary evidence suggests that the low MHPG in the CSF of our depressed patients may not increase significantly even after the patient is substantially recovered. Likewise, the NIMH studies suggest that patients recovered from an acute schizophrenic episode may have significantly decreased dopamine turnover as measured by HVA accumulations in CSF after probenecid (121). Clearly, it would be critical to establish the time course of such alterations in amine metabolism, pratically whether they preceed the onset of the illness and whether they are maintained for significant periods of time following recovery.

The critical nature of the time course variable is emphasized by the effects of drug treatments on amine metabolites as reviewed earlier. For example, the probenecid–5-HIAA decrease following tricyclic antidepressant treatment is more marked in patients studied before three weeks than in those studied after three weeks, while the probenecid–HVA increase is substantial early in phenothiazine treatment but is minimal or absent later in treatment. These findings suggest that some adaptation or "tolerance" phenomena occurs after the initial, acute effects of the drugs. An analogous process may be operating in untreated episodes of illness; hence it is conceivable that marked biological changes may occur during the early stages only to be attenuated by compensatory mechanisms as the episode continues. Under ordinary conditions patients are hospitalized and studied after the illness episode has been on-going for some time, and thus important biologic changes might not be detected.

Another important aspect of all of these studies involves the challenge of discrepant results. Although it is tempting to ignore them, it would seem more fruitful to pay attention to the fact of the discrepancies per se, and to explore some of the possibilities for understanding them. For example it is largely the European and not the American studies of depression that have reported decreased baseline 5-HIAA and positive responses to treatment with L-tryptophan. It should be considered that these differences may not be due to investigator bias or error but rather may reflect some genetic differences in the populations of patients studied, differences in dietary or other environmental inputs, or perhaps differences in the phase of illness when the data were obtained, as discussed above.

Amine Hypotheses of Affective Illness: Relationship to the Metabolite Data

The hypotheses that an abnormality in one or more brain amine systems may be involved in the pathophysiology of depression and mania have been formulated into the catecholamine hypothesis on the one hand, and the indoleamine (or serotonin) hypothesis on the other hand. Both versions of the amine hypothesis were generated from observations on the clinical effects of drugs known to alter central amine function in animals. Hence reserpine, a depletor of central amines is associated with the onset of depression in some individuals, whereas monoamine oxidase inhibitors that increase levels of both catecholamines and indoleamines in the brains of animals were reported to have some antidepressant activity. Additionally, the tricyclic antidepressants were shown to block the presynaptic uptake of norepinephrine and serotonin, thereby increasing their availability at the receptor site; conversely, lithium, an effective antimanic agent, was found to decrease norepinephrine activity at the receptor by different mechanisms; lithium has also been shown to inhibit dopamine synthesis in brain, whereas its effects on brain serotonin are controversial with reports of both increases and decreases in serotonin synthesis, depending on whether acute or chronic treatment was being examined. These drug effects in animals have been reviewed in detail elsewhere (1–3).

In summary, the amine hypotheses state that depression is associated with a functional deficit of either norepinephrine, dopamine or serotonin at critical synapses in the CNS, whereas, conversely, mania is associated with a functional excess of these amines. Questions concerning the amine hypotheses have been raised (3) including issues of species variation, the assumption of mania and depression as phenomenologically opposite states, the lack of neurochemical or clinical specificity of the drugs upon which the models are based, and the fact that a number of amine-active drugs do not produce the predicted behavioral effect in depressed or manic patients.

The available data on CSF amine metabolites in depression, mania, and normal controls do not support the concept of a straightforward biological continuum with depression at one end (deficiency), normal in the middle, and mania at the other end (excess). With regard to norepinephrine, the NIMH results with MHPG, although controversial, would support the concept of a norepinephrine deficiency in some depressed patients, but not an excess in mania. With regard to serotonin, essentially none of the studies of 5-HIAA in the CSF are consistent with a "too little–too much" model, but much of the data would be supportive of the version of the indoleamine hypothesis with postulates a serotonin deficiency in both mania and depression (80). And finally, in regard to dopamine, while the HVA data could support a hypothesis of a dopamine deficiency in depression, the results in mania are confusing since the baseline studies are confounded by a potential activity artifact, and the studies of HVA accumulation on probenecid in mania show, if anything, a deficit.

Thus, when the various CSF amine metabolite findings in affective illness are considered independently of one another, several "fits" into existing hypotheses can be accomplished. However, as we will discuss below, it may be more meaningful to consider all three metabolites together when attempting to interpret results. Unfortunately, in the case of the urinary studies the question of amine specificity cannot be addressed as it is only in the case of norepinephrine that there is evidence that brain metabolism can be studied.

An additional issue for consideration is the paradox that many of the treatments for depression appear to alter amine metabolism in the same direction that was demonstrated (or hypothesized) to be characteristic of the illness itself. For example, as noted earlier, widely diverse treatments effective in depression—tricyclics, lithium, monoamine oxidase inhibitors, and electroconvulsive therapy—all result in an eventual decrease in 5-HIAA accumulation in the CSF; similarly, tricyclics decrease urinary MHPG excretion. This paradox can be understood if one considers that the measurement of amine turnover reflects presynaptic events. Thus, the increased amine function produced at the synapse by the tricyclic-induced reuptake inhibition is in itself sufficient to further decrease, by feedback mechanisms, what may be initially low presynaptic amine synthesis. Another explanation of the paradox would be based on the possibility that postsynaptic aminergic receptor activity was actually *increased* in some depressed patients, causing feedback regulatory mechanisms to decrease amine turnover presynaptically in an attempt to compensate for the postsynaptic imbalance. Given this situation then, antidepressants might initially work by a direct action on the presynaptic neuron (132), resulting in a further reduction in the turnover of serotonin (and/or norepinephrine), a reduction sufficient to overcome the excessive postsynaptic activity.

Amine Hypotheses of Schizophrenia: Relationship to the Metabolite Data

The possible role of catecholamines has been the major focus of recent speculations on the pathophysiology of schizophrenia (133). For example, on the basis of a great variety of indirect data, dopaminergic overactivity has been hypothesized in schizophrenia. These data rest on several kinds of findings: (1) drugs that increase dopaminergic activity, such as the stimulants (amphetamine, cocaine, and methylphenidate) and the dopamine precursor L-dihydroxyphenylalanine, are capable of precipitating or exacerbating schizophreniform symptomatology; (2) the neuroleptics with relatively few exceptions cause parkinsonian side effects; (3) in animal studies, the neuroleptics in relative proportion to their antipsychotic efficacy block dopamine receptors, increase dopamine turnover, block dopamine mediated increases in cyclic AMP and reverse amphetamine-induced suppression of single dopamine nerve-cell firing (reviewed in ref. 4).

On the other hand, reasoning from a self-stimulation model, Stein and Wise have postulated alterations in noradrenergic function in chronic schizophrenia (134). Consistent with their hypotheses, Wise and Stein have reported that dopamine-β-hydroxylase, the enzyme that converts dopamine to norepinephrine, is reduced in autopsy specimens of patients with chronic schizophrenia (135). Wyatt and Murphy (this volume) review the procedural issues involved in the study of autopsied brain specimens.

Finally, on the basis of the serotonin effects of LSD and related hallucinogens, alterations in the metabolism of this amine have been postulated in schizophrenia (136–141).

The existing data on CSF amine metabolites in schizophrenic patients is only partially consistent with the dopamine hypotheses of schizophrenia. Rather than the predicted increases in dopamine turnover being demonstrable in schizophrenic patients, the studies of Bowers and our own group demonstrate that during or following the acute episode, dopamine turnover may be reduced. Bowers' data suggest that the most severely affected, Schneiderian positive, "process" or poor prognosis patients have the lowest HVA accumulations. This is consistent with our own findings that Schneiderian positive patients have lower HVA accumulations than those without such symptomatology. Clearly, further studies of both acute and chronic schizophrenic patients with various subclassifications and diagnoses are warranted before definitive conclusions can be drawn. Bowers' data are consistent with the hypothesis that functional dopamine may be increased at the receptor site, with a decrease in presynaptic dopamine synthesis secondary to compensatory mechanisms. On the other hand, our data showing decreases during recovery are more compatible with the hypothesis that alterations in dopamine metabolism may reflect an underlying predisposition to the illness, and that during the acute episode HVA may increase from this low level.

An adequate test of the noradrenergic hypothesis of Stein and Wise has not yet been performed in chronic schizophrenic patients. Our own study in acute schizophrenic patients, however, did not demonstrate decreases in the norepinephrine metabolite in CSF; in fact, MHPG tended to be higher in the most acutely psychotic patients. Our MHPG findings are also consistent with recent determinations of VMA in CSF where both acute and recovered schizophrenic had high–normal VMA levels (50).

And finally, is there support in the CSF data for the hypothesized role of serotonin in schizophrenia? Aside from a few earlier studies in small numbers of patients, levels of 5-HIAA in the CSF of schizophrenic patients (either baseline or after probenecid) have not been found to be significantly different from normal or neurologic controls. However, Bowers has reported a significant decrease in probenecid–5-HIAA during psychoses induced by psychedelic drugs.

In summary, the CSF amine metabolite studies to date are most supportive of the dopaminergic hypothesis of schizophrenia. However, compared to affective illness there is a paucity of metabolite data available in schizophrenia, particularly chronic schizophrenia. Thus, there is simply no CSF data available to either support or challenge the noradrenergic hypothesis of chronic schizophrenia as proposed by Stein and Wise.

The Question of Specificity

We can formulate the specificity question (the topic of this symposium) in two ways: first, in regard to "amine specificity," does the evidence in either affective illness or schizophrenia favor a disturbance in a *single* amine system or a *pattern* of alterations in more than one amine system? Secondly, in regard to "illness specificity," does the evidence suggest a specific abnormality (either single amine or pattern of changes) which characterizes depression, mania and schizophrenia and which distinguishes them from each other.

It is perhaps easier to answer the first question. Consistent with what is known about the normal complex functional interrelationships between the multiple amine neurotransmitter systems, the metabolite data do not support a single amine model, particularly in the case of affective illness where the most data are available. Therefore, there is some evidence for alterations in dopamine, norepinephrine and serotonin metabolism in depressive syndromes and suggestive evidence for similar decreases in serotonin and dopamine metabolism in mania as well. The model of amine deficits in parkinsonian patients is noteworthy in this respect. Although it is thought that deficits in dopamine are specifically related to Parkinson's disease and only dopamine replacement with L-DOPA is of therapeutic efficacy, there are significant decreases in serotonin and norepinephrine metabolism as well (142). Perhaps a disturbance originates in a single amine system subsequently producing secondary changes in interrelated systems. On the other hand, the possibility of an abnormality that would affect all amine systems should be considered; such possibilities include an alteration in MAO, in a cofactor common to the synthesis of all three amines, or in a common transport system. An alternative view might postulate "subgroups" corresponding to individual amines; however, in the absence of independent evidence for the existence of a subgroup (i.e., genetic, clinical, or pharmacologic evidence) such postulations remain speculations.

The question of "amine specificity" was, of course, initially raised in regard to the pharmacologic models of affective or schizophrenic illnesses. For example, the amine model of depression based on the reserpine of the MAO inhibitor data is consistent with an involvement of norepinephrine, dopamine, serotonin, or all three. Similarly, the amphetamine–cocaine models for the schizophreniform psychoses are consistent with a role not only for dopamine, but conceivably also for norepinephrine, serotonin, or acetylcholine. The specificity issue becomes more broad when one conceptualizes the biology of the functional psychoses in terms of a complex and changing series of interactions between underlying (predisposing) abnormalities and more acute, superimposed dysfunctions.

The question of "illness specificity" is considerably more complex, and although a full treatment of this issue cannot be undertaken here, a few observations should be made. The efficacy of the pharmacologic treatments of the psychoses is characterized by both specificity and nonspecificity. Thus, lithium is effective in the acute and prophylactic treatment of both mania and depression, while the phenothiazines, the treatment of choice for schizophrenia, are also useful in mania and some cases of agitated depression. In addition, it has been emphasized recently (143) that some drugs, for example, the stimulants, are capable of producing both affective and schizophreniform alterations, and thus, may be useful in conceptualizing a continuum along which the same drugs and/or the same transmitter systems may mediate both euphoric and dysphoric as well as schizophrenic-like processes.

On the basis of both the metabolite data and the overlapping spectra of pharmacologic efficacy, one might postulate that alterations in serotonin metabolism may be more basic to the underlying abnormality in the affective disorders, whereas norepinephrine (and/or dopamine) may be involved in the underlying defect in schizophrenia. On the other hand, when considering the superimposed dysfunctions, activation of dopaminergic systems may be responsible for the eruption either of acute manic or schizophrenic episodes, just as a decrease in norepinephrine could trigger the onset of a depressive episode. Depending on whether they are acute or prophylactic, drugs could interact with either the superimposed or underlying dysfunction or both.

Other potentially testable hypotheses for multiple neurotransmitter alterations in the major psychoses are equally tenable. Not only do the stimulant models mentioned earlier implicate multiple neurotransmitter alterations in the affective and schizophreniform psychoses, but recent data regarding the effect of LSD on amine systems, suggests that not only serotonin, but also norepinephrine and dopamine receptor function may be markedly altered by this hallucinogen (144, 145). On the basis of these data one might speculate that the more floridly hallucinatory psychoses could reflect primarily an alteration in serotonergic systems while the paranoid–catatonic continuum might be more related to alterations in catecholamine systems. In addition, many investigators have suggested that the relative ratio of noradrenergic to dopaminergic dysfunction in schizophrenia is crucial (4,146). Finally, increasing amounts of new data as well as a long historical tradition have emphasized the importance of cholinergic-adrenergic balance in the expression of a wide variety of behaviors. Not only can potentiation of a cholinergic systems with physostigmine reverse cocaine-induced (147) or methylphenidate-induced (148) hyperactivity and stereotypic behavior in animals, but it can also abruptly terminate aspects of manic symptomatology in patients with affective illness and block the stimulant-induced psychotic decompensation in schizophrenic patients as reviewed in detail by Davis (this volume).

An additional approach to the specificity question involves the assessment of biochemical changes in patients studied under conditions where specific aspects of behavior are experimentally manipulated; elsewhere we have discussed in detail the potentials and limitations of these methods (149). The increasing appreciation of the value of various experimental paradigms is opening up fresh approaches to the awesome problem of dissecting behavioral–biochemical relationships in human disease states.

Regardless of whether one employs experimental manipulations, or naturalistic approaches, further advances in this field are dependent upon a continued and expanded interrelationship between those working on the application of new biochemical techniques in patients and those in the rapidly advancing field of the quantification of clinical phenomenology. This critically important but fragile interrelationship has been served well by this symposium.

REFERENCES

1. Schildkraut, J. J., and Kety, S. S. (1967): Biogenic amines and emotion. *Science,* 156:21–30.
2. Bunney, W. E., Jr., and Davis, J. M. (1965): Norepinephrine in depressive reactions. *Arch. Gen. Psychiatry,* 13:483–494.
3. Goodwin, F. K., and Murphy, D. L. (1974): Biological factors in the affective disorders and schizophrenia. In: *Psychopharmacological Agents,* edited by M. Gordon, pp. 9–32. Academic Press, New York.
4. Snyder, S. H., Banerjee, S. P., Yamamura, H. I., and Greenberg, D. (1974): Drugs, neurotransmitters and schizophrenia. *Science,* 184:1243–1253.
5. Klein, D., and Davis, J. M. (1969): *Diagnosis and Drug Treatment of Psychiatric Disorders.* Williams & Wilkins, Baltimore, Maryland.
6. Wyatt, R. J., Termini, B. A., and Davis, J. (1971): Biochemical and sleep studies of schizophrenia: A review of the literature 1960–1970. *Schiz. Bull.,* 4:10–44.
7. Weil-Malherbe, H., and Szara, S. I. (1971): *The Biochemistry of Functional and Experimental Psychoses.* Thomas, Springfield, Illinois.
8. Shaw, D. M., Camps, F. E., and Eccleston, E. G. (1967): 5-Hydroxytryptamine in the hindbrain of depressive suicides. *Br. J. Psychiatry,* 113:1407–1411.
9. Bourne, H. R., Bunney, W. E., Jr., Colburn, R. W., Davis, J. M., Davis, J. N., Shaw, D. M., and Coppen, A. J. (1968): Noradrenaline, 5-hydroxytryptamine, and 5-hydroxyindoleacetic acid in hindbrains of suicidal patients. *Lancet,* 2:805–808.
10. Pare, C. M. B., Yeung, D. P. H., Price, K., and Stacey, R. S. (1969): 5-Hydroxytryptamine, noradrenaline, and dopamine in brainstem, hypothalamus and caudate nucleus of controls and of patients committing suicide by coal gas poisoning. *Lancet,* 2:133–135.
11. Lloyd, K. G., Farley, I. J., Deck, J. H. N., and Hornykiewiez, O. (1974): Serotonin and 5-hydroxyindoleacetic acid in discrete areas of the brainstem of suicide victims and control patients. In: *Advances in Biochemical Pharmacology, Vol. 2,* edited by E. Costa, G. L. Gessa, and M. Sandler. Raven Press, New York.
12. Gottfries, C. G. (1974): Paper read at World Congress of Psychiatry, Section on Biological Psychiatry, October 1974, Munich, Germany.
13. Wise, D., and Stein, L. (1975): Personal communication.
14. Olson, L. (1974): Post-mortem fluorescence histochemistry of monoamine neuron systems in the brain: A new approach in the neuropathology of schizophrenia. *J. Psychiatr. Res.,* 11:199–203.

15. Olson, L., and Ungerstedt, U. (1970): Monoamine fluorescence in CNS smears: Sensitive and rapid visualization of nerve terminals without freeze-drying. *Brain Res.,* 17:343–347.
16. Lovenberg, W., and Engelman, K. (1971): Assay of serotonin, related metabolites and enzymes. *Meth. Biochem. Anal.,* 19:1–34.
17. Goodall, McC., and Alton, H. (1968): Metabolism of 3-hydroxytryptamine (dopamine) in human subjects. *Biochem. Pharmacol.,* 17:905–914.
18. Rinne, U. K., and Sonninen, U. (1968): Dopamine and Parkinson's disease. *Ann. Med. Intern. Fenn.,* 57:105–113.
19. Weil-Malherbe, H., and Van Buren, J. M. (1969): The excretion of dopamine and dopamine metabolites in Parkinson's disease and the effect of diet thereon. *J. Lab. Clin. Med.,* 74:305–318.
20. Calne, D. B., Karoum, F., Ruthven, C. R. J., and Sandler, M. (1969): The metabolism of orally administered L-DOPA in Parkinsonism. *Br. J. Pharmacol.,* 37:57–68.
21. Tyce, G. M., Muenter, M. D., and Owen, C. A., Jr. (1970): Metabolism of L-dihydroxyphenylalanine by patients with Parkinson disease. *Mayo Clin. Proc.,* 45:645–656.
22. Goodall, McC., and Rosen, L. (1963): Urinary excretion of noradrenaline and its metabolites at ten-minute intervals after intravenous injection of *dl*-Noradrenaline-2-C14. *J. Clin. Invest.,* 42:1578–1588.
23. Erwin, G. V. (1973): Oxidative-reductive pathways for metabolism of biogenic aldehydes. In: *Frontiers of Catecholamine Research,* edited by E. Usdin, pp. 161–166. Pergamon, New York.
24. Maas, J. W., and Landis, D. H. (1968): *In vivo* studies of metabolism of norepinephrine in the central nervous system. *J. Pharmacol. Exp. Ther.,* 163:147–162.
25. Schanberg, S. M., Schildkraut, J. J., and Breese, G. R. (1968): Metabolism of normetanephrine-H³ in rat brain-identification of conjugated 3-methoxy-4-hydroxyphenylglycol as the major metabolite. *Biochem. Pharmacol.,* 17:247–254.
26. Maas, J. W., Dekirmenjian, H., Garver, D., Redmond, D. E., and Landis, D. H. (1973): Excretion of catecholamine metabolites following intraventricular injection of 6-hydroxydopamine in the macaca speciosa. *Eur. J. Pharmacol.,* 23:121–130.
27. Ebert, M., and Kopin, I. J. (1975): Origins of urinary catecholamine metabolites: differential labeling by dopamine C14. Abstract. *Clin. Res. (In press.)*
28. Maas, J. W., Fawcett, J., and Dekirmenjian, H. (1968): 3-Methoxy-4-hydroxy-phenylglycol (MHPG) excretion in depressive states. *Arch. Gen. Psychiatry,* 19:129–134.
29. Greenspan, K., Schildkraut, J. J., Gordon, E. K., Baer, L., Aronoff, M. D., and Durell, J. (1970): Catecholamine metabolism in affective disorders III. *J. Psychiatr. Res.,* 7:171–183.
30. Bond, P. A., Jenner, F. A., and Sampson, G. A. (1972): Daily variations of the urine content of 3-methoxy-4-hydroxyphenylglycol in two manic-depressive patients. *Psychol. Med.,* 2:81–85.
31. Jones, F. D., Maas, J. W., Dekirmenjian, H., and Fawcett, J. A. (1973): Urinary catecholamines during behavioral changes in a patient with manic-depressive cycles. *Science,* 179:200–202.
32. Stoddard, F. J., Post, R. M., Gillin, J. C., Buchsbaum, M. S., Carman, J. S., and Bunney, W. E., Jr. (1972): Phasic changes in manic-depressive illness. Presented at the Annual Meeting, American Psychiatric Association, Detroit, Michigan, May.
33. Goodwin, F. K., and Wehr, T. (1975): Unpublished manuscript.
34. Goodwin, F. K., and Beckmann, H. (1974): Paper read at the World Congress of Psychiatry, Section on Biological Psychiatry, October, Munich, Germany.
35. Feighner, J. P., Robbins, E., Guze, S. B., Woodruff, R. A., Jr., Winokur, G., and Murray, R. (1972): Diagnostic criteria for use in psychiatric research. *Arch. Gen. Psychiatry,* 26:57–63.
36. Spitzer, R. L., Endicott, J., and Robbins, E. (1975): Research diagnostic criteria for selected groups of functional disorders. *Psychopharmacol. Bull. (In press.)*
37. Dunner, D. L., Gershon, E. S., and Goodwin, F. K. (1975): Heritable factors in the severity of affective illness. *Biol. Psychiatry (In press.)*
38. Beckmann, H., and Goodwin, F. K. (1975): Antidepressant response to tricyclics and urinary MHPG in unipolar patients. *Arch. Gen. Psychiatry,* 32:17–21.
39. Maas, J. W., Dekirmenjian, H., and Jones, F. (1973): The identification of depressed patients who have a disorder of NE metabolism and/or disposition. In: *Frontiers in Catecholamine Research,* edited by E. Usdin and S. Snyder, pp. 1091–1096. Pergamon, New York.
40. Schildkraut, J. J., Keeler, B. A., Grob, E. L., Kantrowich, J., and Hartmann, E. (1973): MHPG excretion and clinical classification in depression. *Lancet,* 1:1251–1252.
41. Ebert, M., Post, R. M., and Goodwin, F. K. (1972): The effect of physical activity on urinary MHPG excretion in depressed patients. *Lancet,* 2:766.

42. Maas, J. W., Dekirmenjian, H., and Fawcett, J. A. (1971): Catecholamine metabolism, depression and stress. *Nature,* 230:330–331.
43. Schildkraut, J. J. (1973): Catecholamine metabolism and affective disorders: Studies of MHPG excretion. In: *Frontiers in Catecholamine Research,* edited by E. Usdin and S. Snyder, pp. 1165-1171. Pergamon, New York.
44. Roth, R. H., Walters, J. R., and Aghajanian, G. K. (1973): Effect of impulse flow on the release and synthesis of dopamine in the rat striatum. In: *Frontiers in Catecholamine Research,* edited by E. Usdin and S. Snyder, pp. 567–574. Pergamon, New York.
45. Karoum, F., Gillin, J. C., and Wyatt, R. (1975): Personal communication.
46. Mannarino, E., Kirschner, N., and Nashold, B. S. (1963): The metabolism of C^{14} noradrenaline by rat brain *in vivo. J. Neurochem.,* 10:373–379.
47. Glowinski, J., Kopin, I. J., and Axelrod, J. (1965): Metabolism of H^3 norepinephrine in the rat brain. *J. Neurochem.,* 12:25–30.
48. Rutledge, C. O., and Jonason, J. (1967): Metabolic pathways of dopamine and norepinephrine in rabbit brain *in vitro. J. Pharmacol. Exp. Ther.,* 157:493–502.
49. Sharman, D. F. (1969): Glycol metabolites of noradrenaline in brain tissue. *Br. J. Pharmacol.,* 36:523–534.
50. Jimerson, D., Gordon, E. K., Post, R. M., and Goodwin, F. K. (1975): Central norepinephrine function in man: VMA in the CSF. *Sci. Proc. Am. Psychiatry Assoc.,* 128:94–96.
51. Meek, J. L., and Neff, N. H. (1973): Is cerebrospinal fluid the major avenue for the removal of 5-hydroxyindoleacetic acid from the brain? *Neuropharmacology,* 12:497–499.
52. Bowers, M. B., and Cohen, A. (1974): Cited in Bowers, M. B. (1974): Lumbar CSF 5-hydroxyin-doleacetic acid and homovanillic acid in affective syndromes. *J. Nerv. Ment. Dis.,* 158:325–330.
53. Sheard, M. H., Zolonick, A., and Aghajanian, G. K. (1972): Raphe neurons: Effects of tricyclic antidepressant drugs. *Brain Res.,* 43:690–694.
54. Moir, A. T. B., Ashcroft, G. W., Crawford, T. B. B., Eccleston, D., and Guldberg, H. C. (1970): Central metabolites in cerebrospinal fluid as a biochemical approach to the brain. *Brain,* 93: 357–368.
55. Papeschi, R., Sourkes, T. L., Poirier, L. J., and Boucher, R. (1971): On the intracerebral origin of homovanillic acid of the cerebrospinal fluid of experimental animals. *Brain Res.,* 28:527–533.
56. Portig, P. J., and Vogt, M. (1969): Release into the cerebral ventricles of substances with possible transmitter function in the caudate nucleus. *J. Physiol. (Lond.),* 204:687–715.
57. Garelis, E., Young, S. N., Lal, S., and Sourkes, T. L. (1974): Monoamine metabolites in lumbar CSF: The question of their origin in relation to clinical studies. *Brain Res.,* 79:1–8.
58. Curzon, G., Gumpert, E. J. W., and Sharpe, D. M. (1971): Amine metabolites in the human cerebrospinal fluid of humans with restricted flow of cerebrospinal fluid. *Nature New Biol.,* 231:189–191.
59. Guilleminault, C., Cathola, J. P., and Castaigne, P. (1973): Effects of 5-hydroxytryptophan on sleep of a patient with a brain-stem lesion. *Electroencephalogr. Clin. Neurophysiol.,* 34:177–184.
60. Eccleston, D., Ashcroft, G. W., Crawford, T. B. B., Stanton, J. B., Wood, D., and McTurk, P. H. (1970): Effect of tryptophan administration on 5HIAA in cerebrospinal fluid in man. *J. Neurol. Neurosurg. Psychiatry,* 33:269–272.
61. Goodwin, F. K., Post, R. M., Dunner, D. L., and Gordon, E. K. (1973): Cerebrospinal fluid amine metabolites in affective illness: the probenecid technique. *Am. J. Psychiatry,* 130:73–79.
62. Garelis, E., and Sourkes, T. L. (1973): Sites of origin in the central nervous system of monoamine metabolites measured in human cerebrospinal fluid. *J. Neurol. Neurosurg. Psychiat.,* 4:625–629.
63. Weir, R., Chase, T. N., Ng, L. K. Y., and Kopin, I. J. (1973): 5-Hydroxyindoleacetic acid in spinal fluid: relative contributions from brain and spinal cord. *Brain Res.,* 52:409–412.
64. Anderson, H., and Roos, B. E. (1969): 5-Hydroxyindoleacetic acid in cerebrospinal fluid of hydrocephalic children. *Acta Paediat. Scand.,* 58:601–608.
65. Anden, N. E. (1965): Distribution of monoamines and dihydroxyphenylalanine decarboxylase activity in the spinal cord. *Acta Physiol. Scand.,* 64:197–203.
66. Post, R. M., Goodwin, F. K., Gordon, E. K., and Watkin, D. M. (1973): Amine metabolites in human cerebrospinal fluid: Effects of cord transection and spinal fluid block. *Science,* 179: 897–899.
67. Dahlstrom, A., and Fuxe, K. (1965): Evidence for the existence of monoamine neurons in the central nervous system. II. Experimentally induced changes in the intraneuronal amine levels of bulbospinal neuron systems. *Acta Physiol. Scand.* (Suppl. 247, Part II), 64:1–36.

68. Gordon, E. K., Perlow, M., Oliver, J., Ebert, M., and Kopin, I. J. (1975): Origins of catecholamine metabolites in monkey cerebrospinal fluid. *J. Neurochem. (In press.)*

69. Neff, N. H., Tozer, T. N., and Brodie, B. B. (1967): Application of steady-state kinetics to studies of the transfer of 5-hydroxyindoleacetic acid from brain to plasma. *J. Pharmacol. Exp. Ther.,* 158:214–218.

70. Gordon, E. K., Oliver, J., Goodwin, F. K., Chase, T. N., and Post, R. M. (1973): Effect of probenecid on free 3-methoxy-4-hydroxyphenylethylene glycol (MHPG) and its sulfate in human cerebrospinal fluid. *Neuropharmacology,* 12:391–396.

71. Meek, J. L., and Neff, H. N. (1972): Acidic and neutral metabolites of norepinephrine: their metabolism and transport from the brain. *J. Pharmacol. Exp. Ther.,* 181:457–462.

72. Goodwin, F. K., Post, R. M., and Sack, R. L. (1974): Cerebrospinal fluid MHPG in affective illness. *Sci. Proc. Am. Psychiatr. Assoc.,* 127:100-101.

73. Post, R. M., Allen, F. H., and Ommaya, A. K. (1974): Cerebrospinal fluid and Iodide-[131] transport in the spinal subarachnoid space. *Life Sci.,* 14:1885–1894.

74. Feinstrom, J. D., and Wurtman, R. J. (1971): Brain serotonin content: Increase following ingestion of carbohydrate diet. *Science,* 174:1023–1025.

75. Korf, J., van Praag, H. M., and Sebens, J. B. (1972): Serum tryptophan decreased, brain tryptophan increased and brain serotonin synthesis unchanged after probenecid loading. *Brain. Res.,* 42:239–242.

76. Korf, J., van Praag, H. M., and Sebens, J. B. (1975): Tryptophan, tyrosine and cerebral serotonin synthesis after probenecid loading of humans and rats. *Biochem. Pharmacol. (In press.)*

77. Ashcroft, G. W., Crawford, T. B. B., Eccleston, D., Sharman, D. F., MacDougall, E. J., Stanton, J. B., and Binns, J. K. (1966): 5-Hydroxyindole compounds in the cerebrospinal fluid of patients with psychiatric or neurological disease. *Lancet,* 2:1049–1052.

78. Dencker, S. J., Malm, V., Roos, B. E., and Werdinius, B. (1966): Acid monoamine metabolites of cerebrospinal fluid in mental depression and mania. *J. Neurochem.,* 13:1545–1548.

79. Fotherby, K., Ashcroft, G. W., Affleck, J. W., and Forrest, A. D. (1963): Studies on sodium transfer and 5-hydroxyindoles in affective illness. *J. Neurol. Neurosurg. Psychiatry,* 26:71–73.

80. Coppen, A., Prange, A. J., Jr., Whybrow, P. C., and Noguera, R. (1972): Abnormalities of indoleamines in affective disorders. *Arch. Gen. Psychiat.,* 26:474–478.

81. Roos, B. E., and Sjostrom, R. (1969): 5-Hydroxyindoleacetic acid (and homovanillic acid) levels in the CSF after probenecid application in patients with manic-depressive psychosis. *Pharmacol. Clin.,* 1:153–155.

82. Bowers, M. B., Heninger, G. R., and Gerbode, F. A. (1969): Cerebrospinal fluid, 5-hydroxyindoleacetic acid and homovanillic acid in psychiatric patients. *Int. J. Neuropharmacol.,* 8:255–262.

83. van Praag, H. M., and Korf, J. (1971): A pilot study of some kinetic aspects of the metabolism of 5-hydroxytryptamine in depression. *Biol. Psychol.,* 3:105–112.

84. Papeschi, R., and McClure, D. J. (1971): Homovanillic acid and 5-hydroxyindole acetic acid in cerebrospinal fluid of depressed patients. *Arch. Gen. Psychiat.,* 25:354–358.

85. McLeod, W. R., and McLeod, M. (1972): *Indoleamines and Cerebrospinal Fluid in Depressive Illness: Some Research Studies,* edited by B. M. Davies, B. J. Carroll, and R. M. Mowbray. Thomas, Springfield, Illinois.

86. Goodwin, F. K., and Post, R. M. (1972): The use of probenecid in high doses for the estimation of central serotonin turnover in patients with affective illness. In: *Serotonin and Behavior,* edited by J. Barchas and E. Usdin. Academic Press, New York.

87. Roos, B. E. (1972): CSF metabolites and psychopathology. Presented at the College of Neuropsychopharmacology, Las Vegas, Nevada, January 18–22.

88. van Praag, H. M., and Korf, J. (1971): Retarded depression and the dopamine metabolism. *Psychopharmacologia,* 19:199–203.

89. Post, R. M., and Goodwin, F. K. (1974): Studies of cerebrospinal fluid amine metabolites in depressed patients: Conceptual problems and theoretical implications. In: *Biological Aspects of Depression,* edited by J. Mendels. Spectrum Publications, Los Angeles.

90. Wilk, S., Shopsin, B., Gershon, S., and Suhl, M. (1972): Cerebrospinal fluid levels of MHPG in affective disorders. *Nature,* 235:440–441.

91. Post, R. M., Gordon, E. K., Goodwin, F. K., and Bunney, W. E., Jr. (1973): Central norepinephrine metabolism in depressed patients: 3-methoxy-4-hydroxy-phenyl-glycol in the cerebrospinal fluid. *Science,* 179:1002–1003.

92. Shaw, D. M., O'Keefe, R., MacSweeney, D. A. Brooksbank, B. W. L., Noguera, R., and Coppen, A. (1973): 3-Methoxy-4-hydroxy-phenylglycol in depression. *Psychol. Med.,* 3:333–336.

93. Carlson, G. A., and Goodwin, F. K. (1973): Stages of mania. *Arch. Gen. Psychiatry,* 28:221–228.
94. Post, R. M., Kotin, J., Goodwin, F. K., and Gordon, E. K. (1973): Psychomotor activity and cerebrospinal fluid amine metabolites in affective illness. *Am. J. Psychiatry,* 130:67–72.
95. Curtis, G. C. (1972): Psychosomatics and chronobiology: possible implications of neuroendocrine rhythms. *Psychosomatic Med.,* 34:235–256.
96. Sjostrom, R. (1973): 5-Hydroxyindoleacetic acid and homovanillic acid in cerebrospinal fluid in manic-depressive psychosis and the effect of probenecid treatment. *Eur. J. Clin. Pharmacol.,* 6:75–80.
97. van Praag, H. M., Korf, J., and Puite, J. (1970): 5-Hydroxyindoleacetic acid levels in the cerebrospinal fluid of depressive patients treated with probenecid. *Nature,* 225:1259–1260.
98. Bowers, M. B. (1974): Lumbar CSF 5-hydroxyindoleacetic acid and homovanillic acid in affective syndromes. *J. Nerv. Ment. Dis.,* 158:325–330.
99. Korf, J., and van Praag, H. M. (1971): Amine metabolism in human brain: further evaluation of the probenecid test. *Brain Res.,* 35:221–230.
100. Sjöstrom, R. (1972): Steady-state levels of probenecid and their relation to acid monoamine metabolites in human cerebrospinal fluid. *Psychopharmacologia,* 25:96–100.
101. van Praag, H. M., Korf, J., and Schut, D. (1973): Cerebral monoamines and depression: an investigation with the probenecid technique. *Arch. Gen. Psychiatry,* 28:827–831.
102. Bowers, M. B. (1972): Clinical measurements of central dopamine and 5-hydroxytryptamine metabolism. *Neuropharmacology,* 11:101–111.
103. Perel, J. M., Levitt, M., and Dunner, D. L. (1974): Plasma and cerebrospinal fluid probenecid concentrations as related to accumulation of acidic biogenic amine metabolites in man. *Psychopharmacologia,* 35:83–90.
104. Ashcroft, G. W., Blackburn, I. M., Eccleston, D., Glen, A. I. M., Hardley, W., Kinloch, N. E., Lonergan, M., Murray, L. G., and Pullar, I. A. (1973): Changes on recovery in the concentrations of tryptophan and the biogenic amine metabolites in the cerebrospinal fluid of patients with affective illness. *Psychol. Med.,* 3:319–325.
105. Weiss, B. L., Kupfer, D. J., Foster, F. G., and Delgado, J. (1974): Psychomotor activity, sleep and biogenic amine metabolites in depression. *Biol. Psychiatry,* 9:45–54.
106. Asberg, M., Bertilsson, L., Tuck, D., Cronhalm, B., and Sjoquist, F. (1973): Indoleamine metabolites in the cerebrospinal fluid of depressed patients before and during treatment with nortriptyline. *Clin. Pharmacol. Ther.,* 14:277–286.
107. van Praag, H. M., Korf, J., Dols, L. C. W., and Schut, E. (1972): A pilot study of the predictive value of the probenecid test in the application of 5-hydroxytryptophan as an antidepressant. *Psychopharmacologia,* 25:14–21.
108. Post, R. M., and Goodwin, F. K. (1974): Effect of amitriptyline and imipramine on amine metabolites in the cerebrospinal fluid of depressed patients. *Arch. Gen. Psychiatry,* 30:234–239.
109. Bowers, M. B. (1972): CSF 5HIAA and HVA following probenecid in unipolar depressives treated with amitriptyline. *Psychopharmacologia,* 23:26–30.
110. Goodwin, F. K., Post, R. M., and Murphy, D. L. (1973): Cerebrospinal fluid amine metabolites and therapies for depression. *Sci. Proc. Am. Psychiatr. Assoc.,* 126:24–25.
111. Bowers, M. B., and Kupfer, D. J. (1971): Central monoamine oxidase inhibition and REM sleep. *Brain Res.,* 35:561–564.
112. Korf, J., and van Praag, H. M. (1972): Action of *p*-chloroamphetamine on cerebral serotonin metabolism: An hypothesis. *Neuropharmacology,* 11:141–144.
113. Bowers, M. B. (1972): Acute psychosis induced by psychomimetic drug abuse. II. Neurochemical findings. *Arch. Gen. Psychiatry,* 27:440–442.
114. Roos, B. E. (1972): CSF amine metabolites and psychopathology. Presented at the American College of Neuropsychopharmacology, Las Vegas, Nevada, January 18–22, 1972.
115. Sjostrom, R., and Roos, B. E. (1972): 5-Hydroxyindoleacetic acid and homovanillic acid in cerebrospinal fluid in manic-depressive psychosis. *Eur. J. Clin. Pharmacol.,* 4:170–176.
116. Persson, T., and Roos, B. E. (1968): Clinical and pharmacological effects of monoamine precursors of haloperidol in chronic schizophrenia. *Nature,* 217:854.
117. Bowers, M. B., Kleber, H. D., and Davis, L. (1971): Acid monoamine metabolites in cerebrospinal fluid during methadone maintenance. *Nature,* 232:581–582.
118. Persson, T., and Roos, B. E. (1969): Acid metabolites from monoamines in cerebrospinal fluid of chronic schizophrenics. *Br. J. Psychiatry,* 115:95–98.
119. Rimon, R., Roos, B. E., Rakkolainen, V., Alanen, Y. (1971): The content of 5-HIAA and HVA in the CSF of patients with acute schizophrenia. *J. Psychosom. Res.,* 15:375–378.

120. Shopsin, B., Wilk, S., Gershon, S., Roffman, M., Goldstein, M. (1973): Collaborative psycho-pharmacologic studies exploring catecholamine metabolism in psychiatric disorders. In: *Frontiers in Catecholamine Research,* edited by E. Usdin and S. Snyder, pp. 1173–1179. Pergamon, New York.

121. Post, R. M., Fink, E., Carpenter, W. T., and Goodwin, F. K. (1975): Cerebrospinal fluid amine metabolites in acute schizophrenia. *Arch. Gen. Psychiatry (In press.)*

122. Bowers, M. B., Jr. (1973): 5-Hydroxyindoleacetic acid (5-HIAA) and homovanillic acid (HVA) following probenecid in acute psychotic patients treated with phenothiazines. *Psychopharmacologia,* 28:309–318.

123. Bowers, M. B. (1974): Central dopamine turnover in schizophrenic syndromes. *Arch. Gen. Psychiatry,* 31:50–57.

124. Cohen, D. J., Shaywitz, B. A., Johnson, W. T., Bowers, M. B. (1974): Biogenic amines in autistic and atypical children. Cerebrospinal fluid measures of homovanillic acid and 5-hydroxyindoleacetic acid. *Arch. Gen. Psychiatry,* 31:845–853.

125. Carpenter, W. T., Strauss, J. S., and Bartko, J. J. (1973): Flexible system for the diagnosis of schizophrenia: Report from the WHO International Pilot Study for Schizophrenia. *Science,* 182:1275–1278.

126. Chase, T. N., Schnur, J. A., and Gordon, E. K. (1970): CSF monoamine catabolites in drug-induced extrapyramidal disorders. *Neuropharmacology,* 9:265–268.

127. Fyro, B., Helgodt-Wode, B., Borg, S., and Sedvall, G. (1974): The effects of chlorpromazine on HVA levels in CSF of schizophrenic patients. *Psychopharmacologia,* 35:287–294.

128. Bowers, M. B., Jr. (1975): Thioridazine: central dopamine turnover and clinical effects of antipsychotic drugs. *Clin. Pharmacol. Ther.,* 17:73–78.

129. Post, R. M., and Goodwin, F. K. (1975): Tolerance to phenothiazine effects on dopamine turnover in psychiatric patients. *Science (In press.)*

130. Post, R. M., Goodwin, F. K., and Jimerson, D. (1975): Unpublished manuscript.

131. Ackenheil, M., Beckmann, H., Greil, W., Hoffman, G., Markianos, E., and Raese, J. (1974): Antipsychotic efficacy of clozapine in correlation to changes in catecholamine metabolism in man. In: *Phenothiazines and Structurally Related Drugs,* edited by I. S. Forrest, J. Carr, and E. Usdin, pp. 647–657. Raven Press, New York.

132. Bruinvels, J. (1972): Inhibition of the biosynthesis of 5-hydroxytryptamine in rat brain by imipramine. *Eur. J. Pharmacol.,* 20:231–237.

133. Matthysse, S., and Kety, S. S. (editors) (1974): *Symposium on Catecholamines and Their Enzymes in the Neuropathology of Schizophrenia,* May 18–21, 1973, Strasbourg, France. *J. Psychiatr. Res.,* 11:1–364.

134. Stein, L., and Wise, C. D. (1971): Possible etiology of schizophrenia: Progressive damage to the noradrenergic reward system by 6-hydroxydopamine. *Science,* 171:1032–1036.

135. Wise, C. D., and Stein, L. (1973): Dopamine-beta-hydroxylase deficits in the brains of schizophrenic patients. *Science,* 181:344–347.

136. Woolley, D. W., and Shaw, E. (1954): A biochemical and pharmacological suggestion about certain mental disorders. *Proc. Natl. Acad. Sci. USA,* 40:228–231.

137. Freedman, D. X. (1961): Effects of LSD-25 on brain serotonin. *J. Pharmacol. Exp. Ther.,* 134:160–166.

138. Bowers, M. B., (1973): LSD-related states as models of psychosis. In: *Psychopathology and Psychopharmacology,* edited by J. O. Cole, A. M. Freedman, and A. J. Friedhoff, pp. 1–14. Johns Hopkins Press, Baltimore, Maryland.

139. Aghajanian, G. K. (1972): LSD and CNS transmission. *Ann. Rev. Pharmacol.,* 12:157–168.

140. Berridge, M. J., and Prince, W. T. (1974): The nature of the binding between LSD and a 5-HT receptor: a possible explanation for hallucinogenic activity. *Br. J. Pharmacol.,* 51:269–278.

141. Wyatt, R. J., Gillin, J. C., Kaplan, J., Stillman, R. Mandel, H., Ahn, S., VandenHeuvel, W. J. A., Walker, R. W. et al. (1974): N,N-Dimethyltryptamine—A possible relationship to schizophrenia? In: *Serotonin, New Vistas,* edited by E. Costa, G. L. Gessa, and M. Sandler, pp. 299–313. Raven Press, New York.

142. Hornykiewicz, O. (1974): Presented at the Annual Meeting of the American College of Neuropsychopharmacology, San Juan, Puerto Rico, December, 1974.

143. Post, R. M. (1975): Cocaine-psychoses: A continuum model. *Am. J. Psychiatry,* 132:225–231.

144. Pieri, L., Pieri, M., and Haefely, W. (1975): LSD as agonist of dopamine receptors in the striatum. *Nature,* 252:586–588.

145. Von Hungen, K., Roberts, S., and Hill, D. F. (1974): LSD as agonist and antagonist at central dopamine receptors. *Nature,* 252:588–589.
146. Goodwin, F. K., and Sack, R. L. (1974): Behavioral effects of a new dopamine-B-hydroxylase inhibitor (fusaric acid) in man. *J. Psychiatr. Res.,* 11:211–217.
147. Post, R. M., Sanadi, C., and Reichenback, L.: *Unpublished manuscript.*
148. Janowsky, D. S., El-Yousef, M. K., Davis, J. M., and Sekerke, H. J. (1972): Cholinergic antagonism of methylphenidate-induced stereotyped behavior. *Psychopharmacologia,* 27:295–303.
149. Post, R. M., and Goodwin, F. K. (1973): Simulated behavior states: an approach to specificity in psychobiological research. *Biol. Psychiatry,* 7:237–254.

Biology of the Major Psychoses, edited by D. X. Freedman, *Res. Publ. Assoc. Res. Nerv. Ment. Dis.*, Vol. 54. Raven Press, New York 1975.

Critique of Single Amine Theories: Evidence of a Cholinergic Influence in the Major Mental Illnesses

John M. Davis

Illinois State Psychiatric Institute, and University of Chicago, Chicago, Illinois 60637

Biologic theories of mental disease have postulated that the cause of the disorder is a deficit in or an excess of a single neurotransmitter. These are the single-transmitter, single-disease theories. Although it is not unreasonable to suppose that an abnormality in a single transmitter could cause a given mental disease, there are important reasons for considering the development of causal theories that involve more than one amine or transmitter. Virtually every biologic function is controlled by a homeostatic system involving intricate balances of mutual regulations between various regulatory systems. The systems that are particularly pertinent to mental disease are the peripheral sympathetic and the parasympathetic nervous systems. Peripheral autonomic functions are controlled by a balance between the sympathetic and the parasympathetic systems. Balances between different transmitters are involved in the central hypothalamic control of the pituitary releasing factors.

Insight into the mechanism by which two or several factors might combine and result in a psychiatric disease may be gained from consideration of what is known about Parkinson's disease. This disorder has been shown to be caused by a dopamine deficit. Postmortem studies on patients with Parkinson's disease, for example, find low dopamine levels in the appropriate brain centers. However, on a physiologic level, the parkinsonian symptoms are influenced by a balance between the dopaminergic and the cholinergic systems. For example, anticholinergic agents are therapeutically useful in reducing parkinsonian symptoms, whereas physostigmine, a drug that affects the cholinergic system by blocking the destruction of acetylcholine (ACh) and thereby increasing brain levels of ACh, can worsen parkinsonian symptoms in parkinsonian patients. Of course DOPA, through conversion to dopamine, can benefit Parkinson's disease, while neuroleptic drugs can cause pseudo-parkinsonian symptoms in normal persons by blocking dopamine receptors. These two facts suggest that dopamine is the primary causative agent in this disorder. Moreover, since physostigmine did not cause parkinsonian symptoms in normal patients (i.e., patients without Parkinson's disease) in our studies, it would seem that the cholinergic system functions as a secondary, modulating influence on this disorder. Hence, even though the cholinergic system may only modulate but not cause the disorder, a complete description of this disorder should account for the effects of the cholinergic system as well as of the adrenergic system.

Furthermore, we should emphasize that the concept of balance of transmitters may be important in the area of mental disease. Because balances of transmitters are involved in so many physiologic functions, it is reasonable to ask whether an imbalance of transmitters is also involved in schizophrenia, mania, or depression.

To investigate this question, Janowsky and I (1) first considered the traditional, single-transmitter, catecholamine theory of depression, which suggests that mania is associated with high norepinephrine levels and depression with low norepinephrine levels. Following the analogy with Parkinson's disease, we reasoned that the cholinergic system might be expected to modulate the effects of noradrenergic system function. The two-factor hypothesis, then, would be that mania is associated with a high norepinephrine–low acetylcholine level (or function) and depression with a low norepinephrine level modulated by a high acetylcholine level. Hence, it would follow that if one produced an increased acetylcholine level in the brain by using physostigmine, a reduction in mania would result, possibly with the production of depression in patients with pre-existing affective disease.

Following this line of reasoning, we administered physostigmine to both manic and depressed patients and also to schizophrenic patients as controls (after obtaining informed consent). In these studies, neostigmine, which does not pass the blood-brain barrier, was used in equivalent pharmacologic doses to produce equal peripheral effects as an active placebo in a double-blind design. Patients were protected against peripheral cholinergic toxicity by pretreatment with methylscopolamine (2).

The Beigal–Murphy Manic Rating Scale was used to quantitate degree of mania and was completed by raters who were blind as to whether the patient received neostigmine or physostigmine. The patients experienced a marked lessening of their manic disorder following administration of physostigmine (Table 1). No changes were found in patients receiving the placebo neostigmine. Essentially, the manic state was converted to a psychomotor retarded depression. In other words, patients were initially in a manic state, exhibiting typically manic symptoms: rhyming and punning, rapid thought, rapid movements, grandiose ideas. Following physostigmine, the patients slowed down and instead of moving rapidly, moved slowly, talked slowly, appeared lethargic, and reported that they felt drained and without energy. Their subjective feelings were quite marked with respect to such dimensions as feeling lethargic, apathetic, and having "no thoughts in their head," etc. A somewhat less consistent response to this drug were feelings of depression. That is, some manic patients would report that they felt depressed following physostigmine, while some would cry and show other manifestations of depressed affect. These depressed patients tended to show greater psychomotor retardation with more depressed affect.

The most impressive feature of the physostigmine effects was on the level of

TABLE 1. *Changes in symptom with physostigmine*

Affective state	Control	Physostigmine	t	p
Beigel–Murphy manic intensity	15.30 ± 2.09	8.71 ± 1.24	3.67	0.002
Beigel–Murphy euphoria	2.54 ± 0.49	0.73 ± 0.30	4.17	0.001
Talkativeness	2.98 ± 0.28	1.56 ± 0.19	4.16	0.001
Hyperactivity	1.89 ± 0.30	0.83 ± 0.16	4.18	0.001
Cheerfulness	1.44 ± 0.19	0.45 ± 0.15	4.42	0.0007
Friendliness	1.79 ± 0.17	1.10 ± 0.23	2.46	0.02
Grandiosity	0.38 ± 0.22	0.17 ± 0.11	1.16	NS
Flight of ideas	1.98 ± 0.38	0.93 ± 0.24	3.62	0.0025
Happiness	1.71 ± 0.26	0.38 ± 0.16	4.55	0.0006
Depression	0.66 ± 0.20	1.68 ± 0.41	4.03	0.002

motoric activity both in the sense of motor movement and also in the sense of more general rate disturbances (employed in a more general sense to include motor-retarded depression). It affected mood less consistently and produced depressed affect in some but not all patients. Not all manic patients had grandiose delusions to start with, and physostigmine did cause some decrease in grandiosity, although not a statistically remarkable decrease.

The time course of the physostigmine effects is shown in Fig. 1. This is consistent with the biologic half-life of physostigmine and its effects on brain acetylcholine in animals. Patients with other pre-existing affective disturbances experience

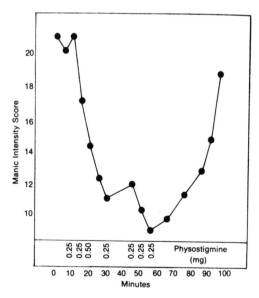

FIG. 1. Time course of changes in Beigel-Murphy manic intensity scale score in case 4, while receiving 2 mg of physostigmine.

a much greater degree of depressive affect following physostigmine intake than do patients with "pure" schizophrenic illness. Hence, there may be some specificity of physostigmine action since patients with affective disorders have more depressed affect following physostigmine than do schizophrenics with no affect disorder. Even patients in a normal volunteer study experienced some depressed affect following medication with physostigmine or experimental cholinesterase inhibitors.

It is a clear observation, however, that the acute dose of physostigmine produces a greater disturbance in rate than in affect or content. There are at least two explanations as to why the rate disturbance changes to a greater degree than does the mood or thought disturbance. First, the rate may be controlled by the amine–cholinergic balance to a greater extent than either the mood or thought functions, a pharmacologic disassociation of several mental functions contributing to the same syndrome. Hence, depression and mania may be disorders that involve more than one mental function and more than one transmitter. Thus, the cholinergic system may be involved in the rate disturbance, while other systems are involved in other aspects of the disorder. A second possible explanation concerns the time dimension. The effects of physostigmine are acute, generally lasting about 1 hr. The very rapid nature of the physostigmine effect may in part be responsible for its failure to alter thought content, in spite of its effect on the other symptoms of mania. It may be that the nature of thought disorder is such that it would not be expected to change instantaneously. For example, acute administration of phenothiazines often reduces extremely agitated behavior in schizophrenic patients within a few hours, but thought disorder may take several weeks or even months to improve.

Although it is appropriate to discuss the specificity of physostigmine's action, it must be remembered that this discussion is speculative at this time, as neither the cause nor the essence (i.e., which symptoms are primary as opposed to secondary) of manic-depressive disease is presently clear. If the rate disturbance (being speeded up or slowed down) is considered to be central to mania and depression, one would conclude that physostigmine is a reasonably specific drug. If thought content, such as the grandiose delusions of mania, is the core symptom, then physostigmine would be considered relatively less specific. In actuality, physostigmine is not a completely specific drug because it influences rate to a greater degree than it does mood or thought content. On the other hand, the drug is not entirely nonspecific. It has an antimanic effect that appears qualitatively different from that of sedation. That is, patients can be heavily sedated but still be manic. For example, clinically severe, life-threatening outbursts of manic excitement have been treated intravenously with barbiturates or high doses of chlorpromazine. In either case patients can be so sedated that they are severely obtunded, almost semicomatose. When they arise from the semicoma state they may stagger to the day room with a toxic gate, slurred speech, etc., while remaining markedly manic in thinking and actions. They are still acutely manic in all respects, but are sedated manic. In contrast, physostigmine does not produce sleep. To say that its action is that of nonspecific sedation would be an inaccurate description. In our view, its degree of specificity is somewhere between completely specific and completely nonspecific. The characterization of its specific action may depend upon assumptions as to what is important in mania and depression. Those who consider the thought content of depression or mania the essence of this disorder are less impressed with the effects of physostigmine than those who place more emphasis on the rate disturbance.

Because cholinergic pathways are involved in many central functions in the brain, one might not expect complete specificity from a drug such as physostigmine. Our inquiry into the mental effects of physostigmine was undertaken to elicit clues regarding the involvement of cholinergic systems in mania and depression. It is also relevant to note that reserpine, which can produce depression in hypertensive patients, has central cholinomimetic properties and that the tricyclic antidepressants, the most effective class of antidepressants, have central anticholinergic properties. Efforts to produce "pure" antidepressants that inhibit the norepinephrine membrane pump without producing anticholinergic blockade have not been successful. It may well be that the anticholinergic properties of the tricyclic antidepressants are a helpful property and contribute to the therapeutic action in a secondary way. Thus, the concept that a single amine, norepinephrine, is the cause of depression may be incomplete with respect to treatment. That is, anticholinergic properties may indeed be helpful in the treatment of depression.

A single-transmitter, single-disease hypothesis also exists for schizophrenia—the so-called dopamine theory of schizophrenia. This model implicitly suggests that high dopamine levels or "functions" produce schizophrenia. It has been noted clinically that injections of psychomotor stimulants can precipitate or worsen schizophrenic episodes in patients with schizophrenic disorders, as evidenced by neurosynthesis interviews in previous years. Using double-blind techniques, Janowsky and I (3,4) compared the effects of placebo to small amounts of intravenous methylphenidate. This psychomotor stimulant produced a marked worsening in schizophrenic illness in patients with active disease as did the administration of *d*- or *l*-amphetamine. The quantitative rating of the severity of psychosis was essentially doubled. This intensification of the psychotic disorder with methylphenidate was regulated by a balance between the dopamine and cholinergic system. Physostigmine, but not neostigmine, administered prior to the methylphenidate prevents the further development of a methylphenidate-induced psychosis. Physostigmine administered after methylphenidate terminates the further intensification of the methylphenidate-induced psychosis (see Fig. 2) (5). Because similar doses of methylphenidate produce a mild euphoria in normals, it seems that schizophrenic patients are unusually sensitive to methylphenidate.

The evidence for the dopamine theory of schizophrenia is that all the antipsychotic compounds block the dopamine receptors. Furthermore, catecholamines are involved in the antipsychotic action of the neuroleptics, since the

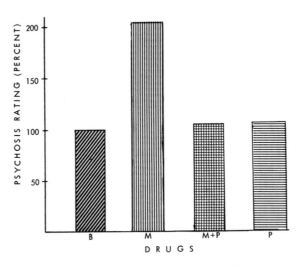

FIG. 2. The effect of methylphenidate (M) i.v.; physostigmine (P), and methylphenidate plus physostigmine (M + P) on psychosis. Psychosis rating expressed as percent of baseline (100%). Methylphenidate markedly worsens psychosis. This is neutralized when physostigmine is added.

catecholamine synthesis inhibitor, α-methyl-p-tyrosine, can potentiate the antipsychotic action of the neuroleptics.

For heuristic purposes, I would like to formulate an alternative to the dopamine theory of schizophrenia. The dopamine theory is, again, a single-transmitter, single-disease theory, i.e., schizophrenia is associated with excessive "functional" dopamine. An alternative explanation would be a two-factor theory of schizophrenia. One factor may involve some other cause, such as the CPK abnormality outlined by Dr. Meltzer in this volume. Just as the cholinergic system may modulate the movement disorder of Parkinson's disease and the rate disturbance of mania and depression, it may be that a dopaminergic system (or a dopaminergic–cholinergic balance) may modulate the disturbance produced by the central factors of schizophrenia. Therefore, there may be two factors in schizophrenia—a central factor, as yet unknown, and a modulating factor under adrenergic–cholinergic control. The antipsychotic agents, by blocking dopamine receptors, affect the adrenergic–cholinergic balance and damp the schizophrenic process. This reduction of the intensity of the schizophrenic symptoms may permit a normal reparative process to take place in connection with other features of the disorder. Schizophrenic illness may remit over the course of 6 weeks or so as, in some broad sense, healing takes place in the other relevant systems, once the process has been damped. I have no evidence to offer for this theory other than the time course of the therapeutic benefit of the neuroleptic drugs. Figure 3 represents the time course on neuroleptic drugs, which Dr. Cole and I prepared, based on data from NIMH Collaborative Studies No. 1.

It seems to me that the slow time course for recovery is a clue to the operation

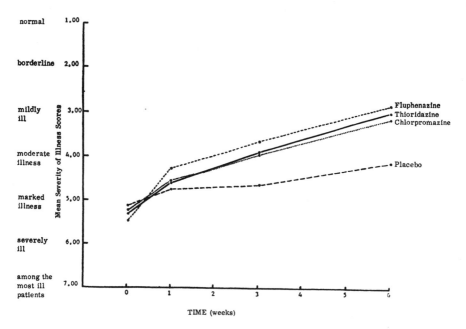

FIG. 3. Severity of illness over time in patients treated with phenothiazines. (Data from NIMH-PSC Collaborative Study I.)

of other factors in schizophrenia besides abnormalities in the dopaminergic–adrenergic system. In addition, there are other clues that may be important in our modulation factor hypothesis (factor 2). Certain schizophrenics appear to have low levels of platelet monoamine oxidase (MAO) (6). Furthermore, this may be under hereditary control. An obvious speculation would be that this is the mechanism by which the hereditary tendency to schizophrenia is transmitted. Furthermore, there is an important relationship between age and MAO; MAO levels are highest in the very young and the very old, and are lowest in adolescents and young adults (7). Thus the natural history of schizophrenia is such that it has its highest incidence in this age period when MAO would be the lowest. This may be a consequence of hormonal changes, but whatever the mechanism, it is interesting that the finding that MAO is lowest in this period (in patients who may, on a hereditary basis, have chronically low levels to begin with) is consistent with our speculation that MAO may play a role in factor 2. It would be expected that MAO, an intracellular enzyme, would be most important in the regulation of intracellular amine levels.

There is further information that implicates abnormalities in stored amines in schizophrenia. Amphetamine is a particularly good releaser of newly synthesized amines. Methylphenidate releases more amines from stores than does amphetamine and is more potent in activating schizophrenia than is amphetamine (8). It is less potent in producing psychomotor stimulation in normals, so this effect is peculiar to the schizophrenic. This is consistent with an hypothesis of an abnormality in the stored dopamine. α-Methyl-p-tyrosine, which blocks the synthesis of dopamine, is ineffective in treating schizophrenia, yet it potentiates the effect of the neuroleptics. Reserpine, which does have antipsychotic properties, interferes with the storage of dopamine. Thus, α-methyl-p-tyrosine is most effective on newly synthesized amines, whereas reserpine is most effective on the amine stores. This further implicates the existence of stored amines in the schizophrenic process.

Whether these theories ultimately prove to be true or false, there is a second spin-off that is important for clinical practice. The pharmacologic concepts underlying these theories are useful in understanding side effects. For example, the concept of cholinergic blockade is useful in explaining the central anticholinergic syndrome. This syndrome can result when multiple anticholinergic agents are administered to psychiatric patients resulting in an addictive anticholinergic effect (9).

In this chapter we have raised the question of whether more than one factor is operative in schizophrenia and in manic-depressive illness. In depression, cholinergic factors may modulate the hypothesized norepinephrine deficit, which does suggest that a complete description of depressive illness may involve more than one transmitter. In schizophrenia, rather than playing a central role as the primary cause, dopamine (or a dopamine–cholinergic balance) might play a role as a modulator. With dopamine blockaded by antipsychotic agents, it is possible that a normal reparative process takes place. It may be important in theorizing to differentiate agents that might modulate a disorder versus those agents that are the principal cause of a disorder.

It is appropriate to add three methodologic cautions in this regard. First, our reasoning, although based upon pharmacologic evidence, is obviously speculative and inferential and should be regarded as such; it is in no sense a well-formed systematically substantiated theory. We feel that it is important to label speculation as such, because it is not unusual in psychiatry for a speculative theory, when it reaches the practitioner, to be taken as an established fact. Dr. Freedman has referred to such theories as "metaneuropsychopharmacology," an apt label; we think it appropriate to generate such theories because of their heuristic value, but only if they are correctly labeled.

A second methodologic caution that applies both to the biochemical theories of schizophrenia and depression concerns the fact that too often these theories are stated in terms of "level" or "turnover." The evidence is based almost entirely on pharmacologic studies that do not point specifically to any given mechanism. For example, it is quite possible that instead of the low norepinephrine level or turnover postulated to occur in depression, the causal mechanism could, in fact, be an impairment or function of the norepinephrine receptor. It is important to recognize that speaking of low norepinephrine in depression or of high dopamine in schizophrenia should really be understood as a shorthand referring to dopaminergic or noradrenergic "function." Even the qualification "free" norepineph-rine in the synaptic cleft is not, strictly speaking, a supportable theory, because most of the evidence would also be compatible with the putative defect being postsynaptic. There are many possible defects that could lower noradrenergic function including (1) low levels or (2) low rates in the synthesis of amines, but also (3) defects in the receptor site, (4) defects in the release process, (5) altera-tions in the membrane transport, and (6) excessive degradation or metabolic alterations resulting in lower noradrenergic function (such as excessive intracellu-lar metabolism).

The third methodologic point concerns our hypothesis that MAO may be low in the brain of schizophrenic patients to a degree that may have a significant effect. It should be recognized that many pharmacologic effects are not apparent until MAO is almost completely inhibited, so there is very real reason to question whether a physiologic lowering of MAO of from 50 to 80% is physiologically significant (if levels were lowered to 1% of normal, it would be reasonable to regard them as physiologically significant). Even though this is a very important criticism of the significance of the observation of low MAO in schizophrenia, it is still possible that the low platelet MAO could be a clue to the biochemistry of schizophrenia in that the same patients could have low central MAO to a degree that was physiologically meaningful. Although this cannot be considered likely, it may be possible. We do not feel that, because MAO is not completely inhibited, it would be absolutely impossible that the hypothesized low MAO in schizophrenia could have any relevance at all. Furthermore, schizophrenia is a disease that has its most frequent onset in late adolescence and the early twenties and a course that indicates that the illness may burn out later in life. MAO levels that have been determined using brains obtained postmortem from elderly schiz-ophrenics, do not necessarily yield data that are relevant to what their MAO levels were when they were young and their schizophrenic illness was active. In other words, biochemical studies of brain functioning from older, burned-out schizophrenic patients may not provide the basis for a good model of schizophre-nia.

In summary, this chapter has suggested that there may be alternative theories in biologic psychiatry to the single-transmitter, single-disease model. For most physiologic functions, homeostatic control is achieved through balances between neurophysiologic systems such as the sympathetic–parasympathetic peripheral autonomic system. We have presented empirical evidence and a discussion of the hypothesis that the central cholinergic system could play a role in mania and depression in modulating the central noradrenergic system. Because alterations of the cholinergic system do not cause parkinsonian symptoms by themselves, but modulate existing symptoms, by analogy with Parkinson's disease, we suggest that the cholinergic system may play a similar modulating role on affect. In discussing biologic theories of schizophrenia, we propose that the dopaminergic system, rather than being the primary cause of schizophrenia, could play a modulatory role, suggesting a two-factor theory of schizophrenia. Furthermore, this modulation of the dopaminergic system in schizophrenia could also involve balances between dopaminergic and cholinergic circuits.

REFERENCES

1. Janowsky, D. S., El-Yousef, M. K., Davis, J. M., and Sekerke, H. J. (1972): A cholinergic–adrenergic hypothesis of mania and depression. *Lancet,* 632–635.
2. Janowsky, D. S., El-Yousef, M. K., Davis, J. M., and Serkerke, H. J. (1973): Parasympathetic suppression of manic symptoms by physostigmine. *Arch. Gen. Psychol.,* 28:542–547.
3. Davis, J. M., and Janowsky, D. S. (1973): Amphetamine and methylphenidate psychosis. In: *Frontiers in Catecholamine Research,* edited by E. Usdin and S. Snyder, pp. 977–987. Pergamon, London.
4. Janowsky, D. S., El-Yousef, M. K., and Davis, J. M. (1973): Provocation of schizophrenic symptoms by intravenous administration of methylphenidate. *Arch. Gen. Psychol.,* 28:185–190.
5. Janowsky, D. S., El-Yousef, M. K., Davis, J. M., and Sekerke, H. J. (1973): Antagonistic Effects of Physostigmine and Methylphenidate in Man. *Am. J. Psychol.,* 130:12.
6. Murphy, D. L., and Wyatt, R. J. (1972): Reduced monoamine oxidase activity in blood platelets from schizophrenic patients. *Nature,* 238:225–226.
7. Robinson, D. S., Davis, J. M., Nies, A., Ravaris, C. L., and Sylvester, D. (1971): Relation of sex and aging to monoamine oxidase activity of human brain, plasma and platelets. *Arch. Gen. Psychol.,* 24:536–539.
8. Scheel-Kruger, J. (1971): Comparative studies of various amphetamine analogues demonstrating different interactions with the metabolism of catecholamines in the brain. Eur. J. Pharmacol., 14:47–49.
9. El-Yousef, M. K., Janowsky, D. S., Davis, J. M., and Sekerke, H. J. (1973): Reversal of antiparkinsonian drug toxicity by physostigmine: A controlled study. *Am. J. Psychol.,* 130:141–145.

Discussion

Iversen: I would like to comment on the important question of the dopaminergic-cholinergic balances which John Davis emphasized in his presentation. I think there is a very interesting issue here concerning some of the neuroleptic drugs. As has been discussed here, the current idea about the mode of action of neuroleptic drugs is that they are all dopamine antagonists. However, some of these drugs are also very powerful anticholinergic agents. Recently in our laboratory in Cambridge, R. J. Miller and C. R. Hiley (*Nature*, 248:596, 1974) estimated the potencies of a series of neuroleptic drugs as antimuscarinic agents. Dr. Snyder and his colleagues at Baltimore have done the same thing and achieved similar results. There are two drugs in particular that are very powerful anticholinergics. One of them is thioridazine, and the other is the more recent neuroleptic drug, clozapine. Both of these stand out among the neuroleptics as being the only drugs in the whole series that we have looked at which are more powerful as anticholinergic agents than they are as antidopaminergic agents. All the others are more powerful dopamine antagonists, especially the butyrophenones, which are virtually devoid of anticholinergic properties.

The interesting correlation here is with the incidence of extrapyramidal side effects, since thioridazine and clozapine appear to stand out clinically as the drugs least likely to induce Parkinson-like side effects. This is a fairly obvious pharmacologic conclusion, as these drugs carry built-in anticholinergic properties, and this is how such symptoms are commonly treated.

In terms of devising new drugs, this sort of consideration may be extremely important, because the two drugs which carry built-in anticholinergic properties do, in fact, show false negatives in many conventional animal tests for antidopamine characteristics. For instance, they do not block amphetamine-induced stimulation of motor activity or stereotyped behavior in animals, despite the fact that they are effective dopamine blockers on a biochemical test system, the striatal adenylate cyclase.

Davis: Dr. Max Fink has asked whether anticholinergics worsen mania, since they help in depression. Anticholinergic drugs produce the central anticholinergic syndrome or so-called atropine psychosis. And I think, as I said in my presentation, that there are many different cholinergic neuronal systems in the brain serving a variety of functions. And what you probably see clinically is an impairment in function that is most susceptible to the drug. I don't think one can answer what happens with manics because other cholinergic systems are more susceptible to anticholinergic agents. And this is important from a different respect. A lot of work with anticholinergics has been done, such as Dr. Fink's work with Ditran. In view of Dr. Iversen's comment, phenothiazines do have anticholinergic properties, particularly, of course, Mellaril, but chlorpromazine and many of the others also have some of these properties.

Now, as pharmacologists, we think of a phenothiazine as a weak cholinergic. But—like chlorpromazine—the weakness may be compared to the potency of cogentin. But patients receive 800 milligrams or two grams of chlorpromazine when they might receive 4 milligrams or 6 milligrams of cogentin. So there they are receiving much more of a "weak" anticholinergic.

And in point of fact patients do develop central anticholinergic psychosis on a combination of psychotropic drugs, all of which have anticholinergic side effects.

Now, normally patients don't die of a central anticholinergic psychosis. They do have disorientation and loss of immediate memory. For example, as Max Fink reported to the Society of Biological Psychiatry years ago, you could potentiate atropine coma with his atropine-like agents by giving chlorpromazine. A patient who has central anticholinergic syndrome that is misidentified as "being crazy," who is then given a massive dose of chlorpromazine—can go into what I think is probably an atropine coma, and then die of a complication of coma.

So, even if these biologic theories are wrong, understanding the biology of the neurotransmitters has implications for treatment in that it allows us to understand and better manage side effects.

Lipton: I'm certainly not surprised by Dr. Davis's findings involving the cholinergic system in psychoses. If one considers that any given neuron (say a noradrenergic neuron which releases norepinephrine exclusively) has inputs from serotonin neurons, from acetylcholine neurons, from other norepinephrine neurons, and perhaps from other transmitter systems as well. Whether or not it discharges will depend upon its input. It is hardly surprising to find that alterations in input from other systems would cause dramatic changes in output, hence symptoms.

We've been concerned with the relationship between the serotonin system and the norepinephrine system. At least in the periphery some evidence is now emerging to the effect that in essential hypertension it is the relationship between those two systems which determines whether or not hypertension exists.

I want to make one or two other comments. One is that I'm struck by what seems to be a symmetry between the amount of time required for the onset of a drug effect and the time required for the termination of the drug effect. There is a wide spectrum of time effects here. In Dr. Davis's work, it's interesting that with methylphenidate he can get an exacerbation of a psychosis in a matter of minutes, but it only lasts an hour. With physostigmine he gets a very rapid diminution of manic effects, but it only lasts an hour.

With reserpine it may take many months to produce a clinical depression. It also can take many months to relieve the reserpine depression. The most clear-cut example is Dr. Gershon's reports of DFP-induced psychosis wherein it apparently takes many months of chronic low-level DFP to induce the psychosis and then many months to relieve it again. I think that symmetry may well be telling us something.

This bears on the question of the difference between the rate of onset of therapeutic effects and the rate of onset of side effects. The rate of onset of side effects is invariably rapid. The rate of onset of therapeutic effects is very slow. Dr. Glowinski now adds chlorpromazine to what we've already known about lithium and imipramine; with all those drugs, pharmacologically, the chronic effects are always smaller than the acute effects. To overstate the case it could almost be said that one begins to get therapeutic effects of drugs at the time at which they are no longer pharmacologically active. That's an overstatement of the case, but the evidence seems to point to the view that clinical effects become manifest when the acute pharmacologic effects are markedly attenuated.

How can we explain that? I don't know that we really have an explanation, but it may have to do with alterations of the equilibria in the other systems. For example an agent that alters the synaptic efficiency of an NE neuron by inhibiting reuptake may well generate long-term changes in the serotonin system or perhaps in some other system. It may also have to do with something that has troubled me for the past several months, namely, that the time course of a therapeutic response to psychotropic drugs is really quite different from the time course response to drugs as we ordinarily encounter them in medicine. For example, ordinarily with digoxin, antibiotics, corticoids, or antipyretics, one gets effects within 24 hours, or at most within 48 hours. But with psychotropic drugs we've got to wait five or six weeks.

The time course of therapeutic response really corresponds much more to that of the time course of response to tissue injury. One doesn't expect to heal a broken leg in 24 hours, or to restore a damaged liver. And one can't help but begin to wonder whether or not there are not types of tissue injury in the psychoses as well. The commonly used terms such as psychic wound, psychic trauma, etc., may be more than a metaphor, even if we can't see them under the microscope. Injuries may occur that can be detected only chemically, and repair of such injuries may involve protein synthesis in receptors or in the neuronal constituents themselves.

Dr. Meltzer has given us a type of tissue injury associated with acute psychosis, with his muscle phenomena. The generation of neuronal endings on that muscle may correspond to a repair process. There may be other examples as well. And I think it may be well worth thinking that pharmacotherapy in psychoses will require shifts in equilibrium, alterations of set points such as occur in essential hypertension. A model such as tissue injury or changes in the equilibrium of multiple interacting systems may come a little closer to telling us what the nature of these illnesses really is from a biologic point of view.

Kety: Although I would agree with much of what Dr. Lipton said in his last few sentences, I think tissue injury is perhaps too harsh a term. I would rather think that the long latency of some of these therapeutic effects may reflect readjustment that is taking place in response to the chronic administration of the drug: re-establishment of homeostasis on the basis of increased receptor sites or increased synaptic connections, changes in enzymes and rates of synthesis, or adjustments that one has to inactivation, which in themselves may be the therapeutic modality rather than the initial and direct pharmacologic effect of the drug. That, I think, is certainly a worthwhile concept to entertain.

We are indebted to Dr. Davis for some very penetrating and compelling studies of the importance of the cholinergic pathways in the major psychoses. But nothing I heard him say really argues against the other transmitter hypotheses, the norepinephrine hypothesis in affective disorder, or the serotonin hypothesis (which incidentally received too little attention at this meeting), or the dopamine hypothesis of schizophrenia. In fact, if one examines what these hypotheses say, they are not at all pretentious. These are not hypotheses that attempt to explain affective disorder or mania or depression or schizophrenia in terms of a monolithic biochemical disorder depending upon one's favorite transmitter. These are very humble hypotheses. They simply suggest the possibility that norepinephrine may be involved in affective disorders, or that hyperactivity of dopaminergic pathways may be involved in schizophrenia. These hypotheses are not intended to suggest that these are the only factors that are involved.

What Dr. Davis has done has been to expand the arena in which these transmitters act. We must recognize that the synapse is an extremely complex site, and that a number of the transmitters that have been discussed and probably many transmitters that haven't even been dreamt of are acting at the synapse.

But what I think is important is that there seems to be a compelling body of evidence at the present time that certain chemical transmitters acting at synapses of the CNS mediate many of the processes involved in the major psychoses. That hypothesis doesn't attempt to explain schizophrenia or manic-depressive illness—it would be pretentious and premature if it did—but it is heuristic in that it suggests areas in which further research should yield valuable information of relevance to these disorders.

Because of the fundamental knowledge which research has provided over the past several decades in many apparently irrelevant areas, certain interesting convergencies have developed. What I find most encouraging about the state of research on mental illness is not that the answers are at hand, but that for the first time crucial and heuristic questions can be asked, and that there are a large number of competent and critical psychiatrists and psychobiologists with the knowledge and methods who can answer them.

Biology of the Major Psychoses, edited by D. X. Freedman, *Res. Publ. Assoc. Res. Nerv. Ment. Dis.*, Vol. 54. Raven Press, New York 1975.

Evidence for Neuroendocrine Abnormalities in the Major Mental Illnesses

Edward J. Sachar

Department of Psychiatry, Albert Einstein College of Medicine, Bronx, New York 10461

Another way of investigating brain function in the psychoses is through the study of neuroendocrine regulation, an approach that offers some special advantages. First, it provides a physiologic measure of actual hypothalamic function. Second, secretions of the various hypothalamic releasing and inhibiting hormones are mediated by the same neurotransmitters implicated in the psychoses: norepinephrine, dopamine, and serotonin. Third, in the absence of good animal models of depression and schizophrenia, hormonal measures have the advantage of being readily applied to humans. Furthermore, pituitary hormones can now be identified according to specificity; they are undiluted by metabolites from other body tissues. Indeed, it may soon be possible to measure the hypothalamic hormones themselves, which would permit us to measure, in blood, substances specifically produced by specific regions of the brain. One of the major limitations of this approach, of course, is that it probably has little value in studying disorders that do not involve the hypothalamus.

Depressive illness, however, has many clinical features suggestive of hypothalamic disturbance—alterations in mood, appetite, libido, aggressive drive, autonomic function, and a diurnal variation in symptomatology. This chapter briefly reviews studies that suggest abnormalities in the regulation of adrenocorticotropic hormone (ACTH) and cortisol, growth hormone, and luteinizing hormone (LH) secretion in unipolar depressive illness.

Both indoleamines and catecholamines appear to be involved in the control of various aspects of ACTH secretion. Although the neuroendocrine literature on this subject is quiet complex, and at times contradictory, there does appear to be strong evidence, developed by Ganong, Van Loon, Scapagnini, and others, that a noradrenergic system normally exerts a tonic, inhibitory influence on hypothalamic centers mediating ACTH secretion (1). We can illustrate this by studies we have performed on monkeys with Marantz, Weitzman, and Sassin (2) (Fig. 1). Equivalent intravenous doses of the adrenergic drugs, *d*- and *l*-amphetamine equally suppressed cortisol secretion—as an index of ACTH secretion. At 60 to 90 min postinjection, plasma cortisol fell to about 60% of control values. Repeating the study (Fig. 2) after pretreatment of the monkeys with pimozide, a specific dopamine receptor blocker, yielded identical results that indicated that the inhibition of cortisol secretion was produced by the noradrenergic effects of both *d*- and *l*-amphetamine.

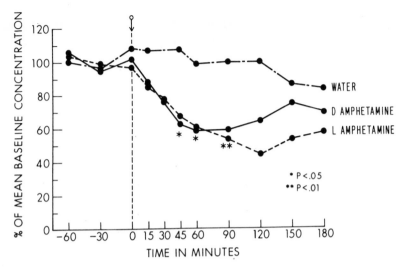

FIG. 1. Plasma cortisol responses to water and to infusions of equimolar amounts of D- and L-amphetamine in six rhesus monkeys. Cortisol values are expressed in percent of mean baseline concentration.

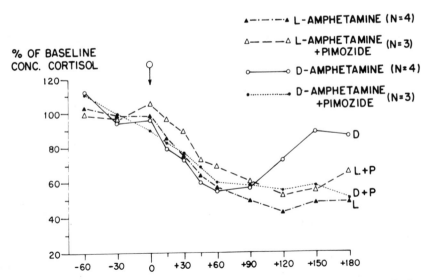

FIG. 2. Plasma cortisol responses to equimolar amounts of D- and L-amphetamine in rhesus monkeys, with and without pretreatment with pimozide.

Conversely, selective depletion of brain norepinephrine in animals prompts hypersecretion of ACTH and cortisol (1). If, as has been hypothesized, some depressed patients have a functional depletion of hypothalamic norepinephrine, one would also expect them to hypersecrete cortisol, particularly during periods when such secretion is normally inhibited.

Of course, it has been known for two decades that many severely depressed patients do secrete excessive cortisol (3). What has remained a question is how much of this hypersecretion is explained by a simple stress response, and how much is a more primary neuroendocrine abnormality. With Drs. Roffwarg, Hellman, Gruen, Altman, and other collaborators (4,5), we have been studying the 24-hr pattern of cortisol secretion in severely depressed unipolar patients, with particular attention to that period of the day when cortisol secretion normally is inhibited, or at least much diminished.

The normal 24-hr pattern of cortisol secretion is apparent in Fig. 3. Plasma cortisol concentration was determined in this normal elderly man every 20 min from blood samples obtained through a cannula. It is seen that cortisol is normally secreted throughout the day in seven to nine discrete episodes that reflect pulses of ACTH secretion and, presumably, pulses of hypothalamic neuroendocrine activity. Note, however, that for about 6 hr—from about 4 hr before to 2 hr after sleep onset—cortisol secretion virtually ceases. It is this period of apparent inhibition that is of particular interest to us in the study of hypersecreting depressed patients.

Figure 4 shows the 24-hr plasma cortisol pattern before and after recovery in a severely depressed woman. Note that during illness plasma cortisol concentration, both at the beginning and end of secretory episodes, is markedly elevated, even during the previously mentioned evening and early morning hours. This disturbed pattern is apparent, even in some patients (Figs. 5 and 6) who are

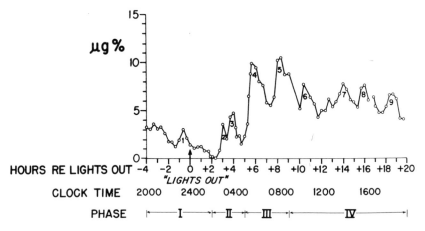

FIG. 3. Twenty-four hour pattern of plasma cortisol concentration in a normal 60-year-old man. Major secretory episodes are numbered.

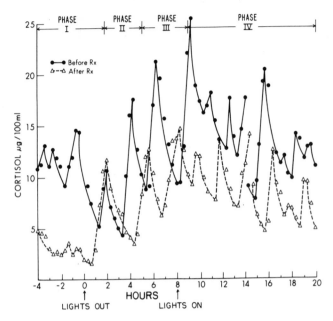

FIG. 4. Twenty-four hour pattern of plasma cortisol concentration in a severely depressed and anxious woman, age 52, before and after clinical recovery. Zero time is time of lights out for sleep.

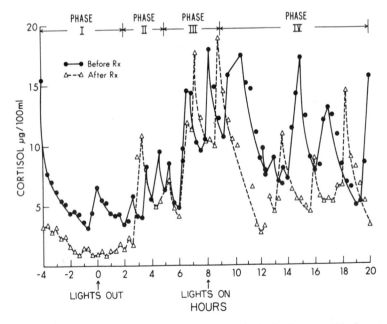

FIG. 5. Twenty-four hour plasma cortisol pattern in an apathetically depressed bipolar man, age 58, before and after clinical recovery. Zero time is time of lights out for sleep.

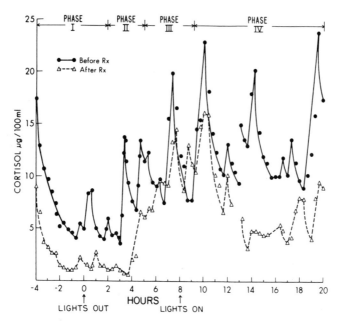

FIG. 6. Twenty-four hour pattern of plasma cortisol concentration in an apathetically depressed woman, age 62, before and after clinical recovery. Zero time is time of lights out for sleep.

predominantly apathetic, rather than emotionally aroused and anxious—which tends to militate against a simple stress explanation.

Figure 7 compares the mean 24-hr plasma cortisol pattern of seven unipolar depressed patients with the mean pattern of 54 normal subjects studied with similar methods by Elliot Weitzman and colleagues. It can be seen that the largest deviations occur not during the period of maximal cortisol secretion, but in the afternoon, evening, and early morning hours, when cortisol secretion normally subsides. This leads to a flattening of the usual circadian fluctuation.

Again, such a pattern would not fit easily with a stress hypothesis, but might fit with a disinhibition hypothesis.

Of course, the early morning hours are also the hours of sleep—and depressed patients characteristically sleep poorly. Perhaps the disturbed sleep of the depressive is stressful, leading to increased cortisol secretion at those times. However, in a study conducted with Ellman, Roffwarg, and others, (6) (Fig. 8) systematic deprivation by awakenings first of REM, then NREM sleep in normals, each for a total of 8 days, did not alter the baseline plasma cortisol patterns. Rubin and colleagues also found no effect of 205 hr of total sleep deprivation on urinary corticosteroid excretion in normals (7). Furthermore, plasma cortisol remains elevated in depressed patients even during sleeping periods. Plasma cortisol concentrations in just those samples drawn during sleep, as determined by EEG, were still significantly higher than were cortisol concentrations in normals during the same hours (5) (Table 1).

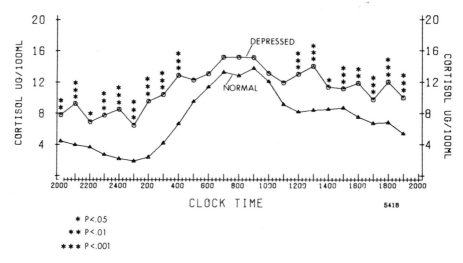

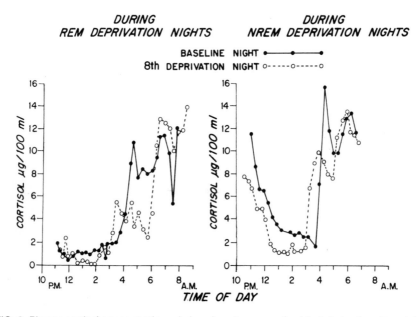

FIG. 7. Mean hourly plasma cortisol concentrations in seven unipolar depressed patients and 54 normal subjects. Individual secretory episodes are obscured in the group means.

FIG. 8. Plasma cortisol concentrations during sleep in a normal subject during baseline nights, and then during the 8th consecutive night of REM deprivation *(left)* and of NREM deprivation *(right)*.

TABLE 1. *Plasma cortisol concentration (μg%) in depressed and normal subjects while asleep*

Time	Normals			Depressed			
	N	Cortisol	S.D.	N	Cortisol	S.D.	P
23:00–24:00	54	2.7	2.9	4	5.5	1.2	NS
24:00–01:00	54	2.2	2.6	5	6.2	2.4	<0.001
01:00–02:00	54	1.9	2.1	6	4.4	1.7	<0.001
02:00–03:00	54	2.4	2.5	6	9.1	4.2	<0.001
03:00–04:00	54	4.2	2.9	7	11.8	3.5	<0.001
04.00–05:00	54	6.7	3.9	4	9.9	0.6	NS
05:00–06:00	54	9.5	3.7	5	10.8	4.4	NS

Such temporal correlations between plasma cortisol concentration and sleep stage must be evaluated cautiously, however, because of the time lags between the secretion of the hypothalamic releasing factor and of ACTH, and then between ACTH and cortisol.

Finally, in another argument against a simple stress hypothesis, Stokes has reported that sedative medication in high doses fails to reduce elevated cortisol levels in many depressed patients (8). Figure 9 shows that a dose of 75 mg chlorpromazine i.m. every 6 hr had no effect upon the elevated and flattened 24-hr plasma cortisol pattern in one of our own agitated depressed patients.

In summary, we certainly do not claim that stress influences on cortisol secretion are absent in depressives, as these have been amply demonstrated by us and others in the past (9,10). It appears, however, that the cortisol hypersecretion in many severely depressed patients may also reflect a central neuroendocrine

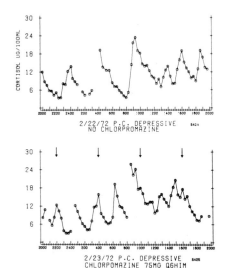

FIG. 9. Twenty-four hour plasma cortisol concentration in a unipolar depressed 65-year-old woman before *(top)* and during *(bottom)* intramuscular injections of 75 mg of chlorpromazine every 6 hr. Arrows indicate time of injections.

disturbance, perhaps related to a functional depletion in hypothalamic norepi-nephrine.

Another hormone system regulated in part by hypothalamic norepinephrine is growth hormone (GH). Whereas different neurotransmitters may be involved in the GH responses to slow-wave sleep, arginine, anxiety, and L-DOPA, there is considerable evidence that the GH response to hypoglycemia is, to a major degree, norepinephrine-mediated, and that depletion of brain norepinephrine inhibits GH responses to hypoglycemia (11). Several laboratories have confirmed our earlier observations of diminished GH responses to hypoglycemia in hetero-geneous groups of depressed patients (12–14). Recently, with Gruen, Altman, Halpern, and Sassin, we studied this response in a highly selected group of primary, unipolar depressed, unmedicated, nonobese, postmenopausal women (15). The use of postmenopausal women eliminates the variable of estradiol secretion, which potentiates the GH response to hypoglycemia as well as to arginine, L-DOPA, and sleep (16).

Figure 10 shows that the GH response to insulin-induced hypoglycemia is significantly reduced in the depressed postmenopausal group compared to age-matched controls. Half the patients failed to achieve even a 5-ng/ml response, which usually is considered to be the minimum adequate response. The difference in response of the two groups cannot be explained by differences in age, weight, or degree of hypoglycemic response. Figure 11 shows that both the absolute and percentage drops in blood glucose from base line were identical in the two groups. These GH findings also appear to support the idea of disturbed neuroendocrine

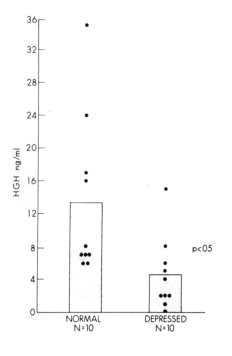

FIG. 10. Maximum HGH increases in re-sponse to insulin-induced hypoglycemia in normal and depressed postmenopausal women.

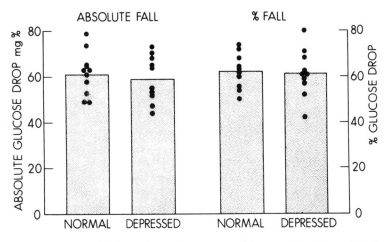

FIG. 11. Maximum drops in blood glucose in normal and depressed postmenopausal women after injection of 0.1 U/kg regular insulin. Drops are expressed in mg% changes from base line, and also as percent of baseline concentration.

function, and possibly of noradrenergic hypoactivity in primary unipolar depression.

Brain catecholamines also play a major role in regulating LH secretion (17). Recently, Ojeda, McCann, and colleagues have shown that norepinephrine mediates the increase in LH secretion after gonadectomy (18). Gonadectomy removes the usual feedback inhibition of LH secretion by estradiol. Postmenopausal women have been shown to secrete no significant amount of estradiol, and they, of course, have markedly elevated plasma LH concentrations, which we have shown cannot be elevated further by administration of an antiestrogen (19). We may, therefore, regard postmenopausal women as functionally gonadectomized; their increased LH secretion can be presumed to be under noradrenergic control. Hence, if postmenopausal women with primary unipolar depressive illness have diminished functional hypothalamic norepinephrine, it might be reflected in reduced LH secretion. With Altman, Gruen, and Halpern, we decided to test this rather far-fetched hypothesis (20). Figure 12 shows that plasma LH concentration was indeed significantly lower in the patients than in the controls. Each LH measure represents the mean of 7 to 11 successive blood samples taken at 15-min intervals in each subject, and all samples from normal and depressed patients were analyzed in duplicate in the same assays. Although these observations need to be replicated, they, too, suggest an alteration in hypothalamic function consistent with the norepinephrine hypothesis.

Could these neuroendocrine techniques also provide an avenue for the study of brain function in schizophrenia? Here we are on much shakier ground. Unlike depressive illness, the clinical phenomena of schizophrenia do not readily suggest a hypothalamic dysfunction that might affect the neuroendocrine system. Other areas of the brain, such as the mesolimbic system, are currently more suspect in schizophrenia. Patients in acute psychotic panic states do secrete very large quantities of cortisol, but this is almost surely a stress response, as we have shown that the cortisol secretion subsides when patients develop an organized delusional system and become calm (21). There have been occasional reports of decreased androgen excretion in schizophrenia, but these have not been reliably replicated. Lebow and Durrell have shown that periodic catatonia is associated with subtle but definite alterations in thyroid function (22)—but this is a rare condition, and there is no evidence that typical schizophrenic illness is associated with thyroid abnormalities.

The hyperdopaminergic hypothesis of schizophrenia does, however, suggest one neuroendocrine possibility. If such dopaminergic hyperactivity is widespread enough to affect the tuberoinfundibular system, it could be reflected in the secretion of prolactin. Dopaminergic influences in the tuberoinfundibular system prompt the secretion of prolactin inhibiting factor (PIF), which suppresses prolactin secretion (23). Hence, L-DOPA ingestion suppresses plasma prolactin, whereas chlorpromazine stimulates prolactin (24). A simple hypothesis, then, would be that schizophrenics would have reduced plasma prolactin levels. However, in a study conducted with Meltzer and Frantz (25) (Fig. 13) plasma prolactin levels in unmedicated severely schizophrenic patients on admission to a hospital did not differ from nonhospitalized healthy control subjects. Furthermore, there were no differences between paranoid and nonparanoid, or between acute and chronic patients. There is one strange aspect in the data, however—psychologic stress is a potent stimulus to prolactin secretion (26), and one would have expected elevated levels in these patients, many of whom were agitated and all of whom were coping with the stress of hospital admission. Hence, this apparent lack of a prolactin stress response might indicate something abnormal about the regulation of prolactin secretion in schizophrenia, although this is highly speculative.

In summary, there appears to be evidence of deviant neuroendocrine function in patients with unipolar depressive illness, although whether it exists in other

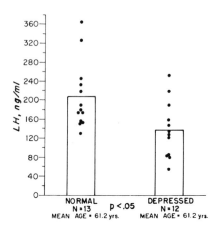

FIG. 12. Mean plasma LH concentrations in depressed and normal postmenopausal women.

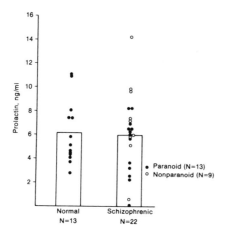

FIG. 13. Morning plasma prolactin concentrations in normal subjects, and in schizophrenic patients on the day of hospital admission.

types of depression remains to be seen. There is no good evidence that neuroendocrine function is affected in a primary way in schizophrenics, but a comprehensive study of these patients, using modern neuroendocrine techniques, has not been done. Hopefully, future neuroendocrine studies of depressed and schizophrenic patients will be conducted with concomitant measures by the other psychobiologic techniques so well described in the previous chapters.

REFERENCES

1. Van Loon, G. R. (1973): Brain catecholamines and ACTH secretion. In: *Frontiers in Neuroendocrinology,* edited by F. W. Ganong and L. Martini, pp. 209–247. Oxford Univ. Press, New York.
2. Marantz, R., Sachar, J., Weitzman, E., and Sassin, J. (1975): Equivalent cortisol and GH responses to *d*- and *l*-amphetamine. *(To be published.)*
3. Sachar, E. J., and Coppen, A. (1975): Biological aspects of affective psychoses. In: *Biology of Brain Dysfunction,* edited by G. Gaull. Plenum, New York. *(In press.)*
4. Sachar, E. J., Hellman, L., Roffwarg, H. P., Halpern, F. S., Fukushima, D., and Gallagher, T. F. (1973): Disrupted 24-hour patterns of cortisol secretion in psychotic depression. *Arch. Gen. Psychiatry,* 28:19–24.
5. Sachar, E. J. (1975): Twenty-four cortisol secretory patterns in depressed and manic patients. In: *Progress in Brain Research,* edited by W. Gispen and D. DeWied. Elsevier, Amsterdam. *(In press.)*
6. Ellman, S. J., Roffwarg, H. P., Sachar, E. J., Finkelstein, J., Kurti, J., and Hellman, L. (1970): Effects of REM deprivation on cortisol and growth hormone levels. *Association for the Psychophysiological Study of Sleep, Santa Fe, New Mexico.*
7. Rubin, R. T., Kollar, E. J., Slater, G. S., and Clark, B. R. (1969): Excretion of 17-hydroxycorticosteroid and vanillylmandelic acid during 205 hours of sleep deprivation in man. *Psychosom. Med.,* 31:68–79.
8. Stokes, P. E. (1972): Studies on the control of adrenocortical function in depression. In: *Recent Advances in the Psychobiology of Depressive Illnesses,* edited by T. A. Williams, M. M. Katz, and J. A. Shield, pp. 199–220. *U.S. DHEW Publ.* 70-9053, Washington, D.C.
9. Bunney, W. E., Mason, J. W., and Hamburg, D. A. (1965): Co-relations between behavioral variables and urinary 17-hydroxycorticosteroids in depressed patients. *Psychosom. Med.,* 27:299–308.
10. Sachar, E. J., Hellman, L., Fukushima, D., and Gallagher, T. F. (1970): Cortisol production in depressive illness. *Arch. Gen. Psychiatry,* 23:289–298.
11. Martin, J. (1970): Neural regulation of growth hormone secretion. *New Engl. J. Med.,* 288:1384–1393.

12. Sachar, E. J., Finkelstein, J., and Hellman, L. (1971): Growth hormone responses in depressive illness: Response to insulin tolerance test. *Arch. Gen. Psychiatry*, 24:263–269.
13. Carroll, B. J. (1972): Studies with hypothalamic–pituitary–adrenal stimulation tests in depression. In: *Depressive Illness: Some Research Studies*, edited by B. Davies, B. J. Carroll, and R. M. Mowbray, pp. 149–201. Thomas, Springfield, Illinois.
14. Mueller, P. S., Heninger, G. R., and McDonald, P. K. (1972): Studies on glucose utilization and insulin sensitivity in affective disorders. In: *Recent Advances in the Psychobiology of the Depressive Illnesses*, edited by T. A. Williams, M. M. Katz, and J. A. Shield, pp. 235–245. *U.S. DHEW Publ.* 70-9053, Washington, D.C.
15. Gruen, P. H., Sachar, E. J., Altman, N., and Sassin, J. (1975): Growth hormone response to hypoglycemia in postmenopausal depressed women. *Arch. Gen. Psychiatry*, 32:31–33.
16. Merimée, T. J., and Fineberg, S. E. (1971): Studies of the sex based variation of human growth hormone secretion. *J. Clin. Endocrinol. Metab.*, 33:896–902.
17. Coppola, J. A. (1971): Brain catecholamines and gonadotropin secretion. In: *Frontiers in Neuroendocrinology*, edited by L. Martini and W. F. Ganong, pp. 129–143. Oxford Univ. Press, New York.
18. Ojeda, S. R., and McCann, S. M. (1974): Evidence for participation of a catecholaminergic mechanism in the post-castration rise in plasma gonadotrophins. *Neuroendocrinology*, 12:295–315.
19. Altman, N., Boyar, R., Gruen, P. H., Halpern, F., Hellman, L., and Sachar, E. J. (Submitted for publication): Effect of clomiphene citrate on plasma LH concentration in postmenopausal women and older men.
20. Altman, N., Gruen, P. H., Halpern, F. S., and Eto, S. (1975): Reduced plasma LH concentration in postmenopausal depressed women. *Psychosom. Med. (In press.)*
21. Sachar, E. J., Kanter S., Buie, D., Engel, R., and Mehlman, R. (1970): Psychoendocrinology of ego disintegration. *Am. J. Psychiatry*, 126:1067–1078.
22. Durell, J., Libow, L., Kellam, S., Shader, R. (1966): Interrelations between regulation of thyroid gland function and psychosis. In: *Endocrine and the Central Nervous System. (Res. Publ. Assoc. Res. Nerv. Ment. Dis.)*, 43:387.
23. Meites, J. et al. (1972): Recent studies on function and control of prolactin secretion in rats. *Rec. Prog. Horm. Res.*, 28:471–526.
24. Kleinberg, D. L., Noel, G. L., and Frantz, A. G. (1971): Chlorpromazine stimulation and L-Dopa suppression of plasma prolactin in man. *J. Clin. Endocrinol. Metab.*, 33:873–876.
25. Frantz, A. G., Kleinberg, D. L., and Nowel, G. L. (1972): Studies on prolactin in man. *Recent Prog. Horm. Res.*, 28:527–573.

Subject Index

A

"Abnormally quiet" state in schizophrenia, 68, 72-75, 299
Acetylcholine, 237-238, 259, 270, 325,
333-335
ACh, *See* Acetylcholine
ACTH, *See* Adrenocorticotropic
hormone
Acute Schizophrenic reaction, 19, 21-
22, 24, 42-44
"Acute" terminology quandary in
schizophrenia, 229
Adenylate cyclase, dopamine-sensitive,
235, 237, 241, 250-251, 274,
278, 297, 343
Adoption studies, 20-23, 43-44, 49, 65,
71
Adrenocorticotropic hormone secretion
cortisol secretion as an index of,
347
noradrenergic system inhibitory
influence on, 347
norepinephrine depletion caused
hypersecretion effect on, 349,
351, 353-354
AER, *See* Average evoked response
Affective disorders
AER augmenting/reducing in,
129-142
amine hypotheses of, 321-322,
324-326, 345
bipolar, 24, 28-30, 113, 136-139,
151-154, 161, 281-283, 290-
291, 301-303, 311-313
CSF amine metabolite studies in,
306-315
dopamine and tricyclic antidepressant role in, 254-255
EEG and evoked potentials in,
101-123
family studies in, 23-24, 28-30,
35-37, 81

Affective disorders *(contd.)*
heterogeneity of, 28-30
muscle fiber, subterminal motor
nerve studies in, 189-206
neuroendocrine abnormalities in
ACTH and cortisol secretion,
347-353
GH response to hypoglycemia,
347, 354-355
LH reduced secretion in, 355
neurotransmitter-related enzymes
in
COMT and MAO, 277-288
physostigmine administration
effects in, 333-337
schizophrenia and
genetically distinct?, 27-39
serum enzyme studies in, 165-188
sleep studies in, 150-157, 161-162
unipolar, 24, 28-30, 113, 135-136,
138-139, 150-154, 161, 281-
283, 290-291, 301-303,
311-313
urinary MHPG in, 301-303
See also, Manic-depressive disorder
Akinesia, 260-261, 263
Aldolase activity increase in sera, 165,
170, 181, 210
Alkaline phosphatase, 170, 190, 192-
195, 201-202
Alpha activity in EEG, 104-106, 109-
111, 118-119
Alpha-methyl-*p*-tyrosine, 305-306,
337-338, 340
Alpha motor neuron abnormalities,
189, 198, 204
American Psychiatric Association,
Diagnostic and Statistical Manual of Mental Disorders, 11,
19-20, 41-42, 229